THE CAIRO GENIZA

THE
CAIRO GENIZA

by

PAUL E. KAHLE
D., D.Litt., D.D., D.H.L., F.B.A.

SECOND EDITION

OXFORD
BASIL BLACKWELL
1959

Printed in Great Britain by
Billing and Sons Limited, Guildford and London
Bound by
Kemp Hall Bindery, Oxford

PAUL ERIC KAHLE

* 23 x 1923 Bonn

† 30 iv 1955 Charlbury/Oxford

PREFACE

THE original form of my book on the Cairo Geniza was in substance delivered as the British Academy Schweich Lectures for 1941. It was published by the Academy in 1947 shortly before the earliest finds of scrolls near the north end of the Dead Sea became known. A German edition of my book was in preparation, but it quickly became clear to me that neither a German translation nor a reprint of the first edition, which was soon called for, would be advisable; it was essential to take into account the new material from the Qumran caves. A second edition was required, but had to wait till sufficient material from the Dead Sea scrolls became available and now it appears in its present form. A German edition of it will be published by the Bibliographisches Institut, Leipzig.

Much has happened since the first edition appeared. I need not say how glad I have been to resume happy contacts with my former country. I have been reinstated as Professor Emeritus of Bonn University, have been nominated Honorarprofessor in the University of Münster and have given many lectures in almost all the German universities.

The greater part of my own library was saved and returned to me after the War in 1948. Besides this, the very great number of photographs of Hebrew MSS which I had collected over the course of many years was again placed at my disposal. Living near and in Oxford has given me easy access to the treasures in the Bodleian Library, where the staff have always been most helpful, and to many scholars from all over the world who come to this city.

In the second edition of my book I have been able to make use of much new material and to discuss many new problems: the importance of the MS fragments brought to our notice from the Cairo Geniza can hardly be exaggerated. Together with what has become and will become available from the caves of Qumran, they have opened quite new prospects. I hope that my book will bear witness to this.

The amount of Geniza material has recently been increased to an extent which could hardly have been foreseen. A few months ago Professor J. Schirmann of Jerusalem sent me an offprint from Tarbīṣ xxvii, 1958 containing (pp. 440 f.) a photograph of a leaf of the Hebrew Ben Sira (xv and xvi 1–9) from MS B (hitherto only MS A of this part of the book was known). The text belongs to a *New Series* of fragments in the Cambridge University Library. In reply to an enquiry of mine concerning this *New Series*, Schirmann writes that he has not so far had time to make a catalogue, as the Geniza fragments which it includes number tens of thousands. He would need several months or even years for the purpose. What he has succeeded in doing during the last two summers is to examine and classify the fragments contained in five large wooden boxes. These fragments he has sorted into fifty-eight cardboard boxes, of which fifty-three contain liturgical poetry, one biblical fragments, one various Hebrew texts, two Arabic material and one printed matter. Some texts of special interest to him, as an expert in Hebrew poetry, he has numbered, catalogued and photographed, and intends to publish, along with material already known from the Geniza, in a special volume.

These fragments belong to the material brought by Schechter to Cambridge. They were so numerous that he left them in the wooden boxes in which they had arrived from Cairo. On my enquiry Professor Schirmann told me that Babylonian and Palestinian supralinear punctuation seldom occurs. Schechter may have put nearly all the supralinear punctuated fragments with the Geniza material already known to us. Possibly as a result of his removal to America as President of the Jewish Theological Seminary in 1901 he found no further opportunity to work on these fragments and they were neglected. At all events this vast quantity of fragments will now become available for study, sixty years after its arrival in Cambridge.

A valuable discussion of the problems raised by D. M. Dunlop in his book *The History of the Jewish Khazars*, Princeton, 1954 (see infra pp. 28–34) is given by V. Minorsky of Cambridge in his article 'A new book on the Khazars', *Oriens* xi, 1958 pp. 122–145.

As to the Arabic Diatessaron, I have tried to show that al-Ghazālī, the great and most influential Islamic scholar, played a decisive role in the formation of one of the two texts we have. In the light of this conclusion it is evident that Georg Graf's five volume *History of Christian Arabic Literature*, which contains much valuable and indispensable material, must be used with the utmost caution. Not only was Graf's linguistic equipment quite inadequate, but he had no critical appreciation of the problems involved.

When I wrote in my first edition (p. 224) of the *excellent* Arabic used by Ibn aṭ-Ṭaiyib, this was simply an allusion to what Marmardji had written and did not represent my own opinion. I have altered the wording in this edition (p. 309). In the Introduction to their edition of Ibn aṭ-Ṭaiyib's great work *al-fiqh an-naṣrānīye*[1] the editors, Wilhelm Hoenerbach and Otto Spies, have given a well-founded judgment about the quality of this Arabic with which I entirely agree.

My particular thanks are due to the Deutsche Forschungsgemeinschaft for the interest they have taken in my research work.

To the many scholars who have helped me in discussion or by raising various problems in correspondence I wish to express my gratitude. I owe an especial debt to my friend and former pupil Dr. Menachem Zulay, the great authority on Hebrew liturgical poetry. Until his untimely death in November 1954 we corresponded frequently about matters arising from the first edition of my book, and it was a particular pleasure to have him and Mrs. Zulay staying with me for some time in September 1954 in Charlbury, when we had many fruitful discussions.

I am further indebted to Professor Rudolf Meyer of Jena University, the distinguished Hebrew grammarian, with whom I have often talked over many questions and who has rendered much assistance in connection with the German edition of this book.

I should like to thank Dr. A. Murtonen of Helsinki particularly for what he has contributed on the Palestinian and Samaritan pronunciation of Hebrew and for his recent observations in America.

With Professor A. Diez Macho of Barcelona University I was in regular correspondence during his two years in America. The photographs of the Palestinian/Tiberian Bible text, published in Appendix III, which he sent me, and his valuable communications on the readings of the original were of great assistance to me.

Mgr. Skehan of the Catholic Institute in Washington, when

[1] Corpus Scriptorum Christianorum Orientalium Vol. 161, Scriptores Arabici 16, Louvain 1956, vol. i p. vi.

we met at Strasbourg in 1956, placed at my disposal the photographs of Greek Bible fragments from Qumran Cave 4.

I have had many profitable conversations about the Targums with Father Georg Schelbert of the Missionary Seminary in Schoeneck near Beckenried (Switzerland). With Dr. S. M. Stern, Fellow of All Souls College, Oxford, I have had many discussions and I am especially grateful to him for his help in understanding problems concerning Saadya. Dr. Naftali Wieder, Professor at The Jews' College, London, has provided me with valuable information on the early Ḳaraites. With Mr. Meir Gertner, of the London School of Oriental and African Studies, I have discussed problems regarding the Tiberian Masoretes and he has kindly written and placed at my disposal some valuable notes on them.

It has been of great importance to me that Mr. Martin Molyneux, M.A., has always been at hand to help in improving the English text and to discuss other problems. Miss Hedwig Herold, who has been my secretary for more than three years, has been invaluable in many ways, and has prepared my manuscript for the printers. Together with my son William she has also compiled the indexes.

It remains for me to acknowledge the kindness of the publisher, who has shown understanding and readiness to accede to my wishes. Nor must I fail to thank Messrs. Billing and Sons, Guildford, who printed the text, and the Clarendon Press, Oxford, for the printing of the appendixes and index.

I dedicate the book to the memory of my son, Paul Eric, whose death so soon after the publication of his work on the *Bala'izah texts* was a very great loss. He had matured into a scholar with whom I regularly discussed all kinds of problems. It was particularly happy for me that his special field was that of Coptic Studies, in which he had become a recognized authority.

CONTENTS

CHAPTER I

GENERAL INTRODUCTION

CHAPTER II

THE HEBREW TEXT OF THE BIBLE

CHAPTER III

THE TRANSLATIONS OF THE BIBLE

APPENDIXES

ABBREVIATIONS

A.K.M.	Abhandlungen für die Kunde des Morgenlandes.
B.A.S.O.R.	Bulletin of the American Schools of Oriental Research.
B.S.O.A.S.	British School of Oriental and African Studies.
B.Z.A.W.	Beihefte für die Zeitschrift für Alttestamentliche Wissenschaft.
H.U.C.A.	Hebrew Union College Annual.
J.B.L.	Journal of Biblical Literature.
J.J.St.	Journal of Jewish Studies.
J.Q.R.	Jewish Quarterly Review.
J.R.A.S.	Journal of the Royal Asiatic Society.
J.T.S.	The Journal of Theological Studies.
O.L.Z.	Orientalistische Literatur Zeitung.
P.G.	Migne, Patrologia Graeca.
R.B.	Revue Biblique.
R.E.J.	Revue des Études Juives.
Th.L.Z.	Theologische Literaturzeitung.
V.T.	Vetus Testamentum.
Z.A.	Zeitschrift für Assyriologie und verwandte Gebiete.
Z.A.W.	Zeitschrift für die Alttestamentliche Wissenschaft.
Z.D.M.G.	Zeitschrift der Deutschen Morgenländischen Gesellschaft.
Z.N.W.	Zeitschrift für Neutestamentliche Wissenschaft.

PART I

General Introduction

CHAPTER I

GENERAL INTRODUCTION

1. The Geniza

THE Cairo Geniza[1] formed part of the Synagogue in Old Cairo, which in early times had been a Christian church dedicated to St. Michael; but in A.D. 882 it was sold to the Jews who converted it into a Synagogue. We are told that Aḥmed Ibn Ṭūlūn, Egypt's ruler from A.D. 868 to 884, demanded from Michael, the 56th Coptic Patriarch, a contribution of 20,000 dinars towards military expenditure. To raise this sum the Patriarch had to sell to the Jews certain church properties such as waḳf-lands, a piece of land on the outskirts of Fusṭāṭ-Miṣr, belonging to the Abyssinians, and a church near the Mu'allaḳa Church in Ḳaṣr ash-Sham'a.[2]

In Ḳaṣr ash-Sham'a, the old Roman fortress near which Fusṭāṭ was founded by the Arabs, there were six Christian churches: Al-Mu'allaḳa, Abū Serge, St. George, St. Mary the Virgin, St. Barbara and St. Michael.[3] St. Michael's was the last one owned by the Melkites after all the other churches throughout Egypt had passed into the hands of the Jacobites. We do not know exactly how long the Melkites used it. 'But the violent antipathy of the two factions no doubt gave a cause of quarrel and conquest to the Jacobites, long before the time when it was made over to the Hebrews.'[4]

Butler describes the Ezra Synagogue—the converted St. Michael's church—in the following way:

> 'The Synagogue is about 65 ft. long and 36 ft. broad, and shows in miniature a Coptic basilica in its simplest and perhaps

[1] Cf. Alexander Marx, 'The Importance of the Genizah for Jewish History', *Proceedings of the American Academy for Jewish Research*, vol. xvi, 1947, pp. 183–204.
In more popular form: Norman Golb, 'Sixty Years of Genizah Research', *Judaism*, Quarterly Journal of Jewish Life and Thought, vol. vi, 1957, pp. 3–16.

[2] Cf. Maḳrīzī, *Khiṭaṭ*, Cairo 1326, vol. iv, p. 397. Abū Ṣāliḥ, *The Churches and Monasteries of Egypt* . . . ed. B. T. A. Evetts, p. 136 of the translation.

[3] They are marked on the map of Ḳaṣr ash-Sham'a, facing p. 155 of vol. i of Alfred J. Butler's *The ancient Coptic Churches of Egypt*, Oxford 1884.

[4] Butler op. cit., vol i, p. 169.

earliest form. If the eastern end has suffered some alteration, the nave, side-aisles and returned aisle with triforium above are unchanged from the old design, though whitewash has long since defaced the splendid colours once blazoned on the walls. In point of detail there is not much of interest remaining, except the fine stucco work about the arch of triumph, the tank or well behind the apse and the carved doors at the end of the south aisle . . . '[1]

Jacob Mann is under a misapprehension when he speaks of two churches sold at this time to the Jews. He is not aware that the names Ḳaṣr ash-Sham'a and Fusṭāṭ apply to the same place and that the former Church of St. Michael is the very church to which the Cairo Geniza belonged.[2]

The Synagogue was renovated in 1890, but the Geniza at the back of the building was left unaltered. It is described as situated at the end of the women's gallery, a sort of room of moderate dimensions without doors or windows; by climbing a ladder one could enter through a hole in the western wall.[3]

However, it is not the room which is of interest to us—in any case it has long since ceased to exist—but what it held. A great number of fragments of MSS and of printed books, documents and letters had been stored there for many hundreds of years. The Jews used to deposit all sorts of written and printed material in such rooms which were provided in or near their synagogues; they were not intended to be kept as in archives, but were to remain there undisturbed for a certain time. The Jews were afraid lest such writings which might contain the name of God should be profaned by misuse. So such written—and in later times also printed—matter was taken from time to time to consecrated ground and buried; thus it perished.

It was by mere chance that the Cairo Geniza was forgotten and its contents so escaped the fate of other Genizas. These old writings have been saved quite contrary to the intention of those who stored them there. When in the course of the last century the Cairo Geniza was rediscovered, the men in charge of the Synagogue to which it belonged made the surprising discovery that there were some queer people in the world who were at-

[1] Butler, op. cit., i, pp. 169 f.

[2] *The Jews in Egypt and in Palestine under the Fāṭimid Caliphs*, vol. i, Oxford 1920, p. 14.

[3] Cf. Elkan N. Adler in *JQR*, ix, 1897, pp. 669 f; S. Schechter, *Studies in Judaism*, vol. ii, Philadelphia, 1908, pp. 5 f.

tracted by the old material, who were willing to pay considerable sums of money for these scraps of dirty parchment and paper, and that even famous universities were keenly interested in the matter.

The Jewish traveller Jacob Saphir heard about the Geniza while he was in Cairo in 1864. He was anxious to visit it in order to make some discoveries, and he obtained permission to enter the room; however, after spending two days there and becoming covered with dust and dirt he abandoned the plan, taking away as a sort of souvenir a few pages belonging to various MSS.[1]

Shortly afterwards during his trip to the Orient, Abraham Firkowitch came to Cairo. This Ḳaraite Jew from the Crimea was of somewhat ill-repute because of the falsifications of dates on tombstones and in Hebrew MSS which he had perpetrated in an endeavour to show that the Ḳaraites had been settled in the Crimea for a longer period than was supposed and that their importance was far greater than had hitherto been acknowledged.[2] Nevertheless the credit goes to Firkowitch for assembling the largest collection of Hebrew MSS now existing in the world. These MSS form the two Firkowitch Collections in the Russian Public Library at Leningrad. The first was sold to the library by Firkowitch himself; the second was acquired by the library in 1876 soon after his death on May 26th 1874.

We may form an idea of the extent of these collections when we are told that in the Second Firkowitch Collection alone the MSS of the Hebrew Bible and the Masora written on parchment number 1,582 and those written on paper 725.[3] To see these figures in their proper perspective we must remember that the British Museum Catalogue records 161 and the Bodleian Catalogue 146 Hebrew Biblical MSS written on parchment and paper, whereas Kennicott who had hoped to use all Hebrew MSS available in the Europe of his time for his great *Vetus Testamentum Hebraice*[4] was not able to collate even one third of the number of MSS which to-day are to be found in this one part of the Leningrad collection.

[1] His experiences are described by him in the report on his journey published under the name of *Eben Saphir* in Lück in 1866; cf. pp. 21 f. He found nothing of importance.

[2] Cf. my book *Masoreten des Westens*, vol. i, 1927, pp. 57 f.

[3] In addition, this collection includes 159 scrolls on parchment or on leather. 4,933 and 1,243 Hebrew and Arabic MSS as well as 344 non-Biblical MSS. However, we must realize that this library lists even a few leaves of a MS as a separate number.

[4] *Vetus Testamentum Hebraice cum Variis Lectionibus*, ed. Benjamin Kennicott, Oxford 1776–80.

The Second Firkowitch Collection is not only extensive but also extremely valuable. It is a well-known fact that Hebrew Biblical MSS dating from the tenth and eleventh centuries are very rare. The so-called Babylonian Codex of the Prophets, dated A.D. 916, belonging to another smaller collection of the Leningrad Library (MS Heb. B 3), has long been regarded as the oldest dated MS of the Hebrew Bible. Aaron ben Moshe ben Asher, the greatest Masoretic authority, who was finally responsible for the exact punctuation and the exact Masora of the Hebrew texts as we have them in our Bibles, lived and worked in the first half of the tenth century.[1] No codices, therefore, which depend on his authority can date from an earlier period. The Codex of the Prophets, preserved in the Synagogue of the Ḳaraites in Cairo, written and provided with punctuation and Masora in A.D. 895 by Moshe ben Asher, Aaron's father, is the oldest dated Hebrew Biblical MS of which we know.[2] But I found in Leningrad in the autumn of 1926, chiefly among the MSS of the Second Firkowitch Collection, not less than fourteen Hebrew Biblical MSS which can be dated between A.D. 929 and 1121, and all of them contain in the main the text as fixed by Aaron ben Asher.[3]

On the other hand the Biblical MSS form only a small part of the Firkowitch Collection in Leningrad. Firkowitch was an expert at ransacking old Synagogues and their Genizas. When, in the summer of 1908, I was in Nāblus for a fortnight working with the Samaritans, the then High-Priest Ya'ḳūb ben Hārūn told me that he well remembered Firkowitch's visit, about forty years before. He spoke with great indignation of the man and the way he had treated the Samaritan priests, taking great quantities of valuable old MSS without paying an adequate price. Nevertheless, it is due to Firkowitch's activity that the Russian Public Library in Leningrad owns the greatest collection of Samaritan MSS in the whole of Europe.[4]

I have not the slightest doubt that a certain number of the MSS in the Second Firkowitch Collection come from the Cairo

[1] Cf. for Ben Asher, *Masoreten des Westens*, vol. i, 1927, pp. 1–15 and the following chapter of this book.

[2] Cf. *Masoreten des Westens*, vol. i, 1927, pp. 15 f. and the following chapter. The MS is kept nowadays in the new Ḳaraite Synagogue in the 'Abbāsīye, Cairo. The head of the Ḳaraite community, the jeweller David Zeki Lischa', showed it to me on Monday, the 20th February 1956.

[3] I have described these fourteen MSS in *Masoreten des Westens*, vol. i, 1927, pp. 56–77 where the facsimiles are also published.

[4] Only the Bible MSS of this collection have so far been described in Russian in a catalogue published by A. E. Harkavy in St. Petersburg in 1874.

Geniza. We are told that Firkowitch did not enter the place but acquired from it bundles of MSS.[1] An expert in MSS, he did not gather material at random. He knew important material when he saw it and no doubt some of the most valuable fragments from the Geniza are in the Second Firkowitch Collection in Leningrad. But Firkowitch's interest lay in concealing the way in which he collected his material and the places whence it came, so that to-day nobody is able to state exactly how many MSS of his collection were taken from the Cairo Geniza.

But the Leningrad Library is in possession of a collection of approximately 1,200 fragments, the so-called Antonin Collection[2] which undoubtedly comes from the Cairo Geniza. It was assembled by Antonin, a Russian Archimandrite of Jerusalem. I examined all these fragments in Leningrad in 1926 and must acknowledge that the Archimandrite had shown a deep understanding of such things and has brought together a very important collection. However, my knowledge of these Geniza fragments is not based only on my short visit of five weeks in 1926. At my request several hundreds of these and other fragments were lent, in a most generous way, to the Oriental Seminar at Bonn University where I could study them at leisure with my pupils.

In 1896 Elkan Natan Adler had an opportunity of entering the Geniza[3] and of taking away with him as much material as could be carried in an old Torah mantle which had been lent to him for the purpose. It was not long before a large number of these MSS were taken to the Library of the Jewish Theological Seminary of America in New York. The Librarian, Professor Alexander Marx, was kind enough to send a generous quantity of volumes containing Biblical fragments to Bonn, where in the nineteen twenties they remained available to me for a time.[4]

Soon after 1890, which year saw the renovation of the Syna-

[1] Cf. Norman Bentwich, *Solomon Schechter, a Biography*. Philadelphia, 1940. p. 139. A. Marx writes (p. 183): It is doubtful whether some of the ancient fragments acquired by the Ḳaraite Firkowitsch . . . came from the Cairo treasure trove'. I am convinced that there can be no doubt.

[2] Harkavy speaks about this Collection in *Отчетъ Императорской Публичной Библиотеки за* 1899 *годъ. С.-Петербургъ* 1903 pp. 75-87. The collection is now called *Evr. III b.*

[3] Adler has described his visit to the Geniza in the *JQR*, vol. ix, 1897, pp. 669–73. Cf. Marx, p. 184.

[4] The MSS which Adler retained in his London library have, since his death, gone to the Library of the Jewish Theological Seminary of America in New York. See on this important Collection now: A. Diez Macho. Importants Manuscrits Hébreux et Araméens aux États Unis, in *VT*, Supplement iv, 1957, pp. 27–46.

gogue in Old Cairo, a general trading was started with the material from the Geniza. Large quantities of fragments were sold, travellers brought them to Europe and in particular to the Bodleian Library in Oxford, where A. Neubauer and A. E. Cowley soon became interested, and made great efforts to acquire material from the Geniza. To-day the Bodleian Library has, next to Cambridge, the largest collection of Geniza fragments, and it is the only library which possesses a printed catalogue of its collections. The second volume of the Bodleian *Catalogue of the Hebrew Manuscripts* is, for the greater part, devoted to the description of these fragments. It is here that we find a detailed list of all those who, in Cairo, acquired fragments for the Bodleian Library; Cowley's catalogue is a fine piece of work.[1] The making of such a catalogue is a very arduous task. As the fragments were delivered to the Bodleian Library they were bound in volumes, chiefly according to the size of the leaves, so that each one of these volumes contains a large number of different fragments. Therefore not only every manuscript mentioned in the catalogue, but nearly every folio of every MS had to be examined and described.

A few fragments found their way to the University Library in Cambridge,[2] and others went to the British Museum,[3] a large quantity was acquired by Professor David Kaufmann of Budapest[4] and a fairly large collection went to the Bibliothèque de l'Alliance Israélite Universelle de Paris, where Israel Lévi was interested in the matter.[5] Some fragments went to the Stadt-Bibliothek in Frankfurt am Main where Dr. A. Freimann was eager to study the material; some other fragments went to Philadelphia where Dr. Cyrus Adler had started a small collection as early as 1891;[6] some were acquired by the Universitätsbiblio-

[1] *Catalogue of the Hebrew Manuscripts in the Bodleian Library*, vol. ii, by A. Neubauer and A. E. Cowley, Oxford, 1906.

[2] These fragments are preserved in the Cambridge University Library as MS Or. 1080, and are kept in several boxes.

[3] Cf. E. N. Adler in *JQR*, vol. ix, 1897, p. 672. Geniza fragments in the British Museum are mentioned in vol. iv, of the Catalogue under the number 4856 as 'fragments from the Genizah in Cairo of biblical, theological, legal, liturgical and secular writings, documents and letters, chiefly in Hebrew'; Nos. 5525–27, 5537, 5542–48, 5554–61 and 7943 are marked with a note, referring them back to No. 4856.

[4] *Genizah Publications in memory of Prof. Dr. David Kaufmann.* In collaboration with Stephen Hahn, Ernest Roth. Ed. Samuel Löwinger, Alexander Scheiber. Budapest, 1949.

[5] I had the opportunity of seeing this collection in the summer of 1927.

[6] B. Halper, *Descriptive Catalogue of Genizah Fragments in Philadelphia.* Philadelphia, 1924.

thek in Strasbourg,[1] others by private collectors. Four thousand fragments, for instance, were collected by a certain Jack Mosseri in Cairo.

The matter took a new turn when, in 1896, the two learned Scottish ladies, Mrs. Agnes Smith Lewis and Mrs. Margaret Dunlop Gibson, returned to Cambridge from one of their numerous journeys to the East. They, too, had bought in Cairo some fragments from the Geniza. These fragments which form a noteworthy collection[2] are now in the Library of the Presbyterian Westminster College in Cambridge which owes its existence largely to the efforts of these ladies. In May 1896 they handed over to Solomon Schechter—at that time Reader in Talmudic at Cambridge University—two leaves, one of parchment and one of paper, both covered with Hebrew lettering.[3]

Schechter ascertained that the parchment belonged to a MS of the Palestinian Talmud[4] and in the paper fragment he discovered a piece of the Hebrew text from the book by Jesus ben Sira (Ecclesiasticus), a Jewish text composed in Hebrew about 200 B.C. We knew this text in its Greek translation as contained in the Septuagint, and in other translations, but hitherto nothing had been known of the text in the original Hebrew. So here was a fragment of a book, once a part of Hebrew literature yet not in the Hebrew Canon, the original Hebrew text of which had been lost for about one thousand years.

This discovery caused a great sensation. It was obvious that where one leaf had been found, more leaves and other important material might also be found. Therefore it was decided—quite secretly—to send Schechter to Cairo so that he might try and bring back to Cambridge whatever he could find in the Geniza. Dr. Charles Taylor, Master of St. John's College, Cambridge, a mathematician who was also greatly interested in Rabbinic studies—he had published for instance a critical edition of the

[1] P. Alejandro Diez Macho, M.S.C., Valiosos manuscritos bíblicos en la Biblioteca Nacional y Universitaria de Estrasburgo. *Estudios Biblicos* vol. xvi, 1957, pp. 83–88.

[2] Cf. S. Schechter 'The Lewis-Gibson Collection', in *JQR*, vol. ix, 1897, pp. 115 ff.

[3] Cf. N. Bentwich, loc. cit. p. 140.

[4] The Fragments of the Palestinian Talmud are published by Louis Ginzberg: *Yerushalmi Fragments from the Genizah.* vol. i, Text with various readings from the *editio princeps*, New York, 1909.

Ginzberg's running commentary began to be published in New York 1941: *Commentary on Berakhot*, Perek 1–4, and comprised three very large volumes. After Ginzberg's death another volume was published. If this commentary should be continued in the same manner it would comprise well over one hundred volumes!

Mishna-tract Pirḳe Aboth, the 'Sayings of the Jewish Fathers'—put the necessary funds for this remarkable journey at Schechter's disposal. Schechter was provided with a letter of recommendation from Cambridge University, addressed to the President of the Jewish Community of Cairo, stating that the journey was undertaken on behalf of the Cambridge University Library. He left for Cairo in December 1896.[1]

A letter of introduction from Elkan N. Adler in London to the Chief Rabbi in Cairo, Rafail b. Shim'on, who had helped E. N. Adler when he had wished to visit the Geniza, brought Schechter in contact with this man[2] through whose influence he received permission to enter the Geniza and take away with him whatever he wanted.

To work in the dark and dusty room was certainly no easy task, but his great energy and enthusiasm enabled him to complete his task within a few weeks.[3] He had permission to take the whole contents with him, but decided to take only the MS fragments and to leave the printed ones. He was interested in hitherto unknown texts which could contribute towards Jewish history and theology, and such material was more likely to be found in MSS than in printed matter. From his point of view we can understand his decision and under the prevailing circumstances only a general selection was possible.[4] We know today that the printed texts also are of importance. Special investigations of printed fragments have revealed very interesting facts about the history of Hebrew printing in the fifteenth and sixteenth centuries.[5] Schechter filled a number of big sacks and large cases with the fragments.[6] The British Embassy in Cairo procured the permit for the export of the material from Egypt and they arrived safely at the University Library in Cambridge even before Schechter himself who returned to Cambridge via Palestine where he visited his relatives.

The Library Syndicate of June 14th 1898 made the following statement concerning the Geniza material:

[1] Cf. Schechter's *Studies in Judaism*, vol. ii, Philadelphia 1908, pp. 3 ff.

[2] Cf. Adler loc. cit. pp. 672 f. The letter of introduction for Schechter was written, as Elkan N. Adler told me, by himself and not by his brother, the Chief Rabbi Dr. Hermann Adler.

[3] Schechter's own report about his journey is to be found in his *Studies in Judaism*. vol. ii, 1908 p. 5 f. Cf. also N. Bentwich loc. cit. pp. 126 ff.

[4] Cf. Schechter loc. cit. p. 6 f.

[5] Cf. J. L. Teicher, 'Hebrew printed Fragments', *Bodleian Library Record*, vol. i, 1939–41, pp. 234–36.

[6] 'Thirty bags', Bentwich loc. cit., p. 130.

Dr. Taylor, Master of St. John's College, and Dr. Schechter, the Reader in Talmudic, have offered to the University on certain conditions the valuable collection of MSS which Dr. Schechter has brought back from the Geniza of Old Cairo with the consent of the heads of the Jewish Community.

Among the more noteworthy treasures which this Collection contains are fragments of the book of Ecclesiasticus in Hebrew and certain Palimpsests of which the underwriting is Greek and which preserve to us unique fragments of the Hexapla and of Aquilas's version of the Old Testament. There, are, moreover, about twenty large boxes of fragments which contain matter of much interest to Semitic scholars; for example, Biblical fragments in an early Hebrew hand presenting in some instances the super-linear punctuation, Liturgical fragments and portions of the Talmud and of commentaries thereon; Historical documents (wills etc.); fragments in Arabic mostly written in Hebrew letters; and a few fragments in Syriac.

The conditions upon which the collection is offered to the University are the following:

1. That the MSS be kept in the University Library as a separate collection, to be called by some such name as the Taylor-Schechter collection from the Genizah of Old Cairo.

2. That the thanks of the University be given to the heads of the Jewish community at Cairo with whose consent the MSS were brought to England.

3. That the collection be not used without the consent of the donors for three years from the date of acceptance by the University.

4. That Dr. Schechter have the right to borrow manuscripts of which Fascimiles are not accessible, from the collection, on giving a receipt to the Library for them.

5. That the University undertake to make such provision as is possible by binding, mounting or otherwise for the preservation of the MSS, and to have them sorted, and a list or Catalogue of them drawn up within ten years from the acceptance of the collection.

6. That the fragments of Ecclesiasticus and those with Greek writing remain in the possession of the donors until after they have brought out complete editions of them.

These proposals were accepted and passed in Senate on November 10th 1898. The Cairo Community received from the Senate of Cambridge University an address in Latin, English and Hebrew, which expressed gratitude 'not only on account of the goodwill with which you received our Reader in Talmudic, but also on account of the conspicuous liberality with which you permitted him to return laden with fragments.'

Cambridge University has done its best to fulfil the conditions under which the collection was offered. Within ten years the fragments were brought into a certain order, they were cleaned and polished, and then either put into large cardboard boxes or bound or mounted between glass, and carefully written lists enable anyone who has to do work on the subject to find everything he seeks within a short time. On the basis of these lists I supply herewith a short survey of the material, which at the same time gives an idea of the Geniza material to be found in other collections.

Fragments contained in boxes (164 boxes):

A. Biblical text, arranged by Biblical books in 37 boxes. Fragments with supralinear punctuation: boxes 38, 39. Colophons, Bible in shorthand, phylacteries, Apocrypha and Pseudepigrapha, boxes 40–5.
B. Versions of the Bible, Trilingual (Hebrew, Aramaic, Arabic) Bible with Targum, Targum alone: 20 boxes.
C. Midrash: Ibn Ezra, Mechilta, Torat Kohanim, Commentaries on the Bible, &c. 7 boxes.
D. Masora: 1 box.
E. Mishna: 4 boxes.
F. Talmud: Text, Commentaries, pointed Talmud text, Maimonides, Halakhot Gedolot, Aruch, Sheeltot, Alfasi, Minor tractates, Sefer Turim, Talmud Yerushalmi, 17 boxes.
G. Responsa in general and Responsa of the Geonim, 2 boxes.
H. Liturgy, originally 18 boxes, now mostly bound up. Of special interest: fragments with Palestinian and Babylonian punctuation.
I. Documents and letters, Bills and Lists, Historical letters, &c. 3 boxes.
K. Miscellaneous: Amulets, Calendars, Catalogues, Children's exercises, Children's Readers, Colophons, Dictionaries, Grammar, Illuminated fragments, Indices, Jottings, Kabbala, Maimonides, Medicine, Magic and Charms, Names, Pedigrees, Poetry, Polemics, Printed Vellum, Saadyana, Vocabularies, Yosippon. Together 27 boxes.

Besides:

Arabic Fragments: Bible, Calendar, Children's Exercise books, Documents, Grammar, Lexicography, History,

Letters and Bills, Liturgy, Masora, Mathematics, Astronomy, Science, Medicine, Philosophy, Poetry, Polemics against the Ḳaraites, Ḳabbala and Amulets, Religious tracts, Midrash and Homilies, Talmud and Rabbinics, Muhammedan fragments, Jottings and so forth. Together 20 boxes.

Fragments in bound volumes. Fragments consisting of a certain number of leaves are classified according to size and contents and the contents correspond to the material contained in the boxes. The process of binding material which was first put into boxes is going on.

Fragments mounted between glass: Single pieces written on parchment and on paper regarded as of special value. There are not less than 1,800 fragments preserved in this way.

According to an approximate calculation made by Schechter about 100,000 fragments were brought from Cairo to Cambridge.[1] Supposing that the material which went to other libraries and collections was just as extensive, we could estimate the total number of fragments to be roughly 200,000. However, it is difficult to make such calculations as they must be regarded as only approximate. In any case it is quite clear that we have to reckon with an amazing quantity of material.

And it is not only the quantity but the quality which must be taken into consideration. Some of the most striking finds have already been mentioned in the report of the Cambridge Library Syndicate. Yet they were only the most conspicuous finds, whereas much material of great importance has only come to be appreciated as such in the course of time; even to-day thorough examination of the fragments results in the most outstanding discoveries. It will still be a long time before this great treasure can be used to its full advantage.

2. The Dead Sea Scrolls

However, before going into detail, I must mention the other great discovery of Hebrew manuscripts which originated in 1947 in caves near the Dead Sea. These manuscripts were first regarded with some mistrust, but in view of the many places in which they were found—eleven caves with manuscripts have been discovered—the large number of manuscripts that came to

[1] *Studies in Judaism*, Second Series. Philadelphia, 1908, p. 9.

light—fragments of about six hundred works are known so far—and the unusual importance that must be ascribed to many of them, any idea of forgery must be dismissed. A good survey of the finds is to be found in the book *Dix ans de découvertes dans le désert de Juda* (Paris 1957) published by the Abbé J. T. Milik, who, according to Père de Vaux, the leader of the excavations and the work on the scrolls, knows the places excavated and the manuscripts discovered better than anybody else. In the Archaeological Museum in Jerusalem (Jordan) an international and interconfessional group of scholars is working on the very large material which was collected from the excavations and from the caves.[1, 2]

The most important finds were made in a number of caves near the site of ruins called Khirbet Qumran which are not, as previously suggested, the remains of a Roman citadel, but rather the one-time centre of a sort of settlement belonging to a religious order. A large cemetery with over one thousand distinguishable graves represents the last resting-place of the members of the order. So far eleven such caves near Khirbet Qumran have been explored in which fragments of MSS have been found; they have been named Qumran Caves 1–11 and it is to be supposed that the discovered texts are parts of MSS which belonged to the religious order and were deposited in the caves by members of it.

The first cave, discovered by Bedouin in 1947, is the best known. A shepherd came upon it when in search of a stray goat. He threw a stone into the cave and this broke one of the earthenware jars which stood there containing MSS. The scrolls had originally been wrapped carefully in linen and deposited in the earthenware jars the lids of which were tightly closed. Obviously when the texts were hidden everything was done to preserve the scrolls as long as possible. The examination of the cave has shown, however, that most of the scrolls once hidden there were removed a long time ago. Judging from the broken pieces there must have been in the cave about fifty jars of which with very few exceptions only the debris remained; of the MSS originally stored only seven, intact or in fragments, have been found. Four of these were taken to America where three of them were published in New Haven in 1950–51 by the American Schools

[1] Cf. 'Le Travail d'Édition des Fragments Manuscripts de Qumran', *RB*, lxiii, 1956, pp. 49–67.

[2] Cf. Christoph Burchard. 'Bibliographie zu den Handschriften vom Toten Meer'. *BZAW* 76, Berlin 1957 (with more than 1550 titles).

of Oriental Research.[1] Subsequently the four MSS have been returned to Jerusalem and together with the remaining three have been acquired by the Hebrew University of Jerusalem which has now started publishing them independently.[2]

On the basis of certain archaeological findings Father de Vaux supposed that the scrolls from the first Qumran cave were hidden there by their owners about A.D. 70 to protect them from the advancing Roman soldiers. It may be possible to account for the contents of one or the other nearby caves in this way, but we have no decisive evidence. With regard to Qumran Cave I it seems to me rather improbable. The careful way in which the MSS were deposited in the cave tells against the surmise; they were obviously put there with the intention of preserving them as long as possible. The logical conclusion is that temporary war measures were not responsible, but that it was a case of a solemn final concealment of the communal library. This could only have taken place when the community was on the point of dying out. When that happened, however, we do not know. We have no account of Jewish history for the period after Josephus. But we know for certain that at the time when Josephus wrote his *Antiquities* and Pliny reported about the Essenes, the religious order was in a vigorous condition and could have had no reason to store its books carefully in a hidden and inaccessible place. Interesting directions for the solemn preservation of a library are to be found in the so-called *Assumption of Moses*, a pseudepigraphical Apocalypse from about the beginning of our era. It reads (i, 16–18, Charles II, 415):

> And receive thou the writing that thou mayst know how to preserve the books which I shall deliver unto thee, and thou shalt set these in order and anoint them with oil of cedar and put them away in earthen vessels in the place which He made from the beginning of the creation of the world, that His name should be called upon until the day of repentance in the visitation wherewith the Lord will visit them in the consummation of the end of the days.

[1] *The Dead Sea Scrolls of St. Mark's Monastery*, vol. i: The Isaiah Manuscript and the Habakkuk Commentary. Edited for the Trustees by Millar Burrows, with the assistance of John C. Trever and William H. Brownlee. Published by the American Schools of Oriental Research, New Haven 1950. vol. iii, Fascicle 2: Plates and Transcriptions of the Manual of Discipline . . . New Haven, 1951.

[2] Eleazar Lipa Sukenik, *Megillot Genuzot* i 1948, ii 1950. *Oṣar ha-Megillot ha-Genuzot* 1954. *A Genesis Apocryphon.* A Scroll from the Wilderness of Judaea, by Nahman Avigad and Jigael Yadin. Jerusalem, 1956.

A solemn concealment of a similar kind is indicated in the case of the Qumran community.

According to examinations of the cave a large number both of very small and also of larger MS fragments must have lain in the cave at the time when the Bedouin shepherd entered it. These fragments were probably remains of MSS which were removed from the cave at an earlier date. They give us a faint idea of the size of the library originally stored there. These recovered fragments have now been carefully examined and published.[1] The MSS of which the fragments are a part must have been removed from the cave a long time ago.[2]

A letter written in the Syriac language by the Nestorian Patriarch of Seleucia Timotheus I (A.D. 726–819) to Sergius, Metropolitan of Elam—the letter is not dated, but must have been written about A.D. 800—relates that trustworthy people had told him of a discovery of books about ten years earlier in a small cave in the rocks near Jericho. The dog of an Arab huntsman had disappeared into the cave and as it did not come out its master entered the cave to look for it and came across the books.[3] He notified the Jews of Jerusalem numbers of whom came to the spot and found the books of the Old [Testament] and others, written in Hebrew.

It seems to me that far more importance has to be attributed to this MS find about the year A.D. 800 than has been done hitherto. Above all it is more than likely that the cave found in 800 was the same as that discovered anew under similar circumstances in 1947. This cave Qumran I is the only one of the caves near Khirbet Qumran in which more or less complete MS scrolls were found. All the other caves, which under the stimulus of the first find were discovered in the course of the next few years, contained only small fragments, sometimes very numerous and of the greatest importance, but no MSS.[4] As we have seen, most

[1] *Discoveries in the Judaean Desert I: Qumran Cave 1*, by D. Barthélemy and J. T. Milik... Oxford, 1955.

[2] I have mentioned this fact in *ThLZ*, 1952, 401 (*Opera Minora*, Leiden, 1956, p. 96).

[3] Professor Oscar Braun of Würzburg published the letter in Syriac with a German translation in *Oriens Christianus*, vol. i, 1901, pp. 299–313. His translation reads: 'A little house in the rock'. This is a misunderstanding, for a cave also serves as an abode and is in this case spoken of as a 'bait' (house). As this cave was rather on the small side, the writer uses the diminutive form 'baitōnā', meaning a small cave.

Johannes Fück drew Otto Eissfeldt's attention to Braun's article who has reproduced and revived the main items of the translation in *ThLZ*, 1949, 598.

[4] MSS have been found in the eleventh Qumran cave, recently discovered, but they were neither wrapped in linen nor deposited in jars. I owe this to the Rev. J. T. Milik.

of the MSS once deposited in Qumran I were removed long ago. It is very probable that this happened about the year 800.

We have to take into account that the Jews in Jerusalem who studied the MSS discovered in about 800 belonged largely to the community of the Ḳaraites which was founded in about 760 by 'Anan, a Davidite, after the influential circles of the Babylonian Jews had refused to make him their leader in the Exile (*Rēš Galūtha*). His ancestry would have qualified him to occupy this position but it seems that he was unfavourably disposed towards the *oral teaching* as codified by the Rabbis in the Mishna and developed in the Talmud. He encouraged his followers to make a personal study of the Bible.

The Ḳaraite community of Babylonia apparently soon found followers in Jerusalem. At all events we hear of a number of Ḳaraite scholars in the course of the ninth century who worked in Jerusalem. This city soon became the spiritual centre of the Ḳaraites and by the second half of the ninth century they had a far greater influence in spiritual matters than the resident Rabbanites. Jacob Mann, with the help of the Geniza material, has proved this beyond doubt.[1] But surely the only explanation of this success lies in the fact that the Ḳaraites had come into possession of old material which they studied eagerly and successfully, whereas the Rabbanite circles took little notice of it because it did not fit in with their teachings. This material would appear to have been the MS scrolls brought to Jerusalem about the year 800 from the cave near Jericho.

Amongst these MSS must have been the so-called *Damascus Document* which was published in 1910 by Solomon Schechter from fragments out of the Cairo Geniza under the title *Fragments of a Zadokite Work*.[2] It contained a text which was entirely different from all Jewish writings we had hitherto known. This was at first rather baffling.

3. The Ḳaraites

But it soon became apparent that there was a close connection between this text and Ḳaraite teaching. Attempts have been made to explain the relationship by suggesting that the *Damascus*

[1] Jacob Mann, *The Jews in Egypt and in Palestine under the Fāṭimid Caliphs*, vol. i, Oxford, 1920, pp. 60 f. Mann, *Ḳaraitica* (*Texts and Studies in Jewish History and Literature*, vol. ii) (a volume of more than 1600 pages), Philadelphia, 1935, pp. 3 f.

[2] *Documents of Jewish Sectaries*, vol. i, Cambridge 1910.

Document was itself indebted to the Ḳaraites.[1] But the text gave the undoubted impression of being ancient. It was not written in the Hebrew of the Rabbis which had to be used for all Hebrew texts written after the beginning of Jewish reorganization subsequent to the destruction of the Temple, but in a language closely resembling the Hebrew of the later books of the Bible. The antiquity of the *Damascus Document* has been confirmed by the discovery of fragments belonging to it in Khirbet Qumran, three such fragments in the sixth cave and fragments of a further seven MSS in the fourth Qumran cave. What is more, the *Manual of Discipline,* found in the first Qumran cave, contains a text closely related to the *Damascus Document* and was evidently widely known: five fragments were found in the third Qumran Cave and fragments of eleven more MSS of the *Manual* were unearthed in the fourth Qumran cave.

The text of the *Damascus Document* must have been the very thing the Ḳaraites had been looking for. Through ʻAnan, their founder, they were unfavourably disposed towards the codified oral teaching of the Rabbis. Here at last was a text which certainly came from priestly circles. They studied the text very carefully, and together with other similar writings which may have reached them from the cave near Jericho it must have greatly influenced the development of their teachings.

That this influence can to a certain extent be traced in detail was confirmed by discussions I had with Dr. Moses Zucker, a pupil of Aptowitzer, who has been for more than twenty years on the staff of the *Seminary Israel Institute,* belonging to the Jewish Theological Seminary of America in New York. We discussed the connection between the *Damascus Document* and the early Ḳaraites. At my request he collected some observations which proved the influence in detail which the *Damascus Document* must have had on a prominent Ḳaraite, Daniel el-Ḳūmisī, who lived and worked in the middle of the ninth century in Jerusalem and was one of the early Ḳaraite settlers there.

In the Geniza fragments, from which Schechter published the text of the *Damascus Document,* we have remains of copies made by the Ḳaraites of the day. The fragments found in the Qumran caves will make possible a new edition of this important text and should enable us in some cases to fill in lacunae and solve textual problems more satisfactorily than we could previously have hoped.

[1] Cf. A. Büchler's review of Schechter's book, in *JQR*, vol. iii, 1912–13, pp. 429–85.

In the *Manual of Discipline* (closely related to the *Damascus Document*) published by the American Schools of Oriental Research in New Haven 1951 according to the MS from the first Qumran cave, directions are laid down to regulate the life of the community of the New Covenant. The same regulations can be found, though a little shorter, in the *Damascus Document*. At times the texts are the same word for word, whilst at other times they reveal discrepancies which are of interest for the history of the community.

In addition, however, the *Damascus Document* contains words of exhortation for which we have so far found no parallel in the MSS from the caves. These passages are particularly interesting because they provide important clues for the history of the community and for the reasons which led to its birth. The translation of the concluding part (VI 11f) runs as follows:

> And all those who have made the resolution not to enter the temple any more or to kindle the fire on the altar in vain, who 'have closed the door', by so doing have fulfilled what God has said (Mal i 10): Oh, that there were some amongst you who would close the door so that no fire may be kindled on my altar in vain![1]

Only the priests were entrusted with kindling fire in the Temple, so these words apply to priests who had resolved not to enter the Temple and not to kindle fire in vain on the altar. They are called the *closers of the door* whom the Prophet Malachi had prophesied. These priests had evidently taken their duties in the Temple very seriously, but had at this time made up their minds to renounce their privileges, withdraw from the Temple and search for a place where they and their followers could live according to their ideals. Their withdrawal must have taken place at the time when the Bnē Ṣadoḳ lost their dominant position in the Temple at Jerusalem, i.e. the time of Antiochus Epiphanes. That the *Damascus Document* belongs to this time was clearly recognized by Eduard Meyer in his *Akademie Abhandlung*, Berlin 1919[2]. In the third chapter of his book *The Zadokite Fragments and the Dead Sea Scrolls*[3] H. H. Rowley has given an excellent survey of the discussion concerning the age of the text and has come to the same conclusion. An identical date has been

[1] I have written about this passage in *ThLZ*, 1952, p. 405. Israel Lévi realized that: 'Ce morceau . . . semble décisif pour l'histoire de la secte'. *REJ*, lxi, 1910, p. 183.

[2] *Die Gemeinde des Neuen Bundes im Lande Damaskus. Eine Jüdische Schrift aus der Seleukidenzeit.*

[3] Oxford, 1952, Chapter iii, pp. 62 ff.

given by Isaak Rabbinowitz[1] in his noteworthy essay about the texts found in the first Qumran cave.

André Michel decides likewise[2] when he discusses the historical interpretation of the Qumran texts and particularly the Habakkuk Commentary.

The priests here called Bnē Ṣadoḳ succeeded the Levites as the priestly class; they were descended from a priest called Ṣadoḳ who had held the office of High Priest at the Temple in Jerusalem in the time of Solomon. Even before the Exile the sacerdotal dignity had been hereditary in the family and it remained so after the Exile. The book of Ben Sira gives us a good idea of the importance of these Ṣadoḳite priests. Proposing to enumerate the important men of Israel, in reality the author writes a panegyric upon its priests. Men like Abraham, Isaac, Jacob, Joseph, even Moses are only given a few lines whereas Aaron and the Aaronites are the subject of long eulogies. They form the centre of the whole passage. The panegyric ends with a hymn to Simon, the last high priest of the Bnē Ṣadoḳ who was held in great esteem and about whom the author writes in a psalm:

> Give thanks unto Him that chooseth the Bnē Ṣadoḳ to be priests;
> For His mercy endureth for ever.

It is understandable that when Ben Sira's grandson made the Greek translation of his grandfather's Hebrew text at the end of the second century B.C., he left out the psalm. By that time the reign of the Bnē Ṣadoḳ in the Temple at Jerusalem had long ceased.

We must keep in mind this high esteem for the old priestly class of the Temple in Jerusalem when we read the *Damascus Document.* The Bnē Ṣadoḳ held an outstanding position amongst the priests who withdrew from the Temple. Ezekiel xliv 15 is quoted where the Levitical priests, the Bnē Ṣadoḳ, are mentioned, and the following comment is made.

> The priests are those who have been converted in Israel and have left the land of Judah. The Levites are those who have joined them. The Bnē Ṣadoḳ are the chosen of Israel whose name will be known until the last day.

[1] *VT*, iii, 1953 pp. 175–185.

[2] A. Michel, *Le Maître de Justice, d'après les documents de la Mer Morte, la littérature, apocryphe et rabbinique*, xv, 335 pp. Avignon, 1954. Cf. the review of the book by R. de Vaux, *RB*, xii, 1955, pp. 299 f.

The *Manual* reads:

> Those who lead a life according to the rules of the Bnē Ṣadoḳ who keep the covenant.

These priests, led by the Bnē Ṣadoḳ, had been deprived of their rights by outsiders who had usurped those rights with the support of the people. A number, probably the most conscientious, had in consequence emigrated and together with their followers sought a new place of worship.

The opponents of these priests who had withdrawn are described as people who built a wall and covered it with unmixed mortar; who built a hedge around the law. Solomon Schechter and Israel Lévi instantly identified them as the Pharisees. I think it is worth while to recall the following words which the discoverer and first editor of the *Damascus Document* writes on page xxviii of his introduction:

> The general impression we receive from the Rabbinic literature, which remains, after all, the only authoritative source for the teachings of the Pharisees, is that they had a deep aversion to all "external writings". . . . Hence it is not likely that they would have indulged in the production of a literature towards which they all maintained a more or less hostile attitude. And this impression is now confirmed by our Text. For whatever difficulties the present unsatisfactory state of our MS may place in the way of the student . . . one thing is certain, that we have to deal here with a Sect decidedly hostile to the bulk of the Jews as represented by the Pharisees. It is a Sect equipped with additional sacred books of its own, a calendar of its own, and a set of laws of its own, bearing upon various commandments of the Scripture.

The foregoing are the words of a man who had a deep historical understanding of the subject. Israel Lévi pronounced much the same verdict. On the other hand, the learned Talmudist Louis Ginzberg, in twelve long articles published in the *Monatsschrift für die Geschichte und Wissenschaft des Judentums*, 1911–14, which, enlarged by an additional chapter, were published in book form,[1] tried to prove that the *Damascus Document* contains nothing which could not have been written by a Pharisee. Even if this were theoretically possible, it would lead here to a complete misinterpretation of the facts. We must not forget that the passage in question is a polemical one. Ginzberg's articles are undoubtedly

[1] Louis Ginzberg, *Eine unbekannte jüdische Sekte I*, New York, 1922.

a source of knowledge for those who can read them critically, and for that reason the forthcoming English translation of the articles which have been long out of print is to be welcomed, all the more as three chapters will be included which up to now have been available only in manuscript.[1] Let us hope it will find discerning readers! In general, however, it must be said that Ginzberg's arguments have obstructed the understanding of the *Damascus Document*. It is opportune to remind ourselves, therefore, that scholars like Solomon Schechter and Israel Lévi from the very first prepared the ground for a real historical assessment of the text.

Hugo Gressmann in his well-known review of Schechter's book misunderstood one essential point[2] and thereby misled Eduard Meyer, who otherwise contributed much towards the proper understanding of the text by his *Akademie Abhandlung* of 1919 mentioned above. What the priests complained about were real changes introduced by the Rabbis which must have given the impression to the priests of destroying the law, although the Rabbis contended that they protected it. This was, it seems to me, rightly appreciated in the main by Rudolf Leszynsky as early as 1912. I think he proved beyond doubt that the *Damascus Document* is strongly anti-Pharisee in regard to vows, marriage laws, the Sabbath, the calendar, the sacrifices, the laws of cleanliness, and oaths, and especially in its attitude towards the Aaronite priests.[3]

We must remember that after the introduction of the law by Ezra who was himself one of the Bnē Ṣadoḳ its interpretation was left entirely in the hands of the priests. This privilege was still substantially claimed by them in the time of Ben Sira. But since the time of Alexander the Great the Greeks had come within the Jewish mental horizon and the Jews had made contact with Greek civilization. The traditional interpretation of the law, practised until then by the priests, was out of date. Lay-people started to take part in its interpretation. Little evidence of this development has come to light hitherto, because the literature

[1] Cf. H. Louis Ginsberg, 'The Dead Sea Manuscript Finds: New Light on *Eretz Yisrael* in the Greco-Roman Period'. in *Israel: Its Role in Civilization*, ed. Moshe David. The Seminary Israel Institute of the Jewish Theological Seminary of America. New York, 1956.

[2] Cf. Gressmann's review of Schechter's book in *ZDMG* lxvi, 1912 pp. 491–505, especially p. 495: Der sonderbare, im Anschluss an Mal. i, 10 geprägte Titel der 'Türschliesser' (6.12) ist mir unverständlich geblieben.

[3] Rudolf Leszynsky, *Die Sadduzäer*, Berlin, 1912, pp. 142–67.

issuing from priestly circles was systematically suppressed and destroyed by the Rabbis in power. In the *Damascus Document* we have for the first time a document which goes back to priestly sources. This accounts for its seeming so unusual when it became known to us. In the eyes of the priests the rulings of the ever increasingly influential Rabbis violated the law. We are inclined to think of relaxations suggesting themselves by customary law. The Rabbis had to try and prove that such changes were no changes at all. They summarized them under the heading of 'oral law' which they gave the required authority by maintaining that it was very ancient and had been revealed to Moses on Mount Sinai together with the 'written law', the Torah.

The great significance of the books found in the caves obviously lies in the fact that they belonged for the most part to the priestly literature. The religious community, in whose possession the books had been, was formed by the followers of those priests who, under protest, had severed their ties with the Temple in Jerusalem. In the new community they retained their dominant influence. We can well understand that the library consisted largely of books which derived from priestly circles and carried on the priestly traditions. Through concealment in inaccessible caves these books were preserved from the Rabbis who managed to destroy the whole literature, in its original language, which dealt with priestly traditions. Parts of it have survived in translations. Often the Christians revised these for Christian purposes and, as Apocrypha and Pseudepigrapha, they have played their part and have had their influence in Christian circles.[1]

When the Ḳaraites studied the MSS brought to Jerusalem from the cave near Jericho, they soon became aware that these were texts from priestly circles considerably older than the texts with the help of which the Rabbis had accomplished the codification of oral teaching in the Mishna and Talmud. It is known that the Ḳaraites appealed to Sadducean texts, and how they had come by such texts presented a real problem. The Sadducees had been dispersed when the Temple was destroyed and the Ḳaraite movement only began in the course of the eighth century. So the handing down of Sadducean teaching must have been achieved by literary means. But what literature was involved?

[1] Cf. Ethelbert Stauffer, 'Probleme der Priestertradition', *ThLZ*, 1956, pp. 135–50. Cf. the instructive remarks about Apocrypha and Pseudepigrapha by Rudolf Leszynsky, *Die Sadduzäer*, Berlin, 1912, pp. 168–279.

All texts appertaining to Sadducean literature had been destroyed by the Rabbis. Josephus, who more than once mentions Sadducean teachings, never came within the purview of the founders of the Ḳaraite community and is certainly never mentioned by them. There remains the Talmud from which we learn a variety of facts about the Sadducees; yet no trace can be found in it of special features which relate Sadducean to Ḳaraite teaching. The connecting link was missing. There can hardly be any doubt that the texts found at the beginning of the ninth century and studied carefully by the Ḳaraites, based on priestly tradition as they are, constitute this connecting link.

The Ḳaraites speak about the MSS from the cave. When Ja'ḳūb al-Ḳirḳisānī in his great work *kitāb al-anwār wal-marāḳib*,[1] written about 937, enumerates the old Jewish sects, he mentions *after* the Samaritans and *after* the Pharisees and Sadducees, but *before* the Christians, a Jewish sect, which he simply calls cave-people (*maghārīya*), explaining that their name is derived from their books which they had found in a cave (*maghār*). The name, which is often misspelt[2] in the various editions of the texts, must have been very well known in the ninth and tenth centuries. Ḳaraite writers use it quite frequently, but it is also known to Muslim writers.[3]

It is more than probable that the members of the religious order who made their centre at the place we call Khirbet Qumrān deposited their MSS in the nearby caves. Maybe they belonged to the religious community which Josephus and Pliny call Essaites or Essenes.

What this religious order called itself we know no better than Ḳirḳisānī; they could only be called *cave-people* after the MSS had been found which they had deposited in the cave (*maghār*). We only learn from the *Damascus Document*, published by Schechter from fragments in the Cairo Geniza which had been copied from scrolls taken out of the cave, that this community was

[1] *Kitāb al-Anwār wal-Marāqib*, *Code of Karaite Law*, by Ya'qūb al-Qirqisānī, ed. Leon Nemoy. New York 1939–45, I, 2, 5–8. Cf. Leon Nemoy, 'al-Qirqisānī's Account of the Jewish Sects and Christianity', *HUCA*, vol. vii, Cincinnati 1930, pp. 325 ff.

[2] Apart from *maghārīya*, there are misspellings such as *maghāriba*, *maqāriba*, *maqārīya* etc.

[3] For instance al-Bīrūnī, *Chronology* . . . Ed. Sachau, p. 284, who quotes as his source of information Abū 'Īsā al-Warrāḳ (died A.D. 909) and Shahrastānī, Mas'ūdī, abu'l-Fiḍā, Maḳrīzī and others. Cf. de Vaux, *RB*, lvii, 1950, pp. 417–29 and the literature quoted by him.

formed by followers of priests who in protest had resigned from service in the Temple. The *Damascus Document* also tells us, and the *Manual of Discipline* confirms, that this community founded by the priests' followers lived under the leadership of the priests. When about the year 800 the MSS were brought to Jerusalem from the cave near Jericho, they made a great impression on the newly-founded community of the Ḳaraites. They saw that these were obviously written by priestly circles and recognized them as Sadducean texts; subsequently they accorded them a great influence in the development of their teaching.

Among the texts brought to Jerusalem from the Jericho caves were, no doubt, the scrolls with the Hebrew text of Ben Sira. We have seen clearly that this text must come from priestly circles. Moreover we can well understand that the Rabbis were not in favour of including such a text in the Hebrew Bible. MSS of the Hebrew text of the book were suppressed at an early date and it took a long time before the text was available again. The chapter: 'Ben Sira's Proverbs in Talmudic and Rabbinic Literature' in Cowley and Neubauer's edition of the Oxford fragments from Ecclesiasticus has proved this unmistakably.[1] When, about A.D. 800, MS scrolls of Ecclesiasticus in Hebrew were brought from the cave near Jericho to Jerusalem, they must have been eagerly studied by the Ḳaraites. We know that the Hebrew text was still available during the ninth and tenth centuries, maybe a little longer. But then the Rabbis seem once more to have succeeded in suppressing it completely. They also saw to it that the copies made between the ninth and eleventh centuries of the old scrolls which had been found in the cave near Jericho disappeared into the Genizas. It was from the Geniza in Old Cairo that the Hebrew of Ben Sira first emerged again.

Since Schechter published in the *Expositor* of July 6th 1896 the historical fragment belonging to the Scottish ladies a large number of fragments from the Geniza have been published—the last one, a fragment of a fifth MS of Ben Sira in Hebrew, as late as 1931 by Joseph Markus in *JQR* xxi, 1931, pp. 223–37 = MS Adler 3597. The material discovered earlier was published in a large critical edition by Rudolf Smend who also brought out a scholarly com-

[1] Cf. Ben Sira's Proverbs preserved in Talmudic and Rabbinic Literature in *The Original Hebrew of a portion of Ecclesiasticus*. . . . Ed. A. E. Cowley and Ad. Neubauer, Oxford, 1897, pp. xix–xxx.

mentary.[1] Smend's conclusions with regard to Ben Sira's Hebrew text are as follows (p. lix):

> . . . that the textual history ceased not long after the Syrian translation had been made can be explained by the fact that the book was read less and less and sank into oblivion in the centres of Jewish scholarship such as Babylonia and Palestine. As a result both the spontaneous corruption of the text and also the blending of the various recensions came to an end. This is one of the reasons why it seems probable that text A, as well as text B and text D originates from Persia. Only the florilegistic text C could have a different origin.

Page lxii reads:

> In many cases we have, next to more recent variants, an older wording which corresponds with Greek readings. On the whole, translations, especially the Greek, not only improve the Hebrew, but generally prove its value or at least its age to a much higher degree than is to be expected from such numerous and thorough corruptions. On the other hand the Hebrew text provides the explanation for two-thirds of the Syrian and the Greek book, at the same time offering most valuable parallels for the interpretation of the third part.

Now, however, after the discovery of the MSS in the caves near the Dead Sea, the matter has assumed a different aspect. Two fragments of scrolls with the Hebrew text of Ben Sira have been found in the second Qumran cave. They give us an idea of the scrolls which were taken to Jerusalem about 800 from the first Qumran cave and which were copied by the Ḳaraites to the best of their ability. Moreover, there is no doubt that Ben Sira's Hebrew text had not only ceased to be read in Babylonia and Palestine, the chief centres of Jewry at that time, as Smend suggests, but also that, generally speaking, Jewish circles had no exact knowledge of it. The Rabbis had systematically suppressed and eliminated it. The Persian marginal notes found in one of Ben Sira's Hebrew MSS do not prove that the Hebrew text had been handed down in Persia, but only that Ḳaraites coming from Persia—there were many of them in Jerusalem in the ninth century—had participated in the copying out of the Hebrew Ben Sira text. How the original Hebrew text compares with the

[1] *Die Weisheit des Jesus Sirach*, erklärt von Rudolf Smend. Berlin 1906. *Die Weisheit des Jesus Sirach*, Hebräisch und Deutsch, herausgegeben von Rudolf Smend, mit einem hebräischen Glossar. *Griechisch-Syrisch-Hebräischer Index zur Weisheit des Jesus Sirach*, von Rudolf Smend. Berlin, 1907.

Geniza fragments has been stated above in Smend's words, and our verdict today would not very much differ. I recommend a short, instructive article by H. L. Ginsberg, 'The Original Hebrew of Ben Sira xii 10–14', in *JBL* lxxiv, 1955, pp. 93–5.

Amongst the texts brought to Jerusalem about 800 was the Aramaic original of the Testament of Levi. Fragments from the Geniza belonging to copies of this text came to Oxford and Cambridge. Old fragments of the Aramaic text have been found in the first as well as in the fourth Qumran cave. J. T. Milik has pointed out that no fragments in the Aramaic or Hebrew originals have been found of any of the other Testaments of the Twelve Patriarchs. He has drawn the correct conclusion that the Testaments of the Twelve Patriarchs which we know represent a later composition based on the typically Jewish Testament of Levi written in Aramaic.[1] This Testament of Levi is therefore another of the texts deriving from priestly circles which, about 800, came into Ḳaraite hands.

It would not be difficult to identify further texts studied by the Ḳaraites in Jerusalem about the year 800. Generally speaking we can assume that they were in possession of all those texts from which little broken-off fragments remained in the first Qumran cave when it was recently rediscovered. The more or less complete MSS, of which we can only form an idea from the broken-off fragments, were taken to Jerusalem; it may be that there were scrolls among them from which no fragments broke off.[2]

In any case these MSS going back to priestly circles must have made a profound impression on the Ḳaraites.

If we consider what Ḳirḳisānī relates concerning the books of the cave dwellers which became available at the beginning of the ninth century, if we further consider that a tremendous amount of work was done on the Bible text by the Tiberian Masoretes during the course of that century, and if finally we realize that this same text, fixed by the Masoretes, was accepted throughout Judaism by Rabbanites and Ḳaraites alike, clearly at a time when the differences between the two parties had not yet come

[1] Cf. J. T. Milik, 'Le Testament de Levi en Araméen'. *RB* lxii, 1955, 398–406. Pierre Grelot, 'Notes sur le Testament Araméen de Lévi', *RB* lxiii, 1956, pp. 391–406. Récemment nous avons pu identifier un second Testament; celui de Naphtali, écrit en hebreu. Le fragment contient la généalogie de Bilha . . . Milik, l.c. p. 32.

[2] An interesting testimony to the growth of the Ḳaraites during the ninth century is provided by the tenth century Ḳaraite author Salmon b. Jeruchim in a passage which I quote *infra* on p. 80 f.

to a head with the controversy between Sa'adya and his opponents, there is hardly room for doubt, I think, that it was the MSS from the cave near Jericho which were responsible for the remarkable growth of the Ḳaraites during the ninth century.

I now return to the discoveries made in the Cairo Geniza and shall deal with a few of the main finds.

Burkitt's scholarly edition of the remains of Aquila's Greek translation of the Bible formed one of the earliest publications of Geniza Fragments.[1] Here for the first time we had continuous texts of at least a few verses from this translation which we had previously known only through quotations by the Church Fathers. They enabled Burkitt to make several important deductions. The publication will retain its importance even after the publication of the much larger fragments of Origen's Hexapla which were discovered by Giovanni Mercati about the same time in a palimpsest of the Ambrosiana at Milan.[2] The 35 folios of the palimpsest contain about 150 verses of the Psalms, and not only in Aquila's translation: five of the six columns of the Hexapla are preserved here, the first column with the Hebrew text in Hebrew letters alone being missing. On the other hand, the Milan fragments are more recent than the Geniza fragments published by Burkitt and they are written in minuscules whilst Burkitt's fragments were in uncials.[3]

4. The Khazars

Another fragment, of wider interest, was published by Schechter in 1913 under the title *An unknown Khazar Document.*[4] The Khazars formed a mighty kingdom to the north of the Caspian and Black Seas. The Arab geographers and historians of the tenth century report many details of their manners and customs, their wars

[1] *Fragments of the Book of Kings according to the Translation of Aquila*, by F. Crawford Burkitt, Cambridge, 1897.—Some fragments of the Hexapla, parts of Psalm xxii, were published by Charles Taylor, *Hebrew-Greek Cairo Genizah Palimpsests*, Cambridge, 1900.

[2] *Atti della Accademia Reale delle Scienze di Torino, vol. xxxi*, Disp. 11, 1895–6. A specimen was published by Ceriani in *Rendiconti del Reale Istituto Lomb. di Scienze e Lettere*, Ser. 2, vol. xxix, 1896. This specimen was republished by E. Klostermann, in *ZAW*, 1896, pp. 336 f.

[3] The work of Giovanni Cardinal Mercati (d. 22. viii, 1957) is now being edited on behalf of the Bibliotheca Vaticana by Professor G. Castellino. I may refer here to the second chapter of my book where I have dealt especially with the Second Column of the Hexapla of which very important parts are to be found in the Milan fragments. See below, pp. 157 f.

[4] *JQR*, New Series, vol. iii, 1912–13, pp. 181–219.

against their Arab, Byzantine and other neighbours. Byzantine, Russian, Armenian and other sources also recount many particulars about them.[1] The most important Arabic source, Ibn Faḍlān's report of his experiences during his journey with the Embassy staff of the Caliph al-Muḳtadir in 921 and 922, was previously only known from excerpts made by Arab geographers of later times, like Yāḳūt and Ḳazwīnī. In 1923 the text of Ibn Faḍlān's report itself was discovered in Meshhed by Aḥmed Zeki Valīdi Togan in the appendix to a MS containing the second volume of Ibn al-Faḳīh's *Kitāb al-buldān*, a text of which we knew before only from extracts which had been published by M. J. de Goeje in *Bibliotheca Geographorum Arabicorum*, vol. v (Lugduni Batavorum 1885).

Aḥmed Zeki Valīdi Togan devoted himself to the study of the report of Ibn Faḍlān in Vienna, where he studied under Alfons Dopsch, the historian, taking his doctorate on Ibn Faḍlān. I succeeded in obtaining his services for the Oriental Seminar in Bonn for some years. He knew very well from personal experience many of the countries about which Ibn Faḍlān writes, and it was of great interest to discuss with him problems arising from Ibn Faḍlān's text. I accepted his book for publication in the *Abhandlungen für die Kunde des Morgenlandes* as a great scholarly achievement.

The great Russian Academician Professor Ignaz J. Kratschkowski (d. 24.1.1951) has dealt with the work of Ahmed Zeki Valīdi Togan in his book on Russian Arabic studies published by the Academy in 1950 (p. 260).[2] According to him the publication of the text of Ibn Faḍlān from the Meshhed MS in 1939 was a scholarly event for Russia. Particularly since the publications of C.M. Frähn in 1823 and 1832 Ibn Faḍlān has been a classical source for the history of Russia. Under the auspices of the Russian Academy A. P. Kowalewski published the Arabic text of Ibn Faḍlān with an exact Russian translation and a commentary in 1939. The text of Ibn Faḍlān as based on a single MS contains many problems, and the differences between the German and Russian translation and explanation of the text have led to much scholarly discussion with the result that already some years ago

[1] Cf. J. Marquart, *Osteuropäische und Ostasiatische Streifzüge*, Leipzig, 1903, pp. 5–27 and, W. Barthold's excellent article 'Khazar' in the *Encyclopaedia of Islam*, vol. ii.

[2] A German translation of the book *Die Russische Arabistik. Umrisse ihrer Entwickelung* übersetzt und bearbeitet von Otto Mehlitz. VEB Otto Harrassowitz, Leipzig, 1957.

a new Russian revision of the text had become necessary. This new edition also has been made by A. P. Kowalewski. It is to be hoped that a new edition of the book of Zeki Valīdi Togan will be made also, which will take into account the problems raised since the first edition was published; this is especially desirable since most of the copies of the first edition were destroyed in Leipzig during the war.

The reports concerning the Khazars given by the Arabic geographer al-Balkhī (died 934) although lost in the original are mostly preserved in the books of al-Iṣṭakhrī (middle of the tenth century)[1] and Ibn Ḥauḳal (*c.* 975).[2] The Khazar kingdom is of special interest for the Jews. It is—apart from the Jewish kingdom in Adiabene (הדיב) in the middle of the first century[3]—the only Jewish kingdom which has come into existence since the beginning of our era. About 1577 a certain Isaac Abraham Akrish published in Constantinople a small pamphlet קול מבשׂר 'Voice of the Messenger of Good News', intended to raise the spirits of the Jews by proving that there are regions where Israel has been blessed with strong and mighty kings; a correspondence is printed here between Joseph, a Jewish king of the Khazars and Chisdai b. Shafrūṭ, a Jewish physician and high official at the Court of the Omaiyad Caliph 'Abdurraḥmān an-Nāṣir, who reigned in Cordova, Spain, from 912–61.[4] Chisdai had received some information about the Jewish kingdom of the Khazars and addressed a letter in Hebrew to the King, asking him various questions about the history and conditions of his kingdom. The letter was introduced by a poem in verse composed by the well-known Hebrew grammarian and poet Menachem b. Saruḳ. King Joseph, in his answer, gave at least some of the required information.

The genuineness of this correspondence has been much dis-

[1] *Viae Regnorum, Descriptio Ditionis Moslemicae, auctore Abu Ishák al-Fárisí al-Istakhrí Bibliotheca Geographorum Arabicorum*, ed. M. J. de Goeje, Pars prima, Leiden, 1870, reprinted 1927, pp. 217–27. In Sir Alfred Chester Beatty's library a valuable MS of the text is to be found in which various new details about the Khazars are recorded. Other MSS in Istanbul are mentioned by H. Ritter in *Islam*, xix, 1931, pp. 55 f.

[2] *Opus Geographicum*, auctore Ibn Ḥauḳal, *Bibliotheca Geographorum Arabicorum*, ed. J. M. de Goeje, Pars secunda, 1875. A new edition based chiefly on the Serai MS 3346, the oldest MS known, was published by J. H. Kramers, Leiden, 1939. For the report on the Khazars see pp. 386–98.

[3] Cf. *infra* Part III, p. 270.

[4] The correspondence published by Akrish has been re-edited by Paul Kokovtsov in his book on the Hebrew Khazar correspondence in the tenth century (*Еврейско-Хазарская Переписка в X веке*), published by the Russian Academy in Leningrad, 1932. In this book critical texts and careful investigations of all documents involved can be found. As Plate 1, Kokovtsov has given a facsimile of pp. 11b–12a of Akrish's book.

puted; in critical circles it has generally been regarded as a late falsification, especially as no trace of the documents published by Akrish could be found, except the text of a MS belonging to Christ Church Library in Oxford which only dated back as far as the sixteenth century. It was Kokovtsov who proved that this text is of great importance.[1]

Among the MSS collected by Firkowitch was the text of the letter sent by King Joseph to Chisdai, which, though generally in accordance with the letter published by Akrish and based on the same original text, is much longer, offering sometimes better readings and adding in some instances new material particularly in the geographical parts. Firkowitch had shown the fragment to Chwolson in 1870. When Firkowitch's collection was taken to St. Petersburg after his death, and included in the Russian Public Library, the document was rediscovered by Harkavy[2] who published a German translation of the text[3] and a little later the Hebrew text.[4] It seems to me very probable that the fragment belonged to the bundles of fragments which Firkowitch had acquired from the Cairo Geniza.[5] Schechter did not think of this possibility, and Kokovtsov does not doubt that it was found in the Crimea.

It has been suggested—by J. Marquart for instance—that this fragment, coming from Firkowitch, has to be regarded with a critical eye, as it may be one of his usual falsifications.[6] Many others have shared this suspicion.[7] But Harkavy was an expert in Hebrew MSS and very well versed in Firkowitch's forgeries. He would certainly not have published the fragment if he had not been sure that it was old. Kokovtsov published a facsimile of the fragment[8] and there can be no doubt that it is really old; but Kokovtsov has proved that the text of the longer version is not always preferable to that of the shorter version, as the first editor

[1] The MS has been described under No. 1454 in the Catalogue of the Hebrew MSS in the Bodleian Library vol. i, p. 870. A facsimile is given by Kokovtsov, Plate 2.

[2] The fragment is now MS Heb. 157 of the second Firkowitch Collection.

[3] 'Ein Briefwechsel zwischen Cordova und Astrachan zur Zeit Swjatoslaws (um 960), als Beitrag zur alten Geschichte Süd-Russlands', in *Russische Revue*, vol. vi, 1875, pp. 69–97.

[4] The Hebrew text appeared in מאסף נדחים, an appendix to the Hebrew periodical *Ha-Melīs*, No. 8, 1879. A Russian translation of the correspondence was published by Harkavy in the periodical *Европейская Библиотека*, tom. vii. 1879 pp. 153–62.

[5] It is very likely that Akrish received the correspondence in Cairo in 1562 on his way from Constantinople to Egypt and published it in 1577. See J. Mann, *Texts and Studies* . . . vol. i, Cincinnati, 1931, p. 8.

[6] Cf. J. Marquart, loc. cit. Marquart could not discover the place where Harkavy published the Hebrew text of the fragment.

[7] The last was Henry Grégoire, in *Byzantion*, vol. ix, 1934, pp. 484–8.

[8] loc. cit. Plate 3.

supposed, and besides, it is very likely that Firkowitch made a few alterations in it.[1]

Schechter found a second Hebrew fragment relating to the Khazars which undoubtedly came from the Cairo Geniza. It is part of a letter which purports to have been written by one of the entourage of the Khazar King. Beginning and end are missing. It has nothing to do with the documents published by Akrish. It mainly contains reports on the conversion of the Khazars to Judaism and many historical and geographical details. That these reports are written in a somewhat fabulous style and that the letter is not very exact in its details is hardly surprising. We cannot expect a letter of this kind to be more exact. Kokovtsov supposes that the text is strongly influenced by the Sepher Josippon, the well-known story-book composed somewhere in Italy on the basis of a Latin translation of Josephus's book on the Jewish War and other sources. This book, however, seems to be somewhat older than Kokovtsov believed,[2] and there are other reasons for accepting the genuineness of the Cambridge fragment. Even Kokovtsov admits that the document is of value as it contains information on Byzantine matters otherwise unknown to us.

That the correspondence published by Akrish must have existed in the eleventh century is proved by the fact that Jehuda b. Barzillai verbally quotes a part of the letter from the Khazar king in his *Sepher ha-ʿIttīm*, a book on the Holiday Seasons, composed about 1100.[3] There can be no doubt that he had the correspondence in front of him in a form very similar to that known to us.

What has been published about the correspondence has for the most part partaken of the nature of apologetic. Either the genuineness is accepted for reasons similar to those which led Akrish in 1577 to publish it,[4] or it is felt that the ideal picture of Chisdai b. Shafruṭ, the man chiefly concerned, does not agree with that of the man who is said to have written the letter to the king of the Khazars, in which case the genuineness of the correspondence is not thought to be in the interests of the Jews.[5]

[1] Cf. the remark of D. A. Chwolson, who had copied the fragment in 1870, reprinted by Kokovtsov loc. cit. p. xvii, n. 5.

[2] J. Mann has shown that Sepher Josippon was already circulating in the time of Chisdai in Spain. Cf. *Texts and Studies*, vol. i, pp. 15 f.

[3] Cf. S. Asaf in *Jeshurun* xi, Berlin, 1924, pp. 113 ff.

[4] Cf. for instance S. Dubnov's article 'Last conclusions on the question of the Khazars', in the Memorial Volume in honour of *S. A. Poznanski*, Warsaw, 1927.

[5] Cf. for instance A. N. Poliak's article 'The Khazar conversion to Judaism', in the Hebrew periodical *Zion*, Jerusalem, 1941.

The Khazar problem came to the fore again in consequence of a long article by Henry Grégoire, published under the title 'Le "Glozel" Khazare'[1] in which he tried to show with great sagacity that the whole Khazar Correspondence had to be regarded as spurious, that it was a kind of later fabrication *ad majorem nationis gloriam.* I indicated to Grégoire a number of points in which he could not be right, and I had the chance of discussing all the problems with him when he visited me in Bonn in December 1937. We decided to make a great joint publication—but political developments made the plan impracticable.

So I proposed to a former Bonn pupil of mine, D. M. Dunlop, that he should take over the work instead. He was a scholar able to deal both with Hebrew and Arabic sources, knew many other languages and had the critical training for so difficult a task.

In 1954, he published his *History of the Jewish Khazars* (Princeton Oriental Series, 16). The most interesting aspect of the Khazar problem is their conversion to Judaism. In chapter v he deals with the numerous Arabic sources which are at our disposal; chapter vi contains a very exact investigation of all details of the Hebrew sources. He has taken great pains to bring out the valuable historical and geographical information provided by the sources and has quite rightly demonstrated that this information cannot be fitted in with the theory that they are later fabrications.

After discussing the origins of the Khazars and their probable connection with the Uigurs, he deals with the clashes between the Khazars and the Arabs in the seventh and eighth centuries. There can be no doubt that the tide of Arab advance was held effectively by the Khazars at the Caucasus.

Dr. Dunlop always critically discusses the problems raised by the facts collected by him, and his book will be an indispensable guide for all who will have to investigate the many difficult problems connected with the Khazars. I do not agree with Sir Gerard Clauson that Dunlop has exaggerated the importance of the Khazars,[2] especially since there really existed some connexion between Khazaria and Khwārizm, as S. P. Tolstov suggested.[3]

It is certainly important that Paul Kokovtsov, an authority to whom we owe the excellent critical edition of the correspondence and a careful investigation of all problems bound up with it, is convinced that in the main the correspondence is genuine.

[1] *Byzantion*, 1937, pp. 225–66. [2] *JRAS*, 1956, pp. 104–7.
[3] S. P. Tolstov, *Auf den Spuren der Altchoresmischen Kultur*, Berlin, 1953.

Moreover we have a good parallel to Chisdai's correspondence in the letter connected with him and published from Geniza fragments by Jacob Mann.[1]

In any case it is clear that the Geniza has preserved some old documents containing a great number of historical and geographical details from a time and a country for which our sources are very meagre. These fragments will have to be investigated very carefully irrespective of their apologetic implications.

5. The Liturgical Poetry of the Jews

So far I have dealt with a number of single fragments of outstanding importance which, when published, attracted great interest and led to fruitful discussion. Not all fragments are of equal importance, but sometimes a fragment becomes very important when studied in connexion with other material. Finally, a systematic investigation of all the material of a particular kind may lead to historical discoveries and conclusions of much greater value than the publication of single fragments from the Geniza. I would like to refer here to the immense mass of material published by Jacob Mann.[2] What he says concerning this material in the Preface to the first volume of his *Texts and Studies* is certainly true:

> All these studies, based as they are on new material, which supplements and illumines the already known, will, it is to be hoped, be appreciated by scholars and students who, like the writer, are averse to fanciful theories spun out as a rule from a minimum of available data. . . . Only by a cautious and laborious inductive method and by adding constantly to our knowledge of the actual realities of the Jewish past . . . can we understand this past fully and truly and ultimately hope to obtain the synthesis that every research worker sets before himself as his ultimate goal. . . . With the widening of the horizon new perspectives are revealed and events, movements, and personalities are placed in a different setting and proportion.

I should like to illustrate this point by some remarks about the

[1] 'Chisdai Ibn Shapruṭ and his Diplomatic Intervention on behalf of the Jews in Christian Europe', *Texts and Studies in Jewish History and Literature*, I, Cincinnati, 1931, pp. 1–30.

[2] Jacob Mann, *The Jews in Egypt and in Palestine under the Fāṭimid Caliphs. A Contribution to their political and communal History based chiefly on Genizah Material hitherto unpublished*, Oxford, vol. i, 1920; vol. ii, 1922—Jacob Mann, *Texts and Studies in Jewish History and Literature*, vol. i, Cincinnati, 1931; vol. ii, Ḳaraitica, Philadelphia, 1935.

liturgical poetry of the Jews; then I shall try to show to what important conclusions we may come concerning the Hebrew text of the Bible through a systematic investigation of the material preserved in the Geniza (*Part II*); finally I shall try to show how this material forces us to see the translations of the Bible: Targum, Septuagint and Peshiṭta, in an entirely new light (*Part III*).

How much the material found in the Geniza has increased our knowledge of the medieval liturgical poetry of the Jews will appear from a few examples. In the introduction to his grammatical treatise *Agron*, of which Harkavy published several fragments from Geniza texts brought to Leningrad by Firkowitch, Sa'adya (882–942)[1] mentions as the 'five early poets' (*ash-shu'arā al-auwalūn*) Yose b. Yose, Yannai, Eleazar Ḳalir, Yoshu'a and Pinḥas. Of these only Eleazar Ḳalir was really known to us by his poetry. He was the author of more than 200 poetical compositions, preserved in the liturgical books of the Jews; Leopold Zunz declared him to have been the lawgiver in this field of poetry.[2]

Not a single poem composed by either of the two poets mentioned by Sa'adya at the end of his list was known to us until a few fragments of Yehoshu'a's[3] and a few more of Pinḥas'[4] poems were discovered in the Geniza. Pinḥas would arouse our special interest if it were confirmed that he is identical with the Tiberian Masorete of the same name who about 800 is known to have been the head of the Rabbinical School in Tiberias. (ראש הישיבה).[5]

To Yose b. Yose only one poem can be ascribed: the 'Aboda for the Day of Atonement' (עבודה ליום הכפורים), a great alphabetical hymn starting with the wonders of creation and dealing with the

[1] Ed. Harkavy p. 51. That Sa'adya was born at the beginning of April 882 and not in 892, hitherto the accepted date, is apparent from a list of his works made after his death by his two sons, Sheerit Alluf and Dosa; the list was made eleven years after Sa'adya's death and has been published by J. Mann, from Geniza fragments, in *JQR*, xi, 1921, pp. 423–8. Henry Malter, in his book *Saadia Gaon, His Life and Works*, (Philadelphia 1921), was only able to speak about it in his postscript (pp. 421–8).

[2] In his *Literaturgeschichte der synagogalen Poesie*, Berlin, 1865, p. 29. That the name of this poet has to be pronounced more correctly as Ḳilir is known from the acrostics in his poems; Ḳilirr would be even more correct (קילירר). The name is derived from Cyrill; Perles has mentioned this fact.

[3] Cf. Menachem Zulay in the article quoted in the next note, vol. i, p. 156.

[4] Cf. Menachem Zulay, *Eine Ḥanukkā-Qerōbā von Pīneḥās hak-Kōhēn*. Mitteilungen des Forschungsinstituts für hebräische Dichtung. Schocken Verlag, vol. i, 1933, pp. 150–74; vol. v, 1939, pp. 121, f.

[5] See *Masoreten des Westens*, vol. i, 1927, p. 37. Jacob Mann, *The Jews in Egypt and in Palestine under the Fāṭimide Caliphs*, ii, 1922, pp. 47 f., i, 1920, p. 58. According to a communication from Dr. Zulay, the identity of the two men cannot be proved.

generations since. Ten verses are devoted to each letter of the alphabet, just as in Psalm cxix where eight verses are devoted to each of the letters. Previously we knew of this poem only through Sa'adya, who had quoted it in his '*Siddur*', his great liturgical work.[1] Liturgical manuscripts with parts of the poem have now been found in the Geniza which are independent of Sa'adya, including one beautiful MS on parchment which contains large parts of the poem. This MS is provided with excellent Palestinian vocalization and is certainly much older than Sa'adya.[2]

Of Yannai a single poetical composition was known from the Maḥzors. Five more were discovered by Israel Davidson on some of the facsimiles of the Geniza-palimpsests of which the underscript contained the fragments of Aquila and the Hexapla published by Burkitt and Taylor.[4] Israel Davidson published these discoveries together with Yannai's poem from the Maḥzors in his *Maḥzor Yannai, A Liturgical Work of the Seventh Century*, ed. from Geniza fragments with notes and introduction and additional notes by Louis Ginzberg, New York, 1919. Since that time many more remains of Yannai's poetry have been discovered on Geniza fragments. A systematical investigation of the more than 10,000 photographs of liturgical Geniza fragments in the Research Institute for Hebrew Poetry in Jerusalem enabled Menachem Zulay to publish in 1938 a large volume of 438 pages with 177 different compositions or fragments thereof. The volume contains more than 800 poems of Yannai, collected from 175 Geniza fragments.[5] In his *Studies of Yannai*, a monograph in which he investigated all problems connected with this poet, Zulay comes to the conclusion[6] that these poems were undoubtedly composed in Palestine and that they must be older than Davidson presumed. They must have been written during the Byzantine suzerainty

[1] Siddur R. Saadya Gaon, *Kitāb ǧāmi' aṣ-ṣalawāt wat-tasābīḥ*. Ed. I. Davidson, S. Assaf, B. I. Joel, Mekize Nirdamim, Jerusalem 1941. Yose b. Yose's poem is included in the liturgy for the Day of Atonement pp. 264–75. Other poems, definitely ascribed to Yose b. Yose, can be found in the liturgy for New Year's Day on pp. 226 f., 228 f., 230 f. These poems differ from the first mentioned in so far as they are rhymed throughout whereas the first ones are not rhymed at all.

[2] It is the Oxford MS Heb d. 55 fol. 12 ff.

[3] In his Academic Dissertation: *Materials for a non-Masoretic Hebrew Grammar*, Helsinki 1958, Dr. A. Murtonen has published on pp. כג–ל the Hebrew text with the Palestinian punctuation of the Geniza Fragment and on pp. 107–14 an English translation of the poem of Jose b. Jose.

[4] See above p. 28, n. 1.

[5] *Piyyute Yannai. Liturgical Poems of Yannai*, collected from Geniza fragments and other sources and published by Menachem Zulay, Berlin, 1938.

[6] In *Studies of the Research Institute for Hebrew Poetry*, vol. ii, Berlin 1936, pp. 213–372.

over Palestine, i.e. in the sixth or at the beginning of the seventh century, before Palestine was conquered by the Arabs in 636.

These poems of Yannai, however, are not the only remnants of liturgical poetry which have come down to us from that time. Zulay has established the fact that the Ḳerobas devoted to the 'Mishmarot' must have been composed during the same period.[1] Mishmarot (sing. Mishmar) is the term for the divisions of priests who took their turn to officiate in the Temple at Jerusalem.[2] The names of these divisions are mentioned in I Chron. xxiv 7–18. After the destruction of the Temple in A.D. 70 we find these priestly families settled in various villages or towns of Galilee, each division in a special place. Here they kept alive the memory of their former service in the Temple, hoping eagerly for the day when the Temple would be rebuilt and they would be able to resume their duties there. The Ḳerobas are devoted to the twenty-four Mishmarot. Each Mishmar is provided with one Ḳeroba for the services of the particular Sabbath day on which the Mishmar would have been in office had the Temple still been standing. This practice must have been in use at that time for the Synagogue services. For us this was surprising news, rites of this kind being mentioned nowhere else.[3]

Of these twenty-four Ḳerobas nearly one-half are preserved in Geniza fragments. Most of them I have published myself,[4] others have been added by Zulay.[5] All the fragments belonged to the same manuscript and no other MS with any portion of these poems is known. From the acrostic in certain parts of the poems Dr. Spanier has proved that they were written by a certain Hedwatha (הדותא or Hedutha?).[6] Nothing else is known about this poet.[7]

[1] Cf. his 'Contributions to the History of the Liturgical Poetry in Palestine', in *Studies* . . . vol. v, 1939, p. 11.

[2] Cf. Emil Schürer, *Geschichte des Jüdischen Volkes* . . . 3rd ed., vol. ii, p. 232; Ed. Meyer, *Entstehung des Judentums*, pp. 168–86; *Ursprung und Anfänge des Christentums* . . . vol. ii, 1921, p. 230.

[3] Fragments dealing with the *Mishmarot* have also been found in Qumran caves 1, 4 and 5, see Milik, *Dix années* . . . p. 37 f.

[4] *Masoreten des Westens*, vol. i, 1927, pp. 1–24 of the Hebrew text, pp. 1–59 of the translation. The text has been published from the Oxford MS Heb d. 63, fol. 82–9 and the Cambridge MS T—S H 16, fol. 2 f.

[5] In *Studies* vol. v. 1939 pp. 113–20, from the Cambridge MS T—S H 2, fol. 2 and the Cairo MS P. 171, 172 of the Moseri Collection.

[6] See *Monatsschrift für Geschichte und Wissenschaft des Judentums*, 1929, p. 68.

[7] Some compositions of a poet with the similar name חדותה are known; one is published by Ismar Elbogen in ציונים, a volume in memory of J. N. Simchoni, Berlin 1929, p. 87, and some others have been found. Zulay has shown that they are of a different kind and have nothing to do with our Hedwatha. Cf. *Studies* vol. v, 1939, p. 112.

I must admit that it was not my special interest in this kind of poetry which induced me to study these poems for many years but problems of Hebrew Grammar. Many of these liturgical MSS in the Geniza are comparatively old and often provided with vowels of the Palestinian system which preceded in Palestine the vocalization developed in Tiberias. Texts of this kind are of importance in so far as they are still more or less independent of the influence of the Tiberian Masoretes who, in the course of the eighth century, began to reorganize the Hebrew language and to bring it into the shape which is familiar to us from our grammars. As early as 1899 A. E. Cowley had presented me with some photographs of the Oxford MS Heb 63. They had to wait for many years until I could begin to study them seriously. Some parts of these poems are written in an exceedingly difficult Hebrew; they are sometimes packed with alliterations and are rich in hints of the Halacha and Haggada. Zulay has shown how closely, for instance, the Ḳeroba of Yannai, devoted to the Seder Gen xxxv.9–xxxvi.43, is connected with the Palestinian Targum of the Pentateuch.[1] These poems are, at least in parts, more artificial than artistic, and time and again I had to discuss them with my collaborators and pupils in Giessen and in Bonn before I could publish the texts. Several of my pupils worked on similar texts and some valuable publications resulted from their studies.[2] This is to be said especially of my pupil and friend Menachem Zulay, who became the great authority in this field of studies; I was very glad when he visited me in England in the autumn of 1954, shortly before his untimely death—a serious loss to scholarship.

The large amount of this poetry preserved in the Geniza enables us to understand much better than before the historical background and the conditions under which it was composed.

[1] In the Appendix to his Bonn thesis (p. 64 ff) Zulay compared a Piut of Yannai, published in *Masoreten des Westens*, vol. i, pp. 24–26 with the text of the Palestine Targum, published (also by me) in *Masoreten des Westens*, vol. ii, pp. 12–14. It is very interesting to note how closely Yannai is following here the text of the Targum.

[2] Cf. M. Kober, *Zum Machzor Yannai* (Jahrbuch der jüdischen lit. Gesellschaft), Frankfurt a.M. vol. 20, 1929; Menachem Zulay, *Zur Liturgie der Babylonischen Juden*. Geniza Texte, herausgegeben, übersetzt und bearbeitet . . . (Bonner Orientalistische Studien ii, Stuttgart 1933); Rafael Edelmann, *Zur Frühgeschichte des Machzors*, (Bonner Orient. Studien vi, 1934); Gustav Ormann, *Das Sünden-Bekenntnis des Versöhnungstages*, Frankfurt a.M., 1934, Falk Bar, *Liturgische Dichtungen*, 1936; Gabriel Davidowicz, *Liturgische Dichtungen der Juden*, 1938 (Bonner Dissertationen) and various other publications. I want here to refer to the last publication in *Sefarad* xv, 1955 p. 287–340; 'Fragmentos de Piyyutim de Yannay en vocalización babilónica' by Diez Macho and Shalom Spiegel.

There can be no doubt that some of its characteristics are due to certain restrictions laid upon the Jews in Palestine at that time and that these restrictions were the consequences of the Edict Περὶ Ἑβραίων, issued in the name of Justinian I as Novella 146 in 553.[1] This Novella regulated the conditions of the Jewish community in the whole Byzantine Empire and has to be regarded as a historical document of the first magnitude, all the more as it was issued at a time from which hardly any other authoritative document in relation to the history of the Jews has been handed down to us. But to study the Novella it must be read in its context. In Appendix I, I give a translation of the whole edict.

We learn from this edict that the Jews in the Byzantine Empire for a long time disagreed among themselves about the way in which Synagogue services were to be conducted. A large number of Greek speaking Jews were dissatisfied because only the Hebrew text of the Scriptures was read in the services, and they demanded that besides the Hebrew text a Greek translation should also be read. Furthermore they objected to the explanations in accordance with the 'Deuterosis' which were given in the services by the interpreters (ἐξηγηταί), and complained about certain teachings they heard there: the denial of the Resurrection, of the Last Judgement, of angels as being created by God.[2] These inter-Jewish controversies were brought before the Byzantine government and in Novella 146 the actual document has come down to us by which the government attempted to settle the quarrels. It was decreed that the Greek translation of the Holy Scriptures should be admitted in addition to the Hebrew text. The Septuagint is given first place as the old and most trustworthy translation, but the translation of Aquila is also admitted. The 'Deuterosis' is strictly forbidden, because it is neither contained in the Holy Scriptures, nor transmitted from of old (ἄνωθεν) by the Prophets,[3] but is an invention of men who were not divinely inspired. Heavy fines were imposed on those who continued to propagate the teachings in question.

[1] *Corpus Juris Civilis*, vol. iii, Novellae. Recognovit Rudolphus Schoell . . . Guilelmus Kroll, 3rd edn. Berlin 1904, pp. 714–718, see below pp. 315–7.

[2] It is most interesting to see, from this official document, the inter-Jewish controversies which were brought before the Byzantine government during the sixth century. Similar controversies led in the eighth century to the Ḳaraite movement.

[3] Earlier on I have pointed to the fact that the Rabbinites gathered all innovations created by them under the heading of *oral teaching*; they codified them in the Mishna and attempted to assert their importance by maintaining that they were old and had been, together with the written law, revealed to Moses on Mount Sinai.

The exact meaning of 'Deuterosis' has been much disputed and it has been interpreted as Targum, as Mishna and Talmud and as Midrash.[1] There can be scarcely any doubt that 'Deuterosis' is a fairly exact Greek translation of 'Mishna'. But the Byzantine authorities seem to have understood by it all material connected with these sources. In the remnants of פירקוי בן באבוי published from Geniza fragments by Louis Ginzberg[2] we have an interesting reference to the changes in Jewish services in Palestine in consequence of the edict. Pirkoi Ben Baboi seems to have been a Persian Jew by birth and to have had a Babylonian education. Towards the end of the eighth century he undertook the task of making the Palestinian Jews accept the authority of the Babylonian Talmud and the Gaonic traditions. (This was the second attempt of its kind, the first one having been made about AD 760 by R. Jehudai Gaon,[3] a great Talmudic authority who had been teacher of Ben Baboi's teacher and to whose authority Ben Baboi refers.) From Ben Baboi's book we learn that the Palestinian Jews had been forbidden to say the Shma', to pray the Tefilla (*Shemone Esre*) and to engage in the study of the Torah. No restrictions were imposed on gatherings in the Synagogues on Saturday mornings, or on the reciting and singing of the 'Ma'mads'. Ben Baboi continues: 'as God has destroyed the kingdom of Edom and abolished the restrictions imposed by it, and as the Arabs have come and the Jews are again permitted to occupy themselves with the Torah, to say the Shma' and to pray the Tefilla, everything in the services ought to be said in its right place, as ordered by the authorities.'[4]

That the term 'Ma'mad', here occurring twice in the Hebrew

[1] The quotations from the Church Fathers have been collected by Hody in his work *De bibliorum textibus originalibus* Oxonii, 1705, pp. 238–240. The most important ones have been arranged by Schürer op. cit. vol. i, p. 113, n. 1 (3rd edition). According to these quotations there can be no doubt that the whole sphere of Jewish tradition was included under Deuterosis. Cf. also Graetz, *Geschichte der Juden*, vol. v, 4th ed. Leipzig 1909, n. 7, pp. 410–13.

[2] *Genizah Studies in Memory of Doctor Solomon Schechter*, ii, *Geonic and Early Karaite Halakah*, by Louis Ginzberg, New York, 1929, pp. 504 ff. According to Epstein, *Tarbiṣ*, vol. ii, pp. 411 f. Pirkoi was Ben Baboi's real name. See however J. Mann in *Tarbiṣ*, vi, 78 f.

[3] Cf. Ginzberg's *Introduction*, p. xiv.

[4] I give here the Hebrew text as Ginzberg published it on p. 551 f.:

וכן אמר מר יהודאי ז̇ל̇ שגזרו שמד על בני ארץ ישראל שלא יקראו קרית שמע ולא יתפלל והיו מגיחין אותן ליכנם שחרית בשבת לומר ולזמר מעמדות והיו אומרים בשחרית מעמד וקדוש ושמע במוסף והיו עושים דברים הללו באונס ועכשיו שכילה הק̇ב̇ה̇ מלכות אדום וביטל גזרותיה ובאו ישמעלים והניחום לעסוק בתורה ולקרא קרית שמע ולהתפלל אסור לומר אלא דבד דבור במקומו כתיקון הכ̇ ז̇ל̇ . . .

Cf. concerning this passage Rafael Edelmann, 'Bestimmung, Heimat und Alter der Synagogalen Poesie' in *Oriens Christianus* iii, vol. 7, 1932, pp. 16–31.

text, is to be understood as meaning liturgical poetry, we see from a note in Yehuda b. Barzillai's 'Sepher ha-'Ittim':[1]

> There was a time when the Jews were forbidden by their oppressors to engage in the study of the Law. The learned men among them, therefore, introduced the custom of mentioning in the course of the prayers the laws of the festivals and the laws of the Sabbath and religious observance and exhorting the common people in regard to them by means of hymns, thanksgivings, rimes (rhymes) and Piyyuṭim.

These texts show the effects of the Novella on the Jewish services in Palestine. When the Jews were forbidden to engage in the study of the law, we must take this as prohibiting the study of Talmud and Mishna, i.e. the 'Deuterosis', regarded as particularly suspicious by the Novella. The study of the Bible was certainly not forbidden them. When we are told that they were forbidden to pray the Tefilla, we must remember that the Palestinian form of this prayer contained the following petition:[2]

> May the apostates have no hope! Mayest Thou speedily, in our days, uproot the kingdom of arrogance! May the Christians (נצרים) and the Heretics (מינים) speedily perish! May their names be effaced from the Book of Life and not be written together with the righteous! Blessed be the Lord who destroys the arrogant.

Nobody can blame the Byzantine authorities for suppressing such a prayer as soon as they became aware of it. It is more difficult to explain why they prohibited the Shma', a kind of creed consisting of Deut. vi, 4–9; xi, 13–21; Num. xv, 37–41, preceded and followed by certain benedictions.[2] Maybe it was regarded as belonging to the 'Deuterosis', as the rules for reciting it were given in the Mishna Berakot (i; 1–4).

But the Jews were not prepared to renounce these elements of their services, so they introduced them into their liturgical poetry. They had to go to work cautiously. Only hints of these elements could be included in the poetry. That is one of the reasons why some of it is so exceedingly difficult; only experts in Talmud and Midrash were able to understand such hints.

[1] The translation given by Davidson in *Mahzor Yannai*, New York 1919, p. xvii, is quoted here.

[2] This form of prayer, disclosed by Samuel Krauss *JQR*, v, 1893, p. 133, has been verified by the Geniza Fragment published by Schechter in ibid. vol. x, 1898, p. 657. Cf. Dalman, *Worte Jesu*, p. 300.

Nevertheless, by reciting, or singing and hearing this poetry in the services they were convinced that they had fulfilled their obligations. We can take it for granted that none of the Byzantine authorities was aware that through these hints the whole 'Deuterosis' was secretly introduced into the services by means of the freely admitted liturgical poetry. Nor do the authorities seem to have realized that the polemic against Edom and Duma in these poems was actually directed against Byzantium. At times, however, doubts seem to have arisen. In an old Leningrad fragment with Palestinian punctuation we read in a Piyut by Yannai:[1]

May the Kingdom of Duma be blotted from the face of the earth
May Roma fall along with all people!

נתוֹש נא מאדמה מלכות דומה ותיפול רומה על כל אוֹמה

The term 'all people' applies to the four kingdoms mentioned by Daniel, which ruled Israel in turn and were later destroyed. The 'kingdom of Duma' is the Byzantine Empire and 'Roma' is Byzantium. It seems that the allusion to the actual government was a little too obvious and the words תיפול רומה were altered into תַּפּוֹל אֵימָה, so that the second half of the sentence now runs thus: 'Make terror fall upon all people!' Polemic of a similar kind can often be found in the poems of Yannai and Hedwatha.

It is clear that this kind of poetry must have been developed in Palestine following the publication of the edict, Novella 146, in 553 and that it lost its motive after the Arab conquest in 636. We can therefore assign Yannai and Hedwatha to this period, thereby making an important contribution to the understanding of their poetry. They developed this kind of liturgical poetry in every way. Later poets like Ḳalir can no longer be declared its 'law-givers' as Leopold Zunz thought. Rather did they imitate and continue the work of their sixth-century predecessors. They make polemical allusions to Byzantium only because such allusions were regarded as integral to this poetic form.

Hedwatha devoted his Ḳerobas to the twenty-four divisions (*mishmarot*) of priests at a time when they performed certain functions. These had long ceased when Ḳalir composed his elegy for the 9th Ab in which the divisions of priests are mentioned.

As Zulay pointed out to me, one can take it that the additions

[1] MS Antonin 369. The text has been published and translated by M. Kober in his thesis pp. 37 and p. 57.

from the elements of the 'Deuterosis', made necessary by the Novella, must have been placed at the end of the Ḳeroba. It seems that the Ḳeroba, in earlier times, ended with the third part, the קדוש. Gustav Ormann, in the unpublished part of his Bonn thesis, indicated this fact. The same arrangement occurs in the Ḳerobas of the Old Spanish Jews, who must have introduced them before the Novella of 553 forced the Jews in Palestine to include the additions and provide a new ending (סלוק); this is an interesting indication of the age of the elements of the Jewish tradition which have survived in Spain.

On the other hand we cannot deal with this Jewish liturgical poetry without referring to the liturgical poetry of other contemporary peoples. The Ḳeroba, the most common form of this poetry, containing the poems for the services of one Saturday or festival day, has a definite and very complicated structure[1] and must have had its own history. But remnants from earlier times which would enable us to study its development are very scarce. The regular use of acrostics in these poems—mostly alphabetical but occasionally indicating the name of the author—is not surprising. Alphabetical acrostics are already to be found in the Old Testament and are in regular use in liturgical poetry.

The metrical form of this poetry is generally the same as the form which we know from the Old Testament. The verse here has a certain number of stresses and is quite unlike the fixed metre of Arabic poetry. Arabic metre was introduced into Hebrew poetry by Dunash b. Labraṭ (who died about 990) and developed by poets of the eleventh and twelfth centuries in Spain such as Ibn Gabirol, Shemuel ha-Nagid and Jehuda ha-Levi. The older liturgical poems (the Piyuts) have no verses with a fixed number of syllables, such as can be found in Syriac poetry. But it is possible that similar metrical forms also existed in old Syriac poetry before verses with fixed numbers of syllables were introduced and, influenced by Ephraem, became the classical form of Syriac metrics.[2]

But the surprising characteristic of the poetry is the rhyme, and the regular use of rhyme in this sixth-century poetry requires explanation. Rhyme is not to be found in the 'Aboda of Yose b. Yose and must have been introduced into Jewish poetry in the

[1] This structure is described by Israel Davidson in his *Mahzor Yannai*, pp. xxvi, ff.

[2] See H. H. Schaeder's essay 'Bardesanes von Edessa', in *Zeitschrift für Kirchengeschichte*, vol. 51, 1932, pp. 47 ff.

period following, exactly when we do not know, but it was *before* the time of poets of the calibre of Yannai and Hedwatha. In most of the poems all verses end with the same rhyme, a method familiar to us from the Arabic Ḳaṣīda of the sixth and seventh centuries. But the first poem of the Ḳeroba is composed in actual stanzas, each having a different rhyme.

Rhyme in this changing form is not entirely unknown to the liturgical poetry of the time. Characteristic examples of it can be found in Byzantium. One is found in the dialogues between Mary and Gabriel and between Mary and Joseph which Proclus (d. in 447) inserted in his great panegyric on the Virgin. These dialogues have the alphabetical acrostic. In order to show the way in which the rhyme is used in this instance, I reproduce the first lines of the beginning of the first dialogue:[1]

Mary: Ἀγνοῶ τοῦ ῥήματος τὸ σαφές
καὶ πῶς γνώσομαι τοῦ πράγματος τὸ θεοπρεπές;
Gabriel: Ἀπαιτεῖς οὖν τὰ ἀγγελικὰ τάγματα
ἄρρητα δημοσιεύειν ῥήματα;
Mary: Βλάβην ἔχει τὰ τῆς ἐπερωτήσεως,
ἐὰν φανερωθῇ τὰ τῆς συλλήψεως;

P. Maas, in discussing this poetry of Proclus, comes to the conclusion that the kind of dialogue it uses must have its origin in a Syriac prototype and that we find such prototype in the Syriac Sugitha, the 'Wechsellied'; he refers to poems of the fifth-century poet Narses.[2] Maas is quite right in maintaining that the form in both cases is almost identical. The difficulty, however, is that these poems by Narses—like all Syriac poems known to us—have a fixed number of syllables in the verse, yet no rhyme. According to Maas the fixed number of syllables in the Syriac is compensated in the Greek by the rhyme. But the rhyme is hardly of Greek origin and if Proclus is here really dependent on the Syriac Sugitha, he must have known an earlier type of it which is lost to us. We have already seen that the verse with a fixed number of syllables was preceded by the verse built up in accordance with the older Semitic type of verse. The Syriac poetry preserved to us is influenced by Ephraem. Since he was regarded as the classical Syriac poet, all older forms of Syriac

[1] See P. Maas in *Byzantinische Zeitschrift*, xix, 1910, p. 292, who refers to Migne, *PG*, lxv, 740 B.

[2] *Syrische Wechsellieder von Narses*. Ein Beitrag zur altchristlichen syrischen Hymnologie . . . herausgegeben, übersetzt und bearbeitet von Franz Feldmann, Leipzig, 1896.

poetry were regarded as imperfect and were destroyed so that practically nothing has been handed down to us. It is very likely that Proclus had Sugithas with this older type of verse as his pattern.

Another question to be considered is whether we can assume that rhyme was used in this kind of verse. Though we do not know any rhymed verses in Syriac, we do know from the few fragments which have come down to us of the older Syriac literature that rhyme was used as a rhetorical element. I would only refer here to Melito, Bishop of Sardis in the second century, who certainly had connexions with the East. The Greek text of his Homily on the Passion has recently been discovered on a papyrus of the fourth century and published by Campbell Bonner.[1] Several Syriac fragments of this Homily were published as early as 1855 by William Cureton[2] and they show groups of rhymed sentences.[3] But we also find such rhymed sentences in the Greek text[4] and it may be that the rhyme was developed in Syriac literature after that time. Yet it is exceedingly difficult to say anything definite, as nothing of the older type of Syriac poetry has been preserved.

The second example we find in the so-called 'Akathistos', a famous Byzantine Kontakion. A Kontakion is a sort of poetical sermon consisting on the average of eighteen to twenty-four stanzas which agree in number of syllables, in accent and syntactic construction. It begins with an allometric stanza, a κουκούλιον. In addition there is within the stanzas a certain correspondence between cola and periods. Finally, acrostic and refrain are obligatory.[5] The Akathistos has been described by W. Christ as 'Hymnus celeberrimus qui ab eo, quod stantes, non sedentes eum cantabant, ἀκάθιστος dictus est, grata memoria praesidium Mariae matris dei prosequitur, quo adiuti Byzantini anno 630 Persas eorumque regem Chaganum,[6] urbem Constantinopolin invadere molientes, muris deiecerunt, deiectosque fuderunt fugaruntque.'[7] The Kontakion itself has no rhyme; but in the Akathistos, stanzas

[1] In *Studies and Documents*, Ed. Kirsopp Lake and Silva Lake, vol. xii, 1940.

[2] *Spicilegium Syriacum*, London, 1855, pp. 49 f.

[3] Cf. my article 'Was Melito's Homily on the Passion originally written in Syriac?' *JTS* xliv, 1943, pp. 52–6.

[4] Cf. E. J. Wellesz, 'Melito's Homily on the Passion: An investigation into the sources of Byzantine Hymnography' *JTS*, vol. xliv, 1943, pp. 41–52.

[5] See Paul Maas, 'Das Kontakion', *Byzantinische Zeitschrift*, vol. xix, 1910, pp. 285 ff.

[6] P. Wittek remarks that Chagan was not the king of the Persians, but the title of the king of the Avares, who at that time besieged the town from the European side.

[7] W. Christ, in *Anthologia Graeca Carminium Christianorum*, adornaverunt W. Christ et M. Paranikas, Lipsiae, 1871, p. lii.

1, 3, 5, 7 &c. have a number of salutations to the Virgin added to them, all formed in exactly the same way, and every two salutations rhyme. The Akathistos is sometimes attributed to Sergius, the Patriarch of Constantinople during the time of the siege. But Paul Maas has shown that it is closely connected with Romanos and must have been composed by him.[1]

Romanos is the great Byzantine poet who, even if he was not the creator of the Kontakion, certainly brought it to its highest perfection. The time of his poetical activity is indicated by the fact that we find in his poems hints of the collapse of the old Hagia Sophia in Constantinople in 532 and of its rebuilding in 537.[2] Maas has recently found a fragment of Romanos on a sixth-century papyrus.[3] The peak period of the Kontakion was, according to Maas, from 536–556, so we can fix the date of the Akathistos in the first half of the sixth century.

In order to show the method of this rhyme I give here the salutations added to the first stanza. The last verse is a refrain repeated at the end of all salutations of this Kontakion.[4]

Χαῖρε, δι' ἧς ἡ χαρὰ ἐκλάμψει
  χαῖρε, δι' ἧς ἡ ἀρὰ ἐκλείψει
Χαῖρε, τοῦ πεσόντος 'Αδὰμ ἡ ἀνάκλησις
  χαῖρε, τῶν δακρύων τῆς Εὔας ἡ λύτρωσις
Χαῖρε, ὕψος δυσανάβατον   ἀνθρωπίνοις λογισμοῖς
  χαῖρε, βάθος δυσθεώρητον   καὶ ἀγγέλων ὀφθαλμοῖς
Χαῖρε, ὅτι ὑπάρχεις   βασιλέων καθέδρα
  χαῖρε, ὅτι βαστάζεις   τὸν βαστάζοντα πάντα
Χαῖρε, ἀστὴρ ἐμφαίνων τὸν ἥλιον
  χαῖρε, γαστὴρ ἐνθέου σαρκώσεως
Χαῖρε, δι' ἧς νεουργεῖται ἡ κτίσις
  χαῖρε, δι' ἧς βρεφουργεῖται ὁ κτίστης
Χαῖρε, νύμφη ἀνύμφευτε

In this connexion it is certainly important to note that the

[1] See *Byzantinische Zeitschrift*, vol. xiv, 1905, pp. 645 f.

[2] P. Maas, 'Die Chronologie der Hymnen des Romanos' in *Byzantinische Zeitschrift*, vol. xv, 1906, pp. 1 ff.

[3] It is pap. gr. Vind. 29 430, published in *Mitteilungen aus der Papyrussammlung der Nationalbibliothek in Wien, Papyrus Erzherzog Rainer*, III. Folge 1939, p. 68; Cf. P. Maas, 'Romanos auf Papyrus' in *Byzantion*, xiv, 1939, p. 381.

[4] The Akathistos is published by Christ and Paranikas in *Anthologia Graeca Carm. Christianorum*, Lipsiae 1871, pp. 140–47 and by J. B. Pitra in *Analecta Sacra Spicilegio Solesmensi parata*, tome i, Parisiis 1876, pp. 250–262. On pages 263–72 Pitra has published another Akathistos 'De B. Virginis Transitu', which shows a further development of the rhyme. But this poem—similar to others—is simply an imitation of the famous Akathistos, and as we do not know when it was composed it is difficult to make use of it.

home country of the great Byzantine poet Romanos was Syria and that he came of a Jewish family.[1] We do not know how far his Jewish education had advanced when he became a Christian. It is difficult to imagine that a man like Romanos did not know at least something of the poetry of his former religion. But the poetry which he may have known must have preceded by nearly a hundred years that of the end of the sixth century known to us from the compositions of Yannai and Hedwatha. The ʻAboda of Yose b. Yose, which I mentioned above, is almost all that remains of such earlier Jewish poetry and it does not seem to be significant in this connexion. However, a great amount of old poetry has been preserved in the Samaritan liturgy. We are familiar with the liturgy from the edition by Sir Ernest Cowley, who was occupied in the preparation of this great work[2] when I first came to know him in 1899. In particular the so-called 'Defter',[3] a kind of Common Prayer, which is the oldest part of this liturgy, contains a number of liturgical poems by the fourth century Samaritan theologian Marḳa.

[1] Paul Maas has proved this: cf. *Byzantinische Zeitschrift*, vol. xv, 1906, p. 31.

[2] The printing of the book was long delayed. Cf. *The Samaritan Liturgy*, ed. A. E. Cowley, two volumes, Oxford, 1909. The work comprises 879 pages of text and 100 pages of introduction. Quite apart from the edition of the text the introduction is also very valuable in which the editor deals with the MSS, gives valuable information about the dates of the texts, provides a grammar to the texts, and furnishes lists of Samaritan high-priests and genealogical tables, a particularly valuable glossary, an index of the initial lines of the poems and an index of the authors.

Liturgical poems for family festivals, which cannot be found in Cowley's edition, have been published by Z. Ben Hajjim in the periodical *Tarbiṣ*, vol. x, Jerusalem, 1939, pp. 190–200 and pp. 333–375, under the title *Samaritan Poems for Joyous occasions*, from two MSS from Jerusalem and one from the British Museum. When in Nāblus in 1908, I had a beautiful MS with these texts copied out for the Berlin Bibliothek.

[3] For the Defter, 'The Common Prayers' pp. 1–92, Cowley has mainly used as a basis (pp. 3–81) a copy of the MS Sam. 3 of the Vatican Library, made by P. Bollig. Since the year 1905 I have owned photographs of the complete MS and can well understand Cowley's opinion of it. The MS probably dates from the 14th century and is one of the most important of all liturgical MSS of the Samaritans. At the same time I am doubtful whether it was expedient to place before an edition of the liturgy which relies chiefly on the text used in present day Samaritan services such a Defter which deviates in the grouping and in other important points from the modern text. Moreover, no instructions for liturgical use such as all other parts of the Samaritan liturgy and modern MSS of the Defter possess are added to the Vatican MS. Also the modern MSS often provide an Arabic translation which is of considerable help in understanding the older Samaritan poems of the Defter. Finally the British Museum owns in MS or 5034 a MS of the Defter of the Samaritan liturgy which is older than the MS of the Vatican. It shows a different order and gives an Arabic translation. About this MS, G. Margoliouth reported in *ZDMG*, vol. li, 1897, pp. 499–507: *An Ancient MS of the Samaritan Liturgy*.

Dr. John Bowman, director of the Hebrew Department of Leeds University, together with several of his students is making a translation, partly also a new edition, of the Samaritan Liturgy; in this way he will be able to make possible the study of this important liturgical material for those interested in liturgical problems, yet not able to understand the often very difficult language of the Samaritan liturgy.

The liturgical poems of Marḳa play even to-day an important role in the Samaritan liturgy.[1] They are composed in the Samaritan language, an Aramaic dialect related to the language spoken in Palestine at the time of the birth of Christianity which has given us a literature written by Jews, Christians and Samaritans.[2] These liturgical poems from the fourth century have acrostics and consist of very evenly formed verses, but they do not rhyme. Yet, at a later date, rhyme also entered the liturgical poetry of the Samaritans, as it had entered the liturgical poetry of the Jews, and came to be there of the same importance. We can see this now in the abundant material found in the Cairo Geniza, much of which goes back to the sixth century.

We must suppose that the Jews also at one time used Aramaic for their liturgical poetry, although nothing has been preserved of it in the liturgical books which we have, for Leopold Zunz[2] has pointed to a large number of Aramaic words in Jewish liturgical poetry and Zulay has drawn my attention to the fact that many litanies, beginning with רחמנא, and written in Aramaic, have been found in the Cairo Geniza. It seems that for the officially used liturgical poems the Jews introduced Hebrew at an early stage. Thus we can only form an idea of the Aramaic liturgical poetry once used by the Jews from the analogy of the Samaritan poems.

[1] Cf. my article 'Die zwölf Marka-Hymnen aus dem "Defter" der Samaritanischen Liturgie', *Oriens Christianus*, 3rd Series, vii, Leipzig, 1932, pp. 77–103;=*Opera Minora*, Leiden, 1956, pp. 196–212.

[2] Cf. my article 'Das zur Zeit Jesu in Palästina gesprochene Aramäisch', *ThR, NF* xvii, Tübingen, 1949, pp. 201–16;=*Opera Minora*, Leiden, 1956, pp. 79–95.

[3] See Leopold Zunz, *Synagogale Poesie des Mittelalters*, 1855, p. 118 and appendix 5, p. 372.

PART II

The Hebrew Text of the Bible

CHAPTER II

THE HEBREW TEXT OF THE BIBLE

1. Introduction. The Translations of the Pentateuch used by the Samaritans

It was in March 1899 that I came to England for the first time. I had published a thesis on the Samaritan Targum of the Pentateuch[1] and hoped to find more material about it in England. I was particularly interested in the Arabic translation of the Pentateuch made by the Samaritans. Abraham Kuenen, the great Old Testament scholar in Leiden, had published, a long time before, Genesis, Exodus and Leviticus in this translation[2], and I intended completing the work by editing Numbers and Deuteronomy. For this purpose I had copied the text of the Berlin MS Petermann 3 and collated with it the three books edited by Kuenen. I had compared the three MSS used by Kuenen, one from Leiden and two from Paris, and had compared the Berlin MS Or Fol 534, written in Samaritan script and containing the Hebrew and Arabic Pentateuch of the Samaritans. I hoped to find further material in libraries in England.

My third purpose was to study Hebrew Biblical MSS with supralinear punctuation. Some time before, G. Margoliouth of the British Museum had published an article in which he had tried to prove that the Yemenite Bible MSS, of which the most important ones were in the British Museum, though provided with Babylonian vowel signs, had nothing to do with the Babylonian text of the Bible and that *Babylonian* was an unsuitable term for this kind of punctuation.[3] These problems could be solved only by studying the MSS themselves.

The first four weeks I stayed as the guest of the Rev. Lic. Dr.

[1] *Textkritische und lexikalische Bemerkungen zum samaritanischen Pentateuch-Targum* (Diss. phil. Halle), Leipzig, 1898.

[2] *Specimen e Literis Orientalibus, exhibens Librum Geneseos secundum Arabicam Pentateuchi Samaritani Versionem ab Abu Sai'do conscriptum . . . e tribus Codicibus edidit Abrahamus Kuenen.* Lugduni Batavorum 1851 . . . *Libri Exodi et Levitici* . . . 1854.

[3] G. Margoliouth, 'The supralinear punctuation, its origin, the different stages of its development and its relation to other Semitic systems of punctuation', in *Proceedings of the Society of Biblical Archaeology*, 7th February 1893.

Gustav Diettrich in Sydenham, London, and collated for him a number of Syriac Biblical MSS in London, Cambridge and Oxford.[1] I studied the rich material in the British Museum, continued these studies for nine weeks in Cambridge, went to Oxford where I stayed seven weeks and returned for a further four weeks to London. I published some fragments of the Samaritan Targum which I had found in England together with other fragments sent to me from Leningrad to Berlin.[2] The greater the amount of material I collected, particularly in Nāblus, Leningrad and Rome, for a publication of the whole Targum, the more difficult did such an edition prove to be. The fact is that almost every MS offers its own particular text. We have here an excellent example of a Targum in an earlier phase through which translations of the Bible usually pass before they reach their final text. It is as if only Itala MSS of the Latin Bible existed and no Vulgate, or as if there were only Old Syriac Gospels and no Peshiṭta. A final revision comparable with the Vulgate or the Peshiṭta was not made by the Samaritans. They attempted it once. In a copy of the Samaritan Targum written in the thirteenth century AD variant readings in great numbers are added in the margins and between the lines.[3] Most of these variant readings can still be found in the MSS of the Targum which have been preserved.[4] A clearly discernible hand has added some variant readings of Targum Onḳelos. This collection must be taken to be a preliminary work towards the creation of a *textus receptus* for this Targum. But the undertaking was never carried out. Arabic had become the language spoken in Palestine and nobody was interested in a uniform text of the Samaritan Targum. The people gradually got accustomed to using the different texts of the Targum concurrently and eventually lost all sense of the differences between the various versions.

[1] Cf. G. Diettrich, *Ein Apparatus criticus zur Pešitto zum Propheten Jesaia. Beihefte zur ZAW*, viii, Giessen 1905, p. ix.

[2] 'Fragmente des Samaritanischen Pentateuchtargums, Herausgegeben und Erläutert'. *ZA*, xvi, 1901, pp. 78–101; xvii, 1902, pp. 1–22.

[3] Of this MS I know 97 fols: 22 fols in the Russian Public Library in Leningrad, MS Sam 182; 43 fols in the British Museum in London MS Or 1442; 30 fols in Trinity College Library Cambridge, MS R 15,56; 2 fols I myself had bought in Nāblus. Photostats of all 97 fols are in my possession.

[4] This was the result of a careful examination of the MS by Lea Goldberg in the Oriental Seminary of Bonn University. She pointed out that the Samaritans at that time, apart from the texts of the Targum which we know from various MSS, had yet another text of the Targum which so far has not been rediscovered. Cf. Lea Goldberg, *Das Samaritanische Pentateuchtargum. Eine Untersuchung seiner handschriftlichen Quellen.* (Diss. Phil. Bonn.=Bonner Orientalistische Studien. Heft 17, Stuttgart 1935.)

That is why the Samaritan priests commissioned by Heinrich Petermann in 1868 to copy the Samaritan Targum produced a mixed text from different MSS taken at random. Petermann, not aware of this fact, collated with this mixed text, which he called *Apographon*, the MSS from which it had been copied, adding the text which in the Paris Polyglot had been printed from the worst known MS of the Samaritan Targum and which, together with Walton's corrections, had been repeated in the London Polyglot. The oldest and most important MSS of this text have either been completely disregarded or are used in a very inadequate way. Carl Vollers, for many years the director of the Khedivial Library in Cairo, who after Petermann's death completed the edition, did not think it necessary to look at the MSS in Nāblus which had provided the basis for the edition.[1]

For decades I tried to assemble the material available in Nāblus, Rome, Leningrad and English libraries. In 1954, my friend Professor Alejandro Diez Macho of Barcelona University, who himself was engaged in preparing a new critical edition of the Targum Onḳelos and to whom I had shown the material for the Samaritan Targum to the Pentateuch, sent to me Father José Ramón Díaz, of the same religious order, who at the time was working in the Pontifical Bible Institute in Rome. I discussed with him the problems of this Targum and put at his disposal the material which I had collected, and he is now preparing a scholarly edition if this important text.[2] This Targum is written in an Aramaic dialect which was spoken in Palestine by the Samaritans. We have at our disposal excellent MSS of this text and the forthcoming edition of the Targum will yield one of the most important sources for the Aramaic spoken in Palestine in the first Christian centuries.

As for the Arabic translation of the Pentateuch used by the Samaritans, after having collated about thirty MSS of this text I came to realize fairly well what had happened. Here we have

[1] *Pentateuchus Samaritanus. Ad fidem Librorum Manuscriptorum apud Nablusianos repertorum edidit et varias Lectiones adscripsit H. Petermann.* Berolini, Genesis 1872. Exodus 1882. Leviticus (quem ex recensione Petermanniana typis describendum curavit C. Vollers) 1883. Numeri (ex recensione Caroli Vollers) 1885. Deuteronium (ex recensione Caroli Vollers) 1891. Vollers, in the preface to Numbers, describes the Apographon as 'neue, um 1868 auf Veranlassung Petermann's von einem Samaritaner besorgte flüchtige Abschrift einer wertvollen Vorlage'. Cf. my article 'Zu den in Nāblus befindlichen Handschriften des samaritanischen Pentateuchtargums', in *ZDMG*, lxi, 1908, pp. 909–12.

[2] Cf. 'Ediciones del Targum samaritano', por José Ramón Díaz M.S.C. (*Estudios Biblicos*, vol. xv, Madrid 1956, pp. 105–8).

a revised version, a *textus receptus* known to have been made by a certain Abū Sa'īd in the second half of the thirteenth century A.D., at about the period when the attempt was made to create a revised version of the Targum. The three MSS used by Kuenen, as also the Berlin MS Petermann 3, contain the text of Abū Sa'īd, but there are many more MSS of this version of the text. They are all written in Arabic letters and show only a few variant readings. Some of them also have the notes of Abū Sa'īd, which Kuenen published for the first three books of the Pentateuch.

But of much greater interest is the text which lies behind this *textus receptus* and we can, to a certain extent, survey its history. The Samaritans know very well that they first used the Arabic version of the Pentateuch made by Sa'adya Gaon. We know quite a number of MSS and fragments in which we find this text written in Samaritan letters. One fragment of it had already been described by Silvestre de Sacy;[1] another one, from Leningrad, has been published by Harkavy.[2] Further fragments I found in Oxford[3] and in a MS now in Manchester.[4] But the most important MS of this text is a Triglot of the Pentateuch in Hebrew, Samaritan and Arabic from the twelfth century; I saw it in Nāblus in 1906 and 1908. Since 1910 it has been kept in the British Museum as MS Or 7562.[5]

These MSS of the Arabic translation of the Pentateuch by Sa'adya, written with Samaritan letters, are of great interest.

[1] Cf. his 'Mémoire sur la Version Arabe des Livres de Moïse a l'usage des Samaritains, et sur les Manuscrits de cette Version' in *Mémoires de Littérature tirés des Registres de l'Academie des Inscriptions et Belles-Lettres*, tome 49, Paris 1808, pp. 1–199; ibid. pp. 117–21.

[2] Cf. MS Sam 179 of the Russian Public Library in Leningrad. The text has been published by Harkavy in his book *Описанiе Рукописей Самаританскаго Пятикнижiя Хранящихся въ Императорской Публичной Библiотекѣ* St. Petersburg 1874, p. 244.

[3] Deut. xi, 2–xxvi, 14 in this version is to be found in the Bodleian MS Or 139, Uss. II, a MS which is composed of various fragments. The text in question was written in the twelfth or thirteenth century A.D.

[4] Deut. 32–34 in Codex ii, described by Edward Robertson on pp. 15–31 of the *Catalogue of the Samaritan Manuscripts in the John Rylands Library Manchester* (1938), contains the Hebrew and the Arabic text of the Pentateuch and is dated 729/1328. I was able to examine the MS closely in Oxford in 1899, where on Cowley's recommendation it was sent from the Bibliotheca Lindesiana which owned it at the time. See my note in *ZDMG*, xcii, 1938, p. 685.

[5] I described the MS on p. lxxxviii f. of the Prologomena to Von Gall, *Der Hebräische Pentateuch der Samaritaner* (Giessen 1918). On the upper part of the folio, showing many additions, a Samaritan priest entered the lost Arabic text according to later versions. The old part of the MS contains the Arabic translation of Sa'adya in Samaritan letters. It may be the oldest MS preserved of Sa'adya's Arabic translation of the Pentateuch. This text has at times been corrected by later hands and it is not always easy to discover the original rendering. One of my pupils tried to make a critical survey of the MS, but alas, without success.

Mostly they are older than the preserved texts written by Jews, and they often still have old renderings of Sa'adya which have been altered in the *textus receptus* by Sa'adya.[1] On the basis of the material which I had collected, Max Katten,[2] in his *Untersuchungen zu Sa'adya's Pentateuch-Übersetzung*, has shown that Jewish authors like Dunash b. Labraṭ (tenth century) Jehuda b. Bal'am (eleventh century), Abraham b. Ezra (died 1167) and Bachja b. Asher (thirteenth century) used Sa'adya's Arabic translation of the Pentateuch in a version which strongly deviates from the later *textus receptus* of this translation—published by J. Derenbourg (Paris 1893)—and often agrees with the Sa'adya text written in Samaritan letters as it is found in the London Triglot. Besides fragments from the Geniza these early Samaritan MSS will have to be investigated carefully[3] for a critical edition of Sa'adya's Arabic translation of the Pentateuch.

But the Samaritans soon began to deviate from Sa'adya's Version. We have a number of MSS which show in an interesting way how this translation was altered more and more by the Samaritans until finally the *textus receptus* of Abū Sa'īd resulted.

[1] Some of these problems are discussed in my book *Die arabischen Bibelübersetzungen* ... Leipzig, 1900, cf. pp. viii ff.

[2] Max Katten's book was published as Giessen Thesis, 1924. A serious investigation of the relation of the Samaritans to Sa'adya has been made by A. S. Halkin under the title 'The Relation of the Samaritans to Sa'adya Gaon' in *Saadia Anniversary Volume* (American Academy for Jewish Research, Texts and Studies, vol. ii), New York 1943, pp. 271–325.

[3] For his edition of Sa'adya's Arabic translation of the Pentateuch Joseph Derenbourg used the text printed in Hebrew letters in the four-language Pentateuch (Constantinople 1546), the text printed in Arabic letters of the Polyglots (Paris, 1646, London 1657) and a Yemenite MS belonging to David Kohen, a Yemenite living in Jerusalem. The same Yemenite MS was the basis for the text published by Yemenite Jews, together with the Hebrew text and the Targum Onkelos, in Jerusalem in 1894–1901 under the title כתר תורה or תאג. The two texts are essentially the same. Derenbourg naïvely identified this text with the text composed by Sa'adya himself. It is in fact a *textus receptus*, written for the convenience of the Arabic speaking Jews in Yemen and based on the translation of Sa'adya.

For a critical edition of this text we cannot rely on two early prints and a Yemenite MS. Apart from the Sa'adya texts used by the Samaritans, the main stress, next to earlier MSS, will have to be laid on the remnants of the translation found in the Cairo Geniza and, as Katten did, quotations from old Jewish authors will have to be carefully considered.

Dr. Moses Zucker, a pupil of Aptowitzer, who is working in the Jewish Theological Seminary of America in New York, intends to publish a new edition of Sa'adya's Arabic translation of the Pentateuch and is also occupied with Sa'adya's commentary on parts of the Pentateuch. When he was in Oxford in the summer of 1956, we thoroughly discussed all the problems of this edition.

I wish also to refer to the Frankfurt Geniza fragment published by Kurt Levy. It shows a version deviating strongly from the usual Sa'adya text. Cf. his book *Zur Masoretischen Grammatik* (*Bonner Orientalistische Studien*, xv, 1936, pp. 18 f) and the article by Rafael Edelmann 'On the Arabic Versions of the Pentateuch' (*Studia Orientalia Joanni Pedersen Septuagenario dicata*, Hauniae 1953, pp. 71–5).

But this *textus receptus* is not to be found in MSS written in Samaritan letters. These have always preserved older forms of the text even to the present day.

When I was in Cambridge I came into contact with Solomon Schechter. He spoke with enthusiasm of the treasures which he had brought to Cambridge from Cairo and gave many details of his journey to Egypt which resulted in his finding them. I often saw him sitting in the large room of the Old University Library, which was at his disposal, surrounded by boxes filled with the (at that time) dirty and crumpled fragments, trying to reduce them to order[1] and telling me of the little discoveries he was making nearly every day. When he realized how interested I was in Biblical texts which were vocalized in an unusual way he gave me some fragments with Palestinian vocalization, the first examples of which had recently been discovered in some Geniza fragments. I carefully copied them. In Oxford I found further fragments belonging to the same MS to which Cowley had drawn my attention. I published these fragments in 1901.[2] Besides this I studied in Cambridge and Oxford, without yet having a real understanding of the problems involved, fragments of the text of the Bible and the Mishna with supralinear punctuation. In Cambridge I also identified some Arabic Geniza fragments at the suggestion of Mr. Jenkinson, the Librarian. I made there the acquaintance of the learned Scottish Ladies, Mrs. Agnes Smith Lewis and Mrs. Margaret Dunlop Gibson, who had had a share in the discovery of the Geniza fragments, and Professor Francis C. Burkitt, who had just published the Aquila fragments from the Geniza, and I met Norman McLean, who was at that time preparing the great Cambridge edition of the Septuagint, and A. A. Bevan with whom as with other scholars I subsequently remained in contact. The material from the Geniza had made a deep impression on me, its importance had become clear to me and I knew that I should have to come back to it over and over again.

This impression was strengthened by what I saw in Oxford and heard in conversations with Cowley and Neubauer. Cowley was occupied at the time in editing the Samaritan liturgy. The

[1] A very characteristic photograph of Schechter sitting in the room of the old University Library and sifting Geniza fragments can be seen in Norman Bentwitch's book, *Biography of Solomon Schechter*, Philadelphia, 1940, p. 142.

[2] 'Beiträge zur Geschichte der Hebräischen Punktation', *ZAW*, xxv, 1901, pp. 273–317; 'Zur Geschichte der Hebräischen Akzente', *ZDMG*, lv, 1901, pp. 167–94.

two big volumes of that work appeared finally in 1909, but he had already some printed proofs of the text which he showed me and which we discussed. I need not say that his great experience in Samaritan matters was very helpful to me. He was also interested in my study of ancient vocalized Hebrew fragments and presented me with some photographs of a fragment of liturgical poetry provided with Palestinian punctuation which—as I have mentioned already[1]—became later of importance to me.

2. The Babylonian text of the Bible

Back in Germany I found the things I had learned during my stay in England of great value for my further studies. When in December 1900 I studied the Hebrew Biblical MSS with supralinear punctuation in the Royal Library at Berlin, I found some Yemenite MSS, but they could not be compared with the much older and better MSS I had seen in the British Museum. But even in the London MSS the Yemenite method of punctuating Hebrew texts was not very helpful as it was entirely based on the Tiberian method. They only render this vocalization in a simplified way by using supralinear signs. What G. Margoliouth had said with regard to the Hebrew text in Yemenite MSS with supralinear punctuation proved to be quite correct.[2]

But there was in Berlin a large fragment of the Ketubim containing parts of the Psalms, Job, Proverbs, Ecclesiastes, Song of Songs, Lamentations, Daniel, Esther, Ezra and Chronicles, and consisting of ninety-four folios of parchment, or fragments thereof, which superficially were punctuated in the Yemenite way—and actually came from Yemen. But on closer examination I found that the vocalization had been systematically altered and that beneath the usual Yemenite punctuation traces of another vocalization, also supralinear, were to be seen which differed in the details from the Yemenite method in a characteristic way. I began to examine the text, a difficult task, and it was nearly two years before I brought out all the details of the original vocalization and was able to write a sketch of Hebrew grammar in accordance with it, which largely differed from the usual Hebrew grammar based entirely on Tiberian punctuation.[3]

[1] *Supra*, Part i, p. 37.
[2] Cf. his article quoted p. 1, n. 3. The Yemenite method of vocalizing the Targum is of much greater importance.
[3] Cf. my book *Der Masoretische Text des Alten Testaments nach der Überlieferung der Babylonischen Juden*. Leipzig 1902.

The great problem was: where did this kind of vocalization come from? I tried to discuss the matter in Berlin with Hermann Strack who, in his youth, had seen MSS with supralinear punctuation in Leningrad and had some experience of Hebrew Biblical MSS.[1] But about the origin of this kind of punctuation he had not the slightest idea. Moritz Steinschneider had no interest in Biblical MSS and all his descriptions of these in the catalogues composed by him are exceedingly poor. He failed to realize the importance of the precious Berlin MS.[2] I studied Hebrew grammarians such as Menachem b. Saruk (died 970), Ḥaiyūj (tenth century), Ibn Ezra (died 1167), David Ḳimḥi (died 1235), and others, without result. Only Sa'adya gave some help. He was born in Egypt, lived for a certain time in Palestine, and became in 928 the head of the Talmudic Academy in Sūra in Babylonia. He knew Palestine and Babylonia well. In his Commentary on Sepher Yeṣīra,[3] the well-known old cabbalistic book, he deals with the different ways of pronouncing Hebrew in Babylonia and Palestine, and there could be no doubt that his statements on the Babylonian pronunciation of Hebrew corresponded in general with the original vocalization in the Berlin MS.[4]

This result was confirmed by other facts. The Masora has preserved a list of the differences in the Hebrew consonantal text used by the Eastern (Babylonian) Jews and the Western (Palestinian) Jews. The Berlin MS always showed the Eastern readings.[5] It was provided with a Masora which clearly differed from the Masora found in Western MSS, including the Yemenite MSS and the Babylonian Codex of the Prophets in St. Petersburg, not only in the way in which the Masoretic notes were

[1] He had published, together with Harkavy, the *Catalog der hebräischen Bibelhandschriften der Kaiserlichen Öffentlichen Bibliothek in St. Petersburg*, Teil I und II, St. Petersburg, Leipzig, 1875. Besides, Strack had published the photographic reproduction of the famous Codex of the Prophets, dated 916; cf. *Prophetarum Posteriorum Codex Babylonicus Petropolitanus*, St. Petersburg and Leipzig, 1876. In the *Zeitschrift für Lutherische Theologie und Kirche* (year 1875, pp. 585–624) he had published some Bible fragments with supralinear punctuation.

[2] Steinschneider describes the MS Or qu 680 in the Berlin Catalogue vol. ii, p. 2 in the following way: 'Pergam. 94 bl., Mittl. Quadrat mit babylonischer Punktation über den Buchstaben, grossenteils abgefaulte Bibelfragmente mit Randmasora, ungeordnet, hauptsächlich Hagiographen (incl. Megillot); Psalmen, Hiob und Sprüche sind strophisch abgeteilt'.

[3] *Commentaire sur le Séfer Yeṣira ou Livre de Création, par le Gaon Saadya de Fayyoum, publié et traduit par Mayer-Lambert*, Paris, 1891. Cf. my remarks on the Sefer Yeṣīra at the end of this lecture, p. 107.

[4] Cf. my book *Der Masoretische Text des Alten Testaments nach der Überlieferung der Babylonischen Juden*, pp. 32 ff.

[5] Ibid., pp. 18 ff.

added to the Biblical words, but in the whole style of the technical terms of the Masora.[1] So we had for the first time an example of real Babylonian Masora. It is true that a large fragment of a Masoretic Commentary on the Pentateuch had already been published in 1885 by Christian D. Ginsburg according to a copy which had been made, ten years before, by H. L. Strack in Leningrad from a MS belonging to the Second Firkowitsch Collection and which had come from the Cairo Geniza. But neither Strack nor Ginsburg had recognized it as a piece of the Babylonian Masora, and Ginsburg had interpreted it wrongly and has completely overlooked its importance.[2] So it was clear that I had found a specimen of a real Babylonian MS of the Bible, unique in comparison with all the hundreds and thousands of Hebrew Biblical MSS so far known. Babylonia had been for centuries the centre of Jewish learning. The Jewish Academies of Sūra and Nehardea, later Sūra and Pumbeditha, were famous. The final redaction of the Mishna had been made there, the Babylonian Talmud regulating every detail of Jewish life up to the present day in an authoritative way had been developed there. The official Aramaic translations of the Bible, Targum Onḳelos on the Torah, Targum Jonathan on the Prophets, had received their definite form there. The Babylonian Gaons were regarded as the recognized leaders of the Jewish world. So it was of the greatest importance that we had now, for the first time, a large piece of the Bible text which undoubtedly came from Babylonia.

After I had published my book on the Berlin MS[3] I suspended my work on these matters for several years. I went to the East where I spent more than five years in Cairo and nearly one year in Palestine; there I was occupied with quite other matters. It was only in 1910, when I was 'Privatdozent' in Halle University, that I was able to resume my studies on the text of the Hebrew Bible.

In the meantime a second genuine Babylonian fragment of the

[1] Ibid., pp. 13 ff.

[2] It is the St. Petersburg Bible MS Firk ii, 1549, of which I have given a facsimile, largely reduced in size, in *Masoreten des Ostens*, plate 16 b. The original consists of 18 parchment leaves, 33 by 26 cm. The text is published and interpreted by Ginsburg in his huge book *The Massorah compiled from Manuscripts*, vol iii, London, 1885, pp. 205–68. How little Ginsburg understood the character of this valuable fragment is to be seen from the fact that in the chapter 'The Massorah, its Rise and Development' (*Introduction to the Massoretico-Critical Edition of the Hebrew Bible*, London, 1897, pp. 287–468) he does not mention the text which he had published 12 years previously. Cf. on Ginsburg's book 'The Massorah . . .' *Masoreten des Ostens*, pp. xiv ff.

[3] Cf. p. 57, n. 3.

Bible had been discovered and published.[1] It belonged to the Second Firkowitch Collection in Leningrad and contained, on four parchment leaves, the text of Job ii 11–ix 32. But here the Babylonian punctuation was not corrected by a later Yemenite hand as in the Berlin MS. As the greater part of the text (Job iii, 7–ix 32) was contained in the Berlin MS also, it was possible to compare the two texts: they supported each other in the best way. It was clear that this kind of punctuation had at one time been in more general use and it was necessary to find more specimens of it. From what I had seen in 1899 in Cambridge and Oxford it was clear to me that in the Cairo Geniza collections, if anywhere in the world, further specimens could be expected. So in 1911 I came back to England, this time with the professed intention of studying Geniza material.

During the twelve years of my absence conditions had much improved. In Cambridge the fragments had been carefully cleaned, smoothed and brought into order, and the lists of the Taylor-Schechter Collection in the University Library proved to be very helpful. In Oxford the second volume of the catalogue of Hebrew MSS had been published[2] and Cowley presented me with a copy. In it he had described as Yemenite all MSS with supralinear punctuation. I was now an expert in these matters and was able to point out to him the great difference between Yemenite and Babylonian punctuation. I found in the Bodleian some very fine specimens of genuine Babylonian Biblical MSS the punctuation and the Masora of which were in good accord with the original punctuation of the Berlin MS. In Cambridge I also found a great number of fragments of the same kind. In the British Museum not a single specimen of a genuine Babylonian text of the Bible could be discovered among all the Geniza fragments which had found their way there.

I returned to Halle with many notes and photographs. At my request several fragments from the Russian Public Library in Leningrad, which Professor Paul Kokovtsov (1861–1942) had kindly indicated, were sent to Halle. Among them I found, besides several Yemenite fragments of no great importance, five fragments with a real Babylonian text and the fragments from

[1] Johannes Weerts, 'Über die babylonisch punktierte Handschrift, No. 1546 der II Firkowitschschen Sammlung (Codex Tschufutkale 3)' Diss. Phil. Halle 1905=*ZAW*, vol. xxvi, 1906, pp. 49–87. Cf. *Masoreten des Ostens*, pp. 141 ff.

[2] *Catalogue of the Hebrew Manuscripts in the Bodleian Library*, vol. ii, by A. Neubauer and A. E. Cowley, Oxford 1906.

Job, published already by Weerts, which needed a new examination.

I had now a broad foundation for the Babylonian text of the Bible. The fragments at my disposal belonged to about sixty different MSS. I published the results of my investigations in my book *Masoreten des Ostens*,[1] edited there a great number of Babylonian texts of Bible and Targum, and added facsimiles of sixteen genuine Babylonian MSS. After the War I continued my search for this material. After 1925 I paid seven separate visits to England; each time I came with new problems, and returned with important material I had found. In 1926 I was for six weeks in Leningrad where, especially in the Antonin Collection of the Russian Public Library,[2] I found many more fragments of these texts. Other specimens I found in the volumes which were sent to me from the Jewish Theological Seminary of America in New York.[3] In 1928 I published a list of the material so far known to me.[4] A special grant from the Prussian Minister of Education allowed me to add to this list facsimiles of seventy more Babylonian Biblical MSS. An improved list of these fragments I published in the Prolegomena to the new edition of Kittel's *Biblia Hebraica*.[5] Here I was able to report on fragments belonging to more than 120 different Babylonian Biblical MSS.

Of most of these MSS only one, two or three folios are known. Larger fragments very seldom exceed twenty folios. The Berlin MS with its ninety-four folios, to which belong seven folios from the Glaser Collection in New York, is a great exception. It was impossible to quote these fragments merely by the shelf-marks of the libraries to which they now belong. Often folios of the same MS had come to different libraries, and nobody could tell which fragments belonged to the same MS. I had therefore to create a special method of quoting them. Some of these fragments exhibit a simpler method of punctuation, others a more complicated one. The first group I designated by the majuscule E (einfach), the second by the majuscule K (kompliziert). A

[1] *Masoreten des Ostens. Die ältesten punktierten Handschriften des A.T. und der Targume, herausgegeben und untersucht.* Mit 16 Lichtdrucktafeln (=Beiträge zur Wissenschaft vom A.T., herausgegeben von Rudolf Kittel, Heft 15, Leipzig, 1913).

[2] cf. supra, p. 7 [3] cf. supra, p. 5.

[4] 'Die hebräischen Bibelhandschriften aus Babylonien'. Mit Faksimiles von 70 Handschriften, *ZAW*, vol. xlvi, Giessen, 1928, pp. 113–37. (100 copies were presented to the 5th German Orientalist Congress, Bonn, 1928.)

[5] *Biblia Hebraica* . . . ed. Rudolf Kittel. Textum Masoreticum curavit P. Kahle, Stuttgart, 1937. Prolegomena, pp. xxx–xxxiii.

minuscule 'a' added to the capital letter indicates that the fragment belongs to the Torah, a minuscule 'b' that it belongs to the Prophets, a minuscule 'c' that it belongs to the Ketubim. It is worth noticing that among the more than 100 MSS to which the fragments belong not a single case is known to me in which a MS contains parts of more than one of these three sections of the Bible. So I had six groups Ea, Eb, Ec, Ka, Kb, Kc, counted (Ea 1, Ea 2, Ea 3 . . . Eb 1, Eb 2, etc.).

Two examples may illustrate how fragments of the same MS came to different libraries: Of Eb 10, a fine MS of the Prophets with simple Babylonian punctuation—a facsimile is to be found in MdO, plate 5—twenty-four folios are known of which ten are in Oxford, bound together with other fragments in MSS Heb d 79 and d 64, four are in Cambridge in Box A 39, 9 of the Taylor-Schechter Collection, seven in Leningrad as MSS Antonin 260, 325, 339, 816, and three are in New York in MS 2021.[1] Of MS Eb 22, an interesting MS of the Prophets, bearing the text of the Targum after each Hebrew verse and provided with simple Babylonian punctuation—a facsimile is to be found in *ZAW*, 1928, plate 47—thirty-six folios are known, of which twenty-five are in Oxford, bound together with other fragments in MSS Heb b. 4, c. 1, d 26, d 49, d 64, four are in Cambridge in Box B 2, 2 of the Taylor-Schechter Collection, seven are in Leningrad as MSS Antonin 280, 908, 909, 910.

The large number of Hebrew Biblical MSS from Babylonia are in their external form very different. Of the eighty-six Babylonian Bible MSS of which I published facsimiles, sixty are without any Masora; only twenty-six have a Masora. In the MSS Ea 7, Eb 26, Ec 1, Ec 4, Ec 5, Ec 11, Ec 12 the notes of the Masora parva are placed between the lines of the Biblical text, exactly above the word to which they belong. In various MSS from Babylonia, which have a Masora magna, the Masora parva is missing (Ea 21, Ka 1, Ka 4, Ka 6, Ka 7, Ka 19). The notes of the Masora magna in the MSS Ec 5, Ec 11 are placed in the margin, next to the Biblical text. As a rule the Masora magna is placed on the lower margin of the Biblical text, but occasionally it is missing in MSS which have a Masora parva (Ka 18, Ka 20).

[1] According to Diez Macho, these fols. of Eb 10, belonging now to MS 504, show Palestinian accents added to the Babylonian text. Cf. *Estudios Biblicos* xiii, Madrid 1954, p. 253. The other folios of Eb 10 do not show any Palestinian accents or vowels, as far as I know.

The Babylonian Masora is written in Aramaic, and Aramaic was also the original language of the Tiberian Masora, although here the Hebrew becomes more and more prevalent. The notes of the Masora parva in Tiberian punctuated MSS are simpler than those in the Babylonian punctuated MSS. Notes of the Masora parva written in the margin of a Babylonian MS always have the form of the Tiberian Masora; they are only found in MSS with complicated Babylonian punctuation (Ka 5, Ka 8, Ka 12, Ka 18, Ka 20, Kc 6). Only one MS of that kind is known to me with simple Babylonian punctuation: Eb 4 (New York) and Eb 8 (Cambridge), facsimile *ZAW*, 1928, plate 38. The Hebrew text is followed by the Targum verse by verse. The signs of the original Babylonian punctuation are used very seldom and it is perhaps the oldest specimen with Babylonian punctuation known to me. A later hand has added Tiberian punctuation to the Hebrew text and Tiberian Masora in the margin.

We can observe clearly in this and other cases the influence of the Tiberian Masora which as time went on penetrated increasingly and eventually eliminated the Babylonian Masora. An interesting example of the incursion of the Tiberian Masora can be seen in the well-known Babylonian Codex of the Prophets in Leningrad from A.D. 916 (Kb 13), which in spite of its being provided with Babylonian vowel signs also has the Tiberian Masora. A few pages of the Codex show Tiberian punctuation.[1]

When C. H. Cornill published *Das Buch des Propheten Ezechiel* (Leipzig 1886)[2] he had carefully collated the text of the St. Petersburg Codex with the usual Tiberian text. He was surprised by the fact that in all the details of punctuation of such a long and difficult text he was able to find only about a dozen slight variations. He concluded that not only the consonantal text but also the punctuation of it was transmitted in Palestine and Babylonia in practically the same way and that the transmission had to be regarded as very constant. We know to-day that this conclusion was wrong. The agreement is to be explained simply by the fact that the St. Petersburg Codex was influenced in every detail by the Tiberian text, and the dozen slight variations found by Cornill are to be regarded merely as details which were overlooked by the Masoretes. This harmonizing of the texts

[1] These are fols. 1b, 212a, 221a, Cf. *ZAW*, 1928, p. 117, n. 1. Prof. Kokovtsov drew my attention to it when we discussed the matter in Leningrad.

[2] Cf. P. de Lagarde's famous review of the book in *Göttingische Gelehrte Anzeigen* 1st June 1886=*Mittheilungen* vol. ii, 1887, pp. 49–64.

is sufficient to explain the survival of the St. Petersburg MS, while all the real Babylonian MSS were lost.

The Tiberian punctuation has in a special way penetrated Yemen. Babylonian Biblical MSS were introduced at an early stage and had accustomed the Yemenite Jews to the Babylonian signs of punctuation. But then a simplified form of Tiberian punctuation made its way which, however, held on to the Babylonian vowel signs and also to the Babylonian shva-sign used for the Tiberian ḥaṭef sounds; it set the vowel signs in a different way and could be regarded as a simplified Tiberian system of punctuation, which had little value for the development of Hebrew vocalization. The old Biblical MSS imported from Babylonia were completely revised according to this method. A good example of this sort of revision is the Berlin MS or qu 680, of the Ketubim in which it is often very difficult indeed to spot the original Babylonian punctuation.

We know that old Yemenite Biblical MSS, particularly the British Museum MS or 1467, sometimes still show genuine Babylonian traditions, particularly in the text of the Targum.[1] Recently, however, the discoveries by Professor Diez Macho in the Library of the Jewish Theological Seminary of America at New York have shown that as late as during the twelfth and thirteenth centuries Biblical MSS were copied in Yemen which reproduced the old Babylonian tradition in the Biblical text as in the Targum text, and that the development of the characteristically Yemenite punctuation analogous to the Tiberian punctuation was effected only at a later stage.[2] Diez Macho worked out that the Babylonian Biblical MSS assembled by me consisted of 521 folios, while he alone has found in New York no less than 567 folios of Babylonian Bible texts. It must be realized, however, that the MSS which I assembled are on the whole much older and mostly come from Babylonia itself, whilst his are mainly copies made in Yemen from Babylonian MSS collected by Elkan N. Adler. Also the quantity of Diez Macho's texts is somewhat reduced by the fact that the Targum and often even the Arabic translation are added to the Hebrew text.

Have we any means of dating with some accuracy such genuine Babylonian Bible texts, of which fragments have been preserved?

[1] Cf. *Masoreten des Ostens*, pp. 213 ff.

[2] A. Diez Macho, 'Importants Manuscrits Hébreux et Araméens aux Etats Unis.' *VT*, Supplement iv 1957, pp. 27–46.

It is obvious that none of these fragments bear a date. Dates are usually written at the end or at the beginning of a MS and the first and last leaves of MSS are the most quickly lost. But the Codex of the Prophets from St. Petersburg seems to me to be a good starting point. It shows that about A.D. 900 the influence of the Tiberian Masoretes was so overwhelming that the Babylonian Biblical MSS had to be adapted to them. We can therefore surmise that MSS with complicated Babylonian punctuation, which have not been adapted, must be older; it is likely that the genuine Babylonian Biblical MSS with simple punctuation must be regarded as even older still.

It seems to me that we shall proceed better if we compare the method of punctuation as used in the genuine Babylonian punctuation with the method used by the Eastern Syrians. Babylonian Jews and Eastern Syrians lived in the same country and it is more than likely that they were in contact with each other.

The simple Babylonian system of punctuation has usually the following six vowel signs:

a = ≺̲, *a* = ⊥̲, *i* = ·̲, *e* = ¨̲, *o* = :̲, *u* = ꜝ̲.

Some of these vowel signs represent Hebrew letters. The vowel ⊥̲ = *a* is a small ע, the vowel ꜝ̲ = *u* a simplified ו, and the vowel ≺̲ = *ā* is to be regarded as a part of the letter א, which as a complete letter is still used in Ea 23 and Ea 24.[1] In the same texts the letter י is used instead of ·̲. The Hebrew letters used in this system make it more than probable that we are dealing with a specifically Hebrew development.

But there is every likelihood that this system was preceded by another which exclusively used dots for its vowels. It can be found in the ancient MS Eb 4 and Eb 8 (belonging to the same MS). In the facsimile of the MS[2] it can be seen that only six words of the Hebrew text and seven words of the Targum text have Babylonian vowel signs. The following signs have been used:

ā = ∸̣, *a* = ∴̲, *i* = ·̲, *e* = ¨̲, *o* = :̲, *u* = ∴̲.

If we remember that the Eastern Syrians used the following vowel signs:

ā = ∴̲, *a* = ∸̣, *i* = ‾.., *e* = ‾⁝, or ‾.., *o* = ȯ, *u* = ọ,

we see that the two systems are so alike as to make it hard to imagine that, coming from the same country, they should have

[1] Facsimiles in *ZAW*, 1928, plates 16 and 17.   [2] *ZAW*, 1928, plate 38.

developed independently of each other. Talking of the Syriac system, H. Ewald made it fairly clear[1] that it must have developed from the diacritical point to be found in MSS of the fifth century and may even have been known to Ephraem (fourth century). The final form of the Eastern Syriac vocalization seems to have existed in the eighth century or even a little earlier, according to Rubens Duval.[2] But we must take into account that the final form is a little further developed than the Hebrew system and that we must probably connect the latter with a slightly earlier form of East Syriac punctuation, which must have existed although so far no traces of it have been found.

3. The Palestinian Punctuation

In Palestine, too, an ancient method of punctuation was used. We call it 'Palestinian punctuation' in accordance with a notice in an Aboth Commentary quoted in *Maḥzor Vitry*,[3] where apart from the other two systems the 'punctuation of the land Israel' (ניקוד ארץ ישראל) is mentioned. That this method of punctuation actually belongs to Palestine is made very plausible in so much as a very similar method is used by the Samaritans in MSS from the twelfth century onwards. The Palestinian signs are:[4]

ā = ˈ̲, *a* = ˉ̲, *i* = ⁚̲, *e* = ⸪̲, (⁖̲ and ⸫̲), *o*, *u* = ∴̲ (∴̲ and ¨̲ or ⁖̲).

The signs used in Samaritan MSS are as follows:[5]

ā = ˈ̲, *a* = ˉ̲, *e*, *i* = ˂̲, *e* = ˇ̲, *o*, *u* = ˆ̲ (or the Arabic sign ʼ̲).

The differences between the two systems are partly to be explained by the fact that we know the Palestinian punctuation from MSS which may have been written in the seventh to ninth

[1] *Abhandlungen zur orientalischen und biblischen Literatur.* Göttingen 1832, pp. 59–77.

[2] In his *Traité de Grammaire syriaque*, Paris 1881, pp. 61–9.

[3] A Maḥzor compiled about 1100 by Simḥa b. Schemuel of Vitry (France). The text of the Maḥzor is published by Hurwitz, Berlin 1889–93. The remark quoted above is to be found on p. 462 of the edition. It was published by Luzzatto in *Kerem Chemed*, iv (1839) p. 203, long before a fragment with this kind of punctuation was known; see *Masoreten des Westens* i, p. 24. Luzzatto adds the note: זה חדוש גדול הצריך עיון וחפוש הרבה

[4] The specimens added in brackets are later developments.

[5] See *Masoreten des Westens*, i. pp. 32 f and my article 'Die Lesezeichen bei den Samaritanern', in *Oriental Studies dedicated to Paul Haupt*, Baltimore and Leipzig 1926, pp. 425–36, = *Opera Minora*, Leiden 1956, pp. 167–79. Fritz Diening *Das Hebräische bei den Samaritanern* (Diss. phil. Bonn = Bonner Orientalistische Studien, Heft 24, Stuttgart, 1938). My article: 'Zur Aussprache des Hebräischen bei den Samaritanern' in *Festschrift Alfred Bertholet*, Tübingen 1950, 281–286 and in *Opera Minora*, Leiden 1956, pp. 180–85.

centuries, whereas Samaritan MSS older than the twelfth century are not preserved.[1] We can take it for granted that the punctuation used by the Samaritans in earlier times bore a closer resemblance to the Palestinian one.[2]

Biblical MSS with Palestinian punctuation are comparatively scarce. Whilst, as we have seen, a large part of the text of the Bible is preserved in Babylonian tradition, I was not able to find more than six MSS of the Bible with Palestinian punctuation.

They are:

1. Fragments of a scroll with parts of Ezek. xiii–xvi.
2. Fragments of a scroll with parts of Ps. xxvii–xxxiii, xxxv–xl, xl–xlvi, lv–lix.
3. Two folios with the last four chapters of Dan.

[1] Only very few Samaritan MSS of the Pentateuch are provided with this type of punctuation. I know the following: (1) MS Sam 101 of the Serai Library in Istanbul (12th century); (2) MS Sam 64 and the small fragment 75 in the Russian Public Library in Leningrad (13th century); (3) a Samaritan Pentateuch in Trinity College Library Cambridge, acquired 1917, dated A.D. 1332; (4) MS Or 6461, of the British Museum in London (14th century).

[2] The oldest MS in book form of the Samaritan Pentateuch known to me is MS Add 1846 in the University Library in Cambridge. It contains a notice that it was sold AH 544 (AD 1149/50) and it may have been written a long time before that. It certainly gives the impression of being considerably older than the Samaritan Pentateuch MSS written since A.D. 1200, of which we know a good many. It was very famous among the Samaritans and had a long history attached to it. On the basis of the material that I put at his disposal, Herr von Gall published the detail about this MS on pages lxxxiv f of his edition of the *Hebräische Pentateuch der Samaritaner*, Giessen 1914–18. But the MS shows no vocalization whatsoever.

Just as little vocalization is to be found in the Pentateuch scrolls, parts of which are older. One of these is to be seen in Sir Frederic Kenyon's book *Our Bible and the Ancient Manuscripts*, London 1939, plate V, facing p. 51; in the new edition of this book, revised by A. W. Adams, Introduction by G. R. Driver, London 1958, Plate xii, after p. 93. This scroll, however, has nothing to do with the famous Holy Scroll, said to have been written by Abisha', the son of Aaron's grandson in the thirteenth year after the Israelites had taken possession of Canaan. This is kept as a great treasure in the Synagogue of the Samaritans in Nāblus. It had been rediscovered at the beginning of the fourteenth century. The various problems connected with it are discussed in my article 'Aus der Geschichte der ältesten Bibelhandschrift' in the Baudissin Festschrift=*BZAW*, xxxiii, Giessen 1918, pp. 247–60.

A complete photograph of the scroll was made in Palestine by request of Professor Fr. Pérez Castro. Cf. his article 'El-Séfer Abišá'', *Sefarad* xiii, Madrid 1953, pp. 119–29, with facsimiles of five columns of the old part of the scroll. On the basis of these photographs I have dealt once more with the old scroll in 'The Abisha Scroll of the Samaritans', in the Pedersen Festschrift: *Studia Orientalia Joanni Pedersen Septuagenario, dicata*, Hauniae 1953, pp. 188–92. On looking carefully at the photograph of the scroll one soon notices that only the end of the scroll is old (end of Numbers to end of Deuteronomy). This is confirmed by a notice in the margin of the original MS of the Samaritan Chronicle al-Tolida, in the possession of the Samaritan High Priest, which says that the rest of the old scroll was destroyed during a storm. A new edition of the Hebrew Pentateuch of the Samaritans is being prepared for the Spanish Polyglot by Professor Fr. Pérez Castro in Madrid. He will publish there the Abisha' scroll and indicate the Samaritan vowel signs as far as they are found in the manuscripts, and the text published by him will be a text really used by the Samaritans, not a reconstructed text like that published by von Gall.

4. One folio with Jer. i and ii.
5. Two folios of fragments with parts of Ps. li–lv, lxix–lxxii.
6. Eight folios with Biblical texts written in abbreviations (סירוגים) containing parts of Isa. and Jer. and Exod. xxviii and xxix. With the exception of 2, I have published these fragments in *Masoreten des Westens*, vol. ii pp. 66–95 and dealt with the problems connected with them on pp. 16–45. There I also gave facsimiles of the various MSS.

The Psalm scroll is of special interest. The fragments are kept under glass in Cambridge (T–S 10, No 52, 53, 54, 58). Only a few vowel signs are used and only one kind of accent. A careful investigation of the originals revealed that even these few signs have been added by different hands and *both* hands adopt different methods. An edition of the fragments of the Psalm scroll has been made by Dr. A. Murtonen in his *Academic Dissertation: Materials for a non-Masoretic Hebrew Grammar*, (Helsinki, 1958) pp. מד–לג. He deals with the text of the Psalm scroll on pp. 22 f of his book. It is clearly to be seen that these biblical texts with Palestinian vocalisation are influenced more or less by the Tiberian method of punctuation, which began to be worked out about 800 and which soon became generally accepted and influenced the texts with the earlier Palestinian vocalisation.

All the more valuable are further fragments which Diez Macho found in the Library of the Jewish Theological Seminary of America in New York.[1] They are the following:

1. MS 594, box B, envelope 12, an incomplete parchment folio, containing on fol. a: Eccles xi 1–9; xii 3–9; on folio b: Lament i 1–4, 7–12. The consonantal text and the Palestinian punctuation, added by the copyist, are written in red-brown ink; the Tiberian signs of punctuation are added in black ink. Professor Diez Macho has kindly put at my disposal a photo of the folio and twice collated my copy with the original. In Appendix III (pp. 336–344) I am publishing this fragment as an instructive specimen of a Biblical text with Palestinian punctuation to which was later added a Tiberian punctuation which gives a very welcome insight into the development of the Tiberian punctuation when it was still in process of formation before it was really

[1] 'Tres nueves manuscritos biblicos "palestinenses".' *Estudios Biblicos* xiii, Madrid 1954, pp. 247–65.

fixed. I am very grateful to Professor Diez Macho for all his help in dealing with this interesting text which he discovered, and I refer to his own observations on pages 251–3 of his article.

2. MS 504, fols. 2, 7, 8. The three folios are part of the Babylonian Biblical text which I have described as Eb 10. When the volume to which it belonged was sent to me from New York in the 1920s, it was marked with the number 2021 and the three folios belonging to Eb 10 are quoted by me in *ZAW* xiv, 1928, p. 125 as Nos. 12, 14 and 21. The folios 7 and 8 (14 and 21 in my enumeration) consist of fragments of folios to which I also added whilst collating them the words 'difficult to read'. Diez Macho restricted himself to the investigation of fol. 2 (12 in my enumeration) and gave reproductions of both its sides. When I collated the folio I also entered the Palestinian signs, but it was Diez Macho who recognized their importance. The other fragments of the MS Eb 10 will therefore also have to be carefully investigated with a view to finding how far Palestinian signs of punctuation have been entered.

The investigation of this folio from Eb 10 made by Diez Macho results in the following important conclusions:

1. To an obviously ancient and valuable Babylonian Biblical text Palestinian accentuation has been added.
2. Besides the Palestinian accents some Tiberian accents (distinctive as well as conjunctive) have been added.
3. The Palestinian writer has also added a few Palestinian vowels which, though few in number, are important as Palestinian corrections of the Babylonian pronunciation.
4. The Palestinian punctuator has added to the Babylonian text several Pesiks and Makkefs, as well as a Tiberian Vowel and a Tiberian Dagesh.
5. We can see that a firm classical system with simple Babylonian punctuation must have existed at the time when the Palestinian system of punctuation was valid and also at the time of the transition from the Palestinian to the Tiberian system of punctuation.

3. MS 504, fols. 10 and 11 with reproduction of 11a and 11b containing Judges xviii, 2–xix 15. Fol. 10 contains the end of Judges (xxi 23–25), the two last verses with Palestinian punctuation, with a colophon: חזק שלום יצחק בר יחיא בר יעקב בר יושיהו.

To the still prevalent Palestinian accents Tiberian accents are already added with a certain regularity.

Another hand, in considerably larger writing, follows with the text from Isa. i, 1–ii, 3 provided, according to Diez Macho, with Tiberian punctuation from the eleventh century, yet retaining some Palestinian accents.

This whole fragment is an exceedingly good example of the transition from the Palestinian to the Tiberian punctuation.

These Biblical fragments with Palestinian punctuation are of great interest to us because they show us what vocalized Bible MSS were like before the Tiberian Masoretes began their work. Although only few Biblical texts with Palestinian punctuation have been preserved, this system of punctuation must have been very general in Palestine. We know texts of Targums with this punctuation,[1] texts of the Mishna,[2] of the Palestinian Midrash,[3] of the Masora,[4] and, above all liturgical texts.[5] The liturgy always tends to be conservative and in liturgical texts this punctuation seems to have prevailed longer.

The chief contribution to the study of texts with Palestinian punctuation has been made by Dr. A. Murtonen. In his *Materials for a non-Masoretic Grammar, I. Liturgical Texts and Psalm Fragments Provided with the So-Called Palestinian Punctuation*, Helsinki 1958, he gives a review of the texts published so far (p. 20) and adds that the largest part of texts that are known with Palestinian punctuation, hitherto unpublished, are published here. He refers to the fact that the vocalisation marks in these MSS are

[1] See Part iii, p. 201.

[2] Apart from the fragment E 1, 107 of the Taylor-Schechter Collection in Cambridge to which I referred in *Masoreten des Westens*, i, pp. 28 f. (parts of Baba Bathra and Sanhedrin) I found another fragment E 2, 76 of the same Collection (parts of Sanhedrin and Shebuoth). It is possible that these fragments belong to different MSS of the Mishna.

[3] Five specimens of the Pesiḳta de Rab Kāhana, Palimpsests written above verses of the New Testament, published by Charles Taylor, *Hebrew-Greek Cairo Palimpsests from the Taylor-Schechter Collection*, Cambridge 1900, Plates ix and x, = T–S E 16,93. The text of the fragments shows many deviations from the text published by Salomon Buber, Lück 1868.

[4] Apart from the Cambridge fragment T–S D 1.12, published in *Masoreten des Westens*, i, p. 29, I found old fragments of the so-called *Ochla we-Ochla* in Leningrad, Firkowitch II, 1551–54. The last of these fragments show a few Palestinian vowel signs. The fragments will be used by Dr. Fernando Diaz Esteban in the new edition of אכלה ואכלה prepared in Madrid.

[5] In the last section of Part i I have referred to these liturgical texts. See further A. Diez Macho, 'Nuevos manuscritos importantes, biblicos o liturgicos, en hebreo o arameo,' A. Manuscritos 'Palestinenses' *Sefarad* xvi 1956, pp. 4–6. A. Diez Macho, 'Un manuscrito "palestinense" en La Biblioteca Nacional de Estrasburgo.' *Sefarad* xvii, 1957, pp. 11–17. A. Diez Macho, 'Importants Manuscrits Hébreux et Araméens aux Etats Unis.' *VT*, Supplement iv, 1957, pp. 27–46.

normally used defectively, i.e. the signs do not always appear where a vowel was to be pronounced. In his MS a (the Bodleian MS Heb. d. 55) he has found 10 folios (4–7, 9–14) which are provided with almost complete vocalisation. His sketch of a Hebrew grammar according to the Palestinian punctuation is mainly based on this MS.

Murtonen has seen that the vocalisation of this MS is made by four hands. The first and the second ones differ from each other, however, only in some isolated instances, so that normally they are treated as a whole. The third hand appears rarely, while the fourth one is Tiberian and, consequently, not taken into account by Murtonen. The other MSS are used to supplement MS a, and their disagreements with the latter are recorded where necessary (p. 25).

Since these texts are liturgical and often difficult to understand, I recommended Murtonen to contact my former pupil and friend Dr. Menachem Zulay, who had become head of the Research Institute for Hebrew Poetry in Jerusalem and the great authority on these studies, and whose death (Nov. 1954) was a very great loss. To his memory Murtonen has dedicated his book.

As for the character of the liturgical texts with Palestinian vocalisation, Murtonen confined himself to recording the most important characteristics and asked Dr. Gustav Ormann[1] in Jerusalem to write an appendix dealing with the special characteristics of the Qerobas of Yannay and Qalir.

In his grammatical sketch Dr. Murtonen deals in the main with texts of the Bodleian MS Heb. d. 55 on the folios indicated above. In the Appendix I am publishing in facsimile fols. 4, 4a, 9, 10, 11, 13, selected by Dr. Murtonen himself, and the Cambridge Psalm fragment T-S 20, 54 in order to enable the reader to study these kinds of texts. For the same reason I am publishing also in the Appendix MS 594, Box B, Envelope 12, described on p. 68, in which the Tiberian punctuation was added to a Palestinian punctuated MS.

Dr. Murtonen is convinced that only a sketch, not a complete Hebrew grammar, can be composed from Hebrew texts with Palestinian vocalisation. The ultimate purpose, as indicated by the title of his book, is a grammar on the basis of all non-masoretic traditions. Of these the Samaritan tradition

[1] Ormann was made Dr. Phil. in Bonn in 1930 for his thesis "Das Sündenbekenntnis des Versöhnungstages", which was published in Frankfurt in 1934.

is the most important, and to enable the reader to study this tradition I am publishing the texts recorded by Helmut Ritter and Artur Schaade from the dictation of the High Priest in Nāblus in the year 1917 which have been put at my disposal by Mrs. Schaade and Professor Dr. Tiemann, the Director of the Hamburg Staatts- und Universitätsbibliothek. Dr. Murtonen has made special studies with the Samaritans and is preparing a Grammar of Hebrew as read by the Samaritans in their services.

But for the non-Masoretic Grammar which he ultimately intends to bring out also, other traditions must be taken into consideration, above all the MSS from the Judaean desert and the Second Column of the Hexapla as deciphered by Giovanni Cardinal Mercati.

With this material I shall deal later on.

4. The Approximate Dates of Texts with Babylonian and Palestinian Punctuation

It would, of course, be of great interest if we could give a date to the development of the Palestinian punctuation. Here again we cannot expect to find a date written on any of the fragments. Nevertheless I believe that an approximate date can be given to them. To achieve this we must start from the vocalization of the Western Syrians.

When, in the course of the eighth century, the Western Syrians introduced Greek vowels as Syriac vowel signs, they used a Greek omicron as sign for Zeḳāfā, a vowel corresponding to the Hebrew Ḳameṣ. This implies that this vowel was pronounced in Western Syria at the time as *o*. Yet we know of an earlier system of vocalization of the Western Syrians which was introduced by James of Edessa (about A.D. 700) and which used an Alif for the same vowel. From this fact Duval correctly concluded that the vowel marked thus was at the time pronounced like an *a*.[1] It seems

[1] Rubens Duval, in his book *Traité de Grammaire syriaque* (Paris 1881, p. 45 f.) writes: The toning of the dull *a* in *o* was a fait accompli when the Greek vowels were used for the notation of the Syriac vowels . . . ; for in this system the Greek *o* (Omicron or Omega) is the sign for a dull Syriac *a*. Was it then the same before the introduction of this system, that is to say, before the second half of the eighth century? One would be tempted to deny it when one considers that James of Edessa amongst the types which he invented . . . reproduced *a* by Alef. Since he took Greek characters as his pattern it would be reasonable to conclude that the Syriac *a* corresponded with the Greek *a*, written as alpha.

Duval also pointed out that this change-over in the pronunciation would have

therefore that it became a general usage in Western Syria after 700 to pronounce the old *a* like an *o*.

A similar change in the pronunciation of the Hebrew vowel as rendered by Ḳameṣ seems to have taken place in Palestine at about the same time. It is certain that when the Tiberian Masoretes developed their punctuation at the beginning of the ninth century, they accepted the pronunciation of the Ḳameṣ as *o* as being correct. Vocalizations like שֳׁרָשִׁים, קֳדָשִׁים can be understood only on the assumption that the words were pronounced like *ḳodoshim*, *shoroshim*. This pronunciation corresponds with that of the Ashkenazic Jews and it is beyond doubt that they carried on the pronunciation of Hebrew as intended by the Tiberian Masoretes.

The Babylonian Masoretes pronounced the Ḳameṣ always like *a*, in the same way as the Eastern Syrians pronounced their Zeḳāfā. In the quoted words they could only use the sign for Ḳameṣ in the second syllable and reproduced the sound which they heard in the first syllable by *u*. In this way they wrote קדשים *ḳudashim*, שרשים *shurashim* and again קדשו *ḳudsho* for Tiberian קָדְשׁוֹ as for them the use of the vowel sign Ḳameṣ in reproducing the open *o* or *u* was not considered. Only in the MSS strongly influenced by the Tiberian Masoretes, as in the Petersburg Codex of the Prophets from A.D. 916 and in later Yemenite MSS, is the Babylonian Ḳameṣ sign also used to mark an open *o*. The influence of the Tiberian system of punctuation penetrates more and more. MSS which show clearly this influence, in spite of the Babylonian vowel signs which they include, cannot be accepted any longer as genuinely Babylonian.

We know that when the Talmudic Academies in Babylonia fell into decay it was Spain which became the centre of Jewish learning. We hear of Babylonian scholars who emigrated to Spain and we also hear of large sums of money which, for instance, were sent to Babylonia by the well-known Jewish physician and statesman Ḥisdaj b. Shapruṭ, for the acquisition of books. Ḥisdaj was one of the confidants of the Spanish Omaijad Caliphs ʿAbdur-raḥmān III an-Nāṣir and his successor an-Nāṣir in the tenth century. The contemporary poet Dunash b. Labraṭ exaggerates

taken place gradually. For the vowels from the Greek pattern introduced by James of Edessa, compare the description which William Wright gives of fols. 37 and 38 of the British Museum MS Add 17217 in no. 996 of his *Catalogue of the Syriac Manuscripts*, iii, 1872, pp. 1169 f.

when he reports that Ḥisdaj spent his entire fortune on books from Sūra (Babylonia). Babylonian Biblical MSS, however, must have been available for the men who revised the Hebrew text of the Complutensian Polyglot at the beginning of the sixteenth century.[1] But Babylonian MSS must have gone to Spain at a much earlier date. We can conclude this from the fact that the usual pronunciation of Hebrew in Babylonia was so firmly established amongst the Jews in Spain that it could not be influenced by a pronunciation which presupposed a Tiberian punctuation. They were not affected by this punctuation, but adhered to the old Hebrew pronunciation which they knew from Babylonia. This is illustrated by a glossary from the ninth century in which about 200 Hebrew words in Latin transcription are mentioned. As Professor Millas Vallicrosa explained in Cambridge at the International Congress of Orientalists, they are rendered in nearly the same way as they were pronounced according to Babylonian tradition and at a time when the Tiberian punctuation was not yet developed.

Also in Palestine the vowel which was later reproduced by Ḳameṣ was not always pronounced like *o*, as the Tiberian punctuation surmises. For this fact we hold definite proofs. One of them is that in the transcribed text as it appears in the second column of Origen's Hexapla and the transcription of Jerome, this sound which corresponds to the later Ḳameṣ is always reproduced by *a*. Also the Samaritans reproduced the sound corresponding to the Ḳameṣ always as *a* and did not join in the change which the Jews and Syrians effected in their pronunciation.

It is very interesting that we can watch this change in the pronunciation when we see the fragments with Palestinian punctuation. In the scroll of Ezekiel (H) the sign corresponding to the later Ḳameṣ is never used to mark an open *o*. To designate this sound the *o* vowel is always used, cf. לאכלה xv, 4, אזניך xvi, 2, ביפיך xvi, 14, 15, 25. The same thing occurs in the Psalm scroll, cf. אזנים xl, 7; חכמה xxxvii, 30; חנני xli, 11; קדשו xxx, 5; In the Jeremiah fragment (K) we find in the same way נכריה ii, 4 and באזני ii, 2; in

[1] Cf. my contribution to *Homenajo a Millas-Vallicrosa*, vol. i, Barcelona 1954: 'The Hebrew Text of the Complutensian Polyglot', pp. 741–751, as well as my contribution to the *Essays presented to Leo Baeck*, London, 1954: 'Zwei durch Humanisten besorgte dem Papst gewidmete Ausgaben der hebräischen Bibel', pp. 50–74 =*Opera Minora*, Leiden, 1956, pp. 128–50) where I tried to prove that these Babylonian Bible MSS as vetustissima exemplaria have been of the greatest importance for the forming of the Hebrew Bible text of the Complutensian Polyglot.

the Psalm fragments (L) we find אֹזנךְ lxxi, 2 and עֹשרו lii, 9. In the fragments from the Piuṭ by Yannai which I published in *Masoreten des Westens*, i, pp. כד–כז, vocalization like כהוקרא, תועקב, בגוזרו יונשב can be found.

But the fragment of Daniel וכשמעי (x, 9) and שרשיה (xi, 3) is written and must obviously be read as *shorashe, ukshom'i*, whereas in the MS with the abbreviated Biblical texts the vowel ـ corresponds entirely with the Tiberian Ḳameṣ and is also used in exactly the same way. I refer here to the examples given in *Masoreten des Westens* ii, p. 33*. The same thing happens in many liturgical texts with Palestinian punctuation. One is justified in drawing the conclusion from these facts that the older fragments with Palestinian vocalization presuppose the pronunciation of this vowel as *a*, the later ones taking the pronunciation as *o*. If we suppose that this change in the pronunciation of Hebrew in Palestine took place at the same time as the change in the pronunciation of Syriac in Western Syria we are able to fix the older and the later fragments with Palestinian punctuation as having been written before 700 and after 750 approximately.

5. The Beginnings of the Tiberian Masora

In a treatise on the Shwa, which must have been composed soon after the fixing of the reading and of the recitation of the Biblical text by the Masoretes of Tiberias, we have a list of Tiberian Masoretes which was first noticed by Firkowitch and was afterwards made known by Harkavy[1] and also by Strack[2] according to Leningrad MS Firk II Paper 145. A similar list of names of Masoretes is to be found in a treatise on the accents in the books of the Psalms, Job and Proverbs, a folio of which is preserved in MS Firk II Paper 146.

Adalbert Merx in his 'Studie zur Geschichte der Masora',[3] made a very scholarly study of these 'fragments from Tschufut-

[1] Harkavy published the texts in הצפירה 1874, No. 15, also in המזכיר 1874, in the *Jahrbücher für Jüdische Geschichte und Literatur*, 1876, and with a detailed discussion in חדשים גם ישנים No. 2.

[2] Strack published the texts in *Theologische Studien und Kritiken*, 1875, pp. 743 f. and 1876, pp. 554 f., as well as in the edition of the Diḳduḳe ha-Ṭe'amim, 1879, pp. 78 f.

[3] Merx's study appeared in conjunction with his 'Bemerkungen über die Vokalisation der Targume' in the *Verhandlungen des V. Internationalen Orientalisten Kongress zu Berlin* 1882, vol. i. pp. 188–225.

kale', in which he tried to arrange the above-mentioned names of Masoretes in groups and assign dates to them. In the treatise on the Shwa the Masoretes are mentioned in connexion with six generations of the Ben Asher family, of which, however, one name has been added between the lines; of the last members of the family we know the dates. To-day we have material to hand, of which Merx could not know anything. His reconstruction of the group of Masoretes is certainly not correct.

Jacob Mann found in Geniza fragments both in Oxford and in London two folios belonging to an Arabic version of the treatise on the Shwa. He published parts of it and pointed out that the Arabic version must be looked upon as the original of the Hebraistic text from Leningrad.[1] In this version only five members of the Ben Asher family are to be found, so the name added between the lines of the Leningrad text must be discounted. Mann's attempt to date the Masoretes undoubtedly represents an improvement upon Merx. I also have discussed these lists of Tiberian Masoretes.[2] They provide information about the time of the Masoretes and tell us something about their kind of activity. But a real understanding of this list is only possible when one studies the whole treatise on the Shwa in which it occurs. At my request the MSS were sent from Leningrad to Bonn and I suggested to Kurt Levy, one of my ablest pupils in Bonn, to go into the matter of these texts in connexion with the Geniza material discovered by Mann. He accepted my suggestion and also discovered further material on the treatise about the Shwa in a Geniza fragment which was brought to the Stadtbibliothek in Frankfurt and which contains a fragment of a second MS of the Arabic text of that treatise. His edition and translation of the treatise and the research which he undertook in connexion with it were a brilliant achievement and it was a tragic fate which prevented him from living to see the conclusion of his book.[3] I published the book from his manuscript. If he had lived to do it himself, he might have included the result of further investigations and added indices. The problems with which the book deals occupied his attention for many years.

[1] Jacob Mann, *The Jews in Egypt and in Palestine under the Fatimid Caliphs*, vol. i, 1920, pp. 55, 58; vol. ii, 1922, pp. 43–9. The Geniza fragments found by Mann are in Oxford (Bodleian MS Heb e 74, fols. 59 & 60 Catalogue 2862, 21) and in the British Museum, London (MS or 5554 A, fols. 28 and 29).

[2] *Masoreten des Westens*, vol. i 1927, pp. 36 f.

[3] Kurt Levy, *Zur masoretischen Grammatik. Texte und Untersuchungen*, Bonner Orientalistische Studien, Heft 15, Stuttgart, 1936.

The Leningrad MS Firk II 145 forms a distinctive whole with its 19 folios. Of the two Arabic MSS we have only remnants, but they are more closely related to the original. The fact that parts of three MSS of the treatise have been preserved shows that we are not dealing with a little known fabrication but that the treatise must have been well known and even famous. The list of the Masoretes is important for the understanding of the treatise, because it becomes apparent that its author feels he stands at a certain distance from their activity. He takes the list as concluded with the name of Aaron b. Asher. But he is not too remote from the Ben Asher family. The treatise makes us realize some of the problems which the Masoretes had to face when they gave the text of the Bible the form which was to be its final one. We can take it that in its style of expression the MS belongs to the early Arabic sources of Hebrew grammar, and it is certain that it was composed before Ḥaijūǧ, who is usually regarded as the first Hebrew grammarian. The list of Masoretes throws light on the character of the treatise, as it is found in similar form in a fragment on the accents which was probably written at nearly the same time. Levy printed this text on pp. 31–3 of his book. The list has a special interest in so far as it shows how fluid the accentuation of the text still was at that time.

Levy, in a very fine investigation, showed how the relation of this treatise to the Diḳduḳe ha-Ṭeʿamim by Aaron b. Moshe b. Asher has to be judged and in what way it is related to the 'Manuel de Lecteur',[1] published by J. Derenbourg. He discusses the problem of how it can be explained that the treatise about the Shwa disappeared later on from the transmission, and he thinks that the cause was its language which later generations found quaint and incomprehensible (p. 40). This may well be one reason. But two further reasons may be added. One is that the writings deal with problems which the Masoretes had to face with regard to fixing the punctuation of the text of the Bible and with different solutions which these problems found. One does not like to be reminded of such differences of pronunciation once the fixed text has been approved and acknowledged. The other reason is that these writings were of Ḳaraite origin. Levy could not know this when he wrote his book, but now there can be no doubt about it.

[1] 'Manuel de Lecteur d'un auteur inconnu, publié d'après un manuscrit venu du Yemen et accompagné de notes', par M. J. Derenbourg (*Journal Asiatique*, vi, 16, 1870, pp. 309–550).

For all further details concerning this treatise I refer to Levy's comments, and only wish to quote the list of the Masoretes, but I do so from the treatise on the Shwa in the form based on the Arabic text which is the original. Levy had to rely on the Hebraistic text of the Leningrad MS when he made his translation, as it is the only one which forms a conclusive whole and we only have a few remnants of the Arabic text. The Arabic text in question has been printed by Mann and by Levy. But Mann could not read the last words of his original and Levy has restricted himself at the end to the quotation of variants, and it is therefore not easy to reconstruct the Arabic text. As it is these final words which matter to me I set them down according to the original as conclusion to the text printed by Mann:

ואמא הד̇א אלקאנון אלד̇י כלאמי פיה אלד̇י חכיתה ענהם אנהם יקרון אשתי אשתים אשתיהם פכולהם מתפקין עליהא בלא כ̇לף בתה וגמיע אהל טבריה הד̇א מעהם באלתלקין ואן כאן עלתה לא יעלמונהא ולא יערפו מא הו . . .

The translation of the passage in question from the treatise on the Shwa is as follows:

> . . . and there is no difference of opinion among them, for they all maintain and agree that this is the correct inspiration which we have taken from the men of the Great Synagogue by truthful tradition. And these are the pupils who have endorsed these declarations:
>
> Abraham b. Rīḳāṭ, and Rīḳāṭ before him and Abraham b. Furāṭ and Pinḥas, the head of the yeshiba. And before him was Ṣemaḥ b. Abī Shaiba and Ṣemaḥ, known as Ibn aṣ-Ṣaiyāra and Rabbi Ḥabīb ben Rabbi Pīpīm and Aḥiyyāhu ha-Kohen ha-Ḥāber from the city of Ma'azzia (Tiberias). And with these was Rabbi Asher, the great master and Neḥemya, his son, and Asher b. Neḥemya and Moshe b. Asher and Aaron b. Moshe and he was the last one in the chain, and it is said that they came from Ezra and other people (קומאן אוכ̇ר) were with them like Rabbi Moshe Mōḥa and Moshe ha-'Azzati (from Gaza), the punctuator and others. And I have only given you their names—may their memory be blessed—because they held different views on many things about Ḳameṣ and Pataḥ and the two and the three (dots: Ṣere, Segol) and the Shwa quiescens and the Shwa mobile. And concerning this rule (*ḳānūn*) of which I treat and about which I have reported concerning them, that they read אשתים, אשתיהם, אשתי, they all agree with it without any difference of opinion and all people from Tiberias do this by inspiration and if there should be a reason for it they don't know it and don't know what it is . . .

The form שתי with Shwa quiescens and following Dagesh lene is, as is well known, a unique case.[1] The author declares that it was generally spoken with a prefixed א.

In the treatise on the accents (Firk II Pap 146) we find the following report on the Masoretes:

> Now concerning its (a kind of Shofar) use in this way, when you see it in many of the manuscripts, do not wonder for it is no mistake, it is only a difference between the first masters like Rabbi Pinḥas, the head of the yeshiba, and Rabbi Ḥabīb b. Rabbi Pinḥas, and Abraham b. Furāt and Abraham b. Rīḳāṭ and Arīḳāṭ before him and Ṣemaḥ b. Abū Shaiba and Moshe Mōḥe, and Ṣemaḥ Abū Slūṭōm (sic!) and Asher b. Neḥemya and Abu'l—'Umaiṭir (עומיטר). These are the pupils of the first whom we mentioned before these masters, whose views one follows and according to whom one transmits. (יקתדא בדאיהם וירֶוא ענהם)[2]

The two lists of Masoretes who joined in making the punctuation of the Hebrew text of the Bible are of great interest to us, even if we do not know much of the bearers of the names. To create a uniform punctuation of the text of the Hebrew Bible was a great achievement which demanded the co-operation of a staff. Both lists point out that for the recitation as well as for the pronunciation of the text various possibilities were under discussion. From the second list we see that the accentuation of the Biblical books in question was still fluid at the time when the list was composed. From the first list we learn that concerning the pronunciation of the vowels different possibilities were considered. We also learn that the authorities mentioned held different views on the pronunciation of the vowels, of the Ḳameṣ and Pataḥ, the Ṣere and the Segol, the Shwa quiescens and the Shwa mobile. I think it is very likely that apart from Tiberian punctuated MSS which showed mainly the punctuation to which we are now accustomed there were also Tiberian punctuated MSS bearing a slightly different punctuation, perhaps one which may be regarded as the predecessor of the punctuation of Codex Reuchlinianus and the large number of related MSS which I discussed together with Dr. R. Edelmann as texts of Ben Naftali, in *Masoreten des Westens* vol. ii 1930, pp. 45*–68*. It is certainly very noticeable

[1] See for instance, J. Barth, in *Nöldeke-Festschrift*, 1906, p. 792.

[2] The Segol in *jurā* refers to the Imāle of ā. Above the line the copyist has written: ויגיד, clearly the Hebrew word which translates the Arabic term.

that in these many MSS the vowels given are used in a different way from what we find in the Biblical texts familiar to us.

The five generations of the Ben Asher family who are mentioned in the first list as the contemporaries of the Masoretes enable us to fix approximately when and where these Masoretes lived. The Codex of the Prophets, completed in 895 in Tiberias by Moshe b. Asher, proves that the work on the Biblical text was finished towards the end of the ninth century. We can go even further and suggest that the text of the Bible was copied in this way somewhat earlier. It is difficult to suppose that the oldest existing dated manuscript of the Hebrew text of the Bible should have been the first to be copied in this way.

Aaron b. Asher, the son of Moshe, was the great authority who in the first half of the tenth century gave to the text of the Bible the detailed form which it was to retain thereafter. He is explicitly named as the last of the chain.

We know with certainty that Moshe b. Asher and his son belonged to the community of the Ḳaraites, and it is therefore very likely that the other members of the Ben Asher family were also Ḳaraites. How many of the Masoretes mentioned in the list belonged to the Ḳaraites we do not know, but one may suppose that there were followers of the Rabbanites among them. Furthermore we must conceive the possibility that Ḳaraites and Rabbanites worked together towards the carrying through of the punctuation of the Biblical text. But it seems that the Ḳaraites were the driving force. Their founder 'Anan had already encouraged them in the study of the Biblical text. It is very likely that the old MSS brought from the cave near Jericho to Jerusalem about 800 gave new impetus to the study of the Bible.

We have an interesting report about the study of the Bible by the Ḳaraites which is written by Selmān ben Jeruḥim soon after 900. It is to be found in the explanation of Psalm lxix, 1. The passage in question has already been published in a Hebrew translation by Pinsker in his *Liḳḳuṭe Ḳadmoniyot* (pp. 21 ff). In view of its importance, Solomon L. Skoss printed it in the Arabic original according to the Leningrad fragment, in his edition of the *Kitāb jāmi' al-alfāẓ* (Agron), the important Hebrew dictionary by David b. Abraham al-Fāsī, the tenth-century[1] Ḳaraite. I was able to use concurrently the Arabic text of the fragment

[1] See *Yale Oriental Series, Researches*, vols. xx, xxi. 1936, 1945. (xxi, p. cxxxvii). Ps xlii-lxxii of the Commentary ed. by Dr. Lawrence Marwick, Philadelphia, 1956.

from the Geniza to be found in the Bodleian MS Heb c 19, fols. 89–96 (Catalogue 2628, 29) to which Dr. M. Zucker drew my attention. I reproduce here the whole passage in translation.[1]

> **למנצח על שושנים** His word: **על שושנים** means that this prayer is uttered for the sake of the devout who are compared to the lilies, as it is written 'as lilies among thorns' (Cant. ii, 2); he has also compared them with the flowers (**נצנים** Cant. ii, 12), the vine, the fig and many plants and fruits, and each one of these has a special meaning which, with God's help, I will explain in the commentary on the Canticle. I say now that these lilies and what is like them begin to grow when winter departs, as it is written: for winter is now past, the rain is over and gone (Cant. ii, 11). Such is the appearance of the devout at the end of the four empires, and their appearance occurs on various occasions with the sole difference that each group arrives in greater strength than the preceding one, until in the end there comes (read: *ilā an*) the remnant.
>
> And in the fourth empire 'Anan appeared. He made the hearts of men responsive and opened their eyes. They had a longing for the book of God, which grew as they dedicated themselves to the study of it, especially as the party of the Rabbanites and their occupation with the Talmud (*bil-gamār*) had made them forget the book of God and their concern with the essential things contained in it. Then Benjamin came and with him an increase of effort and discoveries concerning things in which 'Anan had followed the party of the Rabbanites. After Benjamin the Ḳaraites appeared. With them the study and the correct understanding of the book of God increased. Then people came from East and West, the adherence to religion and the endeavour to know (read: *bil-'ilm*) increased, and they wished to live in Jerusalem and they left their comfort and their homes and lived in the world as ascetics; now they live in Bait al-muḳaddas, (Jerusalem) until among their followers the remnant shall appear: 'the remnant of Israel shall not do iniquity' (Soph. iii, 13) and they are the lilies, and all the devout who have clung to the religion of the book shall be counted among them.

It is very likely that Selmān, in writing his report about the Ḳaraites who were devoting themselves to the study of the Biblical text, had in mind the Tiberian Masoretes and referred to them

[1] The two MSS show the same text. But the Bodleian MS must have been in the hands of a Rabbanite who replaced the eulogy-formula after ענן by writing ענן קד תבע and added after אלרבונין the eulogy-formula זׄ לׄב

in this way. At any rate their work must be regarded as an extraordinary achievement. We learn the importance of their work also from Ḳirḳisānī, who was a contemporary of Selmān b. Jeruḥim. By 'Benjamin', Benjamin an-Nihāwendī is meant who undoubtedly belonged to the great and influential class of the older Ḳaraites. Very few of his writings have been preserved. Yet, when Ja'ḳūb al-Ḳirḳisānī wrote his great work *kitāb al-anwār wal-marāḳib* about the year 937, he must have known a considerable amount of Benjamin's works because in more than 150 places he refers to them and discusses them. We know that Benjamin was already active at the beginning of the ninth century. He is generally acknowledged to have been the second founder of the Ḳaraite community and as such he must have been a remarkable man. He is regarded as the one who first had the courage to use Biblical Hebrew again in his writings instead of the Rabbinic Hebrew which since the reorganization of Jewry had alone been permissible, and we may reasonably suppose that books from the cave near Jericho written in this Biblical Hebrew encouraged him to take this step. With the help of the books from the cave it is very likely that he was able to give new inspiration to the Ḳaraites which enabled them to surpass the Rabbanites in the course of the ninth century in Jerusalem. The importance attached to him is indicated by the fact that he is the only Ḳaraite actually named by Selmān b. Jeruḥim, writing about 900. Benjamin also very possibly gave an impetus to the work of the Masoretes from Tiberias.

6. Moshe ben Asher and his Song of the Vine

In order to prove the Ḳaraite affinities of the Ben Asher Masoretes from Tiberias we have to-day an abundance of material which is decisive. First there is a poem composed by Moshe b. Asher in which Israel is compared with a vine. The first part of the poem, which is in the form of verses having an alphabetical acrostic, is to be found at the end of the Leningrad Codex of the Bible B 19a dated 1009, and follows the Diḳduḳe ha-Ṭe'amim of Ahron b. Asher on fol. 490 of the Codex.

In the Geniza a second copy of the poem was discovered by Dr. Menachem Zulay. The first part of the poem is in the British Museum (Or 5557 I, fol. 40 b). It contains the alphabetical acrostic from א to כ. The continuation is to be found in a Cambridge fragment (Univ. Collection Or 1080, Box V, I). Of these Geniza fragments photographs were made for the Research Institute for Hebrew Poetry in Jerusalem. The Cambridge fragment has the continuation with the verses from ל to ת, followed by verses beginning with the letters מ–ש–ה–ב–נ–א–ש, which indicate as author of the poem Moshe ben Asher; only the last verse, beginning with ר, is missing. As in the Leningrad MS B 19a, after the alphabetical acrostic a verse beginning with ק is to be found; it has been suggested that verses beginning with ח–ז–ק had followed at the end.

Clearly in error the copyist of the Leningrad text passed from the ע-verse to the פ-verse, and the copyist of the Geniza MS passed from the ט-verse to the י-verse. But on the whole, the two MSS supplement each other admirably.

Dr. Zulay placed the fragments of the MS discovered by him at the disposal of Benjamin Klar who published the poem as far as it goes in the Hebrew periodical *Tarbiṣ* xv, 1944, pp. 43 f. The poem is preceded in the Leningrad Codex by the words:

זה הוא תפארת ישראל ותולדות הנביאים שישראל נמשלו בגפן ודליותיה הם
הנביאים ושרשיה הם האבות ויונקותיה הם החכמים מצדיקי הרבים

> This is the adornment of Israel and the genealogy of the prophets in which Israel is compared with a vine of which the branches are the prophets, the roots are the fathers, and the unweaned children are the wise who help the many to righteousness.

I publish here the Hebrew text of the poem with an English translation and refer for text-critical notes to B. Klar's article in Tarbiṣ xv, 1944, pp. 43 f, and I discuss its problems below after the Colophon of Moshe ben Asher's Codex of the Prophets.

The Song of the Vine
by Moshe ben Asher

אַתָּה נָטַעְתָּה גֶּפֶן שׂוֹרֵיקָה מְשׁוּבָּחָה הָיְתָה מִכָּל הַגְּפָנִים
בְּמִגְדַּל דָּוִיר הָיְתָה נְטוּעָה וְאֶרֶז מִלְּבָנוֹן הָיָה בְּתוֹכָהּ
גֶּפֶן יְהוָה שִׁבְטֵי יַעֲקֹב וְאִישׁ יְהוּדָה נְטַע שַׁעֲשׁוּעָיו
דָּלִיּוֹת הַגֶּפֶן הֵם הַנְּבִיאִים וּמִגְדַּל דָּוִיד הוּא הַר צִיּוֹן
הָיְתָה שְׁתוּלָה עַל מַיִם רַבִּים וַתִּגְבַּהּ מְאֹד בֵּין הָעֲבוֹתִים
וְהַגֶּפֶן הַהִיא כָּפְנָה שָׁרָשֶׁיהָ וְעַל מַיִם רַבִּים שִׁלְּחָה קְצִירֶיהָ

זְמֹרוֹת הַגֶּפֶן חֲסִידֵי עוֹלָם הֵם אַבְרָהָם יִצְחָק וְיַעֲקֹב
חַכְמֵי הַגֶּפֶן נְבִיאֵי עוֹלָם מֹשֶׁה וְאַהֲרֹן וּמִרְיָם אֲחוֹתָם
טַרְפֵי הַגֶּפֶן יְהוֹשֻׁעַ וְכָלֵב וְשִׁבְעִים זְקֵנִים וְאֶלְדָּד וּמֵידָד
יְקָבֵי הַגֶּפֶן הֵם שְׁנֵי מִזְבְּחוֹת וְהַהֵיכָל וּדְבִיר לִפְנִים לִפְנָי
כְּמַרְאֵה חָתָן וְכִדְמוּת כַּלָּה כֵּן עֲדַת יְשׁוּרוּן נִגְּשָׁה לְחוֹרֵב
לוּלַבֵי הַגֶּפֶן הָיָה שְׁמוּאֵל אֵלִיָּהוּ וֶאֱלִישַׁע יְשַׁעְיָה וְיִרְמְיָה
מַבּוּעֵי הַגֶּפֶן הָיָה יְחֶזְקֵאל וְהוֹשֵׁעַ וְיוֹאֵל עָמוֹס וְגַם עֹבַדְיָה
נְבִיאֵי חָזוֹן יוֹנָה וּמִיכָה נַחוּם חֲבַקּוּק וְגַם צְפַנְיָה
סְמָדָרֵי הַגֶּפֶן חַגַּי וּזְכַרְיָה וּמַלְאָכִי וְגַם אִישׁ חֲמוּדוֹת
עִנְּבֵי הַגֶּפֶן הֵם בְּנֵי אַהֲרֹן קְדוֹשֵׁי ייי מְשָׁרְתֵי אֱלֹהֵינוּ
פִּרְחֵי הַגֶּפֶן הֵם בְּנֵי לֵוִי מְשׁוֹרְרִים כֻּלָּם בְּנֹעַם כִּנּוֹרוֹתֵיהֶם
צִמְחֵי הַגֶּפֶן הֵם עוֹלָלִים יוֹנְקֵי שָׁדַיִם אֲשֶׁר לֹא טָעֲמוּ חֵטְא
קָנֶה הָיָה סָמוּךְ לַגֶּפֶן הוּא דָוִד מֶלֶךְ יִשְׂרָאֵל
רַבִּים רְשָׁעִים הִכָּה דָוִד בֶּאֱדוֹם וּמוֹאָב בְּעַמּוֹן וּפְלִשְׁתִּים
שָׁרְשֵׁי הַגֶּפֶן יוֹאָב וַאֲבִישַׁי וַעֲשָׂהאֵל וְעָשׂוּ כֻּלָּם כִּגְבוּרָתָם
תְּמִימֵי הַגֶּפֶן הֵם זִקְנֵי בְתִירָה יוֹרְשֵׁי הַנְּבִיאִים יוֹדְעֵי בִינָה
מַיִם עֲמֻקִּים מַבִּיעֵי חִיד[וֹ]ת לִבָּם מַשְׂכִּיל חָכְמָה כְּנַחַל נ(וֹבֵ)עַ
שַׁעֲשׁוּעִים הִתְקִינוּ טַעֲמֵי מִקְרָא בְּשׂוּם שֶׂכֶל וְנִיב מְפוֹרָשׁ
הִקִּיפוּ גָּדֵר לְתוֹרַת אֱלֹהֵינוּ מָסֹרוֹת סְדוּרוֹת לְהַחְכִּים פֶּתִי
בֶּאֱמוּנָתָם יָסְדוּ פֵּירוּשׁ מִקְרָא כְּלָלִים בְּמִצְוֹת בְּלִי לָסוּר מִדֶּרֶךְ
נַפְשָׁם נָתְנוּ עַל תּוֹרַת אֱלֹהֵינוּ לְהַצְדִּיק רַבִּים וּלְהַגְדִּיל תּוֹרָה
אֲפָפוּם צָרוֹת מִמַּלְכֵי יְוָנִים וְהֶגְלוּם וְנִפְּצוּם לְנֹא וּבְנוֹתֶיהָ
שִׁבְטֵי קְדוֹשִׁים נִתְעוֹרְרוּ עֲלֵיהֶם וְחִינְּכוּ נֵירוֹת עַל נְפִילָתָם
קָרֵב יְשׁוּעָה וְתַמְלִיךְ הַגֶּפֶן וְתַעֲקוֹר שׁוֹרֶשׁ כָּל הַמַּמְלָכוֹת:

Translation

א Thou hast planted a precious stock of vine
praised more than all vines.
ב In the tower of David it was planted
and a cedar of Lebanon was in its midst.
ג The vine of God were the tribes of Jacob,
and the man of Judah is his beloved plantation.
ד The branches of the vine are the Prophets,
and the tower of David is the mountain of Zion.
ה It was planted over great waters
and was very lofty among the bushy trees.
ו And this vine bent its roots
and sent out its sprays over great waters.
ז The branches of the vine are the pious of the world;
they are Abraham, Isaac and Jacob.

ח The wise men of the vine are the Prophets of the world
Moses and Aaron and Miriam, their sister.
ט The leaves of the vine are Joshua and Caleb
and the Seventy Elders and Eldad and Medad.[1]
י The vine presses are the two altars
and the Temple and the Holy of Holies.
כ Like the appearance of the bridegroom and the figure of the bride, so did the community of Jeshurun draw near to Ḥoreb.
ל The shoots of the vine were Samuel
Elijah and Elisha', Isaiah and Jeremiah.
מ The sources of the vine were Ezekiel,
Hosea and Joel, 'Amos and also 'Obadiah.
נ The Prophets of vision, Jonah and Micah
Nahum and Habakkuk and Zephaniah.
ס The blossoms of the vine were Haggai and Zechariah
and Malachi and the man of the precious things (Daniel).
ע The grapes of the vine were the sons of Aaron
the holy men of Jhwh, the servants of our God.
פ The shoots of the vine were the sons of Levi,
all singers, with the sweetness of their harps.
צ The buds of the vine were the children,
those sucking the breasts, not having tasted sin.
ק A cane served as support of the vine
that was David, the King of Israel.
ר Many evildoers has David smitten
in Edom and Moab, 'Ammon and Pelishtim.
ש The roots of the vine were Joab and Abishai
and Asahel who all acted in accordance with their strength.[2]
ת The perfect ones of the vine are the Elders of Bathyra,
the heirs of the prophets, who possess knowledge of understanding.[3]
מ Deep waters that utter mysteries;
their heart brings forth wisdom like a flowing brook.
ש As delights they have established the accents of Scripture,
giving sense and interpreting its word.
ה They have erected as a fence round the Torah of our God
well-arranged Masoras to instruct the ignorant.
ב In their faithfulness they have founded the interpretation of Scripture, surrounded by commandments without deviating from the path.

[1] See Num. xi, 26. 27.

[2] Joab, Abishai, Asahel, the sons of Ṣeruya, 2 Sam. ii 18.

[3] זקני בתירה, a Babylonian family which enjoyed Herod's favour and had won through him the presiding place in the Sanhedrin. They were later displaced by Hillel.

ן Their souls they have given for the Torah of our God
to make the many righteous, to extol the Torah.

א Afflictions surrounded them from the kings of the Greeks
and exiled them and dispersed them to No (Egypt) and its provinces (daughter cities).

ש The holy tribes rose up against them
and dedicated lights on their fall.

30 [ר]. . . . .
. . . .
. . . .

ק Bring nearer salvation, let the vine reign,
pluck out the roots of all kingdoms.

The especially important verses of this poem are, as has been shown by Dr. Naftali Wieder, verses 22 and 23. He writes:

> As B. Klar rightly observed, Moses b. Asher traced the chain of Ḳaraitic tradition to the Elders of Bathyra, the spiritual ancestors of Ḳaraism who had inherited the prophetic traditions and transmitted them to the Ḳaraites. The latter are thus in direct line of descent from the prophets.

Wieder shows that it is highly significant that the epithet Moshe b. Asher conferred upon the Elders of Bathyra is precisely *the perfect ones*, which epithet was considered a sufficiently clear identification mark to indicate their religious affiliations. I confine myself here to referring to these remarks of Wieder in *JQR* xlvii, 1956, pp. 97 f. A full discussion is given below in the section: *Psalm cxix and Moshe b. Asher*.

7. Sa'adya and the Masoretes of Tiberias

We have come to know recently that Sa'adya Gaon polemicized against the Ben Asher Masoretes in Tiberias. From the polemic it becomes clear that these Masoretes were Ḳaraites.[1] The first specimen of Sa'adya's polemic had been discovered by Benjamin Manasseh Lewin of Haifa. It is a Piuṭ called from the words with which the first verse begins, אשא משלי. Lewin published the specimen in *Tarbiṣ* iii, 1932, pp. 147–60 and Jacob Mann added some remarks to it (ibid. pp. 380–92). A further fragment

[1] We knew before that a polemic of Sa'adya existed from the *teshubot* of Dunash b. Labraṭ, the poet and grammarian from Spain who had directed an attack against Sa'adya under whom he had studied in Sūra. But nothing of the polemic itself was hitherto known.

was published by Israel Davidson in *Jewish Studies in memory of George A. Kohut* (pp. 9–24 of the Hebrew section), New York, 1935. Lewin subsequently found more material and published it in a small volume under the title אשא משלי לרבנו סעדיה גאון. ספר מלחמות הראשון כנגד הקראים, Jerusalem 1943.[1]

Benjamin Klar has dealt in detail with the problems arising from this polemic in two articles published in *Tarbiṣ* xiv, 1943, pp. 156–73, and xv, 1944, pp. 36–49. He has correctly seen that the Arabic title has to be read *ar-radd 'alā-bni Asher 'Ibrāni* 'the polemic against Ben Asher, Hebrew.' He has shown that the poem of Sa'adya contains a sharp attack on the *Diḳduḳe ha-Ṭe'amim* of which we know that the author was the Masorete Aaron b. Asher. So it was evident to Klar that Aaron b. Asher was the Masorete attacked by Sa'adya.

But the matter is not so simple. A great part of Sa'adya's polemic, as far as it is known, is directed against § 3 of the *Diḳduḳe* which bears the title *seder ha-miḳra* and deals with the three night-watches, identified with Torah, Prophets and Ketubim. The believers are admonished in it to observe the commandments taken from all three parts of the Bible. Rabbanitic teaching ordered the believers to take precepts exclusively from the Torah with the help of the Oral Law as codified in the Mishna. The injunction given in this paragraph of the Diḳduḳe is typically Ḳaraitic. Against this Sa'adya directs his polemic with the utmost energy.

But precisely this paragraph of the Diḳduḳe is older than Aaron b. Asher. We find it written in a prominent way by Moshe b. Asher himself on p. 583 of the Cairo Codex of the Prophets dated 895. It was therefore composed by Moshe b. Asher himself, if he did not take it from an older source. It is the only paragraph of the Diḳduḳe taken over by Aaron b. Asher from his father Moshe. We must therefore reckon with the possibility that Sa'adya also attacked Moshe b. Asher in his polemical Piuṭ.

As is well known, Jacob Mann has proved that Sa'adya must have been ten years older than had been generally assumed, being born in 882 instead of 892. He has shown this on the evidence of a statement of Sa'adya's two sons who declared about

[1] The fragments are found in the Library of Westminster College, Cambridge, in the University Library, Cambridge (T-S H 5 131), in the Bodleian Library, Oxford (MS heb e 45, fol. 11 and 12—Catalogue 2787, 6) and in the British Museum (under No. 5557). I may refer here to my article: The Masoretic Text of the Bible and the Pronunciation of Hebrew, in the *Journal of Jewish Studies*, vol. vii, 1956, pp. 133–152.

eleven years after their father's death (10th May 942) that when he died he was sixty years old less some forty days. Mann found this statement in the Geniza, and reported on it in *JQR*, April 1921.

By this fact all the suggestions which had earlier been put forward about the first decades of his life are rendered useless. Henry Malter, in the Postscript (pp. 421–428) to his book *Saadia Gaon, his Life and Works* (Philadelphia 1921), had reluctantly to withdraw all his conclusions about the early period of Sa'adya's life. What we know about Sa'adya's stay in his native country, Egypt, is that he had developed there into an excellent Arabic scholar who was far better acquainted than any other Jew with Arabic literature and the conditions of the Muslims. We further know that he had to leave his native country and was never again able to return to it. From Egypt he went to Palestine, and it seems that he stayed much longer there than was previously supposed. The only teacher in Jewish studies of whom we know lived in Tiberias, and it is very likely that Sa'adya first came into contact with Ḳaraites in Tiberias. If he had left his native land when he was twenty-three, as generally supposed, he could well have met Moshe b. Asher in A.D. 905, ten years after the latter had finished the Cairo Codex of the Prophets. Moshe had won by then a high reputation. Later he may have come into contact with Aaron his son who had become the greatest authority on all Masoretic matters. Against these two prominent Ḳaraite Masoretes Sa'adya developed his polemic in the form of a Piuṭ of which a considerable part has been found in the Geniza.

We have an important witness to Sa'adya from an Arabic contemporary al-Mas'ūdī who met him together with his former teacher. This is all the more valuable for us as our evidence from Jewish sources is very meagre and confined to two periods only of his life. Al-Mas'ūdī, an Arab historian and geographer who had seen a great part of the world in the first half of the tenth century, and in his works records many interesting experiences, comes to speak in his *kitāb at-tanbīh wa'l-ishrāf*[1] about Sa'adya and reports as follows:

Concerning the Israelites, both the Ashma'ath[2] who are the

[1] The text of al-Mas'ūdī has been published by M. J. de Goeje in *Bibliotheca Geographorum Arabicorum*, vol. viii, Leiden 1894, p. 113.

[2] *Ashma'ath* corresponds to the Aramaic שמעתא used in the Babylonian Talmud for *tradition* and used by al-Mas'ūdī collectively of the Rabbanites. A single Rabbanite is called *ashma'athī*.

many and the great mass, and the 'Ananites[1] who believe in righteousness (*'adl*) and monotheism (*tauḥīd*),[2] in their explanation of the Hebrew books, the Torah, the Prophets and the Psalms (for Ketubim), which are the 24 books, and in their translation into Arabic, rely on a number of Israelites who are held in very high esteem among them, most of whom we have personally met, among them Abū Kathīr Yaḥyā b. Zakarīya, the Kātib, the man from Ṭabarīya, Ashma'athī in belief who died about 320 (932 A.D.), and Sa'īd b. Ja'ḳūb al-Faiyūmī (i.e. Sa'adya), also Ashma'athī in belief, who studied under Abū Kathīr, and whose exegesis of the Bible many of them value most highly. He had differences in 'Irāḳ with the Exilarch (*ra's al-ğālūt*) Dā'ūd b. Zakkai, from the offspring of (king) David, and opposed him. This occurred during the Caliphate of al-Muḳtadir (908–932) and the Jews were divided into two parties regarding them. He was present at a sitting of the Court under the Wezir 'Alī b. 'Īsā and other Wezirs and judges and scholars for the resolution of these differences. When he had won a majority among them the foremost part was played by al-Faiyūmī and they recognized him as leader. He died after 330 (A.D. 941).

al-Mas'ūdī further recounts that he had many discussions with Abū Kathīr in both provinces of the land at that time, al-Filistīn and al-Urdunn, on the problem of abolishing divine laws, and the coming into existence of new conditions which could bring about alterations of previous divine commandments. Ignaz Goldziher pointed out that *a'bada* printed by de Goeje is a mistake for *al-badā'* on the meaning of which Goldziher wrote a very instructive article in the *Encyclopedia of Islam*, vol. i, pp. 527 f.[3]

The report on the differences between Sa'adya and the Exilarch Dā'ūd b. Zakkai, whom Sa'adya strongly attacked in a way which led to the formation of two parties among the Jews, is of great interest. Their differences were heard before the High Court of Baghdād, presided over by the Wezir himself, attended by prominent judges and scholars. 'Alī b. 'Isā Ibn al-Djarrāḥ, is a well-known personality.[4] He was several times the Wezir of the Caliph al-Muḳtadir, his last term of office being January

1 A name formerly given to the Ḳaraites, derived from 'Anan, their founder.

2 The Muslim Mu'tazilites used to call themselves *ahl al-'adl wa't-tauḥīd*; perhaps al-Mas'ūdī's authority was a Mu'tazilite who characterized the Ḳaraites in the same way.

3 I am indebted to Dr. S. M. Stern for drawing my attention to this point.

4 Regarding 'Alī b. 'Īsā see the article of Zettersteen in the *Encyclopedia of Islam* s.v. Ibn al-Djarrāḥ.

to May 928. We may assume that in this period the first session concerned with the Jewish dispute was held. Other sessions must have taken place under his successors whose names are not mentioned by Masʿūdī. The impression is given that the complete hearing lasted for several years and only came to an end when Saʿadya was elected Gaon for the second time definitively.

In this eye-witness report al-Masʿūdī refers to Abū Kathīr and Saʿadya on the basis of personal acquaintance. Tiberias was the capital of the Muslim province al-Urdunn. As Kātib, *secretary*, Abū Kathīr must have had a respected position as one of the many government officials in this capital, and he must have been well informed in Jewish matters—Masʿūdī reports discussions with him in several places, and we may suppose that he was a wealthy man. But he was certainly no expert scholar, so we can understand that nothing is to be found about him in Jewish sources. When Masʿūdī met both of them, the time when Saʿadya had been his pupil was long past.

As for Saʿadya, there can be no question that he was an unusually gifted man. Ability is inborn and cannot be learnt. But Saʿadya developed into an outstanding scholar. For the acquisition of scholarship even the gifted man needs quiet for study. 'Saʿadya was in the habit of travelling' writes Malter (p. 37). Saʿadya had certainly travelled, but we must realize that by travelling one cannot become a scholar. To acquire scholarship one needs a home where books are available. The refugee from Egypt may have found them at the home of Abū Kathīr, and the latter may have advised him how best to make use of them. His own genius soon led him far beyond his teacher, without, however, destroying the good relations between them.

Saʿadya's polemic against the Ben Asher Masoretes of Tiberias certainly embittered the differences between the Rabbanites and the Ḳaraites, to whom the Tiberian Masoretes belonged. As the text of the Bible prepared by the Tiberian Masoretes was accepted by the whole of Judaism, Rabbanites as well as Ḳaraites, we must suppose that this occurred before the polemic of Saʿadya began and the differences came to have such an acute form as we know they assumed in later times.

Benjamin Klar has given in general a correct account of Saʿdya's polemic, but one thing he has completely misunderstood. The Masoretes, especially Moshe b. Asher, are greatly concerned to point out that the punctuation of the text of the Bible fixed by them is in agreement with the way in which the pronunciation of Hebrew was transmitted by Ezra through the men of the Great Synagogue. Moshe b. Asher was certainly aware that the Tiberian punctuation was the work of the Masoretes of Tiberias. Nevertheless he declares that the Masoretes have not added anything to what was transmitted to them nor have they concealed anything. These points were certainly important in order that the punctuation fixed by the Masoretes of Tiberias might be generally accepted. Later speculations which tried to push back the punctuation to the time of Moses on Sinai do not interest us here. What Klar has written on the question whether Ben Asher believed that the punctuation goes back to Moses and Sinai clearly reveals a lack of understanding.

8. Moshe ben Asher and his Codex of the Prophets

It is of the greatest value that we have Biblical Codices which are closely connected with the last members of the Masorete family of Ben Asher. One of the Codices, finished at Tiberias by Moshe b. Asher in 895, is the oldest dated Hebrew Codex of the Bible which has come down to us. Its preservation is to be attributed to the fact that the Codex was, for a very long time, kept and greatly revered in the Ḳaraite Synagogue of Cairo (al-Ḳāhira). During my last stay in Cairo I saw the Codex at 5 p.m. on February 20th 1956 and held it in my hands. The jeweller David Zeki Lisha', president of the Ḳaraite community,[1] showed it to me in the recently built Ḳaraite Synagogue in the 'Abbāsīye (Shāri'a es-Sebīl Khāzindār). This is where the Codex was transferred a few years ago after having been kept for centuries in the old Ḳaraite Synagogue situated in the Muski.

The Codex is beautifully preserved and complete from the first to the last page. It is not bound and is kept in a wooden box made to measure which is locked in a safe. To enable the text of the Codex to be used for the Biblia Hebraica, a photographic copy was made of it at my request in 1926 for the Berlin Staats-Bibliothek.[2] This was bound in seven red half-leather volumes and was at my disposal in Bonn for a long time. Whilst it was to hand I had it re-photographed in the Bonn Orientalische

[1] David b. Yisḥaḳ Alisha', together with Josef b. Abraham Yomṭob, published the book *al-murshid al-amīn* of which Dr. Szyszman kindly let me have a copy.

[2] Dr. med. et phil h.c. Max Meyerhof kindly helped with the making of the photographs.

Seminar before returning the original photographic copy to Berlin. For some years now this re-photographed copy of the Codex has been at my disposal. One of my Spanish pupils, Dr. Fernando Diaz Esteban, who is preparing a new edition of the Masoretic work Ochla we-Ochla, carefully studied the Codex in my house, concentrating on its Masora, punctuation and spelling. He found that everything in the Codex must have been done by one who was a master in his own field and that the Masora which is added to the Codex agrees in all its details with what the Codex itself has to offer. Professor Umberto Cassuto had another photograph of the Codex taken for Jerusalem, and the fact that after his death the text of the Prophets, as contained in the Bible published in Jerusalem in 1953,[1] was corrected according to the Codex of the Prophets by Moshe b. Asher was in accordance with Cassuto's intentions.

We are very well acquainted with the history of the Cairo Codex of the Prophets thanks to the colophons which it contains and which I publish here in original and translation. We learn from a Colophon written by Moshe b. Asher himself (p. 585) that a Ḳaraite living in Jerusalem, called Ya'beṣ b. Shelomo ha-Babli, commissioned the Codex to be made for his own use. He boasts that he has earned the money needed for the payment of the Codex with his own hands—that he did not spend inherited money on the purchase. This is the Colophon on p. 585:

זה הדיפתר מה שזכה יעבץ בן שלמה הבבלי נח נפש ועשה אותו לעצמו להגות
בו מעמלו ומיגיע כפיו ומזיעת אפו לכבוד אלהי ישראל שיאמר יוצר נשמות ויזכהו
להגות בו ולנצור ולשמור כל דבר שיש בו ויתן לו חלק טוב ולב טוב וגורל נעים
בעולם הזה ושׂכר טוב לעולם הבא ויזכה יעבץ בן שלמה נוח נפש לחזות בנועם
ייי ולבקר בהיכלו ויתן לו אלהי ישראל בנים ובני בנים הוגים בתורה ועסוקים
במצוות וכל הברכות הכלולות בתורה ובנבֿ[יאים] ובכתובים יחולו על ראשו ועל
זרעו וכל ישראל בכלל ברכה אמן

The following is a translation of the note:

This is the Codex (*difter*) which it was granted Ya'beṣ b. Shelomo ha-Babli—may his [i.e. the father's] soul find rest—to acquire. He prepared it so that he himself might study it, from the reward of his work, the labour of his hands, the sweat of his face, for the honour of the God of Israel—may the Creator of souls mercifully grant him the study of it, to observe and to keep everything it contains; may He give him a good portion

[1] Cf. my review of the book: 'The new Hebrew Bible, Jerusalem 1953' in *VT*, vol. iii, 1953, pp. 416–20.

and a good heart and a pleasant lot in this world and good reward for the world to come. May Ya'beṣ b. Shelomo—may his soul find rest—be worthy to see the grace of God and to visit His temple (Ps. xxvii, 4). May the God of Israel give him sons and grandsons who study the Torah and who occupy themselves with the Law. And may all blessings which are contained in the Torah and the Prophets and the Scriptures come upon his head and the heads of his offspring and may the whole of Israel be included in the blessing! Amen.

This note is enclosed in a rectangle consisting of the following verses written in small letters: Isa. lix, 21; Joshua i, 8; Isa, lvi, 11. In the diamond above: Ps. cxxi, 7 and 8 are written; in the diamond below: Deut. xxviii, 3 and 4; vii, 14.

From three further notes on pages 582, 583, 588 every one of which is written by a different hand,[1] we learn that a special

(583)

[1] זה הדפתר שמונה נביאים שהקדיש אותו יעבץ בן שלמה בירושלם עיר הקדש אלהים יכונניה עד עולם סלה ללקראין העושים את המועדים על ראות הירח יקראו בו כלם בשבתות ובחדשים ובמועדים לא ימכר ולא יקנה וכל מי שיגנוב אותו (או יוציא אותו מחצר יעבץ בן שלמה יהי אחריתו להכרית בדור אחד ימח שמם) או ימכור אותו או יקנה אותו או יעבוט אותו ארור הוא לאלהי ישראל וכל מי שישמור אותו ויקים מצות יעבץ בן שלמה בעל הדפתר הזה יהוה ישמרהו ויחייהו ואשר בארץ

(p. 583). This is the Codex (*difter*), the Eight Prophets, which Ya'beṣ b. Shelomo consecrated in Jerusalem, the Holy city—may God establish it for ever, Sela! (Ps. xxxxviii, 9)—for the Ḳaraites who celebrate the feasts on seeing the moon. May they all read in it on Sabbaths and at new moons and at feasts. It shall neither be sold nor bought, and may whoever steals it or sells it or buys it or pawns it be cursed by the God of Israel! And whoever preserves it and follows the instructions of Ya'beṣ b. Shelomo, the owner of this Codex (*difter*), may Ihwh preserve him and give him life and make him blessed upon the earth (Ps. xxxxi, 3).

(Added in the margin): Or brings it out of the court of Ya'beṣ b. Shelomo, may his posterity be cut off; in one generation may his name be blotted out (Ps. cix, 13).

(588)

זה הדפתר אשר הקדיש יעבץ בן שלמה ללקראין בירושלם עיר הקדש לא ימכר ולא יגאל ולא יעבט ולא יוציאו אותו מביתו וארורים הם בשם יהוה אלהי ישראל כל מוכריו וכל קוניו וכל מוציאיו מחצר יעבץ בן שלמה בעל הדפתר הזה ולא יאבה יהוה סלוח להם כי אז יעשן אף יהוה וקנאתו בהם ורבצה בם כל האלה הכתובה בספר הזה ומחה יהוה את שמם מתחת השמים: והבדילם יהוה לרעה מכל שבטי יש׳ וכל הקללות הכתובות בכל ספרי המקרא ידבקו בם ובזרעם אמן
וברוכים הם בשם יהוה כל שומריו והקוראים בו בלב אמת יחיו ויראו ישועת ישראל אמן

(p. 588). This Codex (*difter*) which Ya'beṣ b. Shelomo has consecrated for the Ḳaraites in Jerusalem, the Holy city, shall neither be sold nor bought back nor pawned and shall not be brought out of his house. And cursed in the name of the Lord, the God of Israel, be all who steal it and all who buy it and all who bring it out of the court of Ya'beṣ b. Shelomo, the owner of this Codex (*difter*), and may the Lord not be willing to pardon them; rather shall the anger of the Lord flare up and His zeal against them, and all the curses that are written in this book shall lie upon them, and the Lord shall blot out their name from under heaven and the Lord shall separate them for their doom from all the tribes of Israel, and may all the curses that are written in all the books of Holy Scripture cling to them and to their offspring. Amen!

And blessed in the name of the Lord be all those who preserve it and read in it with sincere heart. May they live and see the salvation of Israel. Amen!

(582)

זה הדפתר הנביאים שהקדיש אותו יעבץ בן שלמה אלכלפי בירושלם עיר הקדש אלהים יכונניה עד עולם ללקראין אשר יעשו את המועדים ביראת הירחים יקראו בו כלם ולא ימנע אחד מהם מלקרות בו במקום אשר הוא מונח בו בשבתות ובחדשים ובמועדים ולא ימכר ולא יקנה וכל מי שיגנוב אותו או ימכור אותו או יקנה אותו או יעבוט אותו ארור הוא לאלהי ישראל וכל מי שישמור אותו ויקרא בו יהוה

place was allotted to the Codex; it was kept in the owner's grounds in Jerusalem and nobody was allowed to remove it. The Codex was dedicated to the Ḳaraites who were to have the opportunity of reading the lessons from it on Sabbaths, on the festival of the New Moon and other festivals, and it was expressly stipulated that on such days nobody should be denied access to the Codex.

More than once Cassuto has suggested to me that this Codex was probably only one part of a complete Bible MS, and that this complete Bible Codex was the Ben Asher Codex which Maimonides declared to be the model Codex. Such a theory, however, is impossible because in the note on page 583 of the Codex it is referred to as the *Codex of the Eight Prophets* (Joshua, Judges, Sam., Kings, Isa., Jer., Ezek. XII) and again in the notes on pages 581 and 582 as *Codex of the Prophets*. It never contained anything but the Prophets. Moreover Maimonides saw the Ben Asher Codex in Old Cairo (Miṣrajim), whereas this Codex, when brought to Egypt, was immediately taken to Cairo (al-Ḳāhira).

The Colophon, written on p. 581 in Hebrew cursive, tells us that this Codex of the Prophets was dedicated to the Ḳaraite community (עדת בני מקרא) in the Synagogue of al-Ḳāhira.

זה הספר הנביאים קדש ליוי אלהים אלהי ישׂ הקדיש אותו אחרי גאולתו השר
הגדול דויד בן השר הגדול יפת נכר אלסכנדרי על עדת בני מקרא לקראת בו
בימי השבתות והתעניות בכנסת אלקאהרה תבנה ותכונן ואם הוא או איש מזרעו
יושב ישימהו השמש לפניו: ואין רשות לאדם להוציאו מבית הכנסת כי אם חס
ושלום לצורך וישיבהו בעת ההשקט וכל המחליף התנאי הזה או הקדושה הזאת
ארור הוא ליוי וכל הקללות ידבקו בו וכל השומרו והקורא בו והמשיבו אל מקומו
אחר הרוגז ברוך הוא בשם יוי וכל הברכות והשכר הטוב והשלומות ([1]יחולו) על
ראשו ועל ראש המקדיש השר דויד וזרעו עד סוף כל הדורות וכל ישראל:

The translation of the note is:

ישמרהו ויחייהו ואשר בארץ וכל מי אשר יוציא אותו מחצר יעבץ בן שלמה ימחה מספר חיים ועם צדיקים
אל ימנה אמן
וברוכים הם בשם יהוה כל שומריו והקוראים בו באמת אמן

(p. 582). This is the Codex (*difter*), the Prophets, which Ya'beṣ b. Shelomo al-Khalafi (אלכלפי) has consecrated in Jerusalem, the holy city—may God establish it for ever—for the Ḳaraites, who celebrate the feast at the sight of the moon. They should all read in it and not one shall be hindered from reading in it, in the place where it is deposited, on the Sabbath days, at the new moons and at the feasts. It shall not be sold or bought. May whoever steals it or sells it or buys it or pawns it be cursed by the God of Israel. Whoever preserves it and reads in it shall be preserved by the Lord. May He give him life and make him blessed upon the earth (Ps. 41, 3). Whoever brings it out of the court of Ya'beṣ b. Shelomo shall be effaced from the book of life and not be counted with the righteous ones (Ps. 69, 29) Amen! And blessed in the name of the Lord be all that preserve it and read in it in sincerity. Amen!

[1] The word is altered and cannot be read clearly on the photograph.

(p. 581) This book (*sefer*), the Prophets, is consecrated to the Lord (ליוי) God, the God of Israel. The great lord David, son of the great lord Yefet, known as al-Iskandari, has consecrated it after its redemption for the community of the Ḳaraites (עדת בני מקרא), to read in it on Sabbath days and on fast days in the Synagogue in Cairo (כנסת אלקאהרה)—may it (the city of Jerusalem) be built up and established! And when he or one of his descendants is seated, the server shall set it (the book) before him. And nobody shall be permitted to bring it out of the Synagogue except it is done—may God prevent it—by compulsion, and one shall return it in the time of appeasement. Whoever changes this condition (התנאי) and this holiness (הקדושה) shall be cursed by the Lord (ליוי) and all curses shall come upon him. Whoever keeps it and reads in it and puts it back into its place after the days of unrest, may he be blessed in the name of the Lord, may all the blessings and the good reward and wishes come upon his head and the heads of those who have consecrated it, the lord David and his descendants, until the end of all generations and of all Israel.

The donation of the Codex to the Ḳaraite community of al-Ḳāhira took place אחרי גאולתו 'after its restoration'. These words refer to the seizure of valuable MSS by the Crusaders to which event I shall refer in connection with the next Codex. The seized MSS were released soon afterwards, and this Codex of the Prophets could also be 'restored' and brought to Cairo. We can take it for granted that the Codex has been kept as a valuable treasure in the Synagogue of the Ḳaraites in Cairo for the last 850 years.

The original Colophon which the writer himself added to the Codex on page 586 is the following:

אני משה בן אשר כתבתי זה המחזור שלמקרא על פי כיד אלהי הטובה עלי באר היטב במדינת מעזיה טבריה העיר ההוללה כשהבינו עדת נביאים בחורי יי׳ קדושי אלהינו המבינים כל נסתרות והמשפירים סוד חכמה אילי הצדק אנשי אמנה לא כיחדו דבר ממה שניתן להם ולא הוסיפו מאמר על מה שנימסר להם והעצימו והגדילו המקׄ עשרים וארבעה ספרים וייסדום באמונתם בטעמי שכל בפירוש דיבור בחיך מתוק ביופי מאמר יהי רצון מלפני יוצרנו שיאיר עינינו ויגיה לבנו בתורתו ללמד וללמד ולעשות בלב שלם ובנפש חפצה ולכל ישראל אמן:

נכתב לקץ שמונה מאות שנה ועשרים ושבע שנים לחורבן הבית השני שיאמר יוצר נשמות וישוב עליו ברחמים ויבנהו באבני אקדח וספיר וכדכד בנין שלם בנין מקויים בנין שלא ינתש ולא יהרס ולא ינתץ לעולם ולעולמי עולמים במהרה בימינו ובימי כל ישראל אמן

וכל המשנה מן המחזור הזה או מן הנשתון הזה דבר או מוחק ממנו אות או קורע ממנו דף אלא אם כן יבין וידע שיש בו דבר ששגינו בו בכתב או בניקוד או במסרת או בחסר או ביתר אל יהי לו לא מחילה

ולא סליחה ואל יחזה בנעם יי ולא יראה בטוב הצפון ליריאיו ויהיה כאשה נדה וכמצורע מוסגר לכתת
אברין ולשבור גאון עזו ולכלות בשרו מראי ולשפות עצמותיו שלא יראו אמן

הקורא ישמע והשמע יבין והראה ישכיל שלום

I, Moshe ben Asher have written this Codex (*maḥzor*) of the Scripture according to my judgment 'as the good hand of my God was upon me' (Neh. ii, 8), 'very clearly' (Deut, xxvii, 8), in the city of Ma'azya-Ṭabarīya, 'the renowned city' (Ezek. xxvi, 17), as it was understood by the congregation of Prophets, the chosen of the Lord, the saints of our God, who understood all hidden things and revealed the secret of wisdom, the oak-trees of righteousness (Isa. lxi, 3), the men of faith, who have concealed nothing of what was given to them nor added one word to what was transmitted to them, who have made the Scriptures powerful and mighty, the Twenty-four Books which they have founded in their faithfulness with explanatory accents and clear instruction as to pronunciation with sweet palate and beauty of speech. May it please our Creator to illuminate our eyes and enlighten our hearts by His Torah, that we may learn and teach and act with a perfect heart and a willing mind (1 Chron. xxviii, 9) and for the whole of Israel. Amen!

It was written in the year 827 after the destruction of the Second Temple to which may the Creator of souls be pleased to return in mercy and build up with rubies, sapphires and carbuncles (Isa. liv, 11 f.) as a perfect building, a firmly established building, a building which can neither be pulled down nor demolished nor destroyed in eternity and eternity of eternities, (may it be done) speedily, in our days and in the days of all Israel. Amen!

(The following written by another hand:

Whoever alters a word of this Maḥzor or this writing or erases one letter or tears off one leaf—unless he understands and knows that there is a word in it in which we have erred in the writing or in the punctuation or in the Masora or in defective or in plene—may he have neither pardon nor forgiveness, neither 'let him behold the beauty of the Lord' (Ps. xxvii, 4) nor let him see the good that is reserved for those who fear Him (Jer. xxix, 32). He shall be like a woman in impurity and like a leprous man who has to be locked up so that his limbs may be crushed, the pride of his power be broken, his flesh be consumed away that it cannot be seen and his bones that were covered made bare. (Job xxxiii, 21). Amen!

Whoever reads shall hear; whoever hears shall understand; whoever sees shall perceive. Peace!

I have discussed this Colophon with Dr. M. Zucker from New York and also with Dr. N. Wieder of the Jews' College in London, both of whom are engaged in the study of the early Ḳaraites. There can be no doubt whatsoever that we are here dealing with a characteristic Ḳaraite writing. Dr. Wieder, at my request, put at my disposal a number of valuable remarks which were contained in a letter of his dated the 7th. October 1956 from which I quote the following:

1. The expression עדת נביאים is a reference to the Ḳaraite scholars who maintained that divine illumination had guided them in their exegetic work. Ḳaraite authors of the ninth and tenth centuries, like Daniel al-Ḳūmisī, Sahl b. Maṣliaḥ, Yefet b. 'Alī, and David al-Fāsī claimed divine illumination for the later Ḳaraite scholars, in contrast to the first generations, including even 'Anan, who stumbled over the exegesis of the divine laws (al-Ḳūmisī). This is said to have been prophesied in the book of Daniel where we read (xi, 35): 'some of the Maskīlīm will stumble'. Al-Ḳūmisī refers to the Maskīlīm expressly as to 'prophets who possess knowledge' and he adds: 'they know the Bible through and through and (know) why it was thus and not otherwise written'.

That Ben Asher is referring to the Ḳaraite scholars is quite evident from the title אילי הצדק, the oak-trees of righteousness, a typically Ḳaraite way of describing Ḳaraites. According to Isa. lxi, 3, it is used for those who mourn for Ṣion, and the Ḳaraite scholars in the Holy Land who called themselves *the mourners for Ṣion* אבלי ציון applied this expression as referring to them. עדת נביאים therefore must be translated as the 'Community of Prophets'.

2. Moshe b. Asher's claim that the Ḳaraite scholars 'understand the hidden things' is quite in agreement with the corresponding claim of other Ḳaraite authors. Dr. Wieder refers to Moshe's son Aaron who says, in Diḳdūḳē ha-Ṭe'amim, page 53, that the wise, God-fearing perfect man knows the hidden things of the Torah. For the 'perfect' he refers to his article: 'The Qumran Sectaries and the Ḳaraites', which appeared in *JQR* xlvii, 1956–7, pp. 97–113, 269–292. Thus far Dr. Wieder's comments.

9. Psalm cxix and Moshe ben Asher

I have discussed Moshe b. Asher's *Song of the Vine* and his *Colophon to the Cairo Codex of the Prophets* with Mr. M. Gertner, of London University, and we came to the conclusion that the theological conceptions and terminology of Psalm cxix must have influenced, through the Qumran writings, Ḳaraite literature and the ideas of Moshe b. Asher. We can only hope fully to understand all the implications of the words of Ben Asher in the light of this influence. So I asked Mr. Gertner to write a report summarising the evidence for such an influence; and the report is as follows:

Naftali Wieder has shown that some expressions which can be regarded as key-words in Ḳaraite writings are to be found in Moshe b. Asher's *Song of the Vine*.[1] He has also drawn attention to the importance of Ps. cxix for the Ḳaraites. The expression תמימי דרך, so familiar to Ḳaraite authors, is taken from the Psalm.[2]

The Psalm was, however, of greater importance for the Qumran sect. In the Qumran library quite a number of copies of this Psalm have been discovered.[3] The Qumran authors made a rich use of the Psalm. The expression תמימי דרך was a standard designation for the pious members of the sect.[4]

But the Qumran community did not only make terminological use of the Psalm; they also took over from it one of their basic theological teachings, the teaching that 'knowledge' and 'understanding' of the Torah are given to the pious by God as a gift of grace. Only the man whose eyes are unveiled by God can see the wonderful mysteries of His law. Only if illumination is bestowed on him can he be in possession of the correct understanding of the Torah. God inspires the pious with the true understanding of the Torah.[5]

In a Qumran Midrash on the Priestly Blessing this teaching is clearly expressed; the second verse of the blessing reads in the original (Numb. vi, 25): 'May God make His face to shine upon you, and may He be gracious unto you' (*wiḥunnekka*). In the *Manual of Discipline* (ii, 3) this verse is given in the form of a Midrash paraphrase as follows: 'May He enlighten your heart with understanding of life and may He bless you with eternal knowledge'.[6]

[1] Naftali Wieder, The Qumran Sectaries and the Qaraites, *JQR* xlvii, 1956/7, pp. 97–113, 269–302. These expressions are תמימי דרך (in the Song: תמימי הגפן), מצדיקי הרבים, משכילים.

[2] See Wieder, loc. cit., p. 108.

[3] J. T. Milik, *Dix ans de découvertes dans le désert de Juda*, Paris 1957, p. 26.

[4] See Yigael Yadin, *The War of the Sons of Light*... 1953, pp. 242 f. A. M. Habermann, *'Edah we 'Eduth*, 1952, p. 152.

[5] See Jacob Licht, *The Thanksgiving Scroll*, 1957, p. 42.

[6] Man ii 3: ויאר לבכה בשכל חיים ויחונכה בדעת עולמים
The terms *understanding of life* and *eternal knowledge* correspond exactly to the blessing given in the Synagogue after the reading of the Torah (b. Mas. Sof. 13.8) in which the Torah is called true Torah תורת אמת and eternal life חיי עולם. In the Qumran Midrash שכל and דעת mean the true understanding of the Torah.

Both blessings here mean understanding and knowledge for the true exposition of the Torah.

In the Psalm also the poet asks for enlightenment to understand the Torah and for the gracious gifts of wisdom and knowledge of the Torah in order to be able to see in it wonderful things, that is to say: to understand its true meaning by right exposition. The Psalmist prays: 'Let Thy face shine upon Thy servant and teach me Thy statutes (v. 135). Give me understanding that I may know Thy decrees (v. 125). False ways put far from me and graciously grant me Thy law' (v. 29).

As the Torah was already there and one did not need to ask for it as a gift of grace, the request of the Psalmist must have been for the gift of right interpretation of the Torah. That the understanding and right interpretation of the Torah is to be regarded as a gift of God introduces a new refinement of thought about revelation and is here for the first time clearly expressed. From the Psalm the Qumran teachers must have taken over the idea and thus made use of it in their *intellectualising* interpretation of '*wiḥunneka*'. For originally this expression (*ḥanan*) had nothing to do with spiritual grace. The same holds also of 'making the countenance to shine'. Nor did this originally mean an intellectual enlightenment of the heart. Only after the Psalmist had connected the idea of an enlightenment with the 'teaching' of the law (v. 135) could the passage be interpreted in this way in the Priestly Blessing at Qumran.[1]

The Qumran scrolls had a great influence on the later Ḳaraites. They, also, believed 'that their interpretation of the Bible was the result of special divine inspiration'.[2] We have some evidence that the Ḳaraites had access to the Qumran caves and used a great number of the Qumran writings.[3] There is also internal evidence showing the dependence of the Ḳaraites on Qumran.

(a) In Qumran one particular verse of Psalm cxix especially, in various paraphrases, served as a basis for the idea of inspired Torah interpretation. Wieder has shown that the same verse

[1] From Qumran this new interpretation of *wiḥunnekka* as a gracious gift of knowledge was taken over and included in the Talmudic Midrash; see Sifre, ed. Friedmann, 12a ad loc.—ויחנך בדעת ובבינה ובהשכל: 'may he graciously grant you knowledge, reason and understanding.'

[2] See Wieder, loc. cit. p. 106.

[3] Cf. S. Liebermann, in *Proceedings of the American Academy for Jewish Research*, vol. xx, 1951, p. 402, concerning Rabbi Moses Taku. See also the letter of Timotheus I, the Katholikos, on biblical studies in the ninth century, ed. by Oscar Braun, in *Oriens Christianus*, i, 1901, p. 305, and O. Eissfeldt in *ThLZ* 1949, col. 598.

served[1] as a basis also for the Ḳaraites' emphasis on the inspired Torah interpretation of their own teachers. Verse 18 of the Psalm runs: 'Unveil my eyes that I may behold wonderful things out of Thy Law'. That this verse asks for enlightenment for the right interpretation of the Torah[2] is very obvious when one takes into consideration the already mentioned verses of the Psalmist on the Torah as a gracious gift from God. In Qumran this verse is quite clearly regarded and used in such a sense. The Hodayoth-poet, paraphrasing the Psalm passage, asks: 'How can I see unless thou unveilest my eyes?'[3] And in the Manual xi, 3, a paraphrase of this verse, explained by the idea of enlightenment, runs: ' God has revealed his light from the source of his knowledge and my eye has beheld the wonders of it'.[4]

The same interpretation occurs in Ḳaraite literature. In his commentary on the Ten Commandments, an earlier Ḳaraite teacher, Rabbi Nissi ben-Noaḥ, says:

> 'The Wisdom, which comes from the Torah of the living God, is . . . read by both the wicked and the righteous, but they differ in their interpretations of it, for already (King) David (the Psalmist) said: the knowledge is too wonderful for me. Unveil my eyes in order that I may behold wonderful things out of Thy law.'[5]

(b) The contrasting of the 'true interpreter of the Torah' (מורה צדק) with the 'preacher[6] of lies', possessed by Beliya'al, shows such strong similarity both in style and substance with the same kind of contrast made by the Ḳaraites that there can be no doubt of an influence of Qumran on the Ḳaraites.

[1] See Wieder, loc. cit. 105, 106.

[2] See Targum on Ps cxix 18: גלי עיני ואסתכל פרישן מאוריתך; פרישן means 'wonders', but because of its kinship with פירוש 'exposition' it has obviously been taken to mean 'wondrous expositions'—see Rashi on the verse: דברים נפלאים מפירושי תורתך 'wondrous things of the exposition of Thy Torah'. Cf. also J. L. Seeligmann, in *VT* Suppl. ii, 1953, p. 178, n. 3, who remarks: 'dass hier der Midrash als Exegese vorausgesetzt ist'.

[3] Hodayoth xviii, 19: איכה אביט בלוא גליתה עיני. Exactly the same phrasing we find in a late Midrash to this verse of the Psalm where we read: David said: Master of the world, unveil my eyes that I may behold wondrous things of Thy Torah—for if you do not unveil my eyes—how shall I know . . . אמר דוד : רבונו של עולם גל עיני ואביטה נפלאות מתורתך (Ps. cxix, 18) ואם אין אתה גולה את עיני מנין אני יודע This shows that the same sources must have been known and used by Rabbanite authors too. See above, n. 7 and n. 11.

[4] ממקור דעתו פתח אורו ובנפלאותיו הביטה עיני:

[5] S. Pinsker, *Likkuṭe Ḳadmoniyot*, App. p. 10: והחכמה שהיא מתורת אלהים חיים מחברים בקריאתה . . . הרשעים והצדיקים אבל מתחלפים הם בפתרוניה . . . שכבר דוד . . . אמר: פליאה דעת ממני (Ps. cxxxix, 6) גל עיני ואביטה נפלאות מתורותך. (Ps. cxix, 18)

[6] Pesher Hab. x. 9 מטיף הכזב

In the scrolls of Qumran it is said of the *true teacher*: God has given wisdom to his heart that he may interpret all the words of his servants, the prophets;[1] that he may enlighten the many,[2] to guide them in knowledge and to give them insight into wondrous mysteries and into the truth.[3] On the other hand the *false teacher*, 'the man of derision',[4] poured out for Israel waters of lies and made them go astray in the pathless desert'.[5] For the false interpreters of the Torah 'expounded it with smooth falseness and made the righteous become wicked;[6] and the counsel of Beliya'al was in their hearts,[7] because they uttered smooth words and they tumbled without understanding . . . ' 'They meditated thoughts of Beliya'al to make Thy people exchange Thy Torah . . . for smooth words. . . . They kept the draught of knowledge from the thirsty. . . . And they came to inquire of Thee from the mouth of false prophets, seduced by error. For they spoke of the vision of knowledge that it is not right'.[8]

The same contrast, between the true teacher, whose eyes God illumined and to whom he gave knowledge, understanding and reason, and the false teacher, the son of Beliya'al, to whom God gave neither knowledge nor reason nor understanding and whose 'coarse knowledge' led him to fall into meaningless interpretations of the Torah, we find also among the Ḳaraites:

> 'The wise is a man to whom God gave knowledge, reason, understanding, whose eyes he illumined with insight into the Scriptures . . . He did not err and did not cause to err . . .' The son of Beliya'al is a man to whom God gave no knowledge, no reason, no understanding and no insight, and he erred and caused to err.[9]

If we now turn to the *Song of the Vine*, we see that all the important elements of this teaching about the inspired, true interpretation of the Torah, which was held in Qumran and shared

[1] Pesher Hab. ii, 8–9 נתן אל בלבו חכמה לפשור את כול דברי עבדיו הנביאים.

[2] Zad. Document xvi, 1 ישכיל את הרבים.

[3] Manual ix, 18 להנחותם בדעה וכן להשכילם ברזי פלא ואמת.

[4] Wieder, op. cit. p. 104, quotes a similar expression from Ḳaraite literature כתבי לצות 'writings of derision', where the reference is to *Rabbanite* writings.

[5] Zad. Doc. i, 14–15 איש הלצון אשר הטיף לישראל מימי כזב ויתעם בתוהו לא דרך.

[6] Zad. Doc. i, 18–19: דרשו בחלקות . . . וירשיעו צדיק.

[7] Hodayoth vi 22: ויעץ בליעל עם לבבם.

[8] Hodayoth iv, 7–18.: [כי אמ]רים החליקו למו . . . וילבטו בלא בינה (7) זממו עלי בליעל להמיר תורתכה . . . בחלקות . . . ויעצורו משקה דעת מצמאים (10,11) . . . ויבאו לדורשכה מפי נביאי כזב מפותי תעות (16) . . . כי אמרו לחזון דעת לא נכון (18)

[9] Pinsker, op. cit. p. 10: חכם שנתן לו אל . . . דעת והשכל ובינה והאיר את עיניו במקרא בתבונה . . . לא תעה ולא התעה . . . בן בליעל איש שלא נתן לו אלהים לא דעה ולא בינה לא שכל ולא תבונה . . . ותעה והתעה

by the Ḳaraites, are included and expressed in this poetical song, both in style and substance.

The true teachers, according to Ben Asher, are 'the perfect of the vine' (תמימי הגפן); their knowledge comes to them by divine inspiration, for they are the 'heirs of the prophets' (יורשי הנביאים), they possess 'knowledge of understanding' (יודעי בינה) and are 'uttering mysteries' (מביעי חידות) from their heart, full of understanding wisdom (לבם משכיל חכמה) like a flowing brook (כנחל נובע). They founded the exposition of the Scriptures (יסדו פירוש מקרא) 'without turning aside from the (right) way' (בלי לסור מדרך) in order to make just the many (להצדיק רבים).

The terms תמימי, יודעי בינה[1], משכיל[2], פירוש מקרא[3], בלי לסור מדרך[4] and רבים[5] are standard terms of Qumran. The image of flowing waters for uttering mysteries—which means wondrous interpretations of the Torah—is biblical,[6] but it became a central concept at Qumran, where we already have the *combined* term of 'mashḳeh da'ath'[7] which is not to be found in OT literature.

The phrase: 'They founded (יסדו) the exposition of the Torah by their faithfulness' (be'emunatam) is noteworthy because of the combination of 'yasad' with knowledge, a combination we find for the first time at Qumran.[8]

We have shown here the close ties—both terminological and theological—that link Ps. cxix and the Qumran writings with Ḳaraite teaching and literature. We have demonstrated the affinities of the 'Song of the Vine'—in style and thought—with the Psalm and with Qumran. But there are in the Song two other affinities with the Psalm which deserve proper attention. This is especially so because they are concerned with the signi-

[1] Hodayoth i, 21, מבינתכה, xiv, 12, ואני ידעתי ומבינתך, xv, 12, ואני ידעתי בבינתך 'I knew by your understanding (which you gave me)'; see Jacob Licht p. 245, sub voce בינה

[2] Manual iii, 13, למשכיל להבין ללמד 'for the enlightened to understand and to teach. Zad. Doc. xii 27.28 ואלה החקים למשכיל להתהלך בם these are the statutes for the enlightened to walk according to them. See also Jacob Licht, Hodayoth 174.

[3] Zad. Doc. iv, 7, vi, 16, לעשות כפרוש התורה to act according to the exposition of the Torah.

[4] Zad. Doc. i, 13, סרי דרך ii, 6, סררי דרך; Manual x, 21, סוררי דרך those who hurry aside out of the way.

[5] Zad. Doc. xvi, i ישכיל הרבים he shall enlighten the many. See Habermann 'Edah we Edut 179 sub voce רבים. In our song רבים is combined with להצדיק.

[6] Ps. lxxviii, 2; Prov. xviii, 4.

[7] Hodayoth iv, ii, משקה דעת drink of knowledge, cf. 1 Kor. x, 4.

[8] Manual iii, 1: ביסודי דעת foundations of knowledge, comp. b. Megillah 3a: וחזרו וייסדום they have founded them again. About this reading see Habermann ad locum.

ficance of two basic elements in Ben-Asher's conception of the 'ṭa'ame miḳrā', namely, its *aesthetic* value as far as the proper pronunciation and correct intonation of the words are concerned and its *intellectual* importance for the true understanding and right interpretation of the text. Moreover, these two basic elements also constitute the essence of Ben Asher's description of the 'ṭa'ame miḳrā' in his famous Colophon which actually forms the counterpart in prose to his poem (cf. p. 95).

The first and foremost of these two affinities is the term 'ṭa'ame miḳrā'. 'Ṭa'am' has a number of meanings: taste,[1] intelligence,[2] command,[3] reason or cause,[4] sense or meaning,[5] accent or intonation.[6] Ben-Asher seems to have been the first to create the combined term of 'ṭa'ame miḳrā'. And it is Ben-Asher too who—in the Song and especially in the Colophon—united the basic meanings of 'ṭa'am'—taste and tone, sense and sound—to form the new term 'ṭa'ame miḳrā', including all its exegetical and phonetic implications.

In doing so he must again have had in mind Psalm cxix. One verse of this Psalm runs:

> Teach me good judgment and knowledge,
> for I have faith in thy commandments.[7]

The 'good judgment' (טוב טעם) the Psalmist is praying for was certainly taken to mean, probably after the intention of the Psalmist himself, understanding of the right *interpretation* of the Torah.[8] The Psalmist attributes his worthiness to be granted this intellectual ability to his faithfulness (האמנתי) to the commandments (מצותיך). The same idea we find in Ben-Asher's Song, when he says:

[1] Ex. xvi, 31.

[2] Prov. xxvi, 16.

[3] Jonah iii, 7.

[4] Sir xxv, 18, בלא טעם without any cause or reason. compare b. Sanhedrin 21a: טעמא דקרא 'the reason of the sentence', and b. Pesaḥim 119a: טעמי תורה 'the reasons of the Torah'.

[5] b. 'Abodah Zarah 18a: דברים של טעם 'words which make sense, sensible words'. b. Sanhedrin 34a מקרא אחד יוצא לכמה טעמים 'There are many meanings to one verse'.

[6] Gen. Rabba xxxvi, 12: ושום שכל: אלו הטעמים; ושום שכל (Neh viii, 8) 'these are the intonations'. b. Megillah 3a and Rashi: פסקי הטעמים: הנגינות קרויין טעמים 'The division (of the text) by the accents—the intonations are called accents'. Here we already have the idea that the right accents contribute to the right understanding of the text. Ben Asher on his part elaborated it in detail stressing especially the aesthetic point of view.

[7] Ps. cxix, 66.

[8] In the Greek Bible טוב טעם is rendered by χρηστότητα καὶ παιδείαν 'kindness and education.'

> In their *faithfulness* (באמונתם)[1] they founded the *interpretation* (פירוש) of the Bible, surrounded by *commandments* (מצות).

Ben-Asher's פירוש stands for the Psalmist's טעם.

Now, it is the 'ṭa'ame-miḳrā' which bring about a better *understanding* of the Torah. But in addition to their intellectual significance they also bring the aesthetic 'delight' of correct and beautiful intonation. Ben Asher therefore says:

> As *delights* they established the accents of the Bible, in giving sense to it and in interpreting its word.

That by 'delights' he also refers to the phonetically correct pronunciation and the musically right intonation of the words can be seen from his Colophon. In the Colophon he says:

> They founded them (the Biblical Scriptures) in their faithfulness by accents of reason (בטעמי שכל), by interpretation of the word, by a sweet (taste of the) palate and by the beauty (ביופי) of the expression.

'Ṭa'am' is here employed with all the shades of its various meanings. It is 'reason', 'interpretation' and 'beautiful' intonation.

Moreover, speaking of the 'community of prophets' who by divine inspiration 'understand all hidden meanings',[2] he blends both concepts, the intellectual one of 'understanding' and the aesthetical one of 'beautifying', into one by saying that these inspired teachers are 'beautifying the mysteries of wisdom'.[3] Thus 'Ṭa'am' with its two separate meanings is here defined by a phrase combining them into one single concept. 'Beautifying the mysteries' means *interpreting* the Bible by the beautifying ṭa'ame-miḳrā.

That this combined concept of Ben-Asher is based on the above quoted verse of Ps. cxix becomes obvious when we consider the expression he uses for 'beautifying' המשפירים. This is a Hifil from שפר which as an adjective (שפיר) means both 'good' (or right') and 'beautiful'. Ben-Asher made use of this double—intellectual and aesthetical—meaning of שפר and formed this unusual grammatical form of it not to be found in Hebrew else-

[1] See Pesher Hab. ii 6–9 אשר לוא יאמינו בשומעם את כול הב[אות על]הדור האחרון מפי הכוהן אשר נתן אל ב[לבו חכמ]ה לפשור את כול דברי עבדיו הנביא[ים] who will not believe when they hear all that [will come to pass in] the last generation from the mouth of the priest whom God has given in [the heart wisdom] to *interpret* all the words of his Servants, the Prophets.

[2] עדת נביאים . . . המבינים כל נסתרות, cf Manual v, 11: לא דרשו בחוקיהו לדעת הנסתרות. They did not inquire into his Statutes to know their hidden meaning.

[3] והמשפירים סוד הכמה

where.[1] But the source of this 'ambiguous' expression is to be found in our quoted Psalm verse.

The Psalmist prays for טוב טעם; Targum renders these words by שפיר טעם; and Ben-Asher, then, phrases his definition of טעמי מקרא by playing on the two meanings of both טעם and שפיר. טעם means here for him *sense* and *sound*; and שפיר equally means *right* sense and *beautiful* sound. In this way the strange phrase turns out to be an ingenious feat of blending two different categories of concepts into one covering a special idea.

That טעמי מקרא are a delight (שעשועים) he also borrowed from our Psalm. The term שעשועים occurs several times in this Psalm, and always as a designation of the Torah.[2] For Ben-Asher it might have had the association of a delightful *sound* of the words too.

So there is a direct line from Psalm cxix through Qumran to the Ḳaraites and to Ben-Asher. The fact that at the end of the Song the poet speaks of the 'lights they dedicated at the fall of the Greeks' cannot be used as an argument against Ben-Asher having been a Ḳaraite.[3] True, the Ḳaraites do not acknowledge Ḥanukka as an established festival. But they do not ignore the historical event. In the poem the author only refers to the event of the dedication of lights after the victory. He does not speak of any established festival.

10. The Ben Asher Text of the Bible

From the fact that a Bible text established by Ḳaraite Masoretes was accepted as authoritative throughout Jewry, by Rabbanites and Ḳaraites alike, we must conclude that this acceptance must have taken place at a time when the relations between the two parties had not yet come to the critical stage that we know existed at a later time. But we must also conclude that the text as fixed by the Tiberian Masoretes was regarded as such a supreme achievement that it was beyond comparison. In addition we must remember that the Masoretes of Tiberias called themselves the men of faith who concealed nothing of what was given to them, who added nothing to what had been transmitted to them; they call themselves the God-inspired guardians

[1] Comp. b.'Abodah Zarah 20b and J. Levy s. v. שפר in his dictionaries to Talmud and Targum.

[2] See Ps cxix, 16, 24, 47, 70, 77, 92, 143, 174.

[3] See Moshe Zucker, in *Tarbiṣ* xxvii, 1957, p. 70.

of tradition, who have made the Twenty-four Books of Holy Scripture great and strong, who have added explanatory accents and thus regulated the reading, and by adding the vocalization have provided a clear guidance to the pronunciation with sweet palate and beauty of speech. Their work, as Moshe b. Asher insists at the end, is meant for the whole of Israel.

Such assurances of the Masoretes, to the effect that they confined themselves in their work to passing on what had been transmitted to them, naturally made an impression also in non-Ḳaraite Jewish circles. The Ḳaraite Masoretes had established a reputation for being the experts on Bible texts and what they had achieved was undoubtedly imposing. Until they began to be regarded as suspect, their work was well received and the Bible text as fixed by them was accepted. We must remember that at the time when Moshe b. Asher completed his Codex of the Prophets in Tiberias, Sa'adya, who waged a sharp controversy against the Ḳaraites, was still in Egypt and, according to the new chronology of his life was not more than thirteen years of age. When about ten years or so later he had to flee from Egypt, his native country, he may have met in Tiberias Moshe b. Asher and his son Aaron, the prominent Masoretes. We do not hear anything about that, but it is very likely that it was so, as he wrote his sharp attack against the Ben Asher Masoretes to which I have referred. The Masoretes of Tiberias may have been the first Ḳaraites whom he met. As the polemical Piuṭ of which certain specimens are found in the Geniza did not diminish the respect the Rabbanites had for the text of the Bible established by the Masoretes from Tiberias, we may conclude with certainty that this text of the Bible was adopted by the Rabbanites long before Sa'adya's polemic against the Ḳaraites began. But Sa'adya's polemic resulted in the fact that all information about the Tiberian Masoretes and the text created by them was more and more suppressed. That Sa'adya should already have written in Egypt polemical books against the Ḳaraites is hardly possible.

The other Ben-Asher Codex is the manuscript of the whole Bible which until recently was kept in the Synagogue of the Sephardic Jews in Aleppo but disappeared during the struggle between Arabs and Jews in 1948. It was impossible to ascertain whether it had been burnt together with the Synagogue or whether it had been preserved in part or completely. But now it has been rediscovered. Isḥaḳ Ben-Zvi, the President of the State of Israel, has reported that the greater part of the Codex is again in safety, and photos of two pages (Is. xl and Dt. xxxii) have been published besides the page which had been published in 1887 by Wm. Wickes of which the original is now lost, by Isḥaḳ Ben-Zvi in the periodical *Sinai* (סיני), vol. xliii, 1958; pp. 5–13: שנכתב בארץ ישראל „כתר התורה" של בן־אשר

This Codex has generally been identified with the text to which Maimonides referred when he wrote:[1]

> And as I have noticed a great confusion in all the books which I have seen concerning these matters, and also the Masoretes who have written and composed treatises to enumerate the Setumot and Petuchot differ from each other in these matters because of the divergences in the books on which they relied, I have thought it expedient to set down here all Parashas of the Torah, the closed and the open ones and the forms of poems, so that according to them all books may be ordered and corrected. And the book on which we rely in these matters is the book which is known in Old Cairo (מצרים), which contains all the 24 books, which was kept in Jerusalem many years ago, so that from it all books might be corrected; everyone is accustomed to rely on this book because it was corrected (לפי שהגיהו) and all details were fixed in it (ודקדק בו) by Ben Asher over the course of many years and he corrected it many times, so it is reported, and I have relied on it in the book of the Torah which I have written according to his directions.

From a commentary which Sa'adya b. David al-'Adeni wrote between 1478 and 1484 on Maimonides' *Yad ha-ḥazaḳa* we learn that the Aleppo Codex must have been in Aleppo at any rate during the middle of the fifteenth century and must have been regarded as the one which Maimonides referred to when he wrote his notice quoted above: We read in the commentary:

> The book to which the Gaon refers is still to-day in the city of Ṣoba, i.e. Ḥaleb (Aleppo). It is called '*the Crown*'. It is written on parchment, three columns to the page. At the end is written: 'I am Aaron b. Asher, who has corrected it' . . . and I have myself seen it and read in it . . .[2]

[1] See Maimonides, 'Yad ha-Ḥazaḳa, Hilkot Sefer Tora', Chapter 8, *Masoreten des Westens*, vol. i, p. 11.

[2] It was Dr. Naftali Wieder who drew my attention to this commentary. A part of it is preserved in the Bodleian MS Hunt 372. The notice given above in translation reads on fol. 138v in the original הספר שסמך עליו הגאון ז״ל עדיין הוא היום במדינת צובה והיא חלב ויסמוה אלתאג ומכתוב עלי רק בכל ורקה תלאת דפאה ומכתוב פי אחרה אני אהרון בן אשר שהגהתיו וכו ואני ראיתיו וקראתי בו

Otherwise we know nothing of a colophon written by Ben Asher.[1] But we do know of an important notice at the end of the Codex which gives us the following information:[2] The consonantal text of the Codex was written by Shelomo b. Buyāʿa. Aaron b. Asher had carefully provided the text with punctuation and Masora. A wealthy Ḳaraite from Baṣra, Israel b. Simḥa b. Saʿadya b. Ephraim, bequeathed the Codex to the Ḳaraite community in Jerusalem. There it was to be kept under the special care of two Ḳaraite princes, Yoshiya and Yeḥezḳiya, the sons of the Ḳaraite prince Shelomo b. David b. Boaz. These princes were to appoint a reliable man in Jerusalem to look after the Codex on the spot. During the three great Jewish feasts, Passover, Pentecost and Tabernacles, the Codex was to be brought out and from it the lessons were to be read publicly. Furthermore, every serious scholar, whether Rabbanite or Ḳaraite, was to be given opportunity to consult the Codex for the purpose of correcting other MSS from it, but no one was really to be entitled to study it. The Codex was only to be made accessible in the presence of the reliable man who was in charge of the Codex.

Shelomo b. Buyāʿa was a famous copyist in the first half of the tenth century. A Torah MS in Leningrad written by him, and provided with punctuation and Masora by his brother Ephraim, was finished in 929.[3] It is very likely that the Aleppo Codex was finished at much the same time.

The note recording the donation of the Codex to the Ḳaraites in Jerusalem gives no date. But we can fix the time approximately by the period of office of the Ḳaraite princes mentioned. David b. Boaz, the grandfather of the two princes, to whose care the Codex was entrusted, was a well-known Ḳaraite author who still held the office of Ḳaraite Nasi in the year 993 A.D. when he wrote a commentary on Ḳoheleth.[4] His son Shelomo held the office of Ḳaraite Nasi in 1016, as can be seen from a colophon in which his two sons Yoshiya and Yeḥezḳiya are both mentioned.[5]

[1] See the report of Jacob Berlin in the Hebrew periodical הלבנון 1863, pp. 16, 23; Jacob Saphir in the report about his travel, אבן ספיר vol. i, Lück, 1866, p. 12b; A. E. Harkavy in חדשים גם ישנים no. 6, 1895, p. 7.

[2] I have published and translated this notice according to the best sources in *Masoreten des Westens*, vol. i, pp. 3 f.

[3] No. 17 in the 2nd Firkowitch Collection in Leningrad, see *Masoreten des Westens*, vol. i, pp. 58 f.

[4] Cf. S. Poznanski, *The Karaite Literary opponents of Saadia Gaon*, London, 1908, pp. 18 f. The same, *Babylonische Geonim im nachgaonischen Zeitalter*, Berlin 1914, pp. 127 ff.

[5] No. 225 of the 2nd Firkowitch Collection in Leningrad, see *Masoreten des Westens*, vol. i, pp. 67 f, where I published the Colophon.

The sons themselves are mentioned as holding the office of Nasi in Jerusalem in 1042 and in Cairo in 1055 and 1062.[1] They must therefore have changed their residence between 1042 and 1055. As it was suggested that the princes should appoint a representative in Jerusalem, it is very likely that they were already living in Cairo when the Codex was bequeathed to the Ḳaraites in Jerusalem or at least that they had decided to move there.

A note on the first page of the Codex reads:[2]

אנתקל בחכם אלאפתכאך מן נהב ירשלים עיר הקו׳ . . . לקהל מצרים לכניסת ירושלים . . .

> According to the law of restoration of the booty from Jerusalem, the holy city, it was transferred to the community of Old Cairo, the Jerusalem Synagogue. . . .

'Booty of Jerusalem' refers to those things seized by the Crusaders when they took Jerusalem on July 15th 1099. The seized MSS were released a few years later by King Baldwin. We hear of a thanksgiving service in Jerusalem held on July 13th 1106 in the Synagogue of 'Anan, the founder of Ḳaraism, on the occasion of the release of the seized books.[3]

It is probable that about the same time the codices belonging to the Rabbanites were also released. Many of the seized books were taken to Egypt. We have seen that the Codex of the Prophets written in 895 by Moshe b. Asher was handed over to the Ḳaraite community in Cairo.[4] Now we learn that the Aleppo Codex of a later date was transferred to Old Cairo and handed over to the Jerusalem Synagogue, which, it seems, belonged to the Rabbanites.[5]

[1] Cf. Jacob Mann, *Texts and Studies*, vol. ii, pp. 134 ff.

[2] Cf. *Masoreten des Westens* vol. i, p. 9; Saphir loc. cit., p. 17v prints erroneously אלאפתכאך instead of אלאפתכאך which does not make sense, so it was taken as אלאתפאק to mean *with the consent* (of the princes). The correct reading is to be found in הלבנון and with Harkavy loc. cit., p. 8.

[3] The note is to be found in a Torah scroll belonging to the Ḳaraites and published by Harkavy in the periodical הצפירה 1875, p. 47 f. Cf. J. Mann, *The Jews in Egypt and Palestine*, vol. i, p. 200, n. 1. I gave a translation of the passage in *Masoreten des Westens*, vol. i, p. 10. Mann's doubts of the genuineness of the note (cf. Texts and Studies, vol. ii, p. 137), are unfounded; the date is given as 1037 after the destruction of the temple (=A.D. 1104), 1413 Sel.

[4] See above p. 94.

[5] At the time a Jerusalem Synagogue and a Synagogue of the Babylonians existed in Old Cairo (miṣrajim). Cf. *Masoreten des Westens*, vol. i, p. 10, n. 1.

11. Chr. D. Ginsburg and Seligman Baer

Another Biblical codex connected with the name of Ben Asher is the Leningrad Codex B 19a. That this codex was copied in Old Cairo (מצרים) in 1008 (or 1009), 'from the corrected clear books prepared by the master Aaron b. Moshe b. Asher',[1] is expressly stated by the copyist Samuel b. Jacob himself.[2] For Christian David Ginsburg there was no doubt that this codex was a copy of the Aleppo Codex. He writes:[3]

> In the year 1009, that is, three or four years after it was conveyed to the Jerusalem Congregation at Cairo and most probably in the life-time of the first Trustees, a certain Samuel b. Jacob copied this Standard Codex of Ben-Asher for Meborak Ibn Osdad. This very important copy is now in the Imperial Public Library at St. Petersburg. The name of the Scribe, the place where the copy was made, the honoured person for whom it was transcribed and the date on which it was finished are all most minutely given in the Epigraph of the MS. They are written in the same hand-writing as the MS itself.

But we have seen that the Aleppo Codex was given to the Ḳaraite Community in Jerusalem in the middle of the eleventh century, and that it was brought over to Egypt some years after 1100. In 1897, when Ginsburg wrote his *Introduction*, nothing was known of the time of the Ḳaraite princes mentioned in the colophon, and he misunderstood the notice on the first page of the codex on account of Saphir's mistake in reading it.[4] Ginsburg's reconstruction is therefore wrong, and we have only the following alternatives: either the Aleppo Codex was in Egypt before it was given to the Ḳaraites in Jerusalem, and afterwards was brought back to Egypt at the beginning of the twelfth century, or the Leningrad Codex was copied from other Ben Asher Codices which were in Egypt about 1000 and which later disappeared.[5] Ben Asher certainly prepared several MSS of the Hebrew Biblical text with punctuation and Masora. Besides, Samuel b. Jacob, who copied the Leningrad Codex, declares expressly that he had copied the Codex from several correct and clear codices which had been prepared by the master Aaron b.

[1] Cf. *Catalog der hebräischen Bibelhandschriften* . . . Ed. Harkavy and Strack, 1875, pp. 265 and 269.

[2] The Hebrew words are: מן הספרים המוגהים המבואֹרים אשר עשה המלמד אהרון בן משה בן אשר נוח בגן עדן

[3] Cf. his *Introduction*, pp. 243 f.

[4] See p. 109, note 2.

[5] If such a MS loses its last page it is difficult to recognize it as a Ben Asher Codex.

Moshe ben Asher. If we compare the facsimile of the Aleppo Codex published by Wickes (Gen. xxvi, 34–xxvii, 30) with the Leningrad Codex as printed in the Biblia Hebraica, we find in the punctuation only two differences: at Gen. xxvii, 23 the latter codex reads וַֽיְבָרֲכֵֽהוּ instead of וַֽיְבָֽרְכֵֽהוּ, which is also the reading of both codices elsewhere (Gen. xxvi, 12; xxvii, 27), and at Gen. xxvii, 1, the Aleppo Codex has clearly מֵֽרְאֹת with Metheg, which is missing in the Leningrad Codex not only here but in all the other places where the word occurs (Isa. xxi, 3; xxxiii, 15; xliv, 18; Hab. i, 13; Ps. lxix, 24; cxix, 37). Besides, in six places Metheg is inserted where it is missing in the Aleppo Codex, though this may be explained by the fact that Kittel added some Methegs which were not found in the MS. The differences in the Masoretic notes are greater: two notes of the Leningrad Codex are missing in the Aleppo Codex, and twenty-four of the Aleppo Codex in the Leningrad Codex. This could hardly be explained if the Aleppo Codex was the original of the Leningrad Codex. We must therefore draw the conclusion that the Leningrad Codex and the Aleppo Codex were each copied from different originals worked out by Aaron b. Asher; as we find far more Masoretic notes in the margin of the Aleppo Codex it is more than likely that Aaron b. Asher added in the course of time more masoretic notes to his text of the Bible. Maimonides had heard that Ben Asher had been occupied for many years with the Aleppo Codex and that he had corrected it many times.

It is well known that the genuineness of the two Ben Asher Codices has been disputed. William Wickes, who published the facsimile of one page of the Aleppo Codex mentioned above and who investigated some other readings of the Codex known to him, writes:[1]

> From these few test-passages we may conclude that the statement assigning this Codex to Ben Asher is a fabrication, merely introduced to enhance the value of the same—and that the whole long epigraph with the list of Qaraite names (showing it to be of Qaraite origin), &c., is untrustworthy and undeserving of serious notice.

Adolf Neubauer published facsimiles of two pages of the Cairo Ben Asher Codex of the Prophets. It was clear to him that the text of that Codex was in general the same as that of the Aleppo Codex,

[1] Cf. *A Treatise on the Accentuation of the Twenty-One so-called Prose Books of the Old Testament*, Oxford, 1887, p. IX.

of which Wickes had declared that it had nothing to do with Ben Asher. So he writes:[1]

> But from the mode of accentuation in this MS Drs. S. Baer and Wickes both concluded that it could not have been pointed by a Masorete of the Ben Asher school, the accentuation being against the rules laid down by Ben Asher.

Paul de Lagarde, after having seen the facsimile published by Wickes, writes—I translate the passage:[2]

> According to this (facsimile) the Codex comes from Germany and was written in the fourteenth century, therefore it is worthless for research purposes. I would suggest comparison with the Dresden Codex of the תנ״ך, which was once made available to me at my house, and with plate No. 41 of the Oriental Series of the Palaeographical Society. It should, however, be borne in mind that the facsimile given by Wickes is greatly reduced in size.

To begin with Lagarde: I have not seen the Dresden Codex. Plate 41 of the Oriental Series of the Palaeographical Society presents a facsimile of a Cambridge Codex written in 1345 in Germany. But this Codex is completely different and has nothing whatsoever to do with the Aleppo Codex. Plate 40, however, containing a facsimile of the MS Harl 5720 of the British Museum is similar to it, being described by Ginsburg as one of the oldest Hebrew Biblical MSS of the British Museum; he dates it between 1100 and 1120.[3] Lagarde's condemnation of the Aleppo Codex can be explained only by assuming that he mistook the description of one plate for that of the other.

Neubauer had no judgment of his own in the matter and did not dare say anything against the authority of men like Wickes and Baer. That Wickes depended on Baer's authority in his condemnation of the Aleppo Codex is beyond doubt. Already in his earlier book of 1881 he had acknowledged his 'obligation to Dr. Baer as a personal friend'.[4] In his later book of 1887 he writes in the preface:

> I have once more to express my obligation to my friend Dr. Baer for the valuable assistance which he has willingly rendered

[1] See his article, 'An Account of the Earliest MSS of the Old Testament', *Studia Biblica et Ecclesiastica* III, 1891, pp. 25–7.

[2] *Mittheilungen*, vol. iv, Göttingen, 1891, pp. 17 f.

[3] His *Introduction*, p. 435.

[4] *A Treatise on the Accentuation of the so-called Poetical Books of the Old Testament*, Oxford 1881, Preface.

me. His familiar acquaintance with the Masora, a department of study in which he ranks *facile princeps*—has been of special service to me.

Wickes was so strongly influenced by Baer that he even took over from him the typical Jewish animosity against the Ḳaraites. It is therefore Baer with whom I have to deal here.

Seligman Baer (1825–97) in his early youth seems to have been in contact with Wolf Heidenheim (1757–1832). In any case he inherited some of his MSS and continued his work. They were both convinced that all Masora had been written in order to confirm a Hebrew Biblical text similar to that published by Jacob ben Chaiyim in the second Rabbinic Bible (Venice 1524–25). Generally speaking they both took this text to be identical with the text of Aaron Ben Asher, but they thought that they would be able to improve it with the help of the Masora and to bring it nearer to the ideal Ben Asher text. They actually knew a great deal of Masora and were so devoted to its study that one can almost regard them as in a way continuing the work of the Masoretes, as the last Masoretes. The method used by them consisted in eliminating all difficulties, smoothing out the differences and arriving at a unity in which they saw the 'correct' text of the Hebrew Bible. Their method may be illustrated by two examples.

1. After I had published my article about the traditional pronunciation of Hebrew and the punctuation of the Masoretes,[1] in which I showed amongst other things that in the liturgical fragments provided with Palestinian punctuation the suffix of the 2nd person masc. sing. is always *-ak* and not *-eka*, as vocalized in the Masora, I received a letter from Professor D. Simonsen of Copenhagen in which he pointed out to me that a remnant of the pronunciation *-ak* instead of *-eka* still remains in liturgical poetry, for instance in Seliḥot where the old editions of the German-Polish Maḥzor read: למען אמתָּךְ &c., and only W. Heidenheim (after 1803) introduced אמִתֶּךָ, the form of the suffix in accordance with the Masoretes.[2]

2. In his book משפטי הטעמים, Rödelheim 1808, Heidenheim had pointed out the rules for setting Metheg in Hebrew Biblical MSS. Baer published a German edition of these rules in his article 'Die Metheg-Setzung nach ihren überlieferten Gesetzen dargestellt'.[3]

[1] In *ZAW*, xxxix, 1921, pp. 230–239=*Opera Minora*, Leiden 1956, pp. 38–47.

[2] Cf. *Masoreten des Westens*, vol. i, p. 46, n. 1.

[3] The article was published in *Archiv für wissenschaftliche Erforschung des Alten Testaments*, ed. Adalbert Merx, vol. i, Halle, 1869, pp. 55–67 and 194–207.

Franz Delitzsch, who prepared the article for publication, wrote an introductory notice to it. These rules had been worked out by Heidenheim and Baer from late Hebrew Biblical MSS which were the only ones at their disposal. But they were both firmly convinced that they had found the very rules according to which Ben Asher himself had fixed the correct reading of the text. On the authority of men like Franz Delitzsch these rules were generally adopted and faithfully taken over into our Hebrew grammars. Even a critical scholar like Gotthelf Bergsträsser included them in his *Hebrew Grammar*[1] and illustrated them with some specimens added by himself from the Ben Chaiyim text. When he visited me in Giessen in the spring of 1923, we discussed this part of his *Grammar* and I asked him whether he had ever studied a Hebrew Biblical MS. 'No' was the answer. Thereupon I showed him some photographs of ancient Hebrew Biblical MSS in none of which these elaborate rules for the use of Metheg were observed. He was somewhat surprised and declared that he had not realized that what he had written in his grammar about the use of the Metheg was worthless ('Makulatur').

Baer used to regard the Hebrew Bible MSS which did not set Metheg in accordance with the rules worked out by Heidenheim and himself as not belonging to the school of Ben Asher. Hence his condemnation of the Ben Asher Codices.

The methods followed by Baer in dealing with Masoretic material can best be illustrated by the way in which he made his editions. Aaron b. Asher, under the title *Diḳduḳe ha Ṭeʿamim*, had composed rules for reading and cantillating the text of the Hebrew Bible. Baer edited these rules together with H. L. Strack. But Strack only contributed some bibliographical notes and copies of Masoretic MSS which he had seen and copied a few years previously in St. Petersburg. All the problems of editing the text were left to Baer. Strack was content to share the 'honour' of the edition. The title of the joint edition is typical:

> Die Dikduke ha-Tᵉamim des Ahron ben Moscheh ben Ascher und andere grammatisch-massorethische Lehrstücke zur Feststellung eines richtigen Textes der hebräischen Bibel, mit Benutzung zahlreicher Handschriften zum ersten Male voll-

[1] Some parts of his Grammar are published as 29th edition of Wilhelm Gesenius' *Hebräische Grammatik*. The first fascicle was published in Leipzig in 1918.
As to the criticism of the traditional setting of Metheg, see Rudolf Meyer in his new Hebrew grammar (*Sammlung Göschen*, Berlin 1952) §16, 2.

ständig herausgegeben von S. Baer und H. L. Strack. Leipzig 1879, Verlag von L. Fernau.

Baer did not aim at making a critical edition of the treatise composed by Aaron b. Asher. He had collected Masoretic material of various kinds, written at different times, in order to make it the basis of a 'correct' text of the Hebrew Bible. The problem how far such multifarious material could be attributed to Ben Asher did not trouble him. The rules composed by Ben Asher certainly refer to the Ben Asher text and *not* to the Ben Chaiyim text. But Baer supposed the entire material to be a unity, and as the texts collected by him agreed neither with each other nor with the text which he believed to be the text of Ben Asher, he selected from them what he regarded as 'correct', and what differed he declared to be 'corrupt', 'incomplete' or 'in confusion'.[1] We can hardly agree that with such methods old and difficult Masoretic texts can be edited satisfactorily.[2] Yet it is typical of Baer. Strack was a compiler rather than a critical scholar; he raised no objection to these methods of his colleague.

But Baer did not confine himself to selecting from the material at his disposal what he regarded as being 'correct'. He also freely *altered* readings of his MSS if they did not offer what he took to be 'correct'. In Bonn we came across a very drastic example of Baer's methods. In the preface to the edition of the Diḳduḳe ha-Ṭe'amim a Masoretic compendium is mentioned, called '*Adat Deborim*[3] and composed by a certain Joseph of Constantinople. It was available to him in a copy made by Strack in Leningrad, and the Leningrad MS dated 1207 is the only one we know. The author of this compendium had included the main parts of a treatise registering the slight differences of readings between Ben Asher and Ben Naftali, which treatise was composed by Mishael b. 'Uzziel.[4] Many fragments from this

[1] In the notes to the text published by him remarks such as these can be found: 'In den übrigen Codd. fehlen in einigen diese Sätze ganz, in andern sind bloss Trümmer davon erhalten' (p. 5). 'Von hier an sind in P die Sätze verworren; daher das folgende nach Cod. Cairo and Manuel' (p. 7). 'So dieser Satz richtig in K. In den andern Codd. corrumpiert'. (p. 11). 'So in T 21' (p. 15) the readings of other Codices are not mentioned). 'In den andern Texten fehlt dies alles . . . überhaupt herrscht in diesem Stücke grosse Verwirrung in den Vorlagen' (p. 17). 'Von hier und weiter die Zurechtstellung nach Man(uel) da in den andern Texten die grösst Confusion' (p. 19).

[2] Ginsburg advanced objections to Baer's methods in his *Introduction*, pp. 278–86.

[3] Cf. *Dikduke* . . . pp. xxxii f. The MS is now 'Hebrew-Arabic, paper, 161' of the 2nd Firkowitch Collection.

[4] See *Masoreten des Westens*, vol. ii, pp. 60–2, and *Biblia Hebraica*, Stuttgart, 1937, Prolegomena, pp. vii f.

work are also in Leningrad. I had realized the importance of this text and suggested to one of my pupils, Lazar Lipschütz, that he should investigate and publish it. For this purpose we needed, in addition to the Geniza fragments of the text itself, the MS of *'Adat Deborim*. At my request the MS was sent from Leningrad to Bonn.

Baer had not only used Strack's copy of this book for the edition of *Diḳduḳe ha-Ṭe'amim*, but also for the lists of the differences between the texts of Ben Asher and Ben Naftali, which he had added to the Biblical texts published by him and Franz Delitzsch.[1] In the lists added to these editions since 1880,[2] quotations from *'Adat Deborim* can be found in great numbers. Lipschütz's investigation showed that hardly one of Baer's quotations from this book agreed with the MS from which it had been taken. Baer had altered nearly all these quotations and had brought them into a form which he regarded as the 'correct' Ben Asher text, without saying a word of this somewhat strange method which he had adopted. Franz Delitzsch was so impressed by Baer's great familiarity with the Masora that he completely omitted to make a critical examination of the methods adopted by him and thus gave his authority to Baer's pseudo-editions.

Under the circumstances we need not wonder that William Wickes also was impressed by Baer's acquaintance with the Masora to such an extent that he declared colophons of valuable old Biblical MSS to be *fabrications*, because the text of these MSS did not follow the rules which Baer believed to be those of Ben Asher; nor need we wonder that Neubauer did not dare to say anything against these authorities.

The book of Mishael b. 'Uzziel on the differences between Ben Asher and Ben Naftali proved to be of great importance. From Geniza fragments preserved in Leningrad and Paris and from quotations in *'Adat Deborim* the whole text of the book could be restored.[3] It was also possible to prove that *'Adat*

[1] *Liber Psalmorum.* Textum Masoreticum accuratissime expressit, fontibus Masorae varie illustravit, notis criticis confirmavit S. Baer, Praefatus est edendi operis adjutor Franciscus Delitzsch Lipsiae 1880. See the preface by Delitzsch p. vi.

[2] Psalms 1880, Proverbs 1880, Daniel, Ezra, Nehemia, 1882, Ezechiel 1884, Megillot 1886, Chronicle 1888, Jeremiah 1890, Samuel 1892.

[3] The fragments in Leningrad are in the 2nd Firkowitch Collection, Arabic-Hebrew, paper, nos. 147–153. The Paris fragment is MS IX A. 3 of the Bibliothèque de l'Alliance Israélite Universelle. The first part of the book by Lazar Lipschütz was published as a Bonn thesis for 1937 under the title: *Ben Asher—Ben Naftali. Der Bibeltext der tiberischen Masoreten. Eine Abhandlung des Mischael b. 'Uzziel, veröffentlicht und*

Deborim was written about 1060. Mishael's book, of which a great part had been incorporated in it, must have been older. It is very likely that it was composed as early as the tenth century, not long after the death of the two Masoretes, and Mishael is really very well informed about both of them. He knows, for instance, that both Masoretes occasionally fixed readings in their earlier years which they later altered.

Mishael begins by giving eight general rules[1] for the differences of the two Masoretes and proceeds to give a list of more than 800 instances from all books of the Bible where all the little details are given in which Ben Asher and Ben Naftali differed from each other. The book is an excellent test for Ben Asher and Ben Naftali MSS at that early time.

A careful examination of the Leningrad Bible MS B 19a on the basis of these test passages showed that in about 95 per cent of the cases the MS presented exactly the readings given by Mishael as those of Aaron Ben Asher. The statement of the copyist Samuel b. Jacob that he had made his copy from MSS which go back to Aaron b. Asher was thus confirmed beyond doubt.

The British Museum MS Or 4445, containing a great part of the Pentateuch (Gen. xxxix, 20 to Deut. i, 33), is connected with the name of Ben Asher in so far as on the margin of the MS 'the great master Ben Asher' (מלמד הגדול בן אשר) is several times mentioned.[2] Ginsburg had noticed that the vocalization of this MS differed from that of the text of Ben Chaiyim and was older than it. But as he was convinced that Ben Chaiyim had published the Ben Asher text, Ginsburg suggested that the consonantal text of the codex and the vocalization were written a hundred years before Ben Asher (820–850), and that the Masora was added in the time of Ben Asher, as his name is mentioned without the eulogistic formula (900–40); and G. Margoliouth, in the British Museum catalogue, adopted this somewhat bizarre suggestion. Ginsburg pointed out some features in the writing of the consonants to prove that the codex was written so early.

---

untersucht. I saw in Bonn some printed sheets of the continuation of the book, but not the complete text. But I had a written copy of the whole book and had a few more photos made of the fragments from Leningrad. Some of the fragments which I was able to study while still in Bonn went astray in Leningrad during the last war.

[1] I published a German translation of these eight rules in *Masoreten des Westens* ii, pp. 62–5.

[2] Chr. D. Ginsburg, *Introduction*, London 1897, pp. 249 ff., 469–74. G. Margoliouth's *Catalogue of the Hebrew and Samaritan MSS in the British Museum*, vol. i, London 1899, p. 38.

But Ginsburg was not acquainted with really old Hebrew Biblical MSS, and so he did not know that the features pointed out by him are found in nearly all the known codices of the tenth and eleventh centuries.[1] A careful examination of the British Museum Codex, of which we had a complete photograph in the Oriental Seminar in Bonn, showed that the codex had the readings given by Mishael b. 'Uzziel as those of Ahron b. Asher in his earlier period.

The third codex examined was the Cairo Codex of the Prophets written by Moshe b. Asher and finished in 895 in Tiberias.[2] The result showed that this Codex never had the readings given by Mishael as being characteristic of Aaron b. Asher. It was clear that the little details of punctuation quoted by Mishael were worked out by the son, not by the father. The Cairo Ben Asher Codex represents a kind of text from which Aaron b. Asher started. The British Museum MS is a specimen of the development of the text in the earlier period of Ben Asher's activity; in the specimens from which the Leningrad Codex was copied we may have types of the Hebrew Biblical text in later periods of Ben Asher's activity. It is very likely that the Aleppo Codex is another type of this text, in which the Masora was further developed.

The fact that Mishael b. 'Uzziel composed his book on the differences between Ben Asher and Ben Naftali shows that in his time Moshe b. David b. Naftali was a highly esteemed Tiberian Masorete.[3] In the Geniza remains I found quite a number of fragments of his text, and with the help of these fragments a number of MSS can be identified as containing a text fixed by this authority or later developments of such a text. It thus becomes possible to give a survey of the characteristics of this group of MSS.[4] Only a few of these MSS, however, show all these characteristics. We see in general a tendency to assimilate this text to that fixed by Ben Asher.

On the other hand the Ben Asher text did not remain unaltered. It was influenced by the Ben Naftali text. The Masora always

[1] See the facsimiles of fourteen Hebrew Bible MSS in Leningrad, dated between 929 and 1121, and published in *Masoreten des Westens*, i, plates 17–30.

[2] See above pp. 91 ff.

[3] How little of this Masorete was known in later times can be seen from the fact that Elia Levita called him a 'Babylonian' Masorete (cf. his *Massoreth ha-Massoreth*, ed. Ginsburg, London 1876, p. 114) and that even Ginsburg shared this error, cf. his *Introduction*, p. 267.

[4] Cf. the chapter 'Der Bibeltext des Ben Naftali' in *Masoreten des Westens*, vol. ii, pp. 45–68.

tends to bring differences into unity. The result of this development is a kind of *textus receptus*, which although based on the Ben Asher text, must be regarded as a compromise between the two texts. This text begins to appear from about 1300 and is mostly to be found in MSS of the fourteenth and fifteenth centuries. Such MSS were the basis of the text which was printed in parts and as a whole, chiefly in Italy where the Psalms were the first to be published in Bologna in 1477; but in other countries also, for example, Spain (before 1492) and Portugal (before 1494), such editions of the *textus receptus* were published. The first complete edition of the Hebrew Bible was published in 1483 in Soncino (near Milan) by the Soncino printing press. The Bible published by the same printers in Brescia in 1494 had for the first time the Hebrew accents as well as the vowels. These printings made possible a distribution of the Hebrew Bible hitherto unthinkable. But the printings were mainly limited to reproducing some one or other Hebrew Bible MS in type-print. Lazarus Goldschmidt in his book published in 1950[1] is able to enumerate no less than 39 prints which had appeared up to the year 1518. Nineteen, nearly half of them, were collated by Ginsburg for his greater Bible edition. These early Bible prints have a certain value as incunabula. They show how in ever-increasing measure the people tried to conquer the difficulties of the Hebrew type-print. They are sometimes beautifully decorated, but from the point of view of textual criticism they have no value. To-day we not only have at our disposal the same MSS as these printers had, but much older and more reliable ones.

Also the Bible text which Jacob b. Chaiyim published in the second Rabbinic Bible, brought out by Daniel Bomberg at Venice in 1524–25 and for centuries accepted as the authentic Bible text, is essentially nothing but a carefully prepared form of the *textus receptus*. That represents its value. Obviously Jacob b. Chaiyim tried to endow it with splendour by adding on its margins the comments of the Masora. He was enthusiastic about this Masora and proud of the achievement. But the Masoretic material which he was able to assemble with the means put at his disposal by Daniel Bomberg was not very satisfactory. 'There was not a house where there was not someone dead' (Ex. xii, 30)

[1] *The Earliest Editions of the Hebrew Bible* by Lazarus Goldschmidt, with a Treatise on the oldest Manuscripts of the Bible by Paul Kahle, Aldus Book Company, New York 1950, p. 38.

is applied by him to the Masoretic notes he had found in the manuscripts at his disposal. Jacob boasts of being the first for a long time who had made a special study of the Masoretic material. He is proud of having been able to supplement the incomplete statements of his texts and to correct the faulty ones. He is convinced that he had obtained reliable material for a standard version of the Bible text.

The development, however, really took place in the opposite way. The Masoretic *textus receptus* was fixed long before Jacob b. Chaiyim attempted to compile a correct Masora from imperfect and disparate material; the Masora became correct only when it was adapted to the Masoretic *textus receptus*, in other words when it was brought into agreement with the text which it should have supported.

But there are two impressions of the Hebrew Bible made at the beginning of the sixteenth century which differ from those mentioned above, in so far as their editors tried to prepare scholarly editions of the Hebrew text of the Bible and to produce a critical text of the Bible with the help of old and reliable MSS. They were based on the methods according to which classical texts were edited in those days.

The two editions were edited by Jewish scholars who, after their conversion to Christianity, had supplemented their Jewish learning by thorough study in the humanistic schools, and who now endeavoured to apply their newly acquired knowledge in editing the Hebrew Bible. Both editions are dedicated to Pope Leo X, a son of Lorenzo de Medici who had a real interest in such projects. The texts in question are the one prepared by Felix Pratensis for the first Rabbinic Bible published by Daniel Bomberg in Venice, and the one printed in the Complutensian Polyglot in Alcala in Spain.

12. Felix Pratensis

Felix Pratensis must have become a Christian about 1506 soon after the death of his father who was, we are told, a learned Rabbi. He joined the Order of the Augustinian Hermits at Prato near Florence—hence his name—and here it seems that he thoroughly studied the classical languages.[1] He is described

[1] In Felix Ossinger's *Bibliotheca Augustiniana*, Ingolstadt, 1718, p. 716, we find the following notice regarding him: à Prato, Felix, natione Hebraeus, Alumnus Provinciae Pisarum, Filius Coenobii Pratensis, vixit Saeculo 16. S. Theologiae Magister, ex famoso

as *trium linguarum scientia ac solida eruditione ornatus*. As a teacher of theology he must have been outstandingly efficient in his Order: *adeo in hac scientia profecit ut inter omnes Doctores Theologos similem suo tempore habuerit neminem*. His Latin translation of the Psalms made on the basis of the Hebrew text was acclaimed as a great achievement and went through many editions. When it was first published in 1515 it was approved by the Pope himself.[1]

In Venice Felix had made the acquaintance of Daniel Bomberg,[2] a wealthy and educated Christian merchant from Antwerp who had settled in Venice. Felix had taught him some Hebrew and had aroused his general interest in Hebrew language and literature. He had suggested to him the setting up of a large Hebrew printing press and Bomberg had agreed. The first licence was granted by the Senate of Venice in 1515. As Bomberg was very wealthy the printing press could be started in a big way. In the course of the next decades roughly 200 Hebrew works were printed in this press, amongst them such large ones as the Rabbinic Bibles, the Babylonian and the Palestinian Talmud, the Mishne Tora by Maimonides. These editions even to-day deserve our admiration for their fine execution and their correctness. They are of particular value because they were printed before the censorship intervened.

This famous printing press was founded at the suggestion of Felix Pratensis, a fact which alone shows that he was not only a

---

Hebraeo, Rabbinóque factus Eremita Augustinianus, trium linguarum scientia, ac solida eruditione ornatus, à Reverendissimo P. Generali, Gabriele Veneto, Lector Theologiae constitutus, adeo in hac scientia profecit, ut inter omnes Doctores Theologos similem suo tempore habuerit neminem. Anno 1522, Reverendissimus P. Mag. Generalis praefatus Gabriel Venetiis illum ad Adrianum VI Pontificem Maximum misit, ut negotia nostra tractaret. Multis annis Hebraeorum Concinnator Romae exstitit, è quibus plurimos ad fidem convertit passim enim Hebraeorum flagellum audiebat. Anno 1523, fit auctoritate Pontificia S. Theologiae Magister. Anno 1526 et 28 suae Congregationis Procuratorem egit. Romae, prope centenarius . . . 5, XI, 1559 finem vitae attigit . . .

[1] The wording of the Papal Imprimatur for the Latin translation of the Psalms is printed by me in *Essays presented to Leo Baeck* (London, 1954) pp. 53 f. (=*Opera Minora*, Leiden 1956, p. 131). There, also, is to be found a facsimile of the Latin dedication to the Pope with a German translation (pp. 55 f. and 132–34).

[2] Daniel Bomberg, son of Cornelius Bomberg in Antwerp (the name had originally been: van Bomberghen), was a wealthy merchant who had settled in Venice. At the suggestion of Felix Pratensis (see p. 120, note 1) he had founded a Hebrew printing office in Venice. The first privilege was granted to him in 1515. Between the years 1516 and 1538 Bomberg published 186 Hebrew texts, many of them of very considerable size. In 1538 he had lost in this undertaking all his money ('four millions in gold'). Cf. A. Freimann, 'Daniel Bomberg und seine hebräische Druckerei in Venedig', in the periodical *Zeitschrift für Hebräische Bibliographie*, vol. x, Frankfurt a.M., 1906, pp. 32–6, 79–88.

scholar of renown but also a great personality. This is borne out also by the high esteem which he enjoyed in his Order. When after the death of Pope Leo X it became necessary to discuss matters concerning the Order with the newly elected Pope Hadrian VI, the former Archbishop of Tortosa, Felix Pratensis was sent by the General of the Order, Gabriel Venetus, in 1522 to Spain to look after the interests of the Order. We are also told that he was the Procurator of his Order in the years 1526 and 1528, i.e. Vice-General of the Order; he had in these years the second highest position in his Order. After that Felix lived for some years in great seclusion, and he died after 1550 at the age of nearly one hundred years.[1]

The Rabbinic Bible edited by Felix Pratensis was among the first works to be published by the press. It contains, besides the Hebrew text of the Bible, the most essential Targums, several learned Jewish commentaries on the Biblical books (Rashi, Ibn Ezra, Ḳimḥi) and much important learned material; it consists of 667 large folios. In the dedication to the Pope, Felix Pratensis describes the work he has done on the text of the Bible in the following words:

> Many manuscripts were previously in circulation, but they were deprived of their splendour to such a degree that the number of errors almost equalled the number of words, and nothing was more needed by them than to have their true and genuine splendour restored. That I have attained this result will be acknowledged by all who read this (text).
>
> Daniel Bomberg of Antwerp, who from earliest youth was filled with love of learning and was always versed in the study of the fine arts, having under our guidance tried to study the Hebrew language and made very good progress in it, and also encouraged us in this endeavour—this Daniel, I say, has spared neither trouble nor expense so as to ensure that these books were printed for the general benefit, when they had been correctly prepared by our studies, trustworthiness and care, after a great many manuscripts had been collated—an extremely difficult task which for this reason had hitherto not been undertaken by anyone.

Felix had at his disposal a large number of MSS for his edition. With the help of these MSS he was able to produce a correct text of the Bible, with vowels, accents and reading signs, all based

[1] See p. 120 n. 1.

on the best MSS. From the MSS collated by him he collected a number of *variae lectiones* which he added to the Bible text—beginning with the book of Joshua—as far as his MSS went. Unfortunately we know very little about the character of the MSS at his disposal or about their extent. He only says that some contained many errors, occasionally as many errors as words. Ginsburg took this to be grossly exaggerated, and declared that he had never seen such manuscripts in European libraries. But had he, for instance, really studied the famous Reuchlin Codex of the Prophets in Karlsruhe, which he claimed to have used for his greater edition of the Bible, he could easily have seen that hardly one word of this codex is exactly punctuated as in our Bible editions. Felix could easily have found similar Codices among the older MSS which he consulted.

During the years 1913/14 I had the Codex Reuchlinianus at my disposal for several months while staying in Halle, and had some pages photographed which I always find very useful. The codex has now been made generally accessible in a facsimile edition by Alexander Sperber, *Corpus Codicum Hebraicorum Medii Aevi*, Hauniae 1956, as the first of four codices which bear a similar punctuation, two being in Parma, one in the British Museum (Add 21161) of which I myself have published a specimen, *Masoreten des Westens*, ii, pl. 14 and have had for some thirty years more than fifty photostats. Further specimens of codices of the same kind I have reproduced on plates 13, 15, 16 of *Masoreten des Westens* ii, 1930, and with Dr. Rafael Edelmann I have discussed on pp. 45*-68* of my book many more such codices with the problems connected with them.

When Sperber calls these codices pre-Masoretic, it seems to me he misunderstands the development of the Hebrew text of the Bible. I have shown that the Masoretic text of the Bible was fixed in the ninth century, and we are so fortunate as to have access to model codices coming from the great Masoretic authorities and thereby to the Masora created by them. For the Masora we certainly need no longer the compilations made by Ben Chaiyim in the sixteenth century from heterogeneous sources so full of mistakes that he himself had to confess of them that there was not a house in which there was not one dead.

The value of the codices published by Sperber has to be assessed against this background; codices which can really be declared pre-Masoretic are of a quite different kind.

We do not know what became of the MSS which Felix used. They belonged to Daniel Bomberg and were naturally at hand when Jacob b. Chaijim continued with the work on the Bible text for Daniel Bomberg, though it was not done as Felix would have done it.

Felix was well acquainted with the Masora. He was the first to mark those passages in his Bible text which, fixed by the Masora, had to be read differently from the way in which they were written (qrē and ktīb) and he took careful notice of the letters which, according to the Masora, had to be written differently (majusculae, suspensae, inversae, etc.). Thanks to him a work as fundamentally important for the Tiberian Bible text as the Diḳduḳe ha-Ṭeʿamim by Aaron b. Asher was printed, and he added further important Masoretic material to his Bible text. The idea of compiling a *correct* Masora from the inadequate Masoretic material plus the Masoretic *textus receptus* and of using a compilation of that kind for his Bible text was never conceived by Felix, the scholarly trained humanist. That was left to Jacob b. Chaijim, the refugee from Tunis. But before I go on with the discussion of the latter's work, I must deal with the other scholarly edition of the Hebrew Bible, which was made in Spain at about the same time as the Biblia Rabbinica of Felix Pratensis.

13. The Complutensian Polyglot

The Complutensian Polyglot[1] was produced through the efforts of Francisco Cardinal Ximenes de Cisneros, Archbishop of Toledo. He planned an edition of the Hebrew Bible text in his Polyglot at a time when only Jewish circles were thinking of printing the Hebrew Bible or parts of it. In the prologue to his Polyglot he writes to the Pope, to whom he dedicated the edition:

> Qua in re id aperte Beatitudini tuae testari possumus . . . maximam laboris nostri partem in eo praecipue fuisse versatam, ut et virorum in linguarum cognitione eminentissimorum opera uteremur et castigatissima omni ex parte vetustissimaque exemplaria pro archetypis haberemus quorum quidem tam hebraeorum quam graecorum et latinorum multiplicem copiam variis ex locis non sine summo labore conquisimus.

[1] I refer here to my article: 'Zwei durch Humanisten besorgte, dem Papst gewidmete Ausgaben der hebräischen Bibel', in *Essays presented to Leo Baeck on the occasion of his eightieth birthday*, East and West Library, London 1954, pp. 50–74, also in *Opera Minora*, Leiden 1956, pp. 128–50.

As there were no scholars of Christian birth who had sufficient knowledge of the Hebrew language, he had to consult Jewish scholars for the edition of the Hebrew text. Of these the most famous was Alfonso de Zamora, who was born in 1474 and devoted himself to the study of oriental languages at the University of Salamanca. In 1512 he was appointed professor of oriental languages at the University of Alcala, the place where the work on the Polyglot was carried through, and there he remained until his death, an outstanding authority in his sphere of learning.[1]

Another scholar was Pablo Coronel, born in 1480 in Segovia, who had studied theology at the University of Salamanca. In 1502, when he was already lecturing in Salamanca, he was engaged by the Cardinal to work on the Polyglot and he did so until its completion in 1517. We must assume that he is the man most responsible for the work on the Polyglot. Later he retired to Segovia where he died in 1534.

A third scholar was a certain Alfonso de Alcala, of whom it is said that he had a name as both a lawyer and a physician.[2] That the Cardinal was anxious to use the most correct and the oldest MSS for the text he states in his own letter to the Pope. Alvar Gomez testifies time and again to Alfonso de Zamora's saying that he had acquired seven Hebrew Bible MSS for the Cardinal for the price of 4000 gold coins.[3]

The MSS belonging to the Cardinal were kept in the Collegio de San Ildefonso in Alcala. Those which were still preserved were transferred to the University Library in Madrid when the University of Alcala was removed to that city. Four of them were described by P. Mariano Revilla Rico in his book *La Políglota de Alcalá. Estudio histórico-crítico* (Madrid 1917), pp. 83–5, which he wrote for the occasion of the quater-centenary of the Polyglot. The most important of them is a complete Bible, written on parchment in three columns which, according to Arias Montano,

[1] Professor Pérez Castro, in the introduction to his work '*El Manoscrito Apologetico de Alfonso de Zamora, traducion y estudio*, Madrid 1950, pp. xl–lx dealt in detail with Alfonso de Zamora. We do not know the year of his death, but we do know that he was still alive in 1544, see Pérez Castro, op. cit. p. xxxi.

[2] Cf. the three investigations by Franz Delitzsch, published as Reformationsfest Programmes for the University of Leipzig: i. *Studien zur Entstehungsgeschichte der Polyglottenbibel des Cardinals Ximenes*, 1871; ii. *Complutensische Varianten zu dem Alttestamentlichen Texte*, 1878; iii. *Fortgesetzte Studien zur Entstehungsgeschichte der Complutensischen Polyglotte*, 1886.

[3] Alvar Gomez, *De rebus gestis a Francisco Ximenio Cisnerio, Archiepiscopo Toletano libri octo*, Compluti 1569, fol. 37 v.

was copied at the very latest in the twelfth century and not in 1280, as Ginsburg suspects through mistaking the year of sale for the year of copying the MS.[1]

Franz Delitzsch, in his work *Complutensische Varianten zum Alttestamentlichen Bibeltext* (Leipzig 1878), compared more than ninety passages of the Hebrew text of the Complutensis with the Bible text of Jacob b. Chaiyim, which was generally in use, and he proved that the text of the Complutensis is of a high critical value in contrast with which the text of our editions appears to be in many ways inferior; and needs a thorough revision as the mistakes in it consist not merely of small details which do not impair the sense and understanding of the text.

It is a very remarkable fact that such an outstanding scholar as Franz Delitzsch while realizing the superiority of the Hebrew Bible text as printed in the Complutensis, yet did not understand the reason for it. The obvious explanation is that the humanistically trained Spanish scholars, eager to use *early* codices, had at their disposal Bible MSS based on the old Ben Asher text and not the *textus receptus* of the Hebrew Bible used by Ben Chaiyim. Also, as I shall explain shortly, they had found old Babylonian Bible texts in the old Spanish Synagogues and used them for the Bible text which they published.

Admittedly, the publishers of the Complutensis did not print the old texts as they found them in the MSS at their disposal, but deliberately changed the text in a special way. The Hebrew text of the Complutensis is described by Franz Delitzsch as follows:

> The . . . text . . . has no accents but only vowels and even these are added inadequately and inexactly as the Sheba-sign appears sometimes at the Ḥaṭefs, more often not. The Makkef sign is missing altogether. Of the accents only Athnachta is used, but it is not put under the stressed syllable but after the word, in an ugly way. This Athnachta is used in the books of Job, Psalms and Proverbs instead of the larger dividing accent Mercha-Mehuppach, generally used in these books of the

[1] Ginsburg speaks of the MS in his *Introduction*, London 1897, pp. 771–6, 905-25, Arias Montano, in his *Praefatio de varia in libris hebraicis lectione ac de Mazzoreth ratione atque usu* (Vol. viii of the Poliglota Regia): "Sunt nobis biblia hebraica, ante annos, ut scriptura docet, quadringentos manuscripta, sunt et in Bibliotheca Complutensi nostris antiquiora." Arias Montano seems to have taken the Epigraph of the Codex, published by Ginsburg in his *Introduction*, p. 772, as referring to the acquisition of the Codex by the two physicians R. Isaak and R. Abraham in the year 1280 and to have supposed that the Codex had been written in the twelfth century.

> Bible, so that for instance, in Ps. i, 1, two Athnachtas are used, which is impossible according to our system of accentuation. The Dagesh sign is to be found, but the opposite Raphe-sign is not used at all. These deficiencies are compensated to some extent by two additions . . .

This description, correct in the main, shows what is involved. According to Delitzsch we have to regard these imperfections as excusable defects in printing. In reality the men working in Alcala pursued quite definite aims in their edition of the Hebrew text and carried them through. The essential passage in the prologue to the Polyglot reads as follows:

> Illud est enim considerandum quod in hebraicis characteribus scienter omisimus apices illos quibus nunc utuntur Hebraei pro accentibus. Nam hi cum ad nullam vel significati vel pronunciationis differentiam pertineant, sed ad solam cantus ipsorum modulationem merito a veteribus Hebraeis rejecti sunt; quae in his imitari maluimus . . .
>
> It must be understood that we have deliberately omitted those additional signs which nowadays the Hebrews use as accents. For as these do not refer to any difference of meaning or pronunciation, but only to the modulation of their cantillation, the old Hebrews rightly rejected them. We have intentionally imitated them . . .

It is obvious that the editors of the Polyglot must have had at their disposal Hebrew texts of the Bible showing certain characteristics which are to be found in the Hebrew text of the Polyglot, and there can be no doubt that these were Babylonian texts of the Bible, texts with the simple method of Babylonian vocalization.[1] These do not use Ḥaṭefs but the vowel without the Shwa; they do not use Maḳḳef and certainly no conjunctive accents. They use the accent corresponding to the Tiberian Athnach also in the books of Job, Psalms and Proverbs and place this sign (as also the other accents) not on the syllable of the word which has the stress, but usually after the word. In Babylonian texts of the Bible, distinctive accents were chiefly indicated by small Hebrew letters or parts of letters, and as these signs are not placed over the stressed syllables, we can understand that the editors of the Complutensian Polyglot did not recognize them as accents and could conclude that the old Hebrews did

[1] Cf. my article 'The Hebrew Text of the Complutensian Polyglot', in *Homenaje a Millas-Vallicrosa*, vol. i, Barcelona, 1954, pp. 741–51.

not use accents. The Babylonian manuscripts of the Bible, in which the editors of the Polyglot could not find Hebrew accents, belonged certainly to the *vetustissima exemplaria* and we can understand that humanists like the editors of the Polyglot were inclined to follow in their steps by leaving out the accents in the Polyglot. To-day we know that in this detail they had misunderstood their *vetustissima exemplaria*. It is very likely that Arias Montano refers to these vetustissima exemplaria when he speaks of the *manuscripta nostris antiquiora* in the Complutensian Library.

Professor Millas-Vallicrosa, at the International Congress of Orientalists at Cambridge in September 1954, referred to a Spanish glossary from the ninth century containing about 200 Hebrew words in Latin transcription which certainly cannot be explained on the basis of the Tiberian punctuation. They show certain similarities to the vocalization of Babylonian Bible MSS and would thus prove that Babylonian Bible MSS were already present in Spain during the ninth century. That would naturally be of great interest. As far as I am concerned, the main value of these transcriptions of Hebrew words lies in the fact that they reproduce a pronunciation of Hebrew from pre-Tiberian times, which is what we must expect, as the Tiberian punctuation was only developed in the course of the ninth century.

It is probable that the Babylonian Bible MSS which, as *vetustissima exemplaria* were used by the editors of the Complutensis, belonged to the seven MSS acquired by Alfonso de Zamora for the Cardinal. In my contribution to the Festschrift for Leo Baeck[1] I indicated how these old MSS were lost in Spain.

It is interesting to observe how the humanistically trained editors of the Hebrew text of the Polyglot, in their eagerness to make use of *old* texts, managed to acquire the same two forms of text which even to-day form the main source for an edition of the Masoretic text of the Hebrew Bible: the Ben Asher text fixed in the tenth century and the text in circulation in Babylonia one hundred years earlier.

The editors of the Complutensis modified the Tiberian punctuation of the Ben Asher text according to older Babylonian MSS and thus arrived at a compromise which does justice to neither original, and which, in the form in which it was published, must be described as useless. The two forms of text in question are

[1] *Essays presented to Leo Baeck on the occasion of his Eightieth Birthday*, London 1954, pp. 71 ff. (=*Opera Minora*, Leiden 1956, pp. 148 ff.).

valuable and each has a history in relation to Masora and punctuation. They must be published and investigated separately, if one is to do them justice. It is quite understandable that the Hebrew text of the Complutensis as such had no future.[1] Arias Montano, in the Antwerp Polyglot, greatly modified the Hebrew text and made it agree to a great extent with the *textus receptus* of the Hebrew Bible published by Bomberg in Venice. And the text of the first Rabbinic Bible published by Felix Pratensis was replaced by the *textus receptus* published by Jacob b. Chaiyim in the second Rabbinic Bible, though it largely formed the basis of the latter.

14. The Textus Receptus

I now return to this Bible edition of Jacob b. Chaiyim. The more the *textus receptus* was developed in the course of the fourteenth and fifteenth centuries, the more the study of the Masora was neglected. In the end, the Masora was superfluous for this text. One continued to add Masoretic notes to the MSS of the Bible texts, because one had got used to seeing the Bible text surrounded by such notes. But for the most part they were merely decorative. They were written in the shape of flowers and ribbons and are generally full of mistakes. Credit must be given to Jacob for having revived the serious study of the Masora. First he had to search for MSS. In the Europe of the early sixteenth century there were no libraries which kept valuable MSS for the use of scholars. He had to rely on the material which his patron Daniel Bomberg ordered to be bought for this purpose. In the preface to his edition he speaks in words of the highest appreciation of the liberality shown in the matter of these purchases. But the MSS assembled by these acquisitions were disappointing. The Masoretic notes were in great disorder; he had to improve, to add and to assemble as well as he could. Correct MSS were probably also to be found in his time. But these do not seem to have come his way. We only hear that he used the book Ochla we-Ochla. Otherwise it can be seen that he had acquired very varied material. It was mainly Palestinian, but Babylonian material was also amongst it.[2] It was not easy for

[1] The Complutensis was published only after the Cardinal's death, in 1522, after Felix Pratensis in Spain had consented to it, cf. *Homenajo a Millas Vallicrosa*, vol. i, 1954, p. 744.

[2] To give an example: in the Masora parva for Lev. xviii, 15 we read in the Rabbinic Bible כל סחופי בצירי: siḥpa in the Babylonian Masora is the name for Athnach In the Tiberian Masora the name is unknown.

him to find his way in it and quite often he had to make his own Masora.

Such a Masora, which he assembled and corrected and even partly invented, he added to the Bible text which he printed. He was convinced that there was only *one* correct Masora—the one he had added to the Bible text—and that the Bible text on the margins of which he had added the Masora was in the main the text as fixed by the great Masoretic authorities in Tiberias, particularly Aaron b. Asher in the first half of the tenth century. Jacob had never seen an old Bible MS and could not possibly detect the clear difference between his text and the text of Ben Asher.

It is strange that the text published by Jacob b. Chaiyim was generally accepted as the definitive Bible text. Attempts, however, have been made to construct an independent Bible text on the basis of MSS. The most important of these was the great collection of critical notes made from Spanish MSS by Solomon Norzi in his critical apparatus called *Minḥat Shai* which was finished in 1626 and published for the first time in Mantua in 1742, of which I shall speak later, and the Hebrew Bible published by Johann Heinrich Michaelis in Halle in 1720, the text of which was still taken as a basis for instance by Bernhard Stade in his *Hebräisches Wörterbuch zum Alten Testament*, which he edited with Carl Siegfried (Leipzig 1893); for some time the parts of the Bible which Seligman Baer published stood in fairly high repute because they were edited under the aegis of Franz Delitzsch—I have dealt with these above. But then came Christian David Ginsburg who with great emphasis declared the Ben Chaiyim text to be the only one which could be used. He clearly saw the unreliability of Baer's study of the Masora. In his *Introduction to the Masoretico-critical Edition of the Hebrew Bible* (London 1897), he declares the Ben Chaiyim text, which he reprinted in 1894 for the Trinitarian Bible Society, to be the only Masoretic text worth considering. No editor of the present day should be allowed to diverge from this text without giving definite reasons in each case (p. 963). He could lavish no higher praise on his great new edition of the Hebrew Bible, which began to appear on the occasion of the Centenary of the British and Foreign Bible Society in 1908 and continued to come out until 1926, than that the text of the Bible which he reprinted was an exact replica of the Ben Chaiyim text.[1] And yet he pretends to

[1] 'The text presented in this book is that of the first edition of Jacob ben Chaiyim's Massoretic Recension, printed by Bomberg at Venice in 1524–5. No changes have

have collated no less than 73 MSS and 19 old printings in its preparation.

Nobody would be inclined to regard a classical text, printed at the beginning of the sixteenth century, as the best text available. The New Testament published about this time by Erasmus has to-day historical interest only. It is inconceivable that such a complicated text as that of the Hebrew Bible should have been satisfactorily edited by a man who, more than 400 years ago, relied on late and inaccurate MSS, was overwhelmed with other work, and spent hardly two years on the job. The text is printed together with all sorts of Targums and commentaries on 952 folios, about 1900 folio pages, and is supposed to have been completed in the astonishingly short time of about 15 months.[1] Yet this text has been accepted almost up to the present day as the only authoritative text!

15. The Biblia Hebraica

I was in Leningrad in October and November 1926, studying Hebrew Biblical MSS and Geniza fragments in the Russian Public Library, when I received a letter from Rudolf Kittel in which he asked me what text he should use for the new *Biblia Hebraica* which he was in course of preparing.

'I think we shall have to print the Ben Chaiyim text again', he wrote to me. I had just found in Leningrad a number of dated Hebrew Biblical MSS written between 929 and 1121[2], all of which showed a text generally in accordance with the Masoretic text fixed by Aaron b. Asher and certainly not in accordance with the Ben Chaiyim text. It was clear that this was the Masoretic Bible text as used at that time. On the other hand, I could hardly think it probable that Masoretes working on the Hebrew text of the Bible in the period between 1000 and 1500 would have done anything to it which was based on really old tradition.

---

been made in it beyond the correction of obvious errors as indicated by the MSS collated', so we read in the 'advertisement' with which each part of the edition is prefaced. The Pentateuch appeared in 1908, the earlier and later Prophets in 1911. After Ginsburg's death the edition was completed by H. E. Holmes and A. S. Geden in 1926. With regard to this edition I refer to *Masoreten des Ostens*, pp. xiv–xvii, *Masoreten des Westens*, vol. i, p. 18, n. 2 and *infra* pp. 136ff.

[1] According to Freimann, op. cit. p. 35, the Bible was printed in less than eight months. Lazarus Goldschmidt pointed out to me that this was incorrect and proved that the fifteen months mentioned above were correct. Cf. also W. B. Stevenson in *Transactions of Glasgow University Oriental Society*, vol. v, 1930, p. 46.

[2] See *Masoreten des Westens*, vol. i, pp. 56–77, and the reproductions, plates 17–30.

The Leningrad Codex B 19a proved to be a reliable source for the Ben Asher text. The Codex was copied in 1008 or 1009, only a few decades after Aaron b. Asher's death. It represents the oldest dated MS of the complete Hebrew Bible which has come down to us. The writer of the Codex, Samuel b. Jacob, expressly states in the colophon of the Codex that he copied the Codex from correct clear MSS prepared by Aaron b. Moshe b. Asher. So I suggested to Kittel that he should print the text of Aaron b. Asher in the *Biblia Hebraica* and take the Leningrad MS as its basis. Previously I had discussed the matter with an extremely understanding official, Mr. I. A. Bytchkow, who was in charge of the MSS in the Library, and I gathered that it would be possible to have the Codex in Germany for a time.

To the memory of I. A. Bytchkow, my friend Ignaz Kratshkowski (1883–1951) dedicated the first chapter of his book on *Arabic Manuscripts* (1946), and included a good photograph of Bytchkow (1858–1944). He says of him: Slowly and quietly appears the notable figure of the custodian of the MS treasures, like the spiritus movens, always ready to help, to counsel, to provide information, who had already during his lifetime won a place in the history and legends of the Library. The date of a rare jubilee revealed like a searchlight the path he had trod, and then suddenly there shone in bright light what Iwan Afanojewitsh had done for his country, for science and for all scholars. . . .

I myself belonged to this last category when I was working in the autumn of 1926 for some weeks in the Library, and it was largely due to the valuable help and co-operation of I. A. Bytchkow that my visit to Leningrad was perhaps the most successful journey made in my life.

On my return from Russia in November 1926 I went to Leipzig to visit Kittel at his request. I showed him the photographs of the Hebrew Biblical MSS of the tenth to the twelfth centuries which I had had made in Leningrad and told him why I was convinced that these MSS contain in the main the Ben Asher text. He looked at them and was soon convinced that I was right. He invited me to publish the Ben Asher text for the new edition of the *Biblia Hebraica*. Eventually, after some deliberation, I accepted on condition that the Bible text according to Ben Asher should be published together with the Masora belonging to it. I considered it necessary that the Masora which Aaron b. Asher, the greatest of the Masoretes of Tiberias, had added to his text of the Bible should be added to the text established by him, and that this Masora should replace the Masora compiled by Jacob b. Chaiyim from inadequate material of a different kind and brought into agreement with the *textus receptus*. This was not the *correct* Masora which Jacob b. Chaiyim and his successors up to Wolf Heidenheim and Seligman Baer had dreamed of possessing; nor could this Masora be compared with the large amount of Masoretic material which Christian David Ginsburg had assembled from MSS of different date and kind without understanding the real problems. It was the Masora added by the copyist from reliable MSS of Aaron ben Asher himself a few decades after his death, a collection of Masoretic material which could serve as a basis for comparison with other kinds of Masora: the compilation of Jacob b. Chaiyim, the Masora of Ben Naftali, the various forms of Babylonian and Palestinian Masora and other forms.

Kittel agreed. It was not altogether easy to get the approval of the committee of the Württembergische Bibelanstalt, which since 1920 had taken charge of the publication of Kittel's Biblia Hebraica, to publish the text of Ben Asher with its Masora instead of the Ben Chaiyim text used hitherto. But Kittel had some influence on the committee and besides, we succeeded in obtaining a considerable subsidy for publishing the Ben Asher text from the Deutsche Notgemeinschaft after it had become clear that it was an important scholarly work, not simply a new edition of a successful textbook. Thus for the third edition of the Biblia Hebraica the Württembergische Bibelanstalt agreed to print the Ben Asher text, and also its Masora after I had succeeded in getting a special grant for the extra costs. It then became of special concern to the Bibelanstalt to see that the format should be dignified.

Appreciation of the importance and the size of this publication enabled me to obtain the grants for employing a special assistant for the work on the Biblia Hebraica. These grants were provided for more than eleven years, first by the Preussische Kultusministerium, and from 1933 onwards by the Deutsche Notgemeinschaft. The amount of work involved can be estimated when one realizes that the study of the Masora often raised problems the solution of which needed time, and that we had to read five or six proofs of each printed sheet of the Biblia Hebraica, and for each sheet 60 to 80 hours' work was needed: the Biblia Hebraica consists of nearly 100 sheets.

I was able to choose my assistants from among my pupils. From the commencement of the work until the beginning of 1933 I had Dr. Raphael Edelmann who then went to the Royal Library in Copenhagen as a specialist in Jewish studies and has also been lecturer in Jewish studies for many years at the University of Copenhagen. Dr. Kurt Levy succeeded him, one of my ablest pupils. He unfortunately met an early death on 22nd July 1935. From 1935 to 1938 Dr. Falk Bar took over, a particularly conscientious and reliable worker who, in July 1938, returned with his wife to his Polish home from where he could not return.

I then chose Pastor Lic. Hellbardt to work out in detail the Masora Magna of the Ben Asher text. For some years until its closure he had been a lecturer on the Old Testament at the Theologische Schule in Wuppertal. When I left Bonn in March 1939, he had the material for the Masora and continued his work on it. Subsequently he had to join the army, and he was killed in the war. His widow handed over to me the Masoretic material after the war.

My Spanish pupil Dr. Fernando Diaz Esteban of Madrid made in 1954, and again in 1956, a very careful investigation of the Leningrad Codex, the Cairo Codex of the Prophets and other Ben Asher Codices which he was able to study from photographs while staying with me in Charlbury and Oxford. Together with Professor Pérez Castro, with whom I have been in contact in Charlbury and in Madrid, he worked out the details of a critical edition of the Masora Magna. For the new edition of the old Masoretic work known under the title Ochla we-Ochla which he is preparing he will be able to use, besides the Paris MS (Ancien fonds hebr 56) which was published by Frensdorff, the following sources: 1. The MS described by Hupfeld *ZDMG* xxi, pp. 201–20 of the Halle Universitätsbibliothek, MS. Y b, 10 of which he received a very good photograph with the help of Professor Eissfeldt. 2. The text of Ochla we-Ochla on the margins of the Bible MS Erfurt 3. See Lagarde, *Symmicta*, vol. i, 1877, p. 138. The MS is now Berlin MS or fol 1213. It was sent by the Westdeutsche Bibliothek in Marburg, where it is kept at present, to the Instituto Arias Montano in Madrid, so that Dr. Fernando Diaz Esteban could study it there. I also put at his disposal photographs of various old fragments from the Russian Public Library, some of which were quite extensive. Finally, he found in Oxford and Cambridge interesting fragments from the

Geniza of Old Cairo. These fragments show in some parts old Palestinian, in other parts Babylonian punctuation, and these methods of punctuation prove that the Ochla we-Ochla is old and must have existed in pre-Tiberian times.

The Leningrad Codex B 19 a, dated 1008, was taken as the basis for the text of the Biblia Hebraica. At my request the Codex was sent from Leningrad to Germany where it remained for two years, 1927–29. Gottfried Quell in Leipzig, now Professor at Berlin University, made a thorough revision of the text of the former Biblia Hebraica from the original of the Codex and thus constructed the model for printing the text. At the same time he also carefully noted all the corrections as marked in the Codex.[1]

At the expense of the Old Testament Seminar of the University of Leipzig, of which the director was Albrecht Alt, excellent black and white photographs were made of the Codex, and these formed the basis for the study of the Masora and the proof-reading done by me and my assistants at the Oriental Seminar of Bonn University. A reduced copy of the Leipzig photograph was made in the Bonn Oriental Seminar. The original photographs in Leipzig were destroyed in the war.

It was unfortunately impossible to procure a photograph of the Ben Asher Codex from Aleppo. The heads of the community of the Sephardim were convinced that to take photographs of the Codex would desecrate it and that those who gave permission for it to be photographed would most certainly draw all the curses upon their heads which are threatened in the colophons of the Codex. 'Naturalmente è impossibile vincere una tale superstizione collegata nel timore della morte', so Professor Umberto Cassuto wrote to me from Jerusalem, explaining why he had not been able to make full use of the Codex for the edition of the Ben Asher text which he had prepared for Israel. Professors Gotthold Weil and Hellmut Ritter had had the same experience twenty years before when, at my request, they tried to obtain permission in Aleppo to take photographs of the Codex. Nevertheless, Cassuto succeeded with some difficulty in studying the Codex for a few months—the sole expert of modern times to do so—and he entered the readings of the Codex in his Letteris text,

[1] Cf. F. Pérez Castro, 'Corregido y Correcto. El Ms. B 19a (Leningrad) frente al Ms. Or 4445 (Londres) y a Codice de los Profetas de El Cairo'. *Sefarad* xx, 1955, pp. 3–30.

a reprint of the Ben Chaiyim-text, unfortunately not in the Biblia Hebraica.

It is now known that the greater part of the Aleppo Codex is safe. Isḥaḳ ben Zvi, the President of the State of Israel, has reported this in his article „כתר התורה" בן־אשר שנכתב בארץ ישראל" published in the periodical *Sinai*, vol. xliii, 1958, pp. 5–13, to which I have already referred.

In Bonn during my work on the Biblia Hebraica I had at my disposal the first Rabbinic Bible edited by Felix Pratensis in 1517; it had been sent to Bonn by the Library of the Marienkirche in Halle, and I used it for many years; and the second Rabbinic Bible edited by Jacob b. Chaiyim in 1524/5 was lent for the same purpose by the Universitätsbibliothek in Halle. The copy had previously belonged to the University of Wittenberg. I derived great profit from being able to compare these two important editions while I was editing the Ben Asher text. But I was not in the least interested in comparing the further 17 early printings of the Hebrew Bible which Ginsburg claimed to have used for his edition. I have already pointed out why these and similar printed editions are of little value from the point of view of textual criticism.

It was not necessary to use for more than occasional references the seventy-three Biblical MSS, the small differences of which Ginsburg had added to the textus receptus of Ben Chaiyim reprinted by him. I had long discussions with Ginsburg in London when the two volumes of the Prophets in his new edition had just appeared (1911). I asked him how he could use more than seventy MSS for an edition without trying to assign these MSS to different groups. He replied that it was not possible to do so. I agreed that it was really difficult for the later MSS, as these merely represent different stages of the Biblical text developed in the time between the Ben Asher and the Ben Chaiyim texts. They had influenced each other in different ways, and so it was difficult to classify them. But the older MSS which Ginsburg claims to have used represent quite distinct types of text. These texts, moreover, were centuries older than the *textus receptus* edited by Ginsburg. What connexion, for instance, with the *textus receptus*, which begins to appear in MSS after 1300, have MSS such as the earlier Ben Asher text of the Pentateuch preserved in the British Museum MS Or 4445 (beginning of the tenth century), Ginsburg's codex א; or different developments of the

Ben Naftali text, such as those preserved in the Reuchlin Codex of the Prophets (dated 1105) and in the British Museum MS Add 21161 (about 1150), his codices ג and ז; or the interesting specimen of a mixed text in the final development of the Babylonian punctuation, strongly influenced by the Tiberian Masora, as preserved in the Codex of the later Prophets in Leningrad (dated 916), his codex ב; or the oldest Yemenite MSS of the Pentateuch in the British Museum, MS Or 1467 and Or 2363 (twelfth century), his codices ו and ח? To do justice, for instance, to a text like the Codex Reuchlinianus, it would have had to be printed in a column parallel to and alongside of the *textus receptus*, as hardly any word in this codex is vocalized exactly as in the *textus receptus*.[1] Nearly the same could be said of the other MSS mentioned above. Ginsburg certainly knew these circumstances. The value of his edition lies in his collation of later Biblical MSS. For the little details in which they differ from each other Ginsburg has carefully collected a great amount of material, and whoever is interested in such details will find them in Ginsburg's edition, although the way in which they are made available by him makes it somewhat difficult to see the value of this material. For an edition of the Ben Asher text, however, these small differences of later MSS are unimportant.

The difference between the Ben Asher text and that edited by Ben Chaiyim may be illustrated by the following experience.

Dr. David Herzog, chief Rabbi of Steiermark and lecturer and later professor for thirty years at Graz University, was working in 1940 in the Bodleian Library on an old MS of a grammatical treatise composed by Ibn Ezra (died 1167). He was puzzled by the fact that the quotations from the Bible never agreed exactly with the text he found in his Hebrew Bible, a reprint of the Ben Chaiyim text. He asked me how this fact could be explained. I said: 'You cannot expect Ibn Ezra to quote a text which was fixed centuries after him; compare the Ben Asher text which I published in the Biblia Hebraica in 1937'. He had not heard of this edition, so I lent him my copy of it. A few days later he brought the copy back with the remark that the quotations of Ibn Ezra in the old Bodleian copy showed the closest agreement with the Ben Asher

[1] In his article 'Bemerkungen über die Vocalisation der Targume', (*Verhandlungen des Fünften Internationalen Orientalisten Congress*, Berlin, 1881, vol. ii.), Adalbert Merx dealt with the punctuation of the Codex and gave a few examples on pp. 186–88. Now the whole Codex has been published in facsimile in Copenhagen. See above, pp. 79, 123.

text published by me. In the printed editions of the treatises of Ibn Ezra the quotations are 'corrected' according to the *textus receptus* as printed by Jacob b. Chaiyim. This naïve method of textual criticism is generally followed by editors up to the present day. Anyone having to edit a vocalized Hebrew text is ashamed to publish it with the vocalization found in an old MS. He is convinced that it is his duty to adapt the vocalization to the rules of his Hebrew grammar based exclusively on the Ben Chaiyim text. It is clear that these rules are largely affected by the now published Ben Asher text. When Professor Nyberg, the orientalist of Uppsala University, came to the Congress of Orientalists held in September 1938 in Bonn, he told me that he was preparing a new Hebrew grammar according to the Ben Asher text, as no existing Hebrew grammars could be used for that text.

As a matter of curiosity I would like to mention that the editors of Sa'adya's great liturgical work *ǧāmi' aṣ-ṣalāwāt wat-tasābīḥ*, published under the title *Siddur R. Sa'adya Gaon* in Jerusalem, 1941, replaced the method of vocalization according to Ben Asher in the Bodleian MS (Neubauer 668 = Uri 261), on which the edition is mainly based, by a method of vocalization as used by Ben Chaiyim. Sa'adya was a contemporary of the Ben Asher; Ben Chaiyim lived 600 years later!

16. The Ben Asher Bible of the British and Foreign Bible Society

A new Ben Asher text is to be published by the British and Foreign Bible Society, in place of the Letteris Bible published by the Society up to now which is in the main a reprint of the Ben Chaiyim text. The Rev. Norman H. Snaith, of Wesley College, Headingley, Leeds, the editor of the new text, says in an article published in *Vetus Testamentum*, vol. vii, 1957, pp. 207f, that he has based his edition on his study of Spanish MSS in the British Museum, especially MS Or. 2625–2627 (read 2626–2628) and Or. 2375, together with the Shem Ṭob MS in the David Sassoon Library. These MSS have suffered the general fate and have been 'corrected' to the Ben Chaiyim text held to be the true Masoretic text up to my researches.

MS Or. 2626–8 of the British Museum is a beautifully illuminated Hebrew Bible written in Lisbon A.D. 1483, described by G. Margoliouth in his *Catalogue* under No. 62. Chr. D. Ginsburg deals with the MS in his *Introduction* under No. 48. According to Margoliouth it is the most profusely illuminated copy of the Hebrew Bible in the collection of the British Museum, and Chr. D. Ginsburg writes in his *Introduction*, p. 714: 'Of the numerous Codices which I have collated both at home and abroad, this is the most extensively illuminated MS of the Hebrew Bible'.

The second British Museum MS used by Snaith is Or. 2375. But this was written in South Arabia, not in Spain, at about the same time as the first one (A.D. 1460–80), and contains the Hagiographa only (cf. G. Margoliouth *Catalogue*, No. 147, and Ginsburg, *Introduction* No. 47). This MS certainly cannot be called a Spanish (Sephardic) MS.

The third MS used by Snaith is the so-called Shem Ṭob Bible, which is in the possession of the Sassoon family. In the Descriptive Catalogue of the Hebrew and Samaritan MSS in the Sassoon Library (London 1932) it is described as No. 82 on pp. 2–5. The Codex was written in Soria in Spain in the year 1312 in a somewhat peculiar way, so that one could raise doubts whether such a codex should be taken as a basis for an edition of a Hebrew text of the Bible in which nothing of the peculiarities of the codex could be mentioned. I may refer here to the description of the Codex in the Sassoon Catalogue and to that given before by D. Cazès (*REJ* xx, 1890, pp. 80–83) who had seen the Codex in the hands of a Tripoline family in Tunis. The codex must have been in Babylonia for some time in the hands of the later Geonim.[1]

Snaith began his work by studying Norzi's text-critical and masoretic commentary on the 24 books of the Hebrew Bible, called מנחת שי, a work finished in 1626 and printed for the first time in the Hebrew Bible published in Mantua in 1742. He had noticed that the readings of the Bible preferred by Norzi were mostly those found in Spanish manuscripts, and when he saw that these Spanish readings were generally in agreement with the Ben Asher text published by me in Kittel's Biblia Hebraica, he decided to take Sephardic MSS as the basis of his Bible. It will be found, he declares, that the text of his new Bible is very much closer to that published in the *Biblia Hebraica* than to any other text. 'This may be taken, I trust, as good evidence that his text and (mine) are sound representatives of the true Ben Asher tradition. Kahle

[1] See S. Poznanski, *Babylonische Geonim im nachgaonischen Zeitalter* . . . Berlin 1914.

and I have worked from completely different suppositions and we have achieved substantially the same result.'

That Norzi preferred Sephardic readings for the text of the Bible is to be explained by the fact that he had seen that these readings were based on Ben Asher MSS which must have been introduced into Spain at an early period when Spain became the great centre of Jewish learning. These Ben Asher MSS must have been copied by Jews in Spain with great care, and a manuscript of the Hebrew Bible written in Toledo in 1277 formed the chief basis of Norzi's text of the Bible. By comparing this text with the textus receptus of Ben Chaiyim, which he found in the printed Bibles, the great value of his Toledo manuscript became clear to him.

The manuscript used by Norzi is still preserved and accessible. It came into the possession of Johann Bernhard de Rossi. In his *Variae Lectiones Veteris Testamenti*, vol. i, Parmae 1784, p. cxxiii, the codex used by Norzi is described as Codex 782 in the words:

> Codex elegantissimus, accuratissimus, adeoque diligenter ad masorae leges compositus ut perfectissimum masorethici textus exemplar haberi debeat.

In the Parma Catalogue of the de Rossi Codices (vol. ii, Parmae 1803, p. 170) Codex 782 is described in the words:

> sed majus sane est pretium ac laus quae huic codici evenit ex uso critico quem ejus instituit R. Salomon Norzius, celebris elapsi seculi scriptor, tum in procuranda accuratissima Mantuana Bibliorum editione an. 1742, minhad scai מנחת שי communiter dicta, tum in ferendis in commentario, quem subjecit, de lectionum auctoritate perpetuis judiciis. Ubicumque enim proferentur MS Biblia Toletana noster hic codex intelligendus.

Norzi had no text of the Hebrew Bible at hand which was directly connected with Aaron b. Asher. The first codex of this kind was the complete Bible dated Old Cairo (Medīnat Miṣraiyim) 1008 or 1009, which was brought by Abraham Firkowitch to Odessa, first in 1839, and again in 1845 when he handed it over to the *Gesellschaft für Geschichte und Altertümer*; it was described by Dr. Moses Pinner in the *Nachtrag* to the *Prospectus*, Odessa 1845, on pp. 81–92. Later the Codex was brought to the Russian Public Library in Leningrad where it was described in the *Catalog der hebräischen Bibelhandschriften* by Harkavy and Strack, St. Petersburg, 1875, pp. 263–276.

Even this codex does not go back directly to Aaron ben Moshe ben Asher himself; but a certain Shemuel ben Jacob claims to have copied it from correct manuscripts prepared by Aaron b. Asher himself, and it is very likely that such manuscripts were available in Old Cairo some fifty years after Aaron's death. In any case, this is the oldest dated manuscript of the complete Bible that has come down to us, and it is this Codex I took as model of the Ben Asher text published in the Biblia Hebraica. There can be no doubt that here we have the Ben Asher text before us.

The Codex of the whole Bible which was preserved in the Synagogue of the Sephardic Jews in Aleppo was, according to a Colophon, provided with punctuation and Masora by Aaron b. Moshe b. Asher himself. Umberto Cassuto is the only modern scholar who has investigated the original of the Codex in Aleppo, but neither he nor, some twenty years ago, professors G. Weil and H. Ritter on my behalf got permission to take a photo of the Codex. During the struggle between the Jews and the Arabs in 1948 the codex disappeared. The greater part of it is now again in safety. Perhaps it may be possible in the near future to study this Codex more thoroughly.

17. The Text of the Arabic Koran

We have seen that the men who in the first half of the ninth century started to create a uniform punctuation of the text of the Hebrew Bible belonged to the community of the Ḳaraites. It was due to their efforts that within only a few decades the uniformly punctuated text of the Bible came into existence. This was regarded as an outstanding achievement, acknowledged in Palestine and Babylonia, by Rabbanites and Ḳaraites alike, as the authoritative text of the Hebrew Bible which they claimed could be traced back through the men of the Great Synagogue to Ezra. This text so thoroughly ousted everything that had previously existed in Palestine and Babylonia in the way of vocalized texts of the Bible that remnants of the latter have only been preserved in the Cairo Geniza.

We know that about a hundred years before the Masoretes of Tiberias began their task of establishing the correct reading of the Hebrew text of the Bible, their Arab rulers had had similar problems with their Holy Book, the Koran, the word of God revealed to the prophet Muḥammed (who died in 632). The consonantal text of the Koran had been collected shortly after Muḥammed's death, and was brought to its definitive form in the time of the third Caliph 'Othmān (644–55 A.D.). But now the great problem arose, how this text was to be read and recited correctly. Muḥammed was born in Mecca and belonged, like most of his fellow citizens, to the Arab tribe of Ḳuraish. The Arabic spoken by him was that of a citizen of Mecca, and the consonantal text reflects the Arabic spoken there. But the Arabs were accustomed to regard as the model for correct Arabic the language spoken by the Bedouin. In this language the famous pre-Islamic poetry was composed, and every Arab was proud of it. The word of God could not be read in a language inferior to any other. So in the chief centres of Islam at that early time, in Kufa, Baṣra, Medina, and Mecca, an intensive study of Bedouin poetry began. The students of this Arabic went out to the Bedouin in their neighbourhood and collected there as much as possible of their poetry, and the narratives connected with it, mostly reports of the little battles called 'the Days of the Arabs'. The material collected in that way became the basis of the work done by the Arabic readers. They established the model Arabic in every detail, and to this the language of the Koran was adapted. The consonantal text was not altered. But a method of reading the text correctly was developed, and all sorts of signs were added to the consonantal text in order to safeguard a correct reading.[1]

The books dealing with reading the Koran do not mention this early activity of the readers.[2] Books which may have mentioned it are lost. But I discovered in an Arabic MS dealing with the number of the verses of the Koran, belonging to the Collection of Sir Alfred Chester Beatty,[3] a notice which at least reflects this development. It is a quotation from al-Farrā' (who died in 821), one of the greatest authorities on Arabic grammar and on reading the Koran. Some years ago H. Ritter discovered in Istanbul an old MS (fourth century A.H.) of al-Farrā's Commentary on the Koran, the text of which had been dictated by the

[1] It is very likely that the Arabs began to add vowel signs to the text of the Koran in the first century A.H. Cf. O. Pretzl in Nöldeke's *Geschichte des Qorans*, 2nd ed., vol. iii, p. 262.

[2] Not a single treatise of this kind is mentioned by O. Pretzl in his article 'Die Wissenschaft der Koranlesung. Ihre literarischem Quellen und ihre Aussprachegrundlagen', in *Islamica*, vol. vi, Leipzig, 1934, pp. 1–47, 230–46, 290–331.

[3] It is MS Arab. 705, written A.H. 525=A.D. 1130. I have to express my thanks to Sir A. Chester Beatty for his permission to make use of the text.

author during the years 817–19.[1] Otto Pretzl, when referring to this MS,[2] says of the author:

'Die grammatischen Erklärungen von al-Farrā' werden von den Arabern selbst als das Vollendeste angesehen was auf dem Gebiete der Koranwissenschaft geleistet worden ist.'

I give the whole text in an English translation.[3]

Al-Farrā' says:

We have seen that the readers who know the Book (the Koran) and the practice (*sunna*) and are authorities on correct speech are agreed that it (the Koran) came down in the most correct forms of speech. This was opposed by some of those who investigated 'the poetry' and 'the Days of the Arabs'. They said: 'Those who claimed the excellence of the Koran have merely done so in accordance with what God ordained for honouring the Koran. But when we look for correctness of speech, we find it among the Bedouin'.

But in this they disagreed. The people of Kufa said: 'Correctness is to be found among the Asad', because of their vicinity to them. The people of Baṣra said: 'Correctness is to be found among the upper Tamīm and the lower Ḳais from 'Ukl and 'Uḳail'. The people of Medina said: 'Correctness is to be found among the Ghaṭafān', because they are their neighbours. The people of Mecca said: 'Correctness is to be found among Kināna b. Sa'd b. Bekr and Thaḳīf'.

We wished to refer them through traditions, analogy, and example to the superiority of the speech of the Ḳuraish over all other languages. So we said: 'Do not the Ḳuraish surpass the people in the beauty of their stature, in the sagacity of their minds, in the fullness of their bodies?' They said: 'We know that as well as anybody. But sagacity and beauty came to them merely because the Arabs used to come to the sanctuary (the Ka'ba) for Ḥajj and 'Umra (the two parts of the pilgrimage), both their women and their men. The women made the circuit round the House unveiled (*ḥawāsir*) and performed the ceremonies with uncovered faces. So they selected them by sight

[1] 'Philologica ii', by H. Ritter, in *Der Islam*, vol xvii, 1928, p. 249. It is MS Vehbi Ef Nr. 66. The Oriental Seminar of Bonn University possessed a photograph of this important MS.

[2] In the new edition of Theodor Nöldeke's *Geschichte des Qorans*, vol. iii, Leipzig, 1938, p. 247.

[3] Sir Hamilton Gibb kindly revised my translation and made some valuable suggestions in connexion with it. The Arabic text follows below as Appendix iv.

and sought after dignity and beauty. By this they gained superiority besides those qualities by which they were particularly distinguished.'

We said: 'In the same way they were accustomed to hear from the tribes of the Arabs their dialects; so they could choose from every dialect that which was best in it. So their speech became elegant, and nothing of the more vulgar forms of speech was mixed up with it. Do you not see that you will not find in their pronunciation the *'an'ana* of Tamīm[1] or the roughness in speech[2] of Ḳais, or the keskesa[3] of Rabi'a, or the Kesr (the i-vowel) which you hear from Ḳais and Tamīm, like *ti'lamūna*, *ti'lam*, and like *bi'ir*, *shi'ir* with Kesr of ta, ba, sin, shin?[4] Correctness came to them from their selection of pronunciation, just as from their selection of wives'.

And by this we refuted their arguments and reverted to the arguments of those who knew the Koran better than they.

And besides, we have heard that 'Omar b. al-Khaṭṭāb said: 'O Prophet of God, you came to us with a kind of speech of the Arabs which we do not know, although we are really Arabs'. Then the Prophet of God said: 'My Lord taught me, so I learned, and he corrected me, so I acquired correctness; and the superiority of the Koran to every other speech is as the superiority of God to His creatures'.

'Omar b. al-Khaṭṭāb heard a man reading *'atta ḥīnin* in the meaning of *ḥattā ḥīnin*. He said: 'Who taught you to recite thus?' He said: 'Abdallāh b. Mas'ūd.'[5] So he wrote to 'Abdallāh b. Mas'ūd: 'The Koran came down in the language of the Ḳuraish and it came not down in the language of the Hudhail. So do you teach men to recite it in the language of the Ḳuraish and not in the language of the Hudhail.'

[1] MS: *'an'a*; *'an'ana* is substituting 'ain for alif, cf. Lane, s.v.

[2] *'ajrafīye* means rough, guttural speech, cf. Lane, s.v.

[3] According to the Arabic grammarians (see Ibn Ya'īsh, p. 1245) the terms keskese and keshkeshe were used to signify the pronunciation of the suffix -ki alternatively as -kis or -si, and as -kish or -shi. This is mentioned as a characteristic of the language spoken also by the Rabī'a. Cf. K. Vollers, *Volkssprache und Schriftsprache im alten Arabien*, Strassburg, 1906, p. 11.

[4] To use i in these forms instead of a is mentioned as a characteristic of the Tamīm. Cf. the references given by Vollers, op. cit. p. 16.

[5] Ibn Mas'ūd (died about A.D. 652) was one of the earliest companions of the Prophet and knew perhaps more of him than any other Muslim. He was in possession of his own collections of Koranic material and was regarded as a special authority in matters of Koran and Sunna. The Caliph 'Omar had sent him to Kufa to teach Islam. There, he became the apostle of Islam for Babylonia and the East in general. The Hudhail mentioned here are a tribe of the Bedouin living between Mecca and Medina.

Abū Bekr as-Ṣiddīḳ said: 'The I'rāb of the Koran[1] is preferable to me rather than keeping some of its letters.'

Abu Huraira[2] is reported as saying: The Apostle of God said: 'Learn the Koran and hold fast to its strange words.'

Ibn Mas'ūd[3] said: 'Keep to the text of the Koran and adorn it with the best of pronunciations and read it with I'rāb (*a'ra-būhu*); for it is pure Arabic (*'arabīyun*), and God wishes it to be read with I'rāb (*an yu'raba*)'.

'Omar's son[4] beat his son for pronouncing incorrectly (*'ala-l-laḥn*).

Mujāhid[5] said: 'Verily I prefer to err in a verse than to make an error of pronunciation (*an alḥana*) in the Book of God.'

And he said:[6] ''Omar passed by some people who were contending for superiority in shooting. One of them spoke incorrectly (*laḥana*). 'Omar said: "Incorrectness in speech is worse than badness in shooting." '

'Abdalmalik b. 'Omair[7] related that 'Omar b. al-Khaṭṭāb said: 'None shall dictate our copies of the Koran except men of the Ḳuraish and Thaḳīf.'

Muḥammed b. Sa'dān said that 'Abdalwahhāb b. 'Aṭā al-Khaffāf[8] has reported from Sa'īd from Ḳatāda from Zarāra b. Aufā from Sa'd b. Hishām from 'Āisha from the Prophet . . . The expert in reading the Koran ranks with the noble pious recording angels. And he who recites it having an impediment in his speech, so that he says it twice,[9] gets double reward.'

This is a valuable testimony to the influence of Bedouin Arabic on the language of the Koran. Al-Farrā' cannot deny this influence. Correct Arabic is really to be found among the Bedouin. But he cannot admit any alteration in the language of the Holy

[1] I'rāb are the vocalic endings of the Arabic words according to the laws of the grammar of classical Arabic. The recommendation to read the Koran with these vocalic endings presupposes that they were often not read. In modern Arabic these vocalic endings are usually not read, and are observed only when it is intended to speak classical Arabic, adapted to Bedouin poetry and to the language of the Koran.

[2] Abu Huraira died about A.D. 677 in Medina. Nearly 3,500 traditions are attributed to him.

[3] Cf. p. 144, note 5.

[4] i.e. the son of the second Caliph, 'Omar b. al-Khaṭṭāb.

[5] Mujāhid b. Jabr Abu-l-Ḥajjāj, died about 720; cf. about him *Ibn Sa'd's Biographien*, ed. E. Sachau, vol. v, p. 343.

[6] The same tradition, with some variant readings and with other authorities, is mentioned by Ibn Sa'd, ed. E. Sachau, vol. iii, p. 204, l. 16. Cf. K. Vollers, *Volkssprache und Schriftsprache im alten Arabien*, p. 161.

[7] Cf. about him Ibn Sa'd, ed. E. Sachau, vol. vi, p. 220.

[8] Cf. about him Ibn Sa'd, ed. E. Sachau, vol. vii, 2, p. 76.

[9] The Arabic word is explained by 'his tongue sticks fast in doing so'. Cf. Lane, s.v. *ta'ta'a*, according to Tāj al-'arūs. See Ibn Mājah, adab, § 52. (Fück).

Book. For a good Muslim it is a matter of faith that the word of God was revealed in the most correct form of Arabic. Up to a few decades ago, conditions had not changed much since the time of al-Farrā'. When in 1905 Karl Vollers—an expert on classical Arabic and a special authority on modern Arabic as spoken in Egypt[1]—tried to show the influence of Bedouin poetry on the text of the Koran at the International Orientalist Congress in Algiers, his lecture provoked a real revolt among the Muslim members of that congress.[2]

Al-Farrā' found himself in a difficult position. In his capacity as a *grammarian* he could not deny that correct Arabic was closely connected with the poetry of the Bedouin. As a good *Muslim* he was convinced that the word of God was revealed to the Prophet in the best and most correct language. As a *theologian* he could not admit any alteration in the language of the Holy Book. Therefore he had to find a compromise. He antedated the influence of Bedouin poetry to an earlier period. Long before the Koran was revealed to the Prophet, the language of the Ḳuraish had been influenced by the Arabic of the Bedouin. The Ḳuraish in Mecca had heard from Arabic pilgrims all sorts of Arabic speech, and so they had been able to select the best 'just as they had selected their wives'. In this way the Arabic spoken by the Ḳuraish had become the most perfect Arabic. Al-Farrā' can show that this language is superior to any Bedouin Arabic. It has neither a wrong pronunciation of gutturals, nor wrong vowels, both of which occur in some of the dialects spoken by the Bedouin. This ideal Arabic, in reality the result of the work done by the readers of the Koran and the grammarians, was identified by al-Farrā' with the language spoken by the Ḳuraish in the time of the Prophet. In this perfect language the Koran is supposed to have been revealed to the Prophet. Again and again the necessity of correctly reading the holy texts is emphasized in the quotations of al-Farrā'

[1] For many years Vollers was the director of the Bibliothèque Khédiviale in Cairo and made extensive studies of the Arabic spoken in Egypt; cf. his 'Beiträge zur Kenntnis der lebenden arabischen Sprache in Ägypten', *ZDMG*, 41 (1887), 50 (1896), 51 (1897). Later he was a professor at the University of Jena.

[2] See the preface to his book *Volkssprache und Schriftsprache im alten Arabien*, Strassburg, 1906. Vollers was not very cautious in his statements. Even the title of his book is misleading. Muḥammed certainly did not use a *Volkssprache*, but the language of the reputable Ḳuraish in Mecca, and their language cannot be contrasted with a *Schriftsprache* which, after all, was only developed during the following centuries. Cf. the detailed review of his book by Rudolf Geyer in *Göttingische Gelehrte Anzeigen*, 1909, pp. 10–56. But Vollers is certainly right in stating that Arabic as spoken by the Ḳuraish in Mecca differed widely from the ideal Arabic as fixed by the readers of the Koran in accordance with Bedouin poetry.

and one is under the impression that these exhortations were necessary to stop a prevalent habit of lax reading and to enforce an exact reading.

The material assembled by al-Farrā' is richly supplemented by a large book—hitherto quite unknown—composed by al-Ḥasan b. Muḥammed al-Mālikī (died A.H. 438, A.D. 1046), under the title: 'The Introduction to the knowledge of Koran recitation', *at-tamhīd fī ma'rifat at-taǧwīd.* I found a MS of this work in the Collection of rare Arabic MSS of Sir Alfred Chester Beatty (MS J 152, written A.H. 613). In the sixth chapter of the Tamhīd are to be found more than 120 exhortations to read the Koran in a correct manner, with I'rāb, i.e. by taking into consideration all the nominal and verbal endings which are to be found in the classical Arabic language, but which in colloquial Arabic are usually omitted. In my article 'The Qur'ān and the 'Arabīya', published in the *Ignace Goldziher Memorial Volume* Part i (Budapest 1948, pp. 163–184) I discussed this book in detail. I translated and explained the first 67 of the exhortations quoted by al-Mālikī. They are those attributed to the Prophet himself and to his contemporaries. I have also dealt with the whole problem in my article, 'The Arabic Readers of the Koran'.[1]

With my friend Johannes Fück of Halle University I had a very instructive correspondence regarding these traditions. He pointed out that a large number of the traditions found in *tamhīd* are also to be found in the great collection of Ḥadīth Material published by al-Muttaḳī al-Hindī (died about 1567) under the title *Kanz al-'ummāl* (Hyderabad 1894–6), although they are not so impressively grouped together as in the *tamhīd* but are scattered through many chapters in the large book and so are less conspicuous.

Fück also pointed out that none of these traditions are to be found in the works of al-Bukhārī or Muslim and that they hardly can belong to the first century A.H., but cannot be later than the second century A.H., as al-Farrā' is aware of them. It is well known that Islamic traditions cannot be regarded as sayings of those people to whom they are attributed, but they show clearly the problems which affected Muslims at the time when they were attributed to the Prophet and his contemporaries, and for this period they have to be regarded as sources of first rank. The exhortations on correct reading of the Koran quoted by al-Farrā' and al-Mālikī were in particular devoted to the

[1] *Journal of Near Eastern Studies*, Chicago, vol. viii, 1949, pp. 65–71.

reading of the Koran with I'rāb, and this was a real problem in the course of the second century of the Hijra (A.D. 719–815), and particularly in the second half of this period.

Gotthelf Bergsträsser, in his report on reading the Koran in the first centuries of Islam which was published in the new edition of the third part of Theodor Nöldeke's *Geschichte des Qorans*, used as his main source the historical retrospect given by al-Ǧazarī (died 1429 A.D.) in his *kitāb an-našr fi'l-ḳirā'āt al-'ašr* (book of the development in the readings of the Ten). Al-Ǧazarī is justly regarded as one of the chief authorities in his branch of studies. But in a book of so late an author we cannot find a trace of the older traditions on reading the Koran. He does not deal with problems which were shocking for people of a later time. Bergsträsser did not take sufficient account of this fact. Otto Pretzl tried to collect all available material in his *Quellen der Ḳirā'āt-Wissenschaft.*[1] But he had not a single book dealing with these old traditions. He begins with ed-Dānī (died 1073) who was the first exponent of the authentic reading of the Koran and several of whose writings he published in the *Bibliotheca Islamica II and III, 1930 and 1932.* Of the many books listed in the Fihrist by Ibn an-Nadīm, almost nothing is preserved, and it is very likely that such books on reading the Koran were deliberately destroyed because they dealt with problems which had lost their relevance and might offend good Muslims in later times. To these books belonged also Ṭabarī's *kitāb al-ḳirā'āt* the loss of which is deplored by Nöldeke.[2]

The great value of the two books which I discovered in the library of Sir Alfred Chester Beatty consists in the fact that they are the remnants of a literature which had a wide circulation and which for certain reasons disappeared. We can understand the ever recurring exhortation to read the Koran correctly and with I'rāb only if the Koran was at the time widely read incorrectly and without I'rāb and it was necessary to insist on the correct reading of the Koran.

Vollers comments in his book mentioned above (p. 181):

> Of the first importance were I'rāb and pronunciation of Hamza; here every kind of haggling was excluded; both were carried through rigorously, without regard to the dialect, rhyme and culture of the author.

[1] It is in the first chapter of his work, 'Die Wissenschaft der Koranlesung', *Islamica* vi, 1933, pp. 4–47.

[2] *Neue Beiträge zur semitischen Sprachwissenschaft*, Strassburg, 1910, p. 2.

In the quotations of al-Farrā' and al-Mālikī, we find the best confirmation of what Vollers had observed. Theodor Nöldeke sharply criticized Vollers' comments. His main argument against Vollers is:

> If the Prophet and his faithful followers had read the Koran without I'rāb, the tradition of it would not have completely disappeared.

The traditions missed by Nöldeke have played an important role in older books on reading the Koran. These books have mainly disappeared. Exhortations to read the Koran correctly and with I'rāb are the only form in which such traditions can be expected in Islamic sources. We find such exhortations in al-Farrā', and al-Mālikī collected them in his *Tamhīd* in a very impressive way. It is understandable that books of this kind have disappeared, but their loss does not entitle us to disregard these matters completely in a scientific description of the history of reading the Koran, as was done by Bergsträsser and Pretzl in the new edition of the third part of Nöldeke's *Geschichte des Qorans*.

The systematic adaptation of the text of the Koran to Bedouin poetry triumphed over and obliterated the older forms of the Holy Book. For more than 1,200 years, since about 700, this ideal Arabic has been regarded as the original language of the Koran. From this point of view the work of the readers on the text of the Koran can be regarded as that of 'establishing the text in its integrity'.

18. The Hebrew Text of the Bible before the Tiberian Masoretes

After the time of the great Arab conquest in the seventh century the Jews were living in Palestine and in Babylonia, the chief centres of their activity, under Arab rule. In former times Palestine had been for centuries part of the Byzantine empire, and Babylonia had been part of the Sassanid empire. The frontiers had in some ways impeded the exchange of ideas, and that was why different shoots had grown from a common root. From the mainly uniform Mishna text a Palestinian and a Babylonian Talmud had been developed. Besides the old Palestinian Targums written in an Aramaic language well understood in Palestine, official Targums to Torah and Prophets had come into existence in Babylonia. These however were not composed in the Aramaic current in that country, but in the old Aramaic as used from Persian days. This was done in the firm belief that the widest circulation for the Targums would be secured in such a way.

That also different methods of punctuation of Hebrew had been developed in Palestine and in Babylonia we know only from the rich amount of vocalized Biblical texts preserved in the Geniza of Old Cairo.

Before developments in pronunciation parallel to the system established by the Masoretes of Tiberias became known, it was not possible to look beyond the Masoretic system which stood before us as an inexplicable phenomenon. Nobody could say how it came into being, nor how it was developed. It was like a miracle for which one explanation only could be given: the pronunciation of Hebrew as fixed by the Masoretes of Tiberias was handed down by them unanimously and exactly in the form in which it was transmitted to them, and by the long chain of their trustworthy successors every guarantee was given that they had established the text exactly as read from time immemorial, in the golden days when the Temple was still in existence, when sacrifices were offered and services were held there; indeed, ever since the days of Ezra and the men of the Great Synagogue.

The Masoretes did everything in their power to foster this idea. They eliminated all remnants of earlier pronunciation so radically that no pre-Masoretic texts were allowed to be preserved. The first specimens of earlier punctuation to re-emerge were found in the Cairo Geniza, where they had been stored in order to be destroyed. It was contrary to the intention of the Masoretes that these remnants were preserved there. The Masoretes had wished to ensure that the punctuation finally fixed by them should be the only authoritative one and should alone survive. Thus it became possible to regard the text fixed by these Tiberian Masoretes as something to which, in a slightly modified form, the famous words of Vincent of Lerins could be applied:

quod semper, quod ubique, quod ab omnibus traditum erat,

as a text which in this very form had been transmitted always, everywhere, by everybody—just as the ideal text of the Koran has been regarded as its original form for more than 1200 years.

The material preserved in the Geniza gives us the opportunity to go behind this complicated system of punctuation elaborated by the Masoretes.

Since I discovered in a Berlin MS (Or qu 680) from Yemen, more than fifty years ago, the first specimen of a real Babylonian text of the Bible, a great number of such texts have been discovered, chiefly in the Cairo Geniza. Recently, Professor Alejandro Diez Macho, of Barcelona, while working in the Library of the Jewish Theological Seminary of America in New York, found a great deal of new material. We have now at our disposal nearly half the Bible provided with Babylonian punctuation. An interesting report from Ḳirḳisānī[1] who wrote in the first half of the tenth century tells us that the Babylonian reading (*ḳirā'at al-'Irāḳī*) was used in a great part of the world, from ar-Rakka on the Euphrates to the Chinese frontiers, by most people living in Mesopotamia, Khurasān, Fāris, Kirmān, Iṣfahān, Yamāma, Baḥrain, al-Yemen and other countries. Ḳirḳisānī refers for this information to a certain Ja'ḳūb b. Efraim ash-Shāmī of whom we unfortunately know nothing, but it is certain that his report refers to the time before the text fixed by the Masoretes of Tiberias was known and had any authority outside Palestine. It is of some importance that publication is to be expected soon of such texts as are certainly independent of the texts fixed by the Tiberian Masoretes.

For the pronunciation of Hebrew used in Palestine at the time before the Masoretes of Tiberias began their work we can get some information from a few texts of the Bible provided with Palestinian punctuation. These texts, however, had already been influenced by the work of the Tiberian Masoretes—at an early date and in different ways. Comparatively little influenced are the texts written on scrolls to which some Palestinian vowels have been added. I have published the fragments of a Geniza Scroll, a few columns with the text of Ezekiel,[2] and some fragments with the text of the Psalms which I have discussed have been published by Dr. A. Murtonen.[3]

An interesting specimen of a text with Palestinian vocalization worked over by a Tiberian Masorete has been discovered by Professor A. Diez Macho in the Library of the Jewish Theological Seminary of America in New York,[4] containing the end of

[1] *Kitāb al-anwār, wal-marāḳib*, II 16, p. 135. Cf. Georges Vajda, in *Revue des Etudes Juives cvii*, 1946–47, pp. 91 f.

[2] Cambridge, T–S 20. 59 in Masoreten des Westens ii, 1930, pp. 69–72.

[3] Cambridge T–S 10. 52–54, 58, in A. Murtonen, *Materials for a non-Masoretic Hebrew Grammar* . . . Helsinki 1958 (Academic Dissertation) pp. 22f. (MS c), pp. מט-לג.

[4] Diez Macho, Importants Manuscrits Hébreux et Araméens aux États Unis, in *Volume de Congrès. Strassbourg* 1956, *VT*, Supplement IV, Leiden 1957, pp. 27f.

Qohelet and the beginning of Lamentations, and I am publishing it in Appendix iii. We see from it how a text of the Bible to which the copyist of the MS had added some Palestinian vowels and accents has been worked over by a Tiberian masorete at a time when the Tiberian vocalization was still in its early stages. It is fortunate that such a specimen has been preserved to us.

But we have seen that the Palestinian punctuation was used in all kinds of Hebrew texts: in particular a great number of liturgical texts have been preserved and these have not been influenced by the Tiberian Masora. In these liturgical texts a great number of biblical verses are quoted, and when these are written in full and provided with punctuation they provide us with specimens of Hebrew as it was read in Palestine before the Masoretes of Tiberias began their work.

A. Murtonen, in his Academic Dissertation, *Materials for a non-Masoretic Hebrew Grammar I* (Helsinki 1958), has observed that there is a comparatively large manuscript which contains a frequent, in many parts almost complete vocalization; it is the Oxford MS. Heb. d. 55, fols. 4–7, 9–14, his MS a, and he considered it possible, therefore, to compose a sketch of a grammar of the Hebrew language according to the Palestinian tradition, chiefly in connexion with the treatment of the punctuation of this manuscript. In its vocalization four hands appear. The first and second ones differ from each other, however, in some isolated instances only, so that normally they are treated as a whole. The third hand appears rarely, while the fourth hand is Tiberian and, consequently, not taken into account.

The grammatical sketch shows that there are many forms which deviate from the Tiberian forms, or are remarkable in some way. Murtonen has mentioned these deviations so that the reader of his book may be aware of them. But he insists that he has only been able to write a sketch of a grammar from this material. Yet we see that the forms given by him are very often closely related to the Samaritan pronunciation of Hebrew. His intention is to study thoroughly the Samaritan material and to compose a historical grammar of Samaritan Hebrew—this time not a sketch, but a real grammar, as the material will be sufficient for that.

The final aim is, as the title of his book says, to compose a grammar on the basis of all non-masoretic traditions. Of these the Samaritan is by far the most important, but other traditions also must be made use of, in the first instance Dead Sea scrolls in which the pronunciation is marked by plene-writing, and the readings of the Second Column of the Hexapla.

19. The Pronunciation of Hebrew by the Samaritans

It has been established that a pronunciation of Hebrew closely resembling that in the Palestinian texts has been used up to the present day by the Samaritans. This pronunciation of Hebrew is clearly different from the Hebrew fixed by the Masoretes of Tiberias and used by the Jews in all parts of the world. However differently the pronunciation of Hebrew has developed in the different lands, all these forms are based ultimately on the text fixed by the Masoretes, as it is preserved in our Hebrew Bible. The pronunciation of the Samaritans is the only one which is independent of the Masoretic text, and that this pronunciation of the Samaritans goes back at least in part to a very old tradition has been proved by manuscripts from the Dead Sea as far as they show strong plene-writing. I have proved in my contribution to the Festschrift for Alfred Bertholet[1] that the orthography לכמה etc. found for instance in the first Isaiah Scroll has been preserved up to the present day by the Samaritans, although they do not write the ending ה in their texts. They have therefore retained up to the present day a pronunciation clearly found in pre-Christian MSS, but rejected by the Jews already at the time of the reorganization of Judaism after the destruction of the Temple, almost 1900 years ago; for we find no trace of it in the transliterated texts which Origen has included in the Hexapla.

The Samaritans are firmly convinced that the way in which the Torah is read daily in their services has been handed down from father to son from time immemorial. That their pronunciation of Hebrew has not undergone an essential change in the last 600 years can be proved by a number of Samaritan MSS of the Torah provided with vowel signs. I found four of such MSS and entered their vowel signs in my copy of Gall's edition of *Der Hebräische Pentateuch der Samaritaner*, Giessen 1914–18. These entries of mine and some other material and notes by Arthur Schaade, of which I shall speak later, were the basis for the book published by Fritz Diening *Das Hebräische bei den Samaritanern. Ein Beitrag zur vormasoretischen Grammatik des Hebräischen.*[2]

[1] 'Zur Aussprache des Hebräischen bei den Samaritanern'. *Festschrift Alfred Bertholet zum* 80. *Geburtstag*, Tübingen, 1950. pp. 261–65; =*Opera Minora*, Leiden 1956, pp. 180–85.

[2] Bonner Orientalische Studien, no. 24, Stuttgart, 1938.

A new edition of the Hebrew Pentateuch of the Samaritans is being prepared by Professor Pérez Castro in Madrid on the basis of the oldest Samaritan MSS of the Torah not used by Herr von Gall. In particular Pérez Castro will use the famous Abisha' scroll from Nāblus of which he was able to obtain a photograph. That part of it which is old he will publish in facsimile with a transcript.[1] The text of the Samaritan Pentateuch which he intends to edit will be provided with the vocalization of the MS belonging to Trinity College Library, Cambridge, in the text, and that of the other MSS (London, Leningrad, Istanbul) in the notes.

That the Samaritan pronunciation of Hebrew has not undergone much change is also attested by some Arabic writings of the Samaritans dealing with the Hebrew language, to which Nöldeke first drew attention.[2] But at that time our knowledge of the transmission of the pronunciation of Hebrew by the Samaritans was very imperfect and Nöldeke's conclusions taken from these texts require to be modified in several ways.

Quite recently the Arabic texts composed by the Samaritans on their Hebrew language have been published in their entirety by Zeeb Ben Ḥayyim.[3] The two volumes have 666 + ix pages, and more volumes will follow. There is no doubt that some valuable texts have been published here, for instance a kind of vocabulary, listing Hebrew, Arabic and Samaritan equivalents. I have known a manuscript of this text for nearly sixty years, and am glad that it has been included under No. XI on pp. 437–616; it will be quite useful to have this vocabulary to hand. One may, however, ask whether it was necessary to publish all these Arabic texts, most of which are of little importance, and one may also ask for whom a modern Hebrew translation of all these texts will be of help. Jews in Israel unable to read these Arabic texts will certainly not be able to help in the study of them. Although nobody will deny that Z. Ben Hayyim has been very industrious over a period of

[1] F. Pérez Castro, 'El Sefer Abišá'. El antiguo y célebre rollo del Pentateuco Samaritano de Nablus puede, por fin, ser objetode investigación textual', *Sefarad*, xiii, 1953, pp. 119–29, with the reproduction of five columns of the text (Dt. v 25–xiii 19), containing the colophon. Cf. my article 'The Abisha' Scroll of the Samaritans', in *Studia Orientalia Ioanni Pedersen Septuagenario . . . dicata*, Hauniae 1953, pp. 188–92.

[2] Theodor Nöldeke, 'Über einige samaritanisch-arabische Schriften die hebräische Sprache betreffend', *Göttinger Gelehrte Nachrichten*, nos. 17, 20, 1862.

[3] *The Literary and Oral tradition of Hebrew and Aramaic amongst the Samaritans*, vols. i and ii: The Grammatical, Masoretical, and Lexicographical Writings of the Samaritans, critically edited with Hebrew translation, commentary, and introduction. Jerusalem 1957. The Bialik Institute and the Academy of the Hebrew Language.

nearly twenty years in collecting the material for this book, a translation into some European language of one or two of the most important texts with references to the others would have been a more valuable contribution to scholarship. Perhaps this compilation may be of service to a scholar who will prepare a grammar of the Hebrew used by the Samaritans in their divine services. But what shall we do with the translations into modern Hebrew? Besides, for such a grammar many other sources must be taken into account.

Heinrich Petermann tried to transcribe the Samaritan pronunciation of Hebrew as spoken to-day. During his stay in Nāblus he had asked the High Priest ʻAmram to read slowly before him the Hebrew text of Genesis, and he inserted the Hebrew vowel signs into the copy of the Samaritan Pentateuch of Blayney,[1] which he had before him. From this vocalized copy of the text printed in Hebrew letters he made, when he had returned to Germany, a transcription of Genesis in Latin letters. This transcribed text he published and made the basis of his *Versuch einer hebräischen Formenlehre nach der Aussprache der heutigen Samaritaner.*[2]

This transcribed text has some value through the vowels which Petermann had added at the dictation of the High Priest, but it is misleading in its rendering of the consonants, where Petermann followed in the main the rules of the Tiberian Masoretes. And the texts transcribed by Petermann are entirely useless as he omitted to indicate the stress of the words, which differs completely in Samaritan reading from what is indicated in the text of the Tiberian Masoretes.

While I was in Nāblus (three days in 1906 and a fortnight in 1908) I had other problems to discuss with the Samaritans.

In 1917 I received a letter from Hellmut Ritter then in Nāblus; he had known me in his student days in Halle and was aware of my interest in the Samaritans. He had visited the Samaritan High Priest, Isaac b. ʻAmram, the son of Petermann's informant, whom I knew very well, and had given him my greetings. He enclosed a letter from him together with 23 verses from the first chapter of Genesis, which he had written down at the dictation of the High Priest, without realizing their value.

[1] *Pentateuchus Hebraeo-Samaritanus charactere Hebraeo-Chaldaico . . .* ed. Benjamin Blayney, Oxford, 1790. The edition is mainly based on Kennicott.

[2] Abhandlungen für die Kunde des Morgenlandes, Band v, no. 1, Leipzig 1868.

This specimen of transcription was most important. It reproduced not only the vowels as spoken by the Samaritans, which Petermann had already recorded, but also the consonants as pronounced by them. The stress of the words also was carefully recorded. The whole transcription had been done by one who understood that type of work. I asked Ritter to continue with the transcription if it was at all possible. He himself had no time to do it as he had to leave Nāblus shortly afterwards. But he asked Arthur Schaade, who was also serving in Nāblus at the time, to take over. Schaade accepted and worked carefully. He transcribed a large number of chapters from the Torah at the dictation of the priest 'Amram, Isaac's son.

Schaade had become in 1911 Privatdozent in Breslau and in 1913 and 1914 he was Director of the then Khedivial Library in Cairo. After the war he came to Hamburg (1919) as professor of Arabic and began to copy his transcriptions of the Samaritan Pentateuch made in Nāblus. On the 27th October 1922 he sent me a few specimens of it to Giessen together with a letter in which he wrote:

> Herewith 32 pages fair copy of my Samaritan transcriptions, comprising Gen. i, 24–iv, 14; vi, 9–vii, 3. I further have Gen. vii, 4–ix; xi, 1–9; xii; xviii, 1–16; xxii, 1–17; xxxvii; xxxix–xl; Exod. ii–iv, 18. In case you need certain forms from these specimens please let me know. I shall however soon complete the fair copy to start with the phonetical and grammatical explanations of my texts which so far have not gone beyond the first three chapters of Genesis . . .

I copied Schaade's fair copy, and his transcriptions were used and gratefully acknowledged by me and my pupils. My requests for further material did not meet with success. He had turned to his Arabic studies.

Schaade was later again active in Cairo for a few years, this time as a professor at the Egyptian State University; there and again in Hamburg he was busy with other problems. On 22nd October 1952 he died in Hamburg without having continued with his work on his transcriptions.

The Hebrew Bible MSS from the caves near the Dead Sea, provided with strong plene-writing, and special studies on Hebrew texts with Palestinian punctuation made me realize once more the importance of Schaade's transcriptions from 1917. I asked

Frau Schaade about the fate of the material and was told that, together with the other remains of his scholarly work, it had gone to the State and University Library in Hamburg. The Director of the Hamburg Library, Professor Dr. Tiemann, with the consent of Frau Schaade, kindly put them at my disposal with permission to utilize and publish them.

Schaade had only copied a few verses more than he had sent to me in 1922. Using his original transcriptions I copied the texts as Schaade had taken them down in Nāblus in 1917. The papers had suffered a little in the course of the years but in the main it was possible to read them correctly. After having received permission from Hamburg I sent my copies with the originals to Finland to Dr. Murtonen who had recently been for nearly a year in Palestine and had discussed in detail with the Samaritans their pronunciation of Hebrew. As an expert he has prepared the text recorded by Ritter and Schaade for publication, and I publish it in the Appendix.

There is no doubt that Schaade's transcriptions have a lasting value. They were made by a philologist who was an exact phonetician and who had a good scientific grasp of Hebrew. That he was not a specialist in problems of the Hebrew spoken by the Samaritans when he made the transcriptions does not matter. It enhances the objectivity of his work. The same applies of course to the first 23 verses of Genesis taken down by Professor Ritter. He used a slightly different method of transcription. The publication of this material will make a scientific inquiry possible. Dr. Murtonen has discovered in Schaade's notes some entirely new material of which nobody else has any idea.

20. The Second Column of the Hexapla

Much more vocalized Hebrew, independent of the work of the Tiberian Masoretes, is further to be found in the Hebrew text in Greek transliteration taken over as Second Column of the Hexapla by Origen. The palimpsest discovered by Giovanni Mercati in the Ambrosiana in Milan in the nineties of last century which contains about 150 Psalm verses in the second to the sixth columns, the first specimen of a continuous text of the Hexapla found so far, has been very carefully examined by Cardinal Mercati and is now being published by Professor G. Castellino, commissioned by the Bibliotheca Vaticana. The facsimile reproduction of the Milan fragments and the deciphering of the texts by Cardinal Mercati are already in print and have been sent to me by the kindness of Eugène Cardinal Tisserant and Monsignore Anselmo Albareda, Prefetto della Bibliotheca Vaticana. I am very grateful that I was able to study these texts before their definitive publication. Giovanni Cardinal Mercati spent a great part of his life in the study of this material and its publication will enable us to begin a new study of the Hexapla and the whole problem of the Septuagint. His collection of Hexaplaric material from a great many manuscripts will add much to the material published about eighty years ago by Field, and will also give Mercati's commentary on the text which he has deciphered.

Cardinal Mercati has made a special investigation of the Second Column of the Hexapla, containing the Hebrew text in Greek transcription.[1] He tries to prove that this text, transcribed into Greek, comes from Origen himself or was made on his initiative. He thinks that Origen, while copying the first column containing the Hebrew text in Hebrew letters, of which no trace has been found so far, put the Greek transcription immediately next to it. Mercati admits that Origen may have had Jewish helpers for this task. Yet it could not have been at all easy to produce the whole Hebrew Bible in Greek transcription with vocalization. Even if one is prepared to grant to Origen far more knowledge of Hebrew than he himself admits, and if one takes into account that he learned much during the work, the task for a non-Jew must have been enormous.

There can hardly be any doubt that this work was done by Jews who from childhood had read the Bible and knew it almost by heart. The Jews created this text for those of their fellow believers who could not read the non-vocalized Hebrew text. This has been proved by Ludwig Blau in his book *Zur Einleitung in die Heilige Schrift* (Budapest 1894), where he deals on pp. 80–83 with Biblical Codices in foreign characters. Unfortunately Mercati did not see Blau's book, and he depends for his criticism of Blau on an article of Orlinski[2] and on a review written by Blau of Friedmann's book on *Onkelos and Akylas*,[3] but in neither of these is Blau's principal argument given and so I quote the relevant part of what Blau has to say on the matter as follows:

[1] 'Il Problema della Colonna II del Esaplo', Estratto da *Biblica* 28, Città del Vaticano, 1947, pp. 1–30, 175–215.

[2] *JQR*, xxvii, p. 140, n. 10.

[3] *JQR*, ix, 1896/7, pp. 728–30.

I regard the Baraitha Schabbath 115a[1] as the chief proof: 'If they (the Biblical texts) are written in Coptic, Medic, 'Ibric, Elamic or Greek—although it is not permitted to use them for reading, they may be saved from the fire'. As I have already stated above, the reference must here be to specimens of Hebrew texts written in the characters of the languages mentioned, as *'ibrit*, by which normally must be understood the Hebrew language, would otherwise have no meaning. The precept derived from this Baraitha in Soferim 1.7[2] mentions expressly all kinds of writing besides all languages. The little post-Talmudic treatise Sefer Tora 1.8[3] contains the prohibition: one must not write in (old) Hebrew, Medic, Elamic, Greek.

An old-fashioned Rabbi who certainly did not know anything of Origen's Εβραϊκον, Jacob Halevi of Worms, in whose name the editor gives several explanatory remarks, states that the reference here is to foreign forms of writing, not to foreign languages (although the editor himself does not accept this meaning as it is contrary to the Tosaphot). We have here proof that for the simple method of interpretation, this explanation is much more obvious than the generally accepted one referring the Baraitha to foreign languages. Even although the Talmud understood the Baraitha as referring to different languages this cannot prevent us from preferring the simpler interpretation, all the more as we know a Hebrew text in Greek letters in the Hexapla. This proof can be established in the same way also from the Baraitha Megilla 18a[4] where it is said that the scroll of Esther can be read to the Copts in Coptic, to the Hebrews in Hebrew, to the Elamits in Elamitic, to the Greeks in Greek . . . 'If he has read it in Coptic, Hebrew, Elamitic, Medic, Greek, he has not fulfilled his duty'.

The traditions mentioned, Blau believes, show effectively the existence of Biblical books in the Hebrew language written in foreign characters at least by the second century (A.D.). The Second Column of the Hexapla does not owe its appearance to an idea of Origen, as such Graeco-Hebrew Codices existed already before his time. Origen found this kind of text in existence like

[1] היו כתובין גיפטית מדית עברית עילמית יוונית אף על פי שלא ניתנו לקרות בהן מצילין אותן מפני הדליקה.

[2] אין כותבין לא עברית ולא ארמית ולא מדית ולא יוונית כתב בכל לשון בכל הכתובים (כתבים) ולא יקרא בו עד שתהא כתובה אשורית. The same in Massecheth Soferim 1.8 in שלשה ספרים נפתחים, Ed. S. Schönblum (Lemberg 1877) כתב בכל הלשונות בכל הכתובין כלם אין קורין בו.

[3] *Septem libri Talmudici parvi Hierosolytani* . . . ed. Raphael Kirchheim (Frankfurt a. M. 1857 אין כותבים עברית ולא מדית ולא עילמית ולא יוונית.

[4] Baraitha Megilla 18a קראה גיפטית עיברית עילמית מדית יוונית לא יצא.

the Hebrew text and the different translations. Owing to his poor knowledge of Hebrew he was not equipped for the task even with the help of a Jewish assistant. Blau further refers to the general need for such kinds of transliterated texts for the Jews.

The other Semitist with whom Mercati has to do is Joseph Halévy. In an article 'L'origine de la transcription du texte hébreu en caractères grecs dans les Hexaples d'Origène' in the *Journal Asiatique*,[1] Halévy had indicated some passages in the Palestinian Talmud and in Canticum Rabba from which he wanted to prove that the Jews also used the Hebrew text in Greek transcription during the services in the Synagogues, particularly in the Synagogue of Caesarea where Origen lived.

I think it is quite possible that this was done, but it is certain that the passages indicated by Halévy do not prove it. Mercati was quite emphatic when he pointed out that the passages do not contain what Halévy read into them, and there can be no doubt that Cardinal Mercati is right, and he is here in complete agreement with Ludwig Blau who declared already in his book of 1894: 'Other proofs for writing the Hebrew original with foreign characters cannot be given.' We cannot expect in Jewish texts a clear statement on such matters. Since Christianity had become the religion of the State, the Jews' dislike of everything written in Greek had increased to such a degree that we may take for granted that passages which may once have referred to such transcribed texts of the Bible were altered or omitted later.

There is no question that the transcribed text of the Bible as presented in this instance is consistent,[2] and that the text of the transcription agrees in essentials with our Hebrew consonantal text.[3] But a recent discovery has shed new light on the origin

[1] 9 Sér. xvii, 1901, pp. 335–41.

[2] I spoke about it in my book, just mentioned, pp. 44 f. Alexander Sperber, in *HUCA* xii/xiii, Cincinnati, 1937/8, p. 108 contested the consistency of the transcribed text of the second column on the ground that the transcription usually agrees with that of Cod. A of the Septuagint, but at times also with that of Cod. B. But F. X. Wutz had already shown that the transcriptions of personal names in Cod. B usually follow older methods of transcription, whereas the transcriptions of Cod. A have to a great extent been adapted to the system of transcription of the second column. At other times, the transcription of Cod. B has been revised and Cod. A contains older forms of the transcription. In his work, Sperber referred only to the transcriptions of these two Codices of the Greek Bible.

[3] Einar Brønno in his work, 'Studien über Hebräische Morphologie und Vokalismus auf Grund der Mercatischen Fragmente der zweiten Kolumne der Hexapla' (*AKM* xxviii, Leipzig 1943, pp. 445–47) assembled a large number of variants of the transcribed text against the Tiberian Bible text. But only the consonantal texts can really be compared with each other. The Tiberian vocalization did not exist at the time of the transcribed texts, and the Tiberian Masoretes knew nothing of the latter.

and purpose of the transcribed text. In a Greek papyrus of the fourth century, owned in part by Sir Alfred Chester Beatty and in part by the University of Michigan, a homily about the Passover and the Passion has been preserved which was composed by Bishop Melito who in the second century was active in Sardis. Fragments in Syriac of this homily have long been known and were published by William Cureton[1] and by Cardinal Pitra.[2] The homily begins with the words:

> η μεν γραφη της εβραϊκης εξοδου ανεγνωσται και τα ρηματα του μυστηριου διασεσαφηται πως το προβατον θυεται και πως ο λαος σωζεται . . .

> The script of the Hebrew Exodus has been read and the words of the Mystery explained, how the lamb was sacrificed and the people saved . . .

Campbell Bonner, the editor of the Greek text, has investigated the question of how the first words of the homily are to be understood.[3] Obviously one must distinguish here between the reading of the scripture, the paraphrase, and the following sermon (homily).[4] Sir Frederic Kenyon, the editor of the Chester Beatty Papyri,[5] pointed out that the wording of the text really presupposes that the reading of the text of the Bible was done in *Hebrew*. Next followed the Greek translation and only then the sermon. Günther Zuntz, in a special investigation of the matter,[6] tried to prove that Melito's words really presuppose that it was usual to read the lessons from the Old Testament in Hebrew in Christian communities of the second century. He suggested that the

[1] *Spicilegium Syriacum*, London 1855, pp. 49 f.

[2] *Analecta Sacra*, iv, Paris 1883, p. 199.

[3] A great number of writings by Melito are known. 'Very soon the memory of Melito was obliterated in the Greek Church and that can only be explained on the assumption that his writings were not in sympathy with the later dogmatic taste.' (Harnack, *Geschichte der altchristlichen Literatur bis Eusebius*, i, p. 248; on the Syriac fragments, i, p. 250, ii, pp. 358 f.).

In the course of a detailed investigation of the rhetorical rhymes of the homily, to be found as well in the Greek as in the Syriac text, I have pointed to the possibility that the Syriac text may have been the original text of the homily, as these rhetorical rhymes are more often to be found in the Syriac than in the Greek text (see my article: 'Was Melito's Homily originally written in Syriac?' *JTS* xliv, 1943, pp. 52–6). Is it possible that some of Melito's writings were originally written in Syriac?

[4] *Harvard Theological Review*, xxxi, 1938, pp. 175 ff.—The Homily on the Passion by Melito, Bishop of Sardis . . . ed. by Campbell Bonner, *Studies and Documents*, xii, London 1940.

[5] *The Chester Beatty Papyri* . . . Fasc. viii: Enoch and Melito, by Frederic Kenyon. Plates. London 1941.

[6] 'On the Opening Sentence of Melito's Paschal Homily', *Harvard Theological Review*, xxxvi, 1943, pp. 299–315.

Christians adopted this custom from the Jews. For reading the Hebrew original the transcription in Greek letters would surely have suited all Christians and most Jews.[1] This theory also gives a plausible reason for the existence of a Greek transcribed text; it allowed both Jews and Christians to read the lessons from the Old Testament in Hebrew during the service, and this explains why this transcribed text was composed so carefully and consistently and why Origen thought fit to include it in his Hexapla. The texts must have been valued very highly during Origen's lifetime. Melito's Homily was composed about 168; Origen was born about 185. The Greek transcribed text is therefore considerably older than Origen, as Ludwig Blau correctly supposed.

This text, like all the others assembled in the Hexapla, was adopted by Origen from the Jews. A clear proof of this is to be found in the fact that in all the five columns preserved to us the divine name is regularly given as the Tetragrammaton in Hebrew square letters. Hitherto we knew only one very early text of the Septuagint in which this method of rendering the divine name was used, the Papyrus Fouad 266 containing some verses from the last chapters of Deuteronomy.[2] The Papyrus was written in about 100 B.C. But the divine name must have been written in the same way in the Jewish MSS of the Greek Bible which were used by Origen when he compiled the Hexapla. And this way of rendering the divine name was not only used in the text of the Septuagint, but in all the columns of the Hexapla. We have therefore to suppose that this method of rendering the divine name was very widely used in Jewish circles at that time. Origen had certainly not invented it. He only took over what he had found in his Jewish sources, and the Christians copied the texts exactly as Origen had done, and they continued to do so for a long time—the Milan palimpsest was written centuries after Origen, when the Jews had long ago abandoned the method of writing Hebrew with Greek letters, and had ceased to read Greek texts at all. It is very interesting to note that this transcribed text, which was obviously composed by the most official circles of Jewry, and which must have played a very important role among them at one time, should have been preserved for us only because

[1] Cf. S. A. Wifstrand, *Vigiliae Christianae* ii, 1949, p. 217. T. W. Manson in his very instructive review of my Cairo Geniza, *Dominican Studies*, ii, Oxford, 1949, p. 192.

[2] See W. G. Waddell, 'The Tetragrammaton in the LXX', *JTS* xlv, 1944, pp. 158–61. See my article 'Problems of the Septuagint', *Studia Patristica*, Berlin 1957, vol. i, 328–338, with the Appendix by A. Vaccari S.J., ibidem, pp. 339–42.

Origen included it in his Hexapla. But this is not surprising. How many early Jewish texts have been handed down to us only because the Christians went on using them! We need only think of Philo, Josephus, the Apocrypha and Pseudepigrapha which were preserved for us in writing only because the Christians went on reading and copying them. The edition of the fundamental work on these Hexapla fragments by Cardinal Mercati will reveal the true value of these important texts. In order to give an impression of them, I give here as a specimen the text of Psalm xxx (xxix in the Greek Bible) as it has been published by Cardinal Mercati. Little errors of the copyist are corrected as by Mercati. My intention is only to give a general impression of the text. For all details I refer to the publication of Mercati. Above each word in the transliterated text I give the Hebrew word with Tiberian vocalisation as it is to be found in the Hebrew Bible.

Psalm xxx (xxix in the Greek Bible)

לְדָוִד: הַבַּיִת חֲנֻכַּת שִׁיר־ מִזְמוֹר
1. μαζμωρ σιρ ὀννεχαθ αββαιθ λδαυειδ

לִי: אֹיְבַי שִׂמַּחְתָּ וְלֹא דִלִּיתָנִי כִּי יהוה אֲרוֹמִמְךָ
2. ἐρωμεμεχ יהוה χι δελλιθανη ουλω σεμεθ οϊεββαϊ λι

3. יהוה . . .

בוֹר: מִיּוֹרְדֵי־ חִיִּיתַנִי נַפְשִׁי מִן־שְׁאוֹל הֶעֱלִיתָ יהוה
4. [יהוה] εελιθ μεσσωλ νεφσι ἵθανι μεϊωρδη βωρ

קָדְשׁוֹ: לְזֵכֶר וְהוֹדוּ חֲסִידָיו ליהוה זַמְּרוּ
5. ζωημέρου λיהוה ασιδαυ ουωδου λζεχρ κοδσω

בֶּכִי יָלִין בָּעֶרֶב בִּרְצוֹנוֹ חַיִּים בְּאַפּוֹ רֶגַע כִּי
6. χι ρεγε βααφφω ἀϊϊμ βαρσωνω βααρβ ιαλιν βεχι . . .

לְעוֹלָם: אֶמּוֹט בַּל בְשַׁלְוִי אָמַרְתִּי וַאֲנִי
7. ουανι αμαρθι βσαλουι βαλ εμματ λωλαμ

פָּנֶיךָ הִסְתַּרְתָּה עֹז לְהַרְרִי הֶעֱמַדְתָּה בִּרְצוֹנְךָ יהוה
8. יהוה βαρσωναχ εεμεδεθ λααραρι οζ εσθερθα φαναχ
נִבְהָל: הָיִיתִי
αϊθι νεβαλ

אֶתְחַנָּן: אֲדֹנָי וְאֶל־ אֶקְרָא יהוה אֵלֶיךָ
9. ηλαχ יהוה εκρα ουελ αδωναϊ ἐθανναν

הֲיַגִּיד עָפָר הֲיוֹדְךָ שָׁחַת אֶל־ בְּרִדְתִּי בְּדָמִי מַה־בֶּצַע
10. **μεββεσὲ βδαμὶ βρεδεθι ελ σααθ αϊωδέχχα άφαρ αϊεγγιθι**
אֲמִתֶּךָ:
ἐμεθθαχ

לִי עֹזֵר הֱיֵה יהוה וְחָנֵּנִי יהוה שְׁמַע
11. **σμα יהוה ουανηνί (?) יהוה αϊη ὠζηρ λι**

שִׂמְחָה: וַתְּאַזְּרֵנִי שַׂקִּי פִּתַּחְתָּ לִי לְמָחוֹל מִסְפְּדִי הָפַכְתָּ
12. **ἀφαχθ . . . λμαωλ λι φέθεθα σεκκι ουεθαζερηνι σεμα**

לְעוֹלָם אֱלֹהַי יהוה יִדֹּם ולֹא כָבוֹד יְזַמֶּרְךָ לְמַעַן
13. **λαμαν ιζαμμέρεχ χαβωδ οὐλω ιαδομ יהוה ελωαϊ λωλαμ**
אוֹדֶךָּ:
ὠδεχ

A comparison of this pre-masoretic material just discussed with the text fixed by the Masoretes of Tiberias makes it necessary to evaluate the text of the Bible somewhat differently than the Masoretes wished. They claimed to have done nothing more than retain the text uniformly transmitted from the time of Ezra in its purity. In reality they created an ideal form of Hebrew in which in many cases they replaced a pronunciation which they regarded as lax and inaccurate by one which they believed to be more correct, more in accordance with the ideal Hebrew as it might have been spoken in classical times—just as Arab scholars tried to improve the reading of the Koran by adapting it to an ideal Arabic. I will illustrate this side of the activity of the Masoretes by three examples.

21. The Pronunciation of the Gutturals

Whoever compares the transcribed text of the Second Column of the Hexapla printed above with the text written in Hebrew characters as we have it in our Hebrew Bible will come to the conclusion that the men who were responsible for this kind of transcription did not pronounce the gutturals as consonants. This is confirmed by the whole material preserved in the Milan palimpsest, as may be seen in a few specimens taken from other Psalms of the Hexapla:

θενηνι – תַּנְחֵנִי xxxi, 4; βαταθι – בָּטַחְתִּי xxxi, 7; ουβσαλη – וּבְצַלְעִי xxxv, 15; θερε – תִּרְאֶה xxxv, 17; οραχ – אָרְחֶךָ xliv, 19; ιεμρου – יֶחְמְרוּ xlvi, 4; χεσσω – כִּסְאוֹ lxxxix, 30; μηρεμ – מֵרֶחֶם cx, 3; (Field).

Now it may be said: How was it possible to render Hebrew gutturals with Greek letters? That it really was possible may be seen from the much older methods of transcription which we find in certain strata of the Septuagint. I may refer to transcriptions of proper names like Αερνων (ארנון) Jer. xxxi (xlviii) 20 A; Αερμων (חרמון) Deut. iii, 8 and often; Αηλαμ (עילם) I Kings xxix, I A; Αενδωρ (עין דאר) I Chron. viii, 24 A.[1] It is clear that such transcriptions have to be understood as αΕρνων, αΕρμων, αΗλαμ, αΕνδωρ. The *a* prefixed to the guttural which had to be pronounced with the vowel *e* is the attempt to render in Greek script the Hebrew guttural which still must have been heard when this kind of transliteration was made.[2]

In other cases an *i* or *e* was prefixed to the guttural. I may refer here to transliterations like Ιαχειραν (אחירם) Num. xxvi, 42 B; Ιαβινεεμ (אבינעם) Judges iv, 12 A; Ιασον (עצם) Joshua xix, 3 B; Ιεφραθα (עפרה) Joshua xviii, 23 B; Ιακακ (חוקק) I Chron. vi, 75 A; Ελεαδ (אלעד) I Chron. vii, 21 A; Ελεαζαρ (אלעזר), often; Σωβωθ instead of Εωβωθ (אבת) Num. xxxiii, 43 B. Such transliterations are to be understood as ιΑχειραν, ιΑβινεεμ, ιΑκακ, ιΕφραθα, &c., and we can be sure that at the time when they were made the gutturals were still heard by the transcribers.

Besides, in older times the Hebrew letters ח and ע must have been differentiated like the corresponding Arabic letters, so that ח was pronounced sometimes like Arabic *ḥā*, sometimes like Arabic *khā*, and ע sometimes like Arabic *ʿain*, sometimes like Arabic *ghain*. An ע corresponding to *gh* we find, for instance, in words like Γομορρα (עמרה); Γαζα (עזה); Ραγαυ (רעו) Gen. xi, 18 f; Ραγουηλ (רעואל) Num. i, 14 and often; Ραγμα Ezek. xxvii, 22 (A.Q. Ρεγμα), I Chron. i, 9 (רעמה); Γαδερ (עדר) Gen. xxxv, 16 A.D.; Γοθολια (עתליה) often; – a ח corresponding to *kha* in χορραιος (חרי) Gen. xiv, 6 A; Αχιεζερ (אחיעזר) Αχεικαμ (אחיקם) and similar names.

In the Second Column of the Hexapla we never find transcriptions of this kind. These older methods of rendering Hebrew gutturals in Greek transcription had been completely abandoned in the second century when the transliteration preserved in the Second Column of the Hexapla was made; after the gutturals

[1] These specimens as well as the following ones are to be found in the *Concordance to the Septuagint*, by Hatch and Redpath, Supplement, Fasc. i, Oxford, 1900 (photographic reprint Graz 1955).

[2] Perhaps it was actually pronounced (to help the pronunciation of the guttural); in Samaritan such helping vowels *regularly* preceded gutturals before the disappearance of the latter (proved by the position of the stress) [A. Murtonen].

had lost their consonantal value, a new method of transliteration was introduced, and in many manuscripts of the Septuagint Hebrew names were adapted to the rules of transliteration used in the Second Column of the Hexapla. The older methods of transliteration were no longer understood.

An important witness for the pronunciation of Hebrew in Palestine is Jerome. He translated the whole Old Testament from Hebrew into Latin, and he knew a good deal of Hebrew. He was in close contact with learned Jews in Palestine and had carefully observed their methods of pronunciation. Transliterated Hebrew words are to be found in great numbers in his writings. But they cannot be taken as a uniform mass, as has been done for instance by Carl Siegfried in his well-known article published in 1884.[1] Jerome quotes the Hebrew words just as he finds them in the source from which he has taken them, only replacing the Greek letters by Latin ones. There is a great difference in these quotations according as they are taken from the Septuagint, from the old Greek Onomasticon of Philo or Pseudo-Philo, from later sources such as the Second Column of Origen's Hexapla, or from his own transliteration.[2] Of special interest are the statements made by Jerome about the pronunciation of Hebrew in his time. In his *Liber interpretationis hebraicorum nominum*[3] he quotes the word *Gomorra* which he had found both in the old Greek Onomasticon and in the Septuagint, and he adds:

sciendum quod *g* litteram in hebraico non habet, sed scribitur per uocalem ע.

We find a similar notice somewhat later when he quotes the word

[1] Cf. Carl Siegfried, 'Die Aussprache des Hebräischen bei Hieronymus', in *ZAW*, vol. iv, Giessen, 1884, pp. 34–87.

[2] Cf. Franz Wutz, *Die Transkriptionen von der Septuaginta bis zu Hieronymus*, Stuttgart, 1933, who writes concerning Jerome: 'Die Kenntnis der Onomastik hat sich dabei als recht brauchbar erwiesen; denn schon aus den Onomastica Sacra wusste ich, dass Hieronymus nur mit grösster Vorsicht zu benützen ist, da er ein gewaltiges Sammelsurium von Formen aus allen Jahrhunderten eines Zeitraums von 700–800 Jahren bot. Da Hieronymus trotz aller Gelehrsamkeit der historisch-kritische Blick für die Divergenz seiner Materialien fehlte, häuft er Material auf Material, ohne zu ahnen, um was es ging; ja er nahm Stellung gegen alte Formen, ohne zu wissen wie sehr sie durch die alte Orthographie berechtigt waren' (p. 3). This is correct on the whole. But as we now know the changes in the transcription of Hebrew words in the different centuries, the material collected by Jerome is, when used critically, of great importance. Alexander Sperber, in his treatise 'Hebrew based upon Greek and Latin transliterations' (*Hebrew Union College Annual*, vol. xii/xiii, Cincinnati, 1937/8) has dealt with Jerome's methods on pp. 109 f. His article is based to a considerable extent on Jerome.

[3] Published by Paul de Lagarde in *Onomastica Sacra*, 2nd ed., Gottingae, 1887, pp. 26–116; cf. ibid., p. 33, and Sperber, op. cit., p. 110.

Segor[1] and declares that it is the same as *Seor* which he had explained two lines before and adds:

sed sciendum quia *g* litteram in medio non habeat, scribiturque per uocalem ain.

In mentioning the name *Cham*, Jerome remarks:[2]

sed sciendum quod in hebraico χ litteram non habeat, scribitur autem per ח quae duplici adspiratione profertur.

It is clear that in older times Hebrew ח had in certain cases a pronunciation similar to Greek χ, and that in his own time the Hebrew letter, like all the other gutturals, indicated only a vowel. A. Sperber, after a careful investigation of all the evidence concerning the gutturals spoken in Palestine in Jerome's time, comes to the conclusion: 'Gutturals have, therefore, no independent consonantal value, but serve merely to carry the vowel sign.'

We have seen that in the Jewish liturgical poetry of the sixth and seventh centuries[3] the rhyme—along with the acrostic—is an important characteristic. In these poems there are rhyming words ending in ח and ה, and words ending in ח and ע.[4] It seems clear that the poet Hedwatha, who composed in the second half of the sixth century the Ḳerobas on the twenty-four divisions of priests (משמרות), did not pronounce the gutturals. This is confirmed by the way in which Bible fragments with Palestinian punctuation are vocalized. Pontus Leander, in his article 'Bemerkungen zur palästinischen Überlieferung des Hebräischen',[5] says:

From the Palestinian punctuation we may conclude that the

[1] Hebrew צֹעַר, Gen. xix, 22 f. Septuagint Σηγωρ, cf. Lagarde, p. 37.

[2] Lagarde, op. cit., p. 30. Cf. *Hieronymi Quaestiones Hebraicae in libro Geneseos*. E recognitione Pauli de Lagarde, Lipsiae, 1868, p. 13. Concerning the duplex aspiratio mentioned here by Jerome cf. Sperber, op. cit., pp. 110 f.

[3] Cf. above, p. 43 ff.

[4] Cf. *Masoreten des Westens*, i, p. ב, where the words תִּפְתָּח, תפלתה, תנחתה and בעיתה rhyme; p. ד, where תִּנָּרַע, תִּפָּרַע, יקרע, and אזרח rhyme; and p. ח, where [ ]סיח, ופסיח, and ונסוע rhyme (the fourth rhyme is not preserved).

[5] Cf. *ZAW*., vol. liv, 1936, pp. 91–9. The words quoted above in translation may be given here in the German original: 'Die palästinische Punktation lässt darauf schliessen, dass die Laryngale in der Aussprache nicht, oder wenigstens nicht genau, berücksichtigt wurden. . . . Wörter, die auf ח ausgehn, reimen mit denen auf ע. Und sehr oft wird nur ein Vokal geschrieben, wo die späteren Punktationen zwei—einen vor der Laryngalis, den andern nach ihr—zeigen. Diese Fälle sind zu zahlreich, um sich restlos durch Unvollständigkeit in der Vokalschreibung erklären zu lassen; die Laryngalis ist also elidiert und die umgebenden Vokale kontrahiert. . . . Es ist kaum anzunehmen, dass die Laryngalis in solchen Fällen wirklich gesprochen wurde, denn alles deutet darauf hin, dass die Laryngale zu dieser Zeit völlig verloren gegangen oder wenigstens in der Artikulation irgendwie geschwächt waren' (pp. 95 f.).

laryngals (i.e. gutturals) were not, or not exactly, taken into account in the pronunciation; words ending in ח rhyme with those ending in ע. And very often only one vowel is written where the later punctuation shows two, one before and one after the laryngal. These cases are too numerous to be explained by incompleteness in the writing of vowels. The laryngal is also elided and the surrounding vowels contracted.

From the texts published by me, Leander quotes the following specimens: (with א) הארץ, לארץ, הארון, מארץ (mḗreṣ); (with ע) פעלתה, מבעד (mibbad)=מִבַּעַד . . . לעפר=לֶעָפָר, יערה (yērē)=יֵעָרֶה; (with ה) אהבתי, ההרים=הֶהָרִים, להבה=לֶהָבָה; (with ח) מנוחתך=מְנוּחָתֶךָ, נחמתך (nēmātak)=נֶחָמָתֶךָ, תתנחם (titnēm)=תִתְנַחֵם, מרחוק (mērṓk)=מֵרָחוֹק. He adds:

'We can hardly assume that the laryngal was really pronounced in such cases, for everything points to the fact that the laryngal was completely lost at this time or at least weakened in articulation.'

To these examples I may add a few specimens taken from the scroll of the Psalms with Palestinian punctuation of which the text has now been published by A. Murtonen:[1] כאורח (כְּאֶזְרַח) xxxvii, 35; שאול (שְׁאוֹל) xxx, 11; שאלת (שָׁאֲלְתָּ) xl, 7; יעזב (יַעֲזֹב) xxxvii, 28; ויעבר (וַיַּעֲבֹר) xxxvii, 36; בעצמי (בַּעֲצָמָי) xxxviii, 4; להמיתו (לַהֲמִיתוֹ) xxxvii, 32;[2] בהגיגי (בַּהֲגִיגִי) xxxviiii, 4; ובחמתך (וּבַחֲמָתְךָ) xxxviii, 2; תחרש (תֶּחֱרַשׁ) xxxviiii, 13). It is clear that this method of vocalizing the gutturals confirms the result which we reached on the basis of the other Manuscripts.

This method of not pronouncing the gutturals in reading Hebrew (and Aramaic) has been preserved by the Samaritans up to the present day. The Samaritans know how to pronounce correctly all the gutturals when speaking Arabic. But as soon as they begin to recite the Hebrew text of the Bible or the text of their Targum, or to speak Hebrew or Aramaic, the pronunciation of the gutturals—with the exception of א and ע in certain cases—is completely omitted. In the summer of 1908 I worked for a fortnight daily in the Synagogue of the Samaritans in Nāblus and was always in touch with some of their priests, and I often discussed

[1] Cf. my reference to these fragments supra, p. 151, note 3.

[2] In these fragments no vowels are added when the text is written plene.

with them their method of pronouncing Hebrew. They were convinced that they read the holy text exactly as it had been transmitted to them by their forefathers from time immemorial.

The Masoretes who worked on the Hebrew Biblical text at the beginning of the ninth century added to the gutturals a great number of new vowels by which they tried to force the readers of the holy text not to overlook any of the gutturals written in the text of the Bible. 'From the whole system of the Chatef vowels—a creation of the Tiberian Masoretes—we can clearly see how little they were accustomed to a correct pronunciation of the gutturals', remarks Pontus Leander.[1] According to his theory the neglect of the gutturals began in the Aramaic vernacular language, especially in Galilee which was long notorious for its lax pronunciation of these sounds.[2] It spread next into the synagogal reading of the Hebrew Bible in Galilee. But, according to Leander, the Masoretes found the correct method of pronouncing Hebrew in Judæa and introduced it into the reading of the Biblical text by creating vowel signs which they added with great scrupulousness. They failed, however, to establish a correct pronunciation of the gutturals by their methods, and the difficulties they could not master are clearly to be seen in the text they created. Thus far Leander.[3]

I think it quite impossible to differentiate between the pronunciation of Hebrew in Galilee and in Judæa at that time. Before the Masoretes of Tiberias began their work, the centre of Judaism in Palestine had been for centuries Galilee, and not Judæa. The priestly families, among whom we should expect to find the best tradition for reading the text of the Bible, had been settled in Galilee. They lived in Tiberias and the surrounding places. When after the Muslim conquest Jerusalem was reopened to the Jews, the centre of Jewish learning was transferred from Tiberias to Jerusalem. Where should we find men who had preserved a correct pronunciation of Hebrew during these centuries in Judæa? What we hear of the non-pronunciation of the gutturals from Origen and Jerome was transmitted to Origen in Caesarea, and was heard by Jerome from his Jewish teachers in Bethlehem. Both places were situated in Judæa. Can

[1] Op. cit., p. 95 f.
[2] Cf. the well-known stories reported in the Talmud concerning the lax pronunciation of the gutturals. They are mentioned, for instance, by Dalman in his *Grammar* 2nd edn., Leipzig 1905, pp. 57 f.
[3] Op. cit., p. 96.

we really believe that, besides the faulty pronunciation reported by them, there existed a 'correct' pronunciation of the Hebrew gutturals in Judæa of which neither of them has anything to say? And besides, the Babylonian Masoretes introduced a new pronunciation of the gutturals into their text of the Hebrew Bible at the same time as their colleagues in Palestine, although they did not go quite so far as these. Did they also depend previously on a wrong pronunciation prevailing in Galilee?

We can take it for granted that neither in Palestine nor in Babylonia did a clear pronunciation of the Hebrew gutturals exist at the time when the Masoretes began to revise the pronunciation of Hebrew by fixing every detail through very complicated systems of punctuation. There need be no doubt that the impetus for revising the reading of the Hebrew text was given to the Masoretes by the Arab Readers of the Koran. The Koran was recited everywhere in the great Muslim Empire. In Mesopotamia, Kufa and Baṣra were the great centres of work on the correct reading of the Koran. The Dome of the Rock, built 692 by the Caliph 'Abdulmalik (ruled 685–705), directed Muslim pilgrims for many years to Jerusalem instead of to Mecca. In both Babylonia and Palestine the Masoretes had every opportunity of observing the exact methods employed in reading the Koran. We have seen how important the correct reading of the Koran was for every Muslim. The Arab Readers of the Koran were the forerunners of the Masoretes in their work on the text of the Hebrew Bible in Palestine and in Mesopotamia.

We see from the orthography of the Koran that consonantal Alif was not read in early times. In accordance with the language of Bedouin poetry the Koranic readers introduced the small sign Hamza with great exactness into the text of the Koran in order to safeguard a pronunciation of this guttural which they regarded as correct. In this Arabic Hamza we must see the model of all the signs introduced by the Masoretes for safeguarding a correct pronunciation of the newly restored Hebrew gutturals, the Ḥaṭefs, and the Pataḥ furtivum introduced by the Tiberian Masoretes, and the auxiliary vowels introduced by the Babylonian Masoretes. The Arabs had to safeguard the pronunciation of only one guttural, that of the consonantal Alif. The other gutturals were not ignored by the Arabs in reading the Koran. The Masoretes had to introduce a newly created method of pronouncing all the gutturals which had generally been omitted in reading the Hebrew text, just as they are omitted by the Samaritans up to the present day. So the signs introduced by them differed from those used by the Arabs. But Leander is quite right when he says that the signs introduced by the Masoretes were not very successful; the fact, for instance, that, in reading the Bible, the Jews generally pronounce an ע as Aleph and not as 'Ain, may perhaps remind us of the origin of this innovation made by the Masoretes.

22. The final vowels in the Masoretic Text

In the Masoretic text the regular form of the suffix of the second person singular masculine is ־ְךָ, pausal ־ֶךָ, when affixed to a noun in plural ־ֶיךָ; cf. יָדְךָ, pausal יָדֶךָ thy hand, יָדֶיךָ thy hands. Forms of this kind are not found in the Hebrew known from other sources, as will be shown by the following specimens to which I always add the form of the Masoretic text:

(a) *The Second Column of Origen's Hexapla.*

ουεμιναχ וִימִינְךָ xviii, 36; αμμαχ עַמְּךָ xxviii, 9; βαρσωναχ בִּרְצוֹנְךָ xxx, 8; οζναχ אָזְנְךָ xxxi, 3; σεμαχ שִׁמְךָ xxxi, 4; βιαδαχ בְּיָדְךָ xxxi, 6; τουβαχ טוּבְךָ xxxi, 20; σεδκαχ צִדְקֶךָ xxxv, 28; χσεδκαχ (MS: χσεδκαδ) כְּצִדְקְךָ xxxv, 24; οραχ אָרְחֶךָ xliv, 19; ηχαλαχ הֵיכָלֶךָ xliv, 10; αβδαχ עַבְדְּךָ lxxxix, 40; μσιαχ מְשִׁיחֶךָ lxxxix, 39, 52; θελαθαχ תְּהִלָּתֶךָ xxxv, 28; ουανουαθαχ (MS: ουανανaθαχ) וְעַנְוָתְךָ xviii, 37; νεελαθαχ נַחֲלָתֶךָ xxviii, 9; εμεθθαχ אֲמִתֶּךָ xxx, 10; βσεδκαθαχ בְּצִדְקָתְךָ xxxi, 2; εμαθαχ חֲמָתֶךָ lxxxix, 47; βαεμουναθαχ בֶּאֱמוּנָתֶךָ lxxxix, 50; φαναχ פָּנֶיךָ xxx, 8; xxxi, 21; λιριαχ לִירֵאֶיךָ xxxi, 20; ηναχ עֵינֶיךָ xxxi, 23; ελωαχ אֱלֹהֶיךָ xliv, 8; εσδαχ חֲסָדֶיךָ lxxxix, 58; αβδαχ עֲבָדֶיךָ lxxxix, 51; ερωμεμεχ אֲרוֹמִמְךָ xxx, 2; ιζαμμερεχ יְזַמֶּרְךָ xxx, 13; ωδεχ אוֹדֶךָ xxx, 13; אוֹדְךָ xxxv, 18; ουωρεχ וְאוֹרְךָ xxxii, 8; εσχιλεχ אַשְׂכִּילְךָ xxxii, 8; οιβαχ אֹיְבֶיךָ lxxxix, 52; ιελεδεθεχ יְלִדְתִּיךָ cx, 3 (Field).

I know of two exceptions only: αιωδεχχα הֲיוֹדְךָ xxx, 10, with 'nun energicum' (cf. אוֹדֶךָּ Job xl, 14; אוֹדֶךָּ Ps. cxviii, 28). Such forms may have followed special laws. The other form is ιεσαχα יִשְׁעֶךָ xviii, 36.

(b) *Jerome*

Jerome confirms these forms; he reads *ammach*, *echalach*, *iesacha* as in the Second Column of the Hexapla. Cf. further *dodach* דֹּדְךָ Jer. xxxii, 7; *goolathhach* גְּאֻלָּתְךָ Ezek. xi, 15; *amaggenach* אֲמַגֶּנְךָּ

Hos. xi, 8; *dabarach* דְּבָרֶיךָ Hos. xiii, 14; *messiach* מְשִׁיחֶךָ Hab. iii, 13; *alichothach* הֲלִיכוֹתֶיךָ Ps. lxviii, 25 (Field); *malochothach* מַלְאֲכוֹתֶיךָ Ps. lxxiii, 39 (Field): **alechchach* אֶל חִכְּךָ Hos. viii, 1 is erroneously written *alechcha*, and **methech* מֵתֶיךָ Isa. xxvi. 19 is erroneously written *metheca*.

(c) *Liturgical MSS with Palestinian Punctuation*

Here we always find forms of the same kind, cf. ידך, אברתך, בביתך, שירך, בצילך, חופתך; these specimens are to be found in the first four verses of Hedwatha's Ḳeroba on Mishmar Ḥuppa.[1] Forms of this kind are regularly used in all these texts, and, as we have seen,[2] they were used in liturgical MSS and editions provided with Tiberian punctuation also, up to about 1800, when they were 'corrected' by Wolf Heidenheim. It is only since then that in printed texts of the Piuts forms with the sufix ְךָ, ֶיךָ begin to appear.

Even the Biblical text which was before the copyists of these MSS must have had corresponding forms. Usually in these MSS only the beginning of a Biblical verse is quoted, or the text quoted from the Bible is left without vowel signs. But in the fragments of Hedwatha's Ḳerobas Bible quotations are given with full vocalization, and from these I quote the following specimens:[3] ימינך (יְמִינְךָ) Exod. xv, 6; מפניך (מִפָּנֶיךָ); משנאיך (מְשַׂנְאֶיךָ) Num. x, 35; קדשך (קָדְשְׁךָ); עמך (עַמְּךָ) Deut. xvi, 15; מפניך (מִפָּנֶיךָ) Deut. xxxiii, 17; ונתתיך (וּנְתַתִּיךָ) Isa. xlix, 6; בך (בְּךָ) Jer. li, 20; ידך (יָדְךָ) Mic. v, 8; וימינך (וִימִינְךָ); וענותך (וְעַנְוָתְךָ) Ps. xviii, 36; ידך (יָדְךָ); שנאיך (שֹׂנְאֶיךָ) Ps. xxi, 9; לפניך (לְפָנֶיךָ) Ps. xix, 15; כבודך (כְּבוֹדֶךָ) Ps. xxvi, 8; עבדיך (עֲבָדֶיךָ) Ps. cx, 1; וזכרך (וְזִכְרְךָ) Ps. cii, 13; אויבך (אֹיְבֶיךָ); לרגלך (לְרַגְלֶיךָ) Ps. cx, 11; להודיעך (לְהוֹדִיעֲךָ) Prov. xxii, 21.

(d) *Hebrew as pronounced by the Samaritans*

That the suffix was pronounced and is still pronounced by the Samaritans in the same way, we may see from the following specimens:[4]

[1] Cf. *Masoreten des Westens*, vol. i, p. 6 of the Hebrew text.

[2] Cf. Professor Simonsens's notice quoted above, p. 113.

[3] These specimens are to be found on pp. 6, 7, 9, 15, 20, 21 in *Masoreten des Westens*, vol. i, Hebrew text, and on p. 115 of Zulay's publication.

[4] The specimens are taken from the material collected by Schaade and Murtonen. Cf. the article 'The Hebrew spoken by the Samaritans', of Professor Foad Hassanain, in *Bulletin of the Faculty of Arts*, Fouad I University, vol. vi, Cairo, 1942, pp. 47–64.

ábbek אַפֶּיךָ; *ʿāfârak* עפרך (MT עפר) Gen. iii, 19; *mīy(y)êdak* מִיָּדֶךָ iv, 11; *ʿábdak* עַבְדְּךָ xix, 19; *lēbâbak* לְבָבֶךָ xx, 6; *bênak* בִּנְךָ; *yēʾîdak* יְחִידְךָ xxii, 2; *yâdak* יָדֶךָ xxii, 12; *míttak* מֵתֶךָ xxiii, 6; *ḳaláltak* קִלְלָתְךָ xxvii, 13; *bābēṛâk* בְּבָרְחֲךָ xxxv, 1; *mīy(y)ālâsek* מֵחֲלָצֶיךָ xxxv, 11; *rēʿûshak* רֹאשֶׁךָ xl, 13; *fîyyak* פִּיךָ xli, 40; *yēshûfak* יְשׁוּפְךָ; iii, 15; *shûbak* שׁוּבְךָ iii, 19; *nātáttek* נְתַתִּיךָ xvii, 5; *shāmâttek* שְׁמַעְתִּיךָ xvii, 20; *èberrêkak* אֲבָרֶכְךָ xxii, 17; *weshbīyyâk* וְאַשְׁבִּיעֲךָ xxiv, 3; *uberríktek* וּבֵרַכְתִּיךָ xxvi, 24; *shākértek* שְׂכַרְתִּיךָ xxx, 16; *yèfāgâshak* יִפְגָּשְׁךָ xxxii, 18; *ʿābádtek* עֲבַדְתִּיךָ xxx, 26; *ushāʿêlak* וּשְׁאֵלְךָ xxxii, 18; *eshbīyyâk* הִשְׁבִּיעֲךָ l, 6; *gāmâlok* גְּמָלוּךָ l, 17; *shâmak* שָׂמְךָ Exod. ii, 14; *shällâttek* (Piel) שְׁלַחְתִּיךָ iii, 12.

(e) *Bible MSS with Palestinian Punctuation*

These are the fragments H, J, K, L, M, which I published in *Masoreten des Westens*, vol. ii, pp. 66–95, and the Psalm scroll, T.-S. 10, nos. 52, 53, 54, 58 of the Cambridge University Library, published by Murtonen and the texts recently discovered by Professor A. Diez Macho in Barcelona.[1]

In MS H, the scroll with the text of Ezek. xiii, 11–xvi, 31, we find in chapter xvi a great number of specimens with the *feminine* suffix of the 2nd pers. sing., as מכרתיך (מְכֹרֹתַיִךְ) xvi, 3; ומולדתיך (וּמוֹלְדוֹתַיִךְ) xvi, 4; נפשך (נַפְשֵׁךְ) xvi, 5; אותך (אֹתָךְ) xvi, 5, &c. But not a single specimen in the whole fragment is to be found where the masculine suffix is vocalized.

In MS J, two folios with the text of Dan. ix, 24–xii, 14, we find clearly written עמך (עַמֶּךָ) xii, 1, and no specimen is to be found where the suffix is vocalized according to the method of the Tiberian Masoretes. In comparing this fragment we have to be cautious as the signs ⸗ and ⸗ are also used here for the accents corresponding to Tiberian Zaḳef and Rebiʿa. In some instances the vowels are not written or the words are not preserved. It is very likely that we have here a Biblical MS in which the suffix was vocalized in the same way as in the liturgical fragments.

In MS K, one folio with the text of Jer. i, 1–ii, 29, we find invariably forms like אצורך (אֶצָּורְךָ); הקדשתיך (הִקְדַּשְׁתִּיךָ); נתתיך (נְתַתִּיךָ) i, 5; אלהיך (אֱלֹהֶיךָ), יושיעוך (יוֹשִׁיעוּךָ) ii, 28. This MS always gives the vocalization of the suffix in accordance with the Masoretic text.

[1] 'Tres nuevos manuscritos biblicos 'palestinenses',' *Estudios Biblicos*, vol. xiii, 1954, pp. 247–65, 'Un manuscritto 'Palestinense' en la Biblioteca nacional de Estrasburgo'. *Sefarad* xvii, 1957, pp. 11–17.

In MS L, two folios with fragments of Psalms li–v, lxix–lxxii, we find forms like יתצך (יִתָּצְךָ), ושרשך (וְשֵׁרֶשְׁךָ) lii, 7; זעמך (זַעְמֶךָ), אפך (אַפְּךָ) lxix, 25; בצדקתך (בְּצִדְקָתֶךָ) lxix, 28; ישועתך (יְשׁוּעָתֶךָ) lxx, 5; אזנך (אָזְנְךָ) lxxi, 2; תהלתך (תְּהִלָּתֶךָ), תפארתך (תִּפְאַרְתֶּךָ) lxxi, 8. The vocalization of the suffix is in accordance with the Masoretic text.

In MS M, containing Biblical texts written in abbreviation, we find forms like בעשותך (בַּעֲשׂוֹתְךָ) Isa. lxiv, 2; ך (יִשְׁאָלְךָ) Jer. xxiii, 3; ך (אוֹתְךָ) xxv, 15; ך (מִיָּדְךָ) xxv, 28; עך (עַמְּךָ) Isa. lxiii, 14; ך (לְךָ) lxiii, 14; פך (בְּכַפֶּרְךָ) Exod. xxix, 36. There is no doubt that the suffix was vocalized here in accordance with the Masoretic text.

In the scroll of the Psalms we have to differentiate between the vocalization added by the first hand, perhaps the copyist of the consonantal text himself, and a later hand. Only a few vowel signs are added by the first hand. The second hand has added more vowel signs. They are especially found on the fragment T-S xx, 54. Here we find forms like the following: וירוממך (וִירוֹמִמְךָ) xxxvii, 34; חציך (חִצֶּיךָ) xxxviii, 3; ידך (יָדֶךָ) xxxviii, 3; נגדך (נֶגְדֶּךָ) xxxix, 6; נגעך (נִגְעֶךָ) xxxix, 11; צדקתך (צִדְקָתְךָ) xl, 11; ואמתך (וַאֲמִתְּךָ) xl, 11.

We see it must be supposed that we still have MSS from earlier times in which the suffix of the second person singular masc. is treated in the way in which this suffix is marked in the other texts with Palestinian punctuation at our disposal, and it is also clear that those Biblical MSS which were before the liturgical poets were vocalised in the same way without the ending *-a* in these forms, and liturgical texts are always very conservative. On the other hand, the ending *-a* is to be found in the other texts with Palestinian vocalization. We find the same in the fragment discovered by A. Diez Macho in the Library of the Jewish Theological Seminary of America (MS 594 Box B Envel. 12), the fragment of one folio with verses from the end of Ecclesiastes and the beginning of Lamentations which I publish in the Appendix.

That the ending *-a* existed sometimes in Hebrew we see from MSS with plene-writing discovered among the Dead Sea Scrolls like the first Isaiah Scroll from Qumran Cave I, where such forms are very often written with the ending ה. I may refer here to my book *Die hebräischen HSS aus der Höhle*, Stuttgart 1951

p. 74 f. Here an ending *-a* to these forms which at one time existed in Hebrew was lost for centuries and was reintroduced with great regularity by the Tiberian Masoretes, and from there entered also the texts with Palestinian and Babylonian vocalization. It has therefore to be regarded as an innovation made in the eighth century.

What have we to say of this peculiarity of vocalization? In the important chapter viii of his *Studien zur Hebräischen Metrik,*[1] headed 'Versbau und Sprachform', Eduard Sievers writes with regard to these pronominal forms (§207):

> A form such as יָדְךָ *yad^e^chá* is strange in several ways: (1) orthographically, as it does not indicate the final vowel by a supporting consonant; (2) from the point of view of accent, as it supposes an Early Hebrew oxytone, though otherwise in Early Hebrew the principle of penultimate accentuation is the rule; (3) phonologically, as it affirms the preservation of an original final, yet certainly short vowel which otherwise disappears, and in such forms as *lach* (beside *l^e^chá*) has in fact disappeared; (4) morphologically, as it brings about an incomprehensible difference in the treatment of similarly composed word-forms with masculine and feminine suffix (*yad^e^chá* as against *yadéch*); (5) metrically, since certainly not all, but at least very many forms of this type do not suit the anapaestic rhythm of the verse. If blind chance is excluded, how can all these irregularities have coincided in one and the same category? The probability of this coincidence in any case is quite extraordinarily small . . .

Somewhat later (§229) Sievers states:

> that the forms with feminine suffixes such as pron. *lách,* nom. *yadéch, yadáich,* &c., have developed for the most part clearly and regularly, but that the forms with the masculine suffix are quite incomprehensible, at least if one seeks in them the direct continuation of any early Semitic or Hebrew original agreeing with rules and facts otherwise established—and that, after all, is what one has to try first.

Sievers refers to his previous treatment of these problems and sums them up in the following questions:

> If the original threefold case-group *yaduka, yadika, yadaka* was levelled off in Early Hebrew to **yadaka* (as must be considered

[1] 'Metrische Studien, i', in *Abhandlungen der philologisch-historischen Classe der Königlich Sächsischen Gesellschaft der Wissenschaften,* vol. xxi, i, Leipzig, 1901, pp. 288 ff.

> likely) why did it not become, with penultimate accentuation, **yadáka* and later **yadách* (as *yadíki* to *yadéch*)? Why did it become an oxytone contrary to all rules otherwise applying, and develop into *yad*^{e}*chá*? And if it became an oxytone, why does it not follow the usual system of vowel treatment in nominal forms, i.e. why is it *yad*^{e}*chá* and not either *y*^{e}*dachá* (as, for instance, *d*^{e}*barí*) or *yadchá*, *yę́dchá* as in *yędchę́m*? The mere descriptive grouping under 'light and heavy terminations' does not remove the difficulty, but only describes the facts as they stand. Finally, why is it that in the consonantal text this strange *yad*^{e}*chá* is normally written only as ידך as if it had no final vowel, and especially where it would have been advisable for the Masoretes to make a difference in spelling between masculine and feminine forms?

Sievers comes to the final conclusion that all the ְךָ forms of the Tiberian punctuators are to be regarded as late innovations which only began to appear in the time of Origen and Jerome.

But even this innovation must be dated in reality later than Sievers believed. In 1901, when Sievers wrote his *Metrische Studien*, the amount of Hebrew independent of Masoretic punctuation at his disposal was very scanty. He did not know of the texts of the Second Column of the Hexapla discovered in the Ambrosiana in Milan by Mercati, nor of the texts with Palestinian punctuation from the Cairo Geniza, nor the way in which the Samaritans have always read their Torah in their religious services.

On the other hand, we now have, as already mentioned, a certain number of Hebrew manuscripts from the Dead Sea Caves in which an ending ה appears, showing that the *a*-vowel must sometimes have been pronounced in earlier times, but in later times completely disappeared.

When Dr. A. Murtonen visited me in Oxford in May 1958 we discussed the matter. He thought these circumstances could be explained by supposing that at the time when and at the place where the Dead Sea Scrolls were written, two different forms of pronunciation were used: one form, *yāḏāḵ*, the more solemn form of recitation which alone represented a natural development according to the rules of Hebrew grammar, and another form *yāḏkā*, which was a quicker way of pronunciation based on everyday speech, cf. the Dead Sea Scrolls, and Modern Hebrew.

The Masoretes of Tiberias probably followed on this point the

pattern of the Dead Sea Scrolls. It is quite possible that we have
to consider the 'correct Arabic' as the model for this innovation.
It had been introduced into the language of the Koran by the
readers in accordance with the language of Bedouin poetry. It is
very likely that the Prophet, like the people of Mecca, said *baitak*
'thy house', *yadak* 'thy hand', *darabak* 'he struck thee,' *lak* 'to
thee'. The Bedouin said *baituka*, *yaduka* (nominative), *baitika*
vadika (genitive), *baitaka*, *yadaka* (accusative), and they said
darabaka and *laka*. These forms of Bedouin Arabic were introduced
into the text of the Koran by the early Readers, and observed with
great regularity as the only correct ones. The Masoretes followed
the example given by the Arabic Readers and they were convinced—from the example given by the Arabic Readers—that the
forms with a final vowel had to be regarded as the more correct,
and these forms were now confirmed by the orthography of some
manuscripts which had been brought from the cave near Jericho
to Jerusalem in about 800. We have already seen that as
'Ḳaraites' the Masoretes carefully studied these manuscripts and
placed great reliance on them in their reconstruction of Hebrew
grammar.

Such final vowels were also introduced by the Masoretes into
other kinds of forms where they had not been pronounced before.
I may illustrate this by two examples:

In the liturgical texts with Palestinian punctuation the suffix of
the 3rd person singular feminine is always written without the
final vowel when added to a noun in the plural or to a noun
ending with a vowel. In Hedwatha's Ḳerobas on the Mishmarot
we find the following examples in quotations from the Bible:
אמרֹיה (אֲמָרֶיהָ) Prov. i, 21 (p. 6); מִיקְרָאֹיה (מִקְרָאֶהָ) Isa. iv, 5 (p. 6);
כרמֹיה (כְּרָמֶיהָ), נעֹורֹיה (וְעוּרֶיהָ) Hos. ii, 17 (p. 23). In the liturgical
poems themselves we find חֹומֹֹותֹיה (p. 8, cf. חֹומֹתֶיהָ Ps. lv, 11);
שעֹרֹיה (p. 9, cf. שְׁעָרֶיהָ Lam. i, 4, &c.); עלֹֹותֹיה[ת] (p. 14, cf. תְּעָלֹתֶיהָ
Ezek. xxxi, 4); לשֹֹומרֹיה (p. 14); כֹפֹיה (p. 17, cf. כַּפֶּיהָ Prov. xxxi,
13, &c); בֹיכֹורֹיה (p. 17). To these examples I may add some
from the 'Aboda of Jose b. Jose, according to the Oxford MS Heb.
d. 55, fol. 12 ff.: מֹתֹנֹיה (ii, 3; cf. מָתְנֶיהָ Prov. xxxi, 12); מכֹֹונֹיה (ii, 4;
cf. מְכֹונֶיהָ Ps. civ; 5); פֹֹיה (ix, 5; cf. פִּיהָ Prov. xxx, 20, &c.); אמרֹיה
(x, 1; cf. אֲמָרֶיהָ Prov. i, 21, &c., see above). Similar forms can
be found in all liturgical MSS with Palestinian punctuation. In

the Second Column of the Hexapla specimens of this kind are generally not preserved. I know of only one example: αμουδα (עַמּוּדֶיהָ) Ps. lxxv, 4 (Field). It is clear that the Masoretes introduced in these forms too a final vowel which was not spoken before, and it is very likely that this vowel was not pronounced at the time when Hebrew was still a spoken language and Old Testament poetry was composed. I may here refer to §232 of the *Metrische Studien*, where Sievers has shown that all these forms with the final vowel are against the metrical law on which Hebrew poetry was based.

The second example is the 2nd person singular masculine of the perfect. Here also the Masoretes regularly introduced a final vowel which had not been pronounced—or not regularly pronounced—previously. In the Second Column of the Hexapla we find the following specimens:[1]
ναθαθ נָתַתָּה xviii, 41; αφαχθ הָפַכְתָּ xxx, 12; φαδιθ פָּדִיתָ xxxi, 1; ιαδαθ יָדַעְתָּ xxxi, 8; ραϊθ רָאִיתָ xxxi, 8; σαμαθ שָׁמַעְתָּ xxxi, 23; ζαναθ זָנַחְתָּ lxxxix, 39; φαρασθ פָּרַצְתָּ lxxxix, 41; σαμθ שַׂמְתָּ lxxxix, 41; μαγαρθ מִגַּרְתָּה lxxxix, 45.

To these I may add the following forms transcribed by Jerome: *sarith* שָׂרִיתָ Gen. xxxii, 29; *carath* קָרָאתָ Jer. iii, 12; *calloth* קַלּוֹתָ Nahum i, 14. It is true that these forms without a final vowel are not the only ones found in the Second Column. We have here also the following transcriptions with the final vowel: φααλθα פָּעַלְתָּ xxxi, 20; σαφανθα צָפַנְתָּ xxxi, 20; ραειθα רָאִיתָה xxxv, 22; βαραθα בָּרָאתָ lxxxix, 48. It may be that the different pronunciation of these forms was due to the different Hebrew orthography, in so far as forms written in Hebrew with final ה were pronounced with a final vowel. On this assumption we have to suppose that the consonantal text, used by those who created the transcribed text preserved in the Second Column of the Hexapla, differed in some instances from the text which we now have. The same difference is to be found in the liturgical texts with Palestinian punctuation. Here these forms were written without the final vowel when the Hebrew text was written without a final ה. In the Ḳerobas of Hedwatha we find the following examples: ואמרת (וְאָמַרְתָּ) Jer. xxv, 30; הית (הָיִיתָ) Ps. xc, 1; ידעת (יָדַעְתָּ) Ps. cxxxix, 2. But we find also נתתה (נָתַתָּה) Deut. xxvi, 15 and בנתה (בַּנְתָּה) Ps. cxxxix, 2 written with ה and a final vowel. In the liturgical

[1] Cf. A. Sperber's article, quoted above, p. 166, n. 2.

poems themselves such forms are always written with a final ה and therefore also provided with a final vowel. It is clear that in this case also the Masoretes have introduced a final vowel which usually was not pronounced in earlier times; I may here again refer to Sievers's *Metrische Studien*, where he has shown in §227 that the metrical system demands the forms without a final vowel.

23. The Pronunciation of the BGDKPT[1]

Discussing the regulations for the correct utterance of the Shma‘, the Jewish creed consisting of the pericopes Deut. vi, 4–9; xi, 13–22; Num. xv, 37–41, which every Jew must in duty recite at least twice a day, Rabbi ‘Obadya quotes in the presence of Raba (bar Joseph, died 352, one of the greatest Talmudic authorities) the Baraitha, i.e. a Tannaitic statement not preserved in the Mishna:[2]

> וְלִמַּדְתֶּם ‘and ye shall teach’ (Deut. xi, 19) means that in order that your teaching should be perfect a pause (רֶוַח) must be made between the (letters) clinging together (הדבקים). Raba said after him: That is to say על לבבך (Deut. vi, 6); על לבבכם (xi, 18); בכל לבבך (vi, 5); בכל לבבכם (xi, 13); עשׂב בשׂדך (xi, 15); ואבדתם מהרה (xi, 17); הכנף פתיל (Num. xv, 38); אתכם מארע (xv. 41).

Raba enumerates here the eight places where in the Shma‘ a word begins with that consonant with which the previous word ends. In order that such words should not cling together, a pause was to be made between them. Six of the examples given by Raba are quite clear. But two examples, עשב בשדך and הכנף פתיל, are meaningless unless both בs and both פs are pronounced in the same way. If one of these letters had been pronounced as a spirant and the other as a plosive, as the Masora demands, there would have been no danger whatever of their clinging

[1] Cf. my article 'Die Punktation der Masoreten' in *Marti-Festschrift, Vom Alten Testament* (*Beihefte zur Zeitschrift für die Alttestamentliche Wissenschaft*, vol. xli), Giessen, 1925, pp. 167–72; also in *Opera Minora*, Leiden, 1956, pp. 48–53.

[2] Cf. Bab. Talmud, Ber. fol. 16b. The same Tannaitic source is quoted in the Palestinian Talmud, Ber. 2. 4, with the same examples, only בכל לבבך and בכל לבבכם are omitted, and אשר נשבע יהוה Deut. 11, 21 is added. יהוה was read as אדני, an interesting example for the fact that there was no difference in the pronunciation of ע and א at that time in Palestine. But an authority like Raba is not mentioned here. Louis Ginzberg, in his huge *Commentary* (New York, 1941, 3 vols, more than 1,200 pages for Ber. 1–4), discusses these facts at full length. But he is anxious to write his Commentary on very conservative lines, and so he does not dare draw the necessary conclusions.

together. It is therefore obvious that Raba had in mind here a pronunciation which differed from that fixed by the Masoretes. What do we know of the earlier pronunciation of these letters?

In the Second Column of the Hexapla, the Hebrew כ, פ, ת are regularly rendered by χ, φ, θ, as may be seen in the following examples:

1. for כ: χαβωδ כָּבוֹד xxix, 1; οσχι חָשְׁכִּי xviii, 29; θηληχ תֵּלֵךְ xxxii 8; βδερχ בְּדֶרֶךְ lii, 8; ιεχχον יִכּוֹן lxxxix, 38.
2. for פ: φαρασθ פָּרַצְתָּ lxxxix, 41; εφθα אֶפְתַּח xlix, 5; ουιφρου וַיַּחְפְּרוּ xxxv, 26; βααιφη בְּחַנְפֵּי xxxv, 16; βααφφω בְּאַפּוֹ xxx, 6; ιεφφολου יִפְּלוּ xviii, 39.
3. for ת: ναθαθ נָתַתָּה xviii, 41; θεθφαθθαλ תִּתְפַּתָּל xviii, 27, &c.

In the Septuagint, representing in certain particulars older pronunciations, we find:

Hebrew כ, usually rendered by χ, as for instance χαναaν, χαλεβ, Βαρουχ, Αβιμελεχ, Ασχαναζ. But here it is rendered sometimes by κ, e.g. in foreign names as in Κυρος כֹּרֶשׁ and in Hebrew proper names, especially in certain books, as Κενερωθ כִּנֲּרוֹת Joshua xi, 2; Κεζειβ אַכְזִיב 15, 44; Κεαφ (read Κσαφ) אַכְשָׁף 19, 25; Καραφα כְּפַר 18, 24, and besides Ζαχχουρ זַכּוּר we find Ζακχουρ, and we find Ακχω עַכּוֹ Judges i, 31; Σοκχωθ סֻכּוֹת besides Σοχωθ.

Hebrew פ, usually rendered by φ, as for instance Φαραν, Φαραω Φαλεγ, is sometimes rendered by π: Πατροσωνιειμ פַּתְרֻסִים Gen. x, 14; Πετρεφης פּוֹטִיפָר, Πειθω פִּתֹם. Exod. i, 11; θαλπιωθ Cant. iv, 4B, besides Θαλφιωθ ibid Cod. A (=תַּלְפִּיּוֹת); Σαλπααδ צְלָפְחָד Joshua xvii, 3B, besides Σαλφααδ A; Σουπ צוּף 1 Kings i, 1A; Θαπους (for Θαπουε) תַּפּוּחַ 1 Chron. ii. 43B.

Hebrew ת, usually rendered by θ, as in Θαμνα תִּמְנָה or תִּמְנַע, Θαναχ תַּעְנָךְ, is sometimes rendered by τ, cf. Ταναχ Joshua xvii, 11; Τηναθσηλω תַּאֲנַת שִׁלֹה xvi, 6A; Ταφεθ תֹּפֶת Kings xxiii, 10B, &c.

As to the Letters ב, ד and ג:

Hebrew ב is regularly rendered by β in the Second Column of the Hexapla and usually also in the Septuagint, but here we find sometimes φ, cf. Ιακεφ ζηφ יֶקֶב זְאֵב Judges vii, 25; ζηφ זָב Isa. xlix, 4; Δαλαφ (read Αaλαφ) אַחְלָב Judges i, 31.

Hebrew ד is regularly rendered by δ in the Second Column of the Hexapla and usually also in the Septuagint, but here we find, for instance, ματραειθ מַטְרֵד Gen. xxxvi, 39. This letter was pronounced as a spirant in official Jewish circles in the second century A.D. and later is so considered in the Talmud where a

Tannaitic saying is quoted:[1] צריך להאריך באחד 'It is necessary to extend in אחד'. This is explained as meaning that when saying the Shma' the ד in the word אחד must be extended. This is possible only if this letter was pronounced as a spirant, i.e. as *dh*.

Hebrew ג is regularly rendered by γ in the Second Column of the Hexapla and usually also in the Septuagint. But here we find sometimes ϰ, cf. Δωηϰ דּוֹאֵג 1 Kings xxii, 9 B (Δωηγ in A); Ναφεϰ נֶפֶג Exod. vi, 21; Φαλεϰ, Φαλϰ פֶּלֶג Gen. x, 25, xi, 16; Σεϰελαϰ (besides Σιϰλεγ) צִקְלַג Joshua xv, 31 B, cf. xix, 5.

These few examples show that the transcriptions of these letters varied in earlier times. A careful investigation of the whole material would be necessary before we could come to definite conclusions. Both the different books and the different MSS of the Septuagint would have to be examined separately. Very often the method of transcription differs in the same MS in the different books of the Septuagint. From the different transcriptions of these letters we may infer a different pronunciation. We should also have to pay special attention to the problem of how the Greek letters may have been pronounced at the different times when the transcriptions were made.

Such investigations would also be of great value for the Septuagint itself, as the different methods of transliteration would indicate earlier and later strata in its different books and MSS.[2]

Conditions had completely changed by the time the transliterations of the Second Column of the Hexapla were made. The uniform rendering of the BGDKPT letters in this transcription seems to indicate that these letters were pronounced in one way only. For the letter פ this is expressly confirmed by Jerome. In mentioning the Hebrew word אַפַּדְנוֹ Dan. xi, 45, which he transcribes as *apedno*, he says:[3]

Notandum autem quod *p* litteram Hebraeus sermo non habeat, sed pro ipsa utatur *phe*, cuius vim Graecum φ sonat. In isto tantum loco apud Hebraeos scribatur quidem *phe*, sed legatur *p*.

The word אַפַּדְנוֹ is of foreign origin and corresponds to Accad. *apadana*, and seems to have retained a pronunciation of פ which is not to be found in real Hebrew words in Jerome's time.

[1] Cf. Palestinian Talmud, Berakhot 2, 1, Babylonian Talmud, Ber. 13 b.

[2] This has been shown by Wutz in the first part of his book *Die Transkriptionen . . .* cf. above, p. 90, n. 2. Otto Pretzl refers to these problems in his articles 'Septuagintaprobleme im Buche der Richter' and 'Die griechischen Handschriftengruppen im Buche Josua untersucht, nach ihrer Eigenart und ihrem Verhältenis zu einander', in *Biblica*, vols. vii and ix, Roma, 1926 and 1928.

[3] Cf. Siegfried, *ZAW*, vol. iv, 1884, p. 63.

We have already seen that Jerome's transcriptions of Hebrew words have to be regarded with caution.[1] He usually renders Hebrew words as he found them in his Greek sources. We should not be surprised to find in his works Hebrew words transcribed according to very early methods. When we find in his quotations a Hebrew פ rendered by *p*, we have to recognize in them quotations from the Septuagint or from the Greek Onomasticon, where such transliterations are often to be found. When we find in his quotations a Hebrew פ rendered by *ph*, we should recognize an influence of the method of transliteration used in the Second Column of the Hexapla, although sometimes possibly derived from MSS of the Septuagint, in which the transcription of Hebrew names was made to conform with that method. Transcribed Hebrew words in which a Hebrew פ is rendered by *f* are of special interest. In these we must see Jerome's own transcriptions, made to accord with the pronunciation which he heard in Palestine from his Jewish teachers. I may quote here from *Hieronymi Quaestiones Hebraicae in libro Geneseos*[2] the following examples: *marahaefeth* מְרַחֶפֶת i, 2; *afar* עָפָר iii, 14; *nifilim* הַנְּפִלִים vi, 4; *therafim* הַתְּרָפִים xxxi, 19; *Iafeth* יֶפֶת ix, 18; יֶפֶת x, 2; *Fut* פוט x, 2; *Nefthuim* נַפְתֻּחִים x, 13; *Arfaxad* אַרְפַּכְשַׁד x, 24; *Salef* שָׁלֶף x, 26; *Ofir* אוֹפִיר x, 29; *Fanuhel* פְּנוּאֵל (MT. פְּנִיאֵל) xxxii, 31; *Elifaz* אֱלִיפַז xxxvi, 4; *Efratha* אֶפְרָתָה xxxv, 16.

This transcription of Hebrew פ is quite in accordance with Jerome's statement quoted above. There can be no doubt that Jerome (about 330–420) heard in Palestine the very pronunciation of Hebrew פ which Raba, the Babylonian Amora (299–352), presupposes as the correct pronunciation of הכנף פתיל in the Shma', and that this correct pronunciation was *ha-kanaf fethil*, just as the correct pronunciation presupposed by Raba was *'esebh bhesadheka* or, according to what we have seen before, *eesebh bh'sadhakh*. It is quite certain that the double pronunciation of the BGDKPT, fixed as alone 'correct' by the Masoretes in Tiberias and Babylonia, was earlier completely unknown to the most authoritative Jewish circles.

The first indication of a double pronunciation of these letters is to be found in the Sēpher Yeṣīra, the earliest Cabbalistic writing of which we know, a book which has had great influence upon Jewish thought.[3] There is a shorter and a longer text of this

[1] Cf. above, p. 166. [2] ed. Paul de Lagarde, Lipsiae, 1868.

[3] Cf. G. Scholem's article 'Jezira' in *Encyclopaedia Judaica*, vol. ix, cols. 104–11; Sarton, *History of Science*, ii, pp. 367 f.

book, greatly differing from each other. The shorter text is commented on by Jewish authors in the second half of the tenth century and often in later times. On the longer text we have the commentary written by Sa'adya in the first half of the tenth century. We do not know when the book was written. It is certain that Sa'adya regarded the book commented on by him as an old text.

In this book we find a double classification of Hebrew letters,[1] the first on phonetical principles with five groups: (1) אחהע, (2) בומפ, (3) גיכק, (4) דטלנת, (5) זסצרש; the second differentiating between (1) 'the mothers', the three letters אמש, corresponding to the three elements air, water, fire, to the three seasons, &c.; (2) the seven letters with a double pronunciation, the letters בגדכפרת, corresponding to the seven planets, the seven heavens, &c; (3) the other twelve letters with simple pronunciation, corresponding to the twelve signs of the Zodiac, the twelve months, &c.

It is interesting that the letter ר is connected here with the six BGDKFT. Sa'adya reports that he has himself been told that the double pronunciation of ר was only *spoken* in Babylonia; it was both spoken and also indicated in writing in Tiberias. In spite of this statement we find the double pronunciation of the letter indicated in the Babylonian MS or qu 680 of the Berlin Library,[2] and no Tiberian MS is known to me in which the double pronunciation of ר is indicated. The Tiberian Masoretes abandoned this double pronunciation, and under their influence the indication of the double pronunciation of the letter was abandoned in later Babylonian MSS of the Bible also. Later Hebrew grammarians mention the difference in the pronunciation of the letter, but they no longer understand it.[3] We have here an interesting proof of the fact that the Masoretes have altered a pronunciation which, according to Sa'adya, was generally used in his time.

The two pronunciations of the seven letters are called קשה and רך in the Sepher Yeṣīra. This recalls Syriac Ḳushshaiya and Rukkacha, the signs indicating the double pronunciation of the BGDKFT in Syriac. It was the great James of Edessa

[1] Cf. W. Bacher, 'Die Anfänge der hebräischen Grammatik', in *ZDMG*, vol. xlix, Leipzig, 1895, pp. 20–3.

[2] Cf. my book *Der Masoretische Text des Alten Testaments nach der Überlieferung der Babylonischen Juden*, Leipzig, 1902, p. 44. Other older Babylonian Biblical MSS in which ר is provided with Dagesh and Rafe are mentioned in *Masoreten des Ostens*.

[3] I have quoted and discussed these statements in my book of 1902, referred to in footnote 2 above, pp. 38–45.

(640–708) who, as far as we know, was the first to observe the double pronunciation of these letters in the Syriac language, and under his influence signs for the different pronunciations were introduced.[1] The signs indicating the plosive (hard) and the spirant (soft) pronunciation were at first not added regularly to the letters, but only in exceptional cases, and so *two* signs had to be introduced. Later these signs were added regularly to these letters in Syriac MSS.

The fragments of old Hebrew Biblical MSS show the same method. Here also the signs were added only in rare cases. Thus is the presence of the two signs to be explained. In later MSS the two signs were regularly added to all the letters in question. The names of the signs were altered; in the Babylonian Masora they were called Digsha and Ḳifya, in the Tiberian Masora Dagesh and Raphe.[2] But the old names preserved in the Sepher Yeṣīra are valuable hints indicating the origin of this kind of pronunciation. It is very likely that the double pronunciation of the BGDKFT was introduced into Hebrew in the course of the eighth century. The regular introduction of the signs was accomplished in Syriac and Hebrew Biblical MSS during the ninth century. It is a curious coincidence that the oldest dated Masoretic Biblical MS of the Syrians preserved to us, the famous British Museum MS Add. 12138,[3] was written at nearly the same time (899) as the oldest dated Masoretic text of the Hebrew Bible preserved to us, the Ben Asher Codex of the Prophets in the Synagogue of the Ḳaraites in Cairo (895).

24. *Conclusions*

From the three examples referring to the treatment of the Hebrew Bible by the Tiberian Masoretes discussed above, we can draw the following conclusions:

When in the course of the ninth century the Masoretes of Tiberias began their work of adding a consistent punctuation to the text of the Hebrew Bible, they were convinced that it was their duty to give the text of the Bible as correct a form as possible

[1] Cf. Rubens Duval, *Traité de Grammaire Syriaque*, Paris 1881, pp. 112 ff.

[2] Cf. my contribution to Bauer and Leander, *Historische Grammatik der Hebräischen Sprache des Alten Testamentes*, vol. i, Halle 1922, pp. 117–29.

[3] Cf. Theodor Weiss, *Zur Ostsyrischen Laut- und Akzentlehre auf Grund der ostsyrischen Massora—Handschrift des British Museum* (= Bonner Orientalistische Studien, Heft 5) Stuttgart 1933. Here the text of Genesis is reproduced according to the British Museum MS. The earlier references to the MS are mentioned by Weiss.

—just as the Readers of the Koran had been anxious to give the best possible form to the Koran for reading and pronunciation.

The Arab Readers had adapted the text of the Koran, which had been spoken by the Prophet in the language of an educated citizen of Mecca, to a classical form of Arabic based on pre-Islamic Bedouin poetry which they had carefully studied. A large number of exhortations are preserved in which the faithful are taught how much greater value derives from reading the Koran accurately, by observing I'rāb and all details fixed by the Readers, than from reading the text without such corrections.

The Tiberian Masoretes, likewise, created a correct Hebrew text which they indicated by a consistent system of signs added to the consonantal text, thereby regulating in every detail the pronunciation and recitation of the text of the Bible.

The Arab Readers declared again and again that they had done nothing else than restore the word of God to its original purity. They succeeded in causing the disappearance of all the older treatises dealing with the reading of the Koran, so that only those books were preserved which presupposed their accepted method of reading the text of the Koran. It was quite by chance that the two treatises dealing with earlier methods of reading the text came into the Collection of rare Arabic books belonging to Sir Alfred Chester Beatty.

The Masoretes of Tiberias emphasize with all their energy that the form of the text of the Bible which they had fixed was transmitted to them in the most reliable way from the time of Ezra by the men of the Great Synagogue; that they had neither concealed anything nor added anything to what was transmitted to them. What they had intended to do was to make the Scriptures great and powerful, to establish them with explanatory accents and clear pronunciation with sweet palate and beauty of speech.

They secured the abolition or adaptation of all the texts provided with a different kind of punctuation, such as the Babylonian text of the Prophets from Leningrad, or the Yemenite manuscripts. Vocalized texts independent of the text of the Tiberian Masoretes are found only in the fragments of the Geniza, in the texts retranscribed in Greek or Latin letters transmitted by Christians, in the form in which the Samaritans still read the Hebrew text in their Synagogues, and in the ancient Hebrew texts found recently in the caves near the Dead Sea.

These texts are certainly important for understanding the

historical development of the text of the Bible. But up to the present they have hardly been taken into account. The text fixed by the Tiberian Masoretes has been almost the only one considered in the preparation of our Hebrew grammars. Now we know that this text was altered by the Masoretes.

I have tried to show

1. That the Masoretes of Tiberias introduced a number of new vowels to safeguard the newly-established pronunciation of the gutturals. In this task they seem to have followed the example of the Arab Readers of the Koran who introduced the Hamza sign for securing the pronunciation of the consonantal Alif which had not been taken into account in the language of the Koran as previously read.

2. That the Masoretes introduced a number of end-vowels which previously may have existed in Hebrew. We do not know whether the loss of these vowels was caused by an internal linguistic development or by the too powerful influence of the Aramaic vernacular language. But we must realize that the long final vowels had been lost at a time when Hebrew was still a language in daily use. By reintroducing these vowels, the Masoretes probably followed the example set by the Arab Readers when they introduced end-vowels into the text of the Koran in accordance with Bedouin poetry, particularly the I'rāb. Besides, they may have also followed the example of those Dead Sea Scrolls which were brought, in about 800, from the cave near Jericho to Jerusalem.

3. That the Masoretes introduced a double pronunciation of the BGDKPT, a pronunciation of which nothing was known in the most authoritative Jewish circles of previous centuries. The Masoretes may have here followed the Syrians who had created special signs to indicate this double pronunciation which they observed in their spoken language.

The Masoretes therefore corrected and changed the pronunciation of the Hebrew text in three different ways, and they seem to have done so under Arabic, ancient Hebrew and Syriac influence. Consequently we shall have to subject the whole system of Masoretic punctuation to a careful examination. The system has certainly lost much of its authoritative value.[1] What

[1] R. Meyer 'Probleme der hebräischen Grammatik', *ZAW*, 1951, pp. 221–35. The same: 'Zur Geschichte des hebräischen Verbums', *VT*, iii, 1953, pp. 224–235. The same: 'Die Bedeutung der linearen Vokalisation für die hebräische Sprachgeschichte'. *Wissenschaftliche Zeitschrift der Universität Leipzig* (Alt-Festschrift), 1953/54, pp. 67–76.

we need are vocalized Hebrew texts independent of the work of the Tiberian Masoretes.

In the Cairo Geniza we have found rich vocalized Hebrew material independent of their work. The texts with simple Babylonian punctuation have recently been greatly enlarged by the discoveries of Professor Diez Macho, so that we have now almost half the Hebrew Bible with this punctuation. We have seen how this *Irāḳian reading* was used in many parts of the world. It is an important task of scholarship to publish the material available as soon as possible.

Further, the material preserved in the texts with Palestinian punctuation, as far as it can be seen to be independent of the influence of Tiberian punctuation, is of great importance also. The Palestinian material prepared by Dr. A. Murtonen of Helsinki shows how the work on these texts must be done, and the grammar prepared by him on the basis of these texts shows us a form of the Hebrew spoken in Palestine before the work of the Tiberian Masoretes began.

We see that the language which was used here is clearly connected with the form of Hebrew used by the Samaritans in their religious services up to the present day. The Hebrew text recorded in Nāblus by Hellmut Ritter and especially by Arthur Schaade, which I am publishing here in Appendix II, will make possible a real study of this form of language. It is of great significance that plene-written Dead Sea Scrolls have confirmed the antiquity of certain characteristics in Samaritan pronunciation of Hebrew.

The Hebrew texts in Greek transcription taken over by Origen for the Second Column of his Hexapla are also very important. They seem to have been made by the most official Jewish circles and exhibit a form of Hebrew used in the second century. The edition of these texts by Giovanni Cardinal Mercati will make possible a careful study of them and will provide the basis for further research on other surviving transcribed texts, thereby giving an opportunity to see the earlier development of Hebrew pronunciation. They are older than the text of our Bible and with their help we might be able to investigate problems of Hebrew metric in a promising way. We must always realize that the Masoretes of Tiberias were interested in preparing a reliable text for divine service. They did not prepare a basis for metrical studies.

Gotthelf Bergsträsser, in his article 'Ist die tiberiensische Vokalisation eine Rekonstruktion?' (*OLZ* 1924, No. 26) puts the question:

> 'Is such a daring reform as Kahle supposes thinkable in these centuries bound by tradition? Hardly; least of all if the vocalization does in fact go back to the Masoretes. For what we know of their activity shows an obstinate clinging to the smallest details of what was transmitted to them' (referring to my article in *ZAW* 1921, pp. 230–239, = *Opera Minora*, Leiden 1956, pp. 38–47).

What we knew until recently of the activity of the Masoretes is not very reliable as it was impossible to go behind the text which they created. But now, given the material found in the Geniza and having learned to consider other pre-Masoretic material, it should be possible to arrive at a truly historical understanding of their work. The Jews owe the uniform text of the Bible to the work of the Masoretes. Looking back to this final achievement the verdict of Bergsträsser concerning the character of the Masora is understandable. But it has only the same value as, for instance, the statement that the Law codified in the Mishna is identical with the Oral Law revealed, together with the Written Law, to Moses on Sinai. Both are articles of faith to the pious Jew. But science cannot be based on such principles; it must be established on the data of history.

PART III

The Translations of the Bible

CHAPTER III

THE TRANSLATIONS OF THE BIBLE

1. The Targum Onḳelos

When we speak of Targums, the Aramaic translations of the Bible, we think in the first instance of Targum Onḳelos to the Torah and of Targum Jonathan to the Prophets. These are the two official Jewish Targums and there is no doubt that they received the form in which we have them in Babylonia. In the Cairo Geniza quite a number of fragments of these two Targums were found, provided with genuine Babylonian punctuation. This itself shows that they must have circulated in Babylonia. And not the least fragment of any other Targum with this kind of punctuation is known to us. It is clear that only these two Targums were used in Babylonia.

The name *Onḳelos* by which the Targum to the Torah is generally quoted is nothing else than Aquilas. Aquilas was considered to be the author of a Greek translation of the Bible in which the Greek text was adapted as far as possible to the Hebrew original, even to the pedantic rendering of all details. In the Palestinian Talmud the name is written ʿAḳilas (עקילס) and it is given several times as that of the author of the new Greek translation of the Bible. We learn that he was a proselyte (גר), no born Israelite, and that he was a pupil of Rabbi ʿAḳiba. The name is altered in the Babylonian Talmud to *Onḳelos* (אונקלוס), a name which certainly derives from Aquilas. Of Onḳelos several things are told, but generally no Bible translation is connected with the name. There is only one place in the Babylonian Talmud, Megillah 3a, where the Targum to the Torah is attributed to *Onḳelos the Proselyte* אונקלוס הגר, and in the same place *Jonathan ben ʿUzziel* is given as author of the Targum to the Prophets. This reference in the Babylonian Talmud is the *only* evidence for connecting the two Babylonian Targums with these two names.

But the Babylonian Talmud depends here on the Palestinian Talmud,[1] where we find, in Megilla 1.9, information concerning

[1] As demonstrated by Ludwig Blau, in *JQR*, xi, 1897, p. 738f.

the Greek version of Aquilas (עקילס). It was only the Babylonian Talmud that connected the name of Aquilas, altered to Onḳelos, with the Aramaic translation of the Torah, clearly on the assumption that the Targum Onḳelos would help the Aramaic speaking Jews to understand the Hebrew Torah correctly, just as the Greek translation of the Bible attributed to Aquilas was intended to help the Greek speaking Jews to understand the Hebrew Bible.

Concerning the language of Targum Onḳelos, Gustaf Dalman —like others before him—is quite right in pointing out that it corresponds with neither the Aramaic dialect of the Babylonian Talmud, nor the Aramaic dialect of the Palestinian Talmud. He says that it is related to Biblical Aramaic and he thinks that we may take it to be in the main an exact rendering in the language spoken at that time in Judaea. Yet he goes back on his words when he says:[1]

> At the same time the Targum of Onḳelos is not a copy of a translation of the Pentateuch into the Jewish dialect, as spoken by the people, but a scholarly and artificial imitation of the Hebrew original, showing a treatment of the Aramaic language similar to that of the Greek in the translation by Aquila, who belonged to the same circles.

But what Dalman has not seen is that the similarity of the two texts is due to both having been composed in a language which had become the official Aramaic language in the Persian Empire. This official literary Aramaic had originally been only one of the different dialects in circulation. But conditions in the Persian Empire had resulted in one of these dialects becoming the mainly uniform official language. Almost all Aramaic texts known to us are written in it. I would only mention here the Aramaic parts of the Biblical books of Ezra and Daniel, and the Leather Documents from Susa published by G. R. Driver which had been sent by the Achaemenide prince Arsham, the Satrap, to his officials in Egypt,[2] letters important not only for their contents, but also because they originated from non-Jewish circles; they show that the language was at that time in general use in the Persian Empire.

In mainly the same language were written the documents

[1] *Grammatik des jüdisch-palästinischen Aramäisch*, 2nd edition Leipzig, 1905, p. 13.

[2] *Aramaic Documents of the Fifth Century B.C.* transcribed and edited with translation and notes by G. R. Driver. Oxford 1954.

and letters found in the Jewish military colony at Elephantine in Upper Egypt. These have recently been greatly augmented by the texts that Charles Edwin Wilbour, an American Egyptologist who used to spend the winter on his Dahabiye on the Nile, bought in 1893 near Assuan. These papyri came in 1947 to the Brooklyn Museum in New York and were published by Emil G. Kraeling in 1953.[1]

In the same literary language was written the Targum Onḳelos and also for the most part the Targum of the Prophets. But we should not neglect what H. L. Ginsberg of the Jewish Theological Seminary of America in New York has pointed out in his very instructive review of the book of Franz Rosenthal: *Die Aramaistische Forschung seit Th. Nöldeke's Veröffentlichungen* (Leiden 1939)[2].

> But of course, official Aramaic was never absolutely uniform except in intention, and . . . in course of time, especially after the destruction of the Achaemenian empire, became more and more coloured by the spoken language . . . (233) . . . From the Greek period on official Aramaic tended to be coloured more and more by the vernaculars; but so coloured it continued to be employed in writing, by Palmyrenes and Arabs (Nabateans) always and by Jews for certain purposes.

The consequence of this undoubtedly correct observation must certainly be that from the language of texts composed in literary Aramaic we cannot recognize when and where they were written. We can only pick up hints from certain characteristics deriving from the copyists of the texts due to the language spoken by them.

This holds above all for the Targum Onḳelos. We must understand clearly that this Targum was written in literary Aramaic and can tell us nothing at all about the form of the language spoken by the people at the time of the beginning of Christianity. Besides, it is certain that this Targum was not written before the destruction of the Temple, at the time when Judaism was being reorganized. The name under which the Targum is still known records this. The proselyte Aquilas, who provided Judaism after the destruction of the Temple with the

[1] *Aramaic Papyri of the Fifth Century B.C.*, ed. with translations and notes by A. E. Cowley. Oxford at the Clarendon Press 1923. *The Brooklyn Museum Aramaic Papyri.* New Documents of the Fifth Century B.C. from the Jewish Colony at Elephantine, ed. with a historical introduction by Emil G. Kraeling. Published for the Brooklyn Museum by the Yale University Press, New Haven 1953.

[2] *Journal of the American Oriental Society*, vol. 62, 1942, p. 232f.

trustworthy Greek translation of the Bible that bears his name, is the prototype of the proselyte Onḳelos who provided Judaism with the Aramaic translation of the Torah that was to become the authoritative one.

What can be taken as quite certain, though hardly realized even by Gustaf Dalman, is that this Targum composed in literary Aramaic was not of any importance at that time in Palestine. As proof of this it is sufficient for me to give a few sentences from A. Berliner's introduction to his reprint of the Sabbioneta edition of the Targum Onḳelos.[1]

> To procure recognition and respect for this Targum in its country of origin was not possible. For that reason the Targum had hitherto no authority among the scholars of Palestine. It was only referred to in disparagement; one never quoted from it as from the Greek translation. Consequently no quotation from the Targum can be found in the Mishna or in the Jerusalem Talmud.

This surely means that the Targum Onḳelos was without importance in Palestine. If the Targum Onḳelos had originated in Palestine, as Berliner and many others claim, we should have to suppose that even the nearly all-powerful Rabbis who worked for the reorganization of Judaism after the destruction of the Temple, among whom Rabbi 'Aḳiba was one of the most prominent, were not in a position to replace a Targum highly esteemed in Palestine by a newly formed Targum, the Targum Onḳelos.

The other alternative is that the Rabbis working on the reorganization of Judaism in Palestine did not think of replacing the Targum current at that time by a new one, and that the Targum Onḳelos originated in Babylonia. It is certain that it early came into circulation there. We know from the Masora to Targum Onḳelos that manuscripts were in circulation with different readings named after the two Talmudic Academies of Sūra and Nehardea. Since the Academy of Nehardea was destroyed in the course of the third century, we must conclude that the Targum Onḳelos was known and was in circulation in the two Academies before that time.

The Targum Onḳelos was further developed in Babylonia during the following centuries on the basis of Mishna and Talmud, until it finally became the authoritative text that, in the official

[1] Zweiter Theil, Berlin 1884, p. 108f.

literary Aramaic, established the correct Jewish understanding of every passage of the Torah, and was regarded as of the highest authority among the Jews. As such the Targum was brought to Palestine. It was brought there together with other authoritative products of Babylonian Judaism, especially the Babylonian Talmud, and the yearly Parasha-division of the Torah—in Palestine the Palestinian Talmud, the Palestinian Targum, and the three yearly Seder-division had hitherto been used. We learn of various efforts to persuade Palestinian Judaism to take over the Babylonian Talmud and the whole Gaonic tradition, after Babylonia and Palestine, the chief centres of Judaism at that time, had been united under Arab suzerainty. We are told that already at the middle and end of the eighth century such attempts had been made. But far reaching changes of this kind could not be carried through so quickly. In the Cairo Geniza quite a number of fragments of the Palestinian Targum of the Pentateuch were contained that had been used in Palestine before the Targum Onḳelos had been brought there, among them remains of splendid manuscripts in which, after the Hebrew verse of the Torah, the corresponding verse of the Palestinian Targum follows. They show that the demand for Torah manuscripts with the Palestinian Targum was still at that time very strong. One forms the impression that the Targum Onḳelos was scarcely introduced into Palestine before 1000 A.D. But subsequently it became so firmly established that it completely replaced the Palestinian Targum of which fragments only were found in the Cairo Geniza.

It was therefore an exceptional event when Professor A. Diez Macho of Barcelona University discovered a complete copy of the text of the Palestinian Targum in MS Neofiti I of the Vatican Library (450 parchment folios) which was written in Rome at the beginning of the 16th century, making now available to us this long lost Palestinian Targum of the Pentateuch in a way we had not at all expected. I will discuss it further below.

2. The Targum of the Prophets

The name Jonathan given to the Targum of the Prophets is simply a translation of the Greek name Theodotion. To Theodotion was attributed a Greek translation of the Bible that was used by Origen in his Hexapla. We now know that it was a Greek translation of the Bible which was already in circulation in pre-Christian times. The name, hebraized to Jonathan, was given to the so-called author of the Babylonian Targum of the Prophets who was later identified with Jonathan b. ʿUzziel, a pupil of Hillel, with whom, however, it had nothing to do.

In the palimpsest of the Hexapla, discovered by Giovanni Mercati in the nineties of last century in the Ambrosiana of Milan, the Quinta with the various readings of the Sexta is to be found instead of Theodotion. This has been proved by Mercati.[1] The way in which Rahlfs refers to the Milan Fragments:[2]

> Jetzt bin ich durch Mercati's Freundlichkeit in den Stand gesetzt, die Mailänder Fragmente vollständig zu benutzen. Allzugross ist allerdings die Ausbeute bei dem relativ geringen Umfang der Fragmente auch jetzt nicht, doch bieten sie eine erfreuliche Bereicherung unsers Wissens.

reveals a complete lack of understanding of the problems raised by these important texts which, in the view of Eduard Schwartz, will inaugurate a new era in the study of the Hexapla.[3] When Rahlfs published his Septuagint text, he paid no attention whatever to the Hexapla. Cardinal Mercati often told me how disappointed he was by the way in which Rahlfs had neglected the material he had put at his disposal.

In contrast to the Targum Onḳelos *old* parts can be found in the Targum of the Prophets which go far back into pre-Christian times. Both Professor W. H. Brownlee[4] of Duke University, North Carolina and also Dr. Naftali Wieder of Jews' College in London[5] have shown how probable it is that the Habakkuk Commentary found in Qumran Cave I presupposes in several places the Targum of the Prophets. Exact investigation of the Targum to the Prophets must be made as soon as the new edition of it appears, prepared by Dr. Alexander Sperber partly in Bonn.

We know that additional material to the Targum of the Prophets is often cited by Rashi, Ḳimḥi and in the Codex Reuchlinianus (written 1105 A.D.) of which the Targum text was published (without vocalisation) by Paul de Lagarde[6] and which has just

[1] *Studi e Testi* v, 1901, pp. 40f.
[2] *Psalmi cum Odis, Septuaginta*, vol. x, Göttingen 1931, p. 52.
[3] *Zur Geschichte der Hexapla, Nachrichten*, Gesellschaft der Wissenschaften, Göttingen, 1903, Heft 6, p. 7.
[4] 'The Habakkuk Midrash and the Targum of Jonathan.' *IJSt*, 1956, 169–186.
[5] 'The Habakkuk Scroll and the Targum.' *IJSt* iv 1953, 14–18.
[6] *Prophetae Chaldaice.* Paulus de Lagarde e fide codicis reuchliniani edidit Lipsiae, 1872.

been published in a facsimile edition in Copenhagen by A. Sperber.[1] Zunz already wrote in 1832 in his *Die gottesdienstlichen Vorträge der Juden, historisch entwickelt.* Berlin, 1832, p. 79:

> May we not conclude from the agreement of historical evidence and with reference to Haggadic Targum fragments on the books of Judges, Samuel, Kings, Isaiah, Jeremiah, Ezekiel, Micah, Habakkuk, Zechariah, that for all the prophetical books a complete Jerusalem[—i.e. Palestinian]-Targum must have existed?

Professor A. Diez Macho has recently published a fragment of the Targum on Joshua found in the Library of the Jewish Theological Seminary, New York. I had found another fragment of the same text in the Geniza material in Cambridge (Box B 13[12]) of which, at my suggestion, Alastair McIntosh prepared an edition in Bonn. Diez Macho wrote to me a short time ago that he is publishing in a forthcoming number of *Biblica* a new fragment of the Palestinian Targum of the Prophets which he has found.

There can be no doubt that the Targum of the Prophets was in circulation in Babylonia, that like the Targum Onḳelos it received the form we know there, and that it was brought over to Palestine together with the Targum Onḳelos. But it is more difficult to ascertain the fate of the Targum of the Prophets. And it must be investigated anew as soon as material becomes available.

We have in the Targum of the Prophets, besides the translation of the Hebrew text of the Bible, a great deal of material taken from the Midrash which often contains an interesting commentary on the Bible. This midrashic element is almost entirely lacking in the Targum Onḳelos which contains only a word for word translation of the Hebrew text of the Torah, reproducing exactly, however, as we have seen, the interpretation presupposed in Mishna and Talmud. On the other hand, like the Targum of the Prophets, the Palestinian Targum contains, besides the exact translation of the Hebrew text of the Bible, a very full exposition from the Midrash so that the translation of a single verse of the Bible often occupies half a page or more. What Midrashic material we had hitherto comes from a later time, so it is of special importance that the remains of an old Midrash

[1] *Corpus Codicum Hebraicorum Medii Aevi.* Redigendum curavit Rafael Edelmann. Pars II: *The pre-Masoretic Bible,* Discovered in Four Manuscripts Representing a Unique Tradition. I The Codex Reuchlinianus . . . and published with a General Introduction, Detailed Description of the MSS and Basic Conclusions by Alexander Sperber. Copenhagen. Ejnar Munksgaard 1956.

book have become known through their discovery in Qumran Cave I.

3. The Midrash Book from Qumran I

This Midrash Book is contained in the leather scroll in Aramaic that was difficult to open, on account of its fragmentary condition and the uncertainty of its ownership, as long as it was in America. After the scroll had come into the possession of the Jerusalem University it was opened there with great care, and five of the twenty-two columns have now been published under the very misleading title *A Genesis Apocryphon*,[1] about which I have already spoken. What is known of the text deals with stories of the birth of Noah and of the history of Abraham.[2] The biblical history is here paraphrased and expanded; the author wishes to make it in this way more attractive and understandable. Chronological and geographical details that are added fix the text in time and place. On the other hand, in contrast with the book of Jubilees with which the book is undoubtedly connected, the chronology is not worked out according to a preconceived plan. The haggadic parts are organically bound up with the text of the Bible that is to be explained by the different passages of Genesis being brought together or by the help of a suitable story. The explanation in this Midrash book follows verse by verse the Biblical narrative. The impression is given that we have here extensive Midrashic material which it was desired to have at hand. It is perhaps not really an old form of Targum as I have previously said,[3] but one only has to study the Palestinian Targum of the Pentateuch in order to see how much midrashic material is contained in it—in the Aramaic, in the main spoken by the people, in which the Palestinian Targum of the Pentateuch was written.

An attempt to establish the language of this Midrash Scroll has been made by E. Y. Kutscher of the University of Jerusalem.[4] He deals with it in the following way:
1. The linguistic background. 2. The language of the scroll and

[1] *A Genesis Apocryphon*. A Scroll from the Wilderness of Judaea. Description and Contents of the Scroll, Facsimiles, Transcription and Translation of Columns II, XIX–XXII by Nahman Avigad and Yigael Yadin. Jerusalem 1956.

[2] See the excellent characterization of the book given by G. Vermès: *Le plus ancien Midrash sur la Genèse*. Cahiers Sioniens vol. x. See also the valuable notes given by Père de Vaux to the text in *RB* lxiv, 1957, 623-5.

[3] See Matthew Black, 'Die Erforschung der Muttersprache Jesu.' *ThLZ* 1957 p. 664, 668.

[4] 'The Language of the Genesis Apocryphon.' A preliminary Study. *Aspects of the Dead Sea Scrolls. Scripta Hierosolymitana*, volume iv. Publications of the Hebrew University of Jerusalem. Jerusalem 1957.

Middle Aramaic. 3. The language of the scroll and Biblical Aramaic. 4. The language of the scroll: a language in transition from 'Reichsaramäisch' to Middle Aramaic. 5. Influence of Biblical Aramaic on the language of the Scroll. 6. Non-Biblical 'Reichsaramäisch' elements in the Scroll. 7. The Middle Aramaic in the Scroll—Western Aramaic. 8. The Middle Aramaic of the Scroll close to Targum Onḳelos and Christian Aramaic. 9. The language of the Scroll and the Christian Aramaic of Palestine. 10. The language of the Scroll and Samaritan Aramaic. 11. Eastern Elements in the Language of the Scroll. 12. Hebrew elements in the language of the Scroll. 13. Place of Origin of the Scroll. 14. Time of Origin of the Scroll. There follow some remarks on proper names, orthography and on the text.

Kutscher's explanations seem to be very learned, but I am somewhat doubtful about them. On closer examination one can easily see that the linguistic material on the basis of which the examination is made is somewhat restricted. That only 5 of the 22 columns of the Midrash Book are considered is due to the bad condition of the scroll. We know, however, of ten fragments of the Aramaic Enoch and three fragments of the Aramaic Tobit found in cave 4, and we know of other Aramaic texts found among the Dead Sea material and in the Cairo Geniza. The utilization of these texts seems to me much more important for establishing the language of this Midrash Book than the Aramaic inscriptions made in stone by Jews, Palmyrenians and Nabateans, which Kutscher has frequently quoted. One feels that the author has not always realized the principal difference between texts in literary Aramaic and those in the Aramaic spoken in Palestine. Besides, the texts composed by Jews, Samaritans and Christians in the language spoken by the people require new editions and critical investigation before one can use them in the way Kutscher does.

Nevertheless, Kutscher may have in the main correctly established the age of the Midrash Scroll and its localization. It may well be that the scroll discovered in Qumran I was written in the first pre-Christian century, or somewhat later. But I am convinced that it was composed earlier, as it seems to have been presupposed by the book of Jubilees: the text actually found in the first cave may have been a copy of an older original.[1] I also believe

[1] Père de Vaux thinks that it is not proved that the Midrash book is older than the book of Jubilees, but he also ends his review of the book (*RB* lxiv, 1957, p. 624) with the words: 'Les textes de Qumran nous apprennent de plus en plus que cette littérature était riche et que son histoire est complexe.'

myself that the book may have been composed in Palestine; though in the case of a text like this written in literary Aramaic, I do not believe that this can be proved by linguistic arguments, as Kutscher has tried to prove it.

4. Palestinian Aramaic

As for the Aramaic texts composed by Samaritans: since I wrote my thesis[1] sixty years ago on the edition of the Samaritan Targum made by Petermann—Vollers,[2] I have tried to collect reliable material on the Targum in Rome, Nāblus, London, Oxford, Cambridge and Leningrad. Father José Ramón Díaz, of Logroño/Zaragoza, a member of the same order as Professor A. Diez Macho, has made a thorough study with me of material on the Samaritan Targum.[3] I have put at his disposal all the material I have collected, and he has himself collected with care and understanding further material and has worked on it, so we hope soon to have a trustworthy edition of Genesis according to the Samaritan Targum which will soon be followed by the other parts of the Targum. Only when we have a reliable text can a grammar and a lexicon of the Samaritan Targum be written.

On the liturgical Aramaic texts of the Samaritans, published in the main by A. E. Cowley in 1909, Dr. John Bowman, the Head of the Hebrew Department of the University of Leeds, who has discussed the problems with the Samaritans in Palestine, is now working with his collaborators and pupils. He is preparing studies and translations of the whole material for the use of liturgical scholars who are unable to read these ancient and important texts in the original. I have put at Dr. Bowman's disposal all the relevant material that I have collected myself. We may look forward to seeing the work published in the near future.

On the Christian Palestinian Aramaic texts Professor Matthew Black of St. Andrews has worked. His edition of the Christian Palestinian Aramaic Horologion, from a manuscript which I bought about fifty years ago in Cairo for the Berlin Library,

[1] *Textkritische und lexikalische Bemerkungen zum Samaritanischen Pentateuchtargum.* Halle, 1898.

[2] *Pentateuchus Samaritanus.* Ad fidem librorum manuscriptorum apud Nablusianos repertorum edidit et varias lectiones adscripsit H. Petermann. Berlin, i, 1872; ii 1882, iii 1883, iv 1885; v 1891 (iii–v ed. K. Vollers).

[3] José Ramón Días, M.S.C., 'Ediciones del Targum samaritano.' *Estudios Biblicos*, vol. xv, Madrid 1956, pp. 105–108.

has shown that the problems of these texts are somewhat different from what Francis C. Burkitt or Friedrich Schulthess thought.[1]

Regarding the Palestinian Aramaic Pentateuch: as soon as Professor Diez Macho notified me of his discovery of a complete MS of the Targum in MS Neofiti I of the Bibliotheca Vaticana, it was clear to me that a new edition was required of the Geniza fragments of this Targum which I published in 1930. I have had new photographs of the Cambridge fragments made and they have come out extremely well. In addition I have had photographs made of parts of Neofiti I.

Last October, Father Georg Schelbert came to work with me for a year on the Palestinian Targum of the Pentateuch. He had made his studies at the Institutum Biblicum in Rome and subsequently lectured for some years on the Scriptures at Schoeneck near Beckenried NW in Switzerland. He has first been working on the important Cambridge MS T-S 20, 155 (MS A), a Geniza fragment of a parchment scroll containing the Palestinian Targum on Exodus xxi-xxiii of which the Palestinian punctuation gives a very exact indication of the vocalisation of the Targum. With the help of the complete Targum it is certainly much easier to read and to complete the Geniza fragments. He has subsequently begun to work on the other fragments.

Besides the Geniza fragments published by me, other fragments have been found. Professor A. Marx sent me some photographs which were studied at my suggestion by Alastair McIntosh in Bonn. Other fragments have been discovered in New York by A. Diez Macho who has already published some of them.[2] He has rightly shown that these Geniza fragments published by us are of particular importance because their language is free from the influence of the Babylonian Targums. Moreover, these fragments—with their excellent vocalisation—will be the chief source for a grammar of the Palestinian Targum. The complete MS of the Targum is with the exception of one page without vocalisation.

Professor Diez Macho is preparing an edition of the complete MS Neofiti I with all the many marginal notes, especially variae lectiones, for the Spanish Polyglot Bible, and the Bibliotheca

[1] *A Christian Palestinian Syriac Horologion* (Berlin MS. Or. Oct. 1019). Texts and Studies, Contributions to Biblical and Patristic Literature (New Series i), ed. Matthew Black. Cambridge, University Press, 1954.

[2] 'Nuevos fragmentos del Targum Palestinense,' *Sefarad* xv, 1955, pp. 31–39. More fragments will be published in the Memorial Volume for Renée Bloch.

Vaticana has decided to bring out a facsimile edition of MS Neofiti I to which Diez Macho will write an introduction in Latin and Hebrew.

We shall also have to take into account other material of this Targum which was known to us before: the so-called Fragmenten-Targum and the Targum Pseudo-Jonathan. We now know the Fragmenten-Targum to be a collection of Midrashic material from the Palestinian Targum which people did not want to lose after the Targum Onḳelos had become the authoritative Targum in Palestine. I have discussed with Professor M. Black the importance of a new edition of this Fragmenten-Targum on the basis of the material now available, and such an edition is now being prepared.

It is to be hoped that an able scholar will also be found to deal with the Targum Pseudo-Jonathan. Hitherto it has been supposed that this Targum was made up of the Targum Onḳelos in which material from the Palestinian Targum had been inserted. As we now have complete copies of both these Targums, we are interested to see how far the Palestinian Targum may have been modified in this process. We must not forget, however, that the Palestinian Targum of the Pentateuch never had an official, uniform text; there were always different texts in existence. We must not think that the single preserved manuscript, (Add 27 031 of the British Museum) which was published by M. Ginsburger, Berlin 1903, contains all that ever existed in the Targum Pseudo-Jonathan. We know that very late events are mentioned in this manuscript. For instance in Gen xxi 21 two wives of the Prophet Muhammed are mentioned.

How important the material can be that is still contained in this Targum Pseudo-Jonathan is shown by an example which Abraham Geiger has provided in Excursus II to his '*Urschrift*' of 1857. I quote it here as given by Theodor Nöldeke in his book *Die Alttestamentliche Literatur* . . . Leipzig 1868, p. 256:

> The passage is from Deut xxxiii 11 ומשנאיו מן יקומון '. . . and those who hate him shall not stand again' is translated by: ולא יהי לסנאיו דיוחנן כהנא רבא רגל למקום '. . . and those who hate Joḥanan, the highpriest, shall not have a foot to stand on'. The 'highpriest Joḥanan' is in Jewish writings the usual designation of the great ruler John Hyrcanus. This translation must have been made during the time of his government (135–105 B.C.), because in later times the narrow-mindedness

of the spiritual rulers of the Jewish people discredited the memory of this hero in such a despicable manner, because he had not followed their opinions, that it was impossible to refer to his name after his death. We still find in this Targum all sorts of interpretations rejected in the normative writings of the Jews such as the Mishna; they go back therefore to an earlier time.

I would like to refer here to A. T. Olmstead's article 'Could an Aramaic Gospel be written?'[1]

The translation of this passage in the Pseudo-Jonathan Targum would be:

> 'Bless, Yahweh, the substance' of the House of Levi, because they give a tithe of the tithes and accept with good will 'the work of the hands' of Elijah the priest, who is sacrificing on Mount Carmel. 'Smite through the loins' of Ahab his enemy, and the neck of the false prophets 'who rise up against him'. There shall be no foot on which to stand for the enemies of John the high priest.

See Olmstead loc. cit. p. 62. He adds:

> That this is the prayer of a contemporary for John Hyrcanus immediately after the conquest of the Samaritans, is specifically indicated. That this is not a part of the original text should be equally clear from the context; the original must be earlier than the interpolation and, as found in the fragments (i.e. the Fragmenten-Targum), must therefore be not later than the beginning of the second pre-Christian century.

So we would have here a possibility of dating a part of the Targum Pseudo-Jonathan.

5. The Wensinck Material

As for the language, we have also to investigate the Aramaic parts of the Palestinian Talmud. These two sources have been taken into consideration by the late Professor A. J. Wensinck of Leiden. In the last years of his life (he died in September 1939) he made a special study of the language spoken in Palestine at the time of the beginning of Christianity there. When I saw him for the last time at his Institute in Leiden in Summer 1938, he showed me the extensive collections of slips he had made for this purpose. He had written down on slips all the words occur-

[1] *Journal of Near Eastern Studies*, Chicago, i, 1942, pp. 41–70. I refer especially to pp. 60–62 which deal with the supposed age of the Targum.

ring in the Palestinian Targum in so far as it was available at that time, collecting in this way lexicographical and grammatical material. He had taken into consideration the Greek equivalents and was just working on the Aramaic parts of the Palestinian Talmud according to its first edition (1523). I was able to see the material collected by him and we discussed the problems to which it gave rise. He was deeply impressed because the word *rabbuni*, which occurs twice in the Gospels and had not hitherto been found in any rabbinic text, is to be found quite often in the fragments of the Palestinian Targum. Unfortunately a serious illness made it impossible for him to go on with these studies.

After the war, I had the opportunity of discussing the future of this material with Professor F. A. H. de Boer at a meeting of the Old Testament Society in Cardiff in 1946. In 1947 I further discussed the matter with Mrs. Wensinck in Leiden, and with her consent and that of Professor de Boer the whole collection was sent to me in England for some years. I copied all the slips collected by Wensinck for a Palestinian Aramaic Dictionary in a bound volume and thus obtained a valuable collection which, in spite of its incompleteness, has been of great help, through its great number of references, to my pupils and helpers and to myself. It will have to be taken as the basis for a dictionary of Palestinian Aramaic. Other parts of the material I sent to Leeds University for the use of my two former pupils, Dr. M. Black and Dr. J. Bowman, who were both working at that time in Leeds University. Under their guidance Dr. T. Jansma worked on the material in Leeds, and when he, after his return to Holland, was nominated Professor of Hebrew in Leiden, I sent the whole Wensinck-material back to Leiden where it is now preserved in Professor Jansma's Institute under the superintendence of Professor de Boer. We look forward to seeing the observations made by Wensinck put to use in the near future to further the study of Palestinian Aramaic.

As for the material to be found in the Palestinian Talmud, Kutscher has pointed out that we should rely not on a printed edition, but as far as possible on manuscripts, and he has suggested taking for this purpose the edition of the Geniza material from the Palestinian Talmud edited by Louis Ginzberg, New York 1909.[1] It is reasonable that we should take the oldest ma-

[1] Studies in Galilean Aramaic (Hebrew), *Tarbiṣ* xxi, 1950, pp. 192–3, offprint pp. 1–2; xxii, 1950, pp. 62–3, offprint pp. 26f.

terial that we have for this purpose. But from Ginzberg's edition we can form no idea of the great differences between the fragments of the Palestinian Talmud that we know. If a useful study of this material from the Palestinian Talmud is to be made, it will be necessary to refer to the originals, or to photos of the originals.

Other material in Palestinian Aramaic is to be found in the Aramaic parts of the Midrash *Bereshit Rabba*. Hugo Odeberg has based his own edition of *The Aramaic Portions of Bereshit Rabba, with Grammar of Galilean Aramaic* (Lund 1939) on the edition published by Theodor and Albeck. Theodor, however, had not used the oldest and best MS for his edition, but he had mentioned the various readings in the apparatus. Kutscher has used for Bereshit Rabba the MS Heb. 30 of the Vatican library, a MS from the Palatina.[1] He has studied this manuscript in a microfilm and has shown that it is written in genuine Palestinian Aramaic, and he has even found a few Palestinian vowels in it. Such vocalisation is also to be found in Geniza fragments of Bereshit Rabba of which I possess photographs. To mention only one which seems to me of especial importance: No 958 of the Antonin Collection in Leningrad, a palimpsest with a Christian Palestinian text written underneath, containing a great number of Palestinian vowel signs. It is essential, as Kutscher rightly says, to utilize for the Aramaic texts the oldest sources of the Midrash available.

6. Exod. xxii 4,5 in the Targum

The most important evidence for Palestinian Aramaic as regards language and matter is to be found in the Geniza fragments containing the Palestinian Targum,[2] and of particular importance for its orthography and vocalisation is the fragment of the leather scroll from Exod. xxi–xxiii. It provides the foundation for the study of the language, when it is taken together with the other Geniza fragments and the complete Targum as contained in the Vatican MS Neofiti I.

An important passage of the Mishna enumerates four kinds

[1] Albeck has given a description of this MS in his introduction to *Bereshit Rabba*, Berlin 1931, pp. 163, 107–8, 137. Cf. Umberto Cassuto, *Codices Vaticani Hebraici*, Vatican, 1956, pp. 36–8.

[2] A new edition of the fragments published in *Masoreten des Westens*, ii, 1930, prepared in the main by Georg Schelbert, will come out in one of the next Supplements of *VT*.

of damage which can be done to a neighbour's field: the cattle (שור) (Exod. xxi, 35ff.,) and the cistern (בור) (Exod. xxi, 33), and there cannot be any doubt that the verses xxii 4 and 5 refer to the other kinds of damage. The text of the two verses in the Revised Version (here counted as vv. 5 and 6) is:

> 5. If a man shall cause a field or vineyard to be eaten, and shall let his beast loose, and it feed in another man's field; of the best of his own field, and of the best of his own vineyard, shall he make restitution.
> 6. If fire break out, and catch in thorns, so that the shocks of corn, or the standing corn, or the field, be consumed; he that kindled the fire shall surely make restitution.

This translation agrees in the main with the official interpretation of the text and is presupposed in Mishna and Talmud. The difficulty in this explanation of the text lies in the fact that words of the same Hebrew root בער which occurs in both verses are taken in vs 4 in the sense of 'cause to be eaten', 'beast' and 'feed', and in vs 5 'that kindled', 'the fire'.

In the Palestinian Targum as we find it in the Cambridge fragment and as it lies complete before us in the Vatican MS Neofiti I, the Hebrew words in both cases are understood as 'fire' and 'to burn' or 'light.' This translation is also given, for instance, by Bruno Baentsch in his *Kommentar zum Alten Testament*, Göttingen, 1900, and in the modern American translation, ed. J. M. Powis Smith, by J. Meek who has:

> If a man in burning over a field or vineyard lets the fire spread so that it burns in another man's field, he must make restitution with the very best of his own field or vineyard. If fire breaks out and catches in a thorn-hedge so that the shocks of grain or the standing grain or the field itself is consumed, he who lit the fire must make restitution.

In the Palestinian Targum of the Pentateuch the Hebrew words are taken in both cases as 'fire' and 'to be consumed', and the verses have to be translated as by Meek. There can be no question that the Palestinian Targum of the Pentateuch takes Exod. xxii 4 and 5 as referring in both cases to a kind of damage caused by fire. It shows a clear understanding of the passage which contrasts with the rulings of the Mishna. That is only possible if the translation is much older than the Mishna.

The fundamental importance of this passage of the Targum

became clear to me through a discussion with my old friend and lecturer from Giessen, Dr. J. J. Weinberg, when I visited him in Berlin where he had become Rector of the Rabbinic Seminary. In the course of our conversation I realized how difficult it must be for a Talmudic Scholar, as he was, to accept an interpretation of a passage of the Bible which conflicted with the rules of the Mishna, even if it was contained in an old Geniza text—the only source available to us at that time. How intensively he studied the problem of the right interpretation of this passage is shown by the fact that he devoted the entire first volume of his *Investigations in the Talmud* מחקרים בתלמוד Berlin 1938 to the elucidation of these two verses of the Bible and their rendering in the Palestinian Targum. He came to the conclusion that either the text of the Targum is corrupt, or the first יקידתה has by analogy with Hebrew בעירה to be understood as cattle. But we certainly have to take the passage in the way Abraham Geiger has understood similar divergent explanations of the Bible text in the Palestinian Targum.

Since in the second century B.C. an addition to the Targum was made which cannot have been made later than the second century B.C., the Targum must have existed at that time. And the divergent interpretation in the Targum of Exod. xxii 4.5 leads to the same conclusion, as we have mentioned. In his *Urschrift* (1857) Abraham Geiger examined over a hundred passages in the material of the Palestinian Targum available to him.

Th. Nöldeke wrote at the time:

> Geiger, who has performed a great service to the correct evaluation of the Targum and in general of the old translations of the Bible, has also shown that in the so-called Jerusalem Targum important remains are still to be found of the oldest Targum along with passages of a quite different time.

We can to-day go further since we now have the oldest Targum itself in its entirety, and not in a later revision. This Targum, as we now have it, can be regarded as being nearly in the same form as when it was in circulation at the time of the beginning of Christianity. We must only bear in mind that it never had a fixed text of the kind to which we are accustomed from Targum Onḳelos. Even the oldest Geniza fragments containing this Targum differ greatly from one another where we have the same text of the Bible preserved in different fragments. On the other hand we have seen that the interpretation of the Targum in the old Geniza fragment in Cambridge, diverging from the interpretation of the Mishna, is exactly the same as in the MS of the complete Targum dating from the sixteenth century. It is only in the Targum Pseudo-Jonathan that the passage is altered in accordance with the Targum Onḳelos.[1]

We have seen that the Targum must have been in circulation by the second century B.C. On account of its language and the Midrash material it contains, the Targum must have enjoyed great popularity and we can safely say that it was this Targum which prevented the later Targum Onḳelos from establishing itself in Palestine.

Abraham Geiger writes at the end of his observations on the Palestinian Targum (Excursus II, *Urschrift* p. 480):

> Serious and impartial investigation in this field will lead even in other respects to fruitful results for Jewish history.

This judgement will be shared by everybody who studies these old and in the main pre-Christian Jewish texts. We can learn many more details from them than from the material collected by Billerbeck or Bonsirven. Their voluminous works only serve to indicate what the conditions were at the time of the reorganization of Judaism after the destruction of the Temple: they show us how the Rabbis rebuilt Judaism for the future.

In the Palestinian Targum of the Pentateuch we have in the main material coming from pre-Christian times which must be studied by everyone who wishes to understand the state of Judaism at the time of the birth of Christianity. And we possess this material in a language of which we can say that it is very similar to that spoken by the earliest Christians. It is material the importance of which can scarcely be exaggerated.

[1] I may refer here to the excellent article of Georg Schelbert: 'Exodus xxii 4 im Palästinischen Targum' *VT*, viii, 1958, pp. 253–63.

THE SEPTUAGINT

1. The Letter of Aristeas

The Greek translation of the Bible has always been regarded as something unique, as the first attempt to translate a long text into a foreign language. The story told in the letter of Aristeas is well known. The famous Demetrius Phalereus, said to have been the Royal librarian, aroused the interest of King Ptolemy II Philadelphus (284–47 B.C.) in the Jewish Law, and the king wished to have a Greek translation of it in his library. Aristeas, a senior Court official, was sent to Jerusalem. The Jewish High Priest Eleazar selected six elders from each of the twelve tribes of Israel and sent them to Alexandria, together with an exact copy of the Hebrew Torah, written in golden letters on exquisitely prepared parchment. We are told that the king gave seven banquets to these elders, questioning ten of them at each of the first five banquets, and eleven of them at each of the last two banquets, as a result of which he ascertained that these elders were superior to the Greek philosophers. He then put at their disposal a spacious house on the island of Pharos, which was connected with Alexandria by the Heptastadion. Here they accomplished their great task: seventy-two elders translated in seventy-two days the entire Pentateuch in such a marvellous way that at the end they were all found to agree on every detail of the translation.

As long as people were convinced that the Greek translation of the Law was made on the order of a king, they could find in this command a sufficient reason for the translation having been made. But for more than 250 years we have known that the story must be regarded as legendary.[1] To-day there can be no doubt that the Greek translation of the Law was not made by order of a Ptolemaic king, but that it became a necessity for the Jewish Communities in Egypt in view of the great number of their Greek-speaking members who no longer understood Hebrew. The translation was not made by Palestinian Jews, but by Jews who were

[1] See Humphrey Hody, *Contra historiam Aristeae in LXX Interpretibus Dissertatio*, Oxford 1685. Hody summed up his arguments in his book: *De Bibliorum textibus originalibus*, Oxford 1705.

familiar with the Greek language as spoken in Egypt. Aristeas' letter, which was clearly intended to glorify the Jewish people and the Jewish Law, was not written by a pagan, a high official of a Ptolemaic king, but by a Jew who was greatly interested in recommending the translation of the Law of which he speaks. He deals with the time of Ptolemy Philadelphus as a time long past and did not live—as the letter claims—in the first half of the third century B.C., but much later.

The author of the letter of Aristeas is generally well informed about the time in which he lived. On the other hand, W. W. Tarn has shown that he has used older material. The questions said to have been put to the Jewish scholars by King Ptolemy II, were probably part of an essay on the kingdom περὶ βασιλείας, written in the third century B.C. which unlike Aristeas' letter was not propaganda. The older book seems to have been well known among the Hellenistic Jews. With its help Aristeas tried to compose an apologetic work by showing (§235) that the Jews could beat the Greek philosophers on their own ground.[1]

The letter of Aristeas must be regarded as a Jewish story of a similar literary genre as the books of Jonah, Esther, Judith and Tobit. But while the first two of these books were included in the Hebrew and the last two in the Greek Bible, the letter was not included in any form of the Holy Scriptures. Yet it must have been well known. Josephus used it in the twelfth book of his Antiquities and the Christians found in the letter welcome information on the Greek Bible which they used.

The letter only deals with the Jewish Law and was written in connection with a Greek translation of it. This fact has not been sufficiently stressed since the letter's genuineness was disproved. We have to seek the reasons why the letter was written and cannot confine ourselves, like H. St. J. Thackeray,[2] to searching in the

[1] W. W. Tarn, *The Greeks in Bactria and India*, Cambridge, 1938, pp. 414–35 (in the second edition, Cambridge, 1951, a few appendices have been added). Tarn has shown some striking parallels in the 'Questions of Milinda', i.e. Menander, the Greek king in India (about 175–150 B.C.). Menander is said to have put the questions to the Indian sage Nagasena. We know the story from the Milindapañha, a Pali text written by an Indian Buddhist. Among the four persons mentioned in the introduction to the Milinda we find a Demetrius and an Antiochus, the names having been adjusted to Devamantiya and Anantakaya in order to make some sort of sense in the Pali. Demetrius is here the main character. Menander's questions must have been made public soon after his death. It is quite possible that Demetrius was adopted from this source by Pseudo-Aristeas. He identified him with the famous Demetrius of Phaleron, who, however, was probably dead before King Ptolemy's rule began. For all details see Tarn's book.

[2] Thackeray, *The Septuaginta and Jewish Worship*, Schweich Lectures of the British Academy for 1920, London 1923, p. 11.

letter for details which might be regarded as *credible*. We read in the letter (§§ 308–11):[1]

> When the work was completed, Demetrius collected together the Jewish population in the place where the translation had been made, and read it over to all, in the presence of the translators, who met with a great reception also from the people, because of the great benefits which they had conferred upon them. They bestowed warm praise upon Demetrius too, and urged him to have the whole law transcribed and present a copy to their leaders. After the books had been read, the priests and the elders of the translators and the Jewish community and the leaders of the people stood up and said, that since so excellent and sacred and accurate a translation had been made, it was only right that it should remain as it was, and no alteration should be made in it. And when the whole company expressed their approval, they bade them pronounce a curse in accordance with their custom upon anyone who should make any alteration either by adding anything or changing in any way whatever any of the words which had been written or making any omission. This was a very wise precaution to ensure that the book might be preserved for all the future time unchanged.

It is obvious that the letter describes a translation of the Jewish Law officially approved and accepted by the Jewish Community of Alexandria: no addition; no omission; no revision; cursed be he who makes any alteration! The version to which the letter refers was an authoritative one, and there can be no doubt that the letter itself was propaganda for it.[2]

We are familiar with propaganda. Nobody makes propaganda for something a hundred or more years old. Propaganda is made for something contemporary. We can be sure that the translation had just been made when the letter of propaganda was written. When we know the date of the letter, we know that of the translation also.

The letter has been ascribed to various dates, mostly on subjective grounds which prove nothing. A few impartially observed facts have recently been indicated by Elias Bickermann.[3] He has shown that certain formulas in documents quoted in the

[1] I quote from H.T. Andrews' translation in Charles' *Apocrypha and Pseudepigrapha* ... Oxford 1913, vol ii, pp. 83 ff.

[2] Cf. my 'Untersuchungen zur Geschichte des Pentateuchtextes', in *Theologische Studien und Kritiken*, 1915, p. 413=*Opera Minora*, Leiden 1956, p. 14.

[3] 'Zur Datierung des Pseudo-Aristeas' *ZNW*, xxix, 1930, pp. 280–96.

letter cannot be found in a document before 145 or after 127 B.C. The letter must therefore have been written in the second half of the second century B.C. Sir Harold Idris Bell whose opinion I asked on this argument wrote to me that Bickermann's deductions agreed with his own general impressions, and he added: 'His argument seems to me most convincing, for it is on such minutiae too unimportant to be thought of by the average man that a forger most often trips up'. But Bickermann's arguments for the year 127 are not so conclusive. Momigliano tried to fix the *terminus ad quem* at about 100 B.C.[1] and W. W. Tarn agreed with him. With regard to Bickermann, Tarn writes: 'His valuable examination of the formula in the Royal letters puts the work within the limits 145–100 B.C., though strictly speaking the facts he gives p. 289, n. 1, prove a date *c.* 100. His dating before 127 depends entirely . . . on the implication in a phrase of Pseudo-Aristeas that Idumea was not part of Palestine, 127 being the date of its annexation to the Maccabean realms. But Bickermann himself has shown that much of Pseudo-Aristeas's description of Palestine is simply a compound of the Old Testament and of ideas about the ideal state. . . . The independent Idumea is only O.T. Edom. . . .[2]

But whether the letter was written before 127 or *c.* 100 B.C. is not so important. In any case we must face the fact that the Greek translation with which the letter deals was finished towards the end of the second century B.C.

Now it is clear that the Jews in Alexandria must have had a Greek translation of their Law at a much earlier period. But the translation for which the letter makes propaganda was not the *first* Greek translation of the Law. It was a revision of already existing translations. The letter, however, attempts to show that it was the first translation ever made. So it antedates this translation by 150 years. Nevertheless, a number of hints as to earlier translations can be found in the letter. In his memorandum (§30) to the king, Demetrius reports that he has taken great care to collect all kinds of books for the library and he continues:

> The books of the Law of the Jews (with some few others) are absent. They are written in the Hebrew characters and language and have been carelessly interpreted (ἀμελέστερον σεσήμανται)

[1] Cf. Arnoldo Momigliano, 'Per la data e la caratteristica della lettera di Aristea', *Aegyptus*, xii, 1932, pp. 161–73.
[2] Cf. Tarn's book *The Greeks in Bactria and India* . . . p. 425.

and do not represent the original text (καὶ οὐχ ὡς ὑπάρχει) as I am informed by those who know; for they have never had a king's care to protect them.

The words ἀμελέστερον δὲ . . . σεσήμανταὶ 'rather carelessly written', are not clear and οὐχ ὡς ὑπάρχει 'with deviations from the original text' is at least not good Greek. But it seems that the author has deliberately chosen somewhat obscure expressions.

The words 'rather carelessly' (ἀμελέστερον) can only be taken as referring to earlier *translations*, for one can hardly suppose that Demetrius was interested in any form of the Hebrew of the Pentateuch, nor would he suggest that the *Hebrew* copies had been made carelessly.[1] The end of the letter makes it even plainer that allusion is being made to earlier translations. The author tells us (§§ 314–16) that the Greek historian Theopompos and the Greek tragic poet Philodectos had quoted the Jewish Law in their writings, but that God had inflicted heavy penalties upon them because the translations used by them had been inadequate. With regard to Theopompos the words explicitly used are 'some of the earlier, but imperfect translations of the Law' (τίνα τῶν προηρμηνευμένων ἐπισφαλέστερον ἐκ τοῦ νόμου). The two abovementioned Greek authors lived in the fourth century B.C. So the letter implies that at that time a Greek translation of the Jewish Law or at least of parts of it was already in circulation.

So we see that the letter itself contains hints of earlier translations in spite of all the author's efforts not to refer to them. We shall have to visualize the origin of the Greek translation of the Jewish Law in Egypt in a similar way to the origin of the Aramaic translation of the same Law in Palestine. As the Jews in Palestine translated the Law into Aramaic, the language which since Ezra's days had been spoken in that land, so the Jews in Egypt

[1] Bickermann tried to understand the text in this way. He wrote in his article The colophon of the Greek book of Esther' (*JBL*, lxiii, 1944, p. 345, n. 24): 'The passage is misunderstood by translators and commentators who try to find here a hint of a previous Greek version while the author clearly speaks of the original text of the Law.' But it seems that the misunderstanding is on Bickermann's side. σεσήμανται is certainly not *copied*, and the whole letter tends to show the royal sympathy for the Greek *translation*, not for the Hebrew *original* which after all was imported from Palestine. What Bickermann says about the date of the colophon, i.e. that the words 'In the fourth year of Ptolemy and Cleopatra's reign' refer to Ptolemy XII Auletes and Cleopatra, his wife and sister and that therefore the colophon was written between the 12th September 78 and the 11th September 77 B.C. seems convincing. But he is definitely wrong when he takes λευείτης to be the proper name of 'Levitas', although the suggestion goes back to Saul Liebermann. The verb εἰσήνεγκεν is singular. Furthermore the word εἶναι, quoted by Bickermann certainly does not mean to *exist actually* and cannot be translated in this way. But both items are essential for the understanding of this interesting colophon.

translated the same Law into Greek, the language spoken there. It is probable that oral, extempore, translations were made originally. Then the translations began to be written down. The first copies were probably not very perfect. The beginning is always hard. The definition *rather inexact*, in the letter of Aristeas ἀμελέστερον, is probably quite to the point. Perhaps the copyists tried as best they could to improve the text to make the style and matter conform to the original. In this way circumstances may have been created such as are quite familiar to us from the Palestinian and Samaritan Targums.

2. The Bible Commission in Alexandria

We have to suppose that at a certain period the need for an authorized Greek text of the Jewish Law arose among the influential Jewish circles in Alexandria. The need may have been met by basing the Greek version on a Hebrew text procured from Palestine. The commission entrusted with the revision of the Greek Bible text consisted of experts, mainly Jewish scholars from Egypt, but there may have been one or more Hebrew scholars from Palestine. It is very likely that the commission worked on the island of Pharos. Philo gives an account of an annual festivity held there to celebrate the translation:

> For this cause there is held to this day every year a festival and assembly on the island of Pharos to which not only Jews, but multitudes of others sail across, to pay reverence to the spot on which the translation first shed its light and to render God thanks for a benefit, ancient yet ever new. After the prayers and thanksgivings some pitch tents on the shore, others recline in the sand, regaling themselves under the open sky with their relatives and friends and regarding the beach on that occasion as more luxurious than a palace. (*De Vita Mosis*, ii. 41–3. I quote Colson's translation.)

Such a festival could hardly have been instituted without some justification. But the commission entrusted with the translation was presumably selected by the Jewish community of Alexandria and must have worked for as long as was necessary in order to agree on a uniform text. The statements to the effect that the translation was made by order of a king from a beautifully prepared parchment on which the Hebrew text was written in golden letters, that the translation was done by a commission of seventy-two members, six from each of the tribes of Israel, and that it was completed in seventy-two days are all embellishments of the letter designed to underline the importance of the translation and to help with its dissemination. Swete pointed out how remarkable it was that the translation should first have been presented to the Jewish community and only afterwards to the king who is said to have ordered it.[1]

We are told that the community in Alexandria declared the translation to be authentic and that they made sure it should be preserved and not altered. In certain Jewish circles in Alexandria admiration for the translation increased with the passage of time. We may remember Philo's comments, about 150 years after Aristeas wrote his letter:[2]

> Sitting here (on the island of Pharos) in seclusion . . . they became as it were possessed, and, under inspiration, wrote, not each several scribe something different, but the same word for word, as though dictated to each by an invisible prompter. . . . The clearest proof of this is that, if Chaldeans have learned Greek, or Greeks Chaldean, and read both versions, the Chaldean and the translation, they regard them with awe and reverence as sisters, or rather one and the same, both in matter and words, and speak of the authors not as translators but as prophets and priests of the mysteries, whose sincerity and singleness of thought have enabled them to go hand in hand with the purest of spirits, the spirit of Moses.

These remarks of Philo obviously refer to the Greek standard text of the Jewish Law, for which Aristeas wrote his letter of propaganda. Philo himself knew too little Hebrew to be able to read the Law in the original. This explains his verdict that it is absolutely the same whether one reads the Hebrew or the Greek text. He has little understanding for philological problems, and speaks as a devoted theologian with special philosophical interests, not realizing that his own quotations from the Greek Torah deviate widely from the text approved by the Jews of Alexandria.

3. The Prologue of Ben Sira

But we possess the testimony of an expert who had personal experience of translating a Hebrew text into Greek and who was living in Alexandria at the time when the Commission of Alex-

[1] H. B. Swete, *Introduction*, p. 20.

[2] *De Vita Mosis*, ii, 37–40.

andria was working on the Greek text of the Bible. I refer to the grandson of Ben Sira who translated his grandfather's Book of Wisdom from Hebrew into Greek. In the Prologue to the translation which he has written in the Egyptian κοινή he reports that he had come to Egypt in the eight-and-thirtieth year of king Euergetes. The king in question was Euergetes II Ptolemy VII Physkon. The years of his reign are counted as from 170 B.C. Ulrich Wilken has shown that when an author mentions the name of a ruler and puts ἐπί immediately after the year, he thereby indicates that at the time of writing the ruler was dead.[1] Euergetes II died in 116 B.C., so we can assume that the grandson's prologue was not written before that. According to Bickermann's calculation it was written about 110 B.C.[2] During the more than twenty years which he had spent in Egypt the grandson had taken the opportunity not only to study the κοινή then spoken there, and to write the prologue in this medium, but also to acquire a knowledge of the Greek used for translation from Hebrew—a much more complicated language—which he himself used, after the model of Bible texts familiar to him, for his Greek version of his grandfather's Book of Wisdom. He writes that he had ample opportunity to learn and had therefore considered it his duty to make every effort and spare no trouble to translate his grandfather's work. He had spent many sleepless nights and much learning on the task of finishing the book and having it published. Nevertheless he feels obliged to apologize for certain imperfections in the translation and he does so in the following words (I use the translation in Charles' *Apocrypha and Pseudepigrapha*):

> Ye are entreated, therefore, to make your perusal with favour and attention, and to be indulgent, if in any parts of what we have laboured to interpret we may seem to fail in some of the phrases. For things originally spoken in Hebrew have not the same force in them when they are translated into another tongue.

Yet the grandson is quite aware that the translations of the Bible, though he had taken them as his model, laboured under the same difficulties.

> And not only these, but the Law itself, and the Prophecies, and the rest of the books, have no small difference when they are spoken in their original form.

[1] *Archiv für Papyrusforschung*, iii, 1908, p. 351; Bickermann, *ZNW*, xxix, 1930, p. 285.

[2] *JBL*, lxiii, 1944, p. 343.

These are the words of one who knows from his own experience the difficulties involved in the translation of a Hebrew text into Greek. The same imperfections which he admits exist in his own work are also to be found in the translations of his predecessors. When he mentions the *translation of the Law*, he obviously has in mind the standard edition of the Greek Law, the subject of Aristeas' letter. We have seen that this translation was made shortly before the grandson's translation. That he mentions next after the Law, in his prologue, the Prophets and the rest of the Books, goes to show that the translation of these books must have immediately followed the translation of the Law and that Ben Sira was convinced that it had been made under similar circumstances. Ben Sira's grandson regards himself as the immediate successor of the Bible translators and we can take it for granted that he was in Egypt when some of the biblical translation work was still being done.

I make these last statements with certain reservations. Professor Kilpatrick has drawn my attention to the fact that there are reasons to suppose the prologue may not be genuine. It is true that the prologue is not to be found in the oldest form of the old Latin translation, that it is missing in some Greek cursive MSS and that other MSS have a different prologue which was undoubtedly written at a later date. It is not very easy to see the import of these facts, as the hitherto existing editions of the Greek text of Ben Sira are quite inadequate. A critical edition meets with great difficulties, as the Hebrew text as well as the Greek translations have undergone drastic revisions. The Cambridge scholar J. H. A. Hart speaks of a revision of the text made by the Pharisees. Most likely he is right. I have already pointed to the fact that this text, coming from priestly circles, had to be adapted to conditions which had developed after the Bnē Ṣadoḳ had ceased to have influence in the Temple. Yet it is certain that we are not dealing with only one revision. Hart has pointed correctly to the problems which arise from Clement of Alexandria's quotations and has on the whole done very valuable preparatory work.[1] As far as I can see it is mainly the revised texts which exhibit the differences in the prologue.

Furthermore, the prologue of Ben Sira's grandson is the only document earlier than A.D. 70 which mentions the threefold

[1] *Ecclesiasticus. The Greek Text of Codex* 248, ed. with a textual Commentary and Prolegomena by J. H. A. Hart, Cambridge 1909.

canon of the Old Testament: Law, Prophets and Writings. Yet we must take into consideration that generally speaking we know very little of this time, and also that the few lists of books of the Old Testament which we have, are of Palestinian origin, including what is possibly the oldest list available to us, a Hebrew-Aramaic list, discovered only a few years ago by the Dominican Father, Professor Jean-Paul Audet (Ottawa), in MS 54 of the Library of the Greek Patriarchate in Jerusalem, dated A.D. 1058. This is the codex from which Philotheos Bryennius published the text of the Didache (Constantinople 1883). Epiphanius was familiar with the list and Audet has proved that it must be very old and that it seems to refer to books written partly in Hebrew and partly in Aramaic.[1]

The prologue of Ben Sira's grandson was written in Egypt and, as I have shown, at the time when the revision of the Greek Bible text in Alexandria had just been completed. It is very probable that the threefold Canon of the Books of the Bible was known in Egypt at a much earlier date than in Palestine. I feel that it is difficult to doubt the genuineness of the prologue, because it is not easy to find a motive which would explain its later authorship and inclusion. Also the critical way in which Ben Sira's grandson speaks of the Greek translation of the Jewish Law is much more easily understandable if written immediately after its completion than later, when the Aristeas letter and its propaganda had had their effect.

4. The Cairo Papyrus Fouad 266

We are in the happy position of possessing a sample of the revision of the Greek Torah, made in the second part of the second century B.C., which must have been written shortly after completion of the revision. It is the Cairo Papyrus Fouad 266 of which a few verses from Deut. xxxi and xxxii have had our attention drawn to them and been published by W. G. Waddell in order to show that in this Papyrus scroll the divine name was written as the Tetragrammaton in Hebrew square letters.[2]

Professor Kilpatrick informed me of a few more fragments of this papyrus reproduced in America, not very well, but recogniz-

[1] The books of the Bible are mentioned in the list in the following order: Gen., Exod., Lev., Jos., Deut., Num., Job, Jud., Ps., 1, 2 Sam., 1, 2 Kings, 1, 2 Chron., Prov., Eccles., Cant., Jer., xii Proph., Isa., Ezek., Dan., 1, 2 Esra, Est. The list is published and all problems examined by J-P. Audet in *JTS* NS, i, 1950, pp. 135–54.

[2] 'The Tetragrammaton in the LXX', *JTS*, xlv, 1944, pp. 157–61.

ably. They all show the Tetragrammaton.[1] I asked Father A. Vaccari S.J. of the Pontifical Biblical Institute in Rome to assess the character of the text of this papyrus. He replied as follows:

> Without doubt the papyrus belongs to the group of the uncials A B F and has nothing to do with the Hexaplaric or Lucianic recensions or later minuscules. Its position between the groups of B A F and the related minuscules is not so clear and it seems to waver between them. But if we consider that the codex deviates from Codex Vaticanus (B), where this MS stands alone i.e. has its special version and not one of a group, and if we consider further the important conformity with B and the minuscule a_2 in a number of places, I would suggest that the codex must be included in the group B and the minuscule a_2. It must also be regarded as superior to these two MSS, because it does not agree with the deteriorations which in B are individual mistakes and in the minuscule a_2 are to be ascribed to influences from classes. The text of the papyrus contains old elements which disappeared later from the tradition.

Such was the result of Father Vaccari's examination. His detailed report has been published as an Appendix (pp. 339–42) to my article 'Problems of the Septuagint' in *Studia Patristica*, Berlin 1957, vol. i, pp. 328–38. What Vaccari has shown is that we have here a Greek Bible text in a papyrus scroll which exhibits the text of the Septuagint in a more reliable form than the Codex Vaticanus and the codices nearest related to it. The papyrus was written about four hundred years earlier than the Codex Vaticanus.

Unfortunately we cannot compare this Cairo Papyrus scroll, written by Jews about 100 B.C., with the Chester Beatty Codex of Numbers and Deuteronomy, written by Christians in the first half of the second century A.D., because what is known of the Cairo Papyrus scroll has not been preserved in the Chester Beatty Codex. As to its date, the codex stands half way between the Cairo Papyrus scroll and the Codex Vaticanus (B). Sir Frederic Kenyon has proved that in Numbers the codex is nearest related to Codices B and a_2, in Deuteronomy to the Codices A and a_2 of the Septuagint.[2] The efforts of my friends in Cairo, Professor

[1] *New World Translation of the Christian Greek Scriptures*, rendered from the Original Languages by the New World Bible Translation Committee. A.D. 1950. Publishers: Watchtower Bible and Tract Society Inc. International Bible Students Association. Brooklyn, New York, U.S.A. Foreword, pp. 13 and 14. (Dr. Abraham Spiro kindly procured a copy of the book for me.)

[2] *The Chester Beatty Biblical Papyri . . . Fasciculus V, Numbers and Deuteronomy*, by Frederic G. Kenyon. Text, London 1935.

A. S. Atiya and Dr. Mohammed Mostafa, to obtain more information about the place where the Papyrus scroll is now kept, were unsuccessful; nor was I able, during my own stay in Cairo in February 1956, to find out any more about it.

We have some more samples of Greek Bible texts, written by Jews for Jews, which have been discovered in recent times. They are of an essentially different nature from the Cairo Papyrus scroll, mentioned above, but for this very reason are of particular importance.

5. The Manchester Papyrus Greek 458

One is Papyrus Greek 458 of the John Rylands Library in Manchester, remains of a papyrus scroll with fragments from Deut. xxiii–xxviii. They were incorporated in a mummy sarcophagus and had to be extracted with great care. The papyrus has been published by C. H. Roberts.[1] This papyrus was written about the middle of the second century B.C. and is the oldest fragment of a Greek Bible known to us. To fix the character of the text, it has been compared with the main uncial MSS of the Septuagint, but the result was negative.[2]

It was Father Alberto Vaccari S.J. of the Pontificial Biblical Institute in Rome who was able to shed light on the mystery.[3] He proved that the text of the papyrus is most closely related to the Greek text of the Bible which we are accustomed to connect with the name of the martyr Lucian of Samosata (died 7th January A.D. 312). We know that Lucian revised the Greek text of the Bible which was in use during his lifetime. The Lucianic text presents a special recension of the Greek Bible and Paul de Lagarde published the historical books of the Greek Bible[4] according to this version while, independently, Frederic Field determined the MSS according to which the Lucianic text could be published. With regard to the historical books of the Bible he came to exactly the same conclusions as Lagarde.[5]

[1] *Two Biblical Papyri in the John Rylands Library, Manchester.* By C. H. Roberts, Manchester 1936.

[2] As an example take the examination by H. G. Opitz and H. H. Schaeder: 'Zum Septuaginta-Papyrus Rylands Greek 458.' *ZNW*, xxxv, 1936 pp. 115–17.

[3] A. Vaccari S.J., 'Fragmentum Biblicum Saeculi II ante Christum', *Biblica*, xvii 1936, pp. 501–4.

[4] *Librorum Veteris Testamenti Canonicorum Pars Prior Graece*, Pauli de Lagarde studio et sumptibus edita. Gottingae 1883.

[5] *Originis Hexaplarum quae supersunt . . . Fragmenta* . . . concinnavit emendavit et multis partibus auxit Fridericus Field. Oxonii, 1875. Tomus I, pp. lxxxiv ff.

Lucian began his studies in Edessa and continued them in Antioch, and it was there that he became the great authority on the Greek text of the Bible. Some of the material available to him on which he based the revision which bears his name must have been fairly old. We find in the Manchester Papyrus a text related to the Lucianic text of the Bible written some five hundred years before Lucian himself.

If the letter of Aristeas was written about 100 B.C. as propaganda for a Greek Torah which had been completed only a little earlier, the Manchester Papyrus must have been written before the Alexandrian Committee commissioned by the Jews began its work. I have discussed the matter with reference to the Rylands Papyrus in my article 'Problems of the Septuagint' in *Studia Patristica*, Berlin 1957, vol. i, pp. 328–38. C. H. Roberts wrote to me, when I sent him my paper:

> I found the tentative conclusions to which you came convincing and it has since occurred to me that they would provide an explanation for something which has always puzzled me, why such a beautifully written scroll of Deuteronomy should have been destroyed and treated as scrap (even being used for a crocodile mummy) in the way that the Rylands fragment was treated. If about the middle of the second century B.C. a more or less 'authorised' version of the Law was produced in Alexandria, accompanied by vigorous efforts to ensure that it superseded existing texts, then a complete explanation of the treatment of the Rylands papyrus is supplied. On chronological grounds it would fit admirably; the indications are that it was in the second half of the second century that the Rylands MS was re-used and the text of Deuteronomy may very well have been written in the first half of the century.

There can be no doubt that we must reckon with earlier translations into Greek of the Hebrew Bible. With the different passages in the letter of Aristeas which refer to such earlier translations I have already dealt. It is, moreover, well known that an earlier Greek translation of the Hebrew Bible was mentioned by the Jewish philosopher Aristobulus of Alexandria in a book which he dedicated to King Ptolemy Philometor (184–141 B.C.), fragments of which are preserved by Clement of Alexandria[1] and by Eusebius.[2]

[1] *Stromata*, i, 150, 1–4.

[2] *Praeparatio Evangelica*, ix, 6; xiii, 12. The texts are reprinted for instance by Swete, *Introduction*, Cambridge 1900, 2nd ed. 1914, pp. 1 f, and by Wellhausen in the 4th edition of Bleek, *Einleitung in das A.T.*, 1878, p. 573.

That the report of Aristobulus was not influenced by the letter of Aristeas was shown by Wellhausen, who refers to the fact that Aristobulus regards the whole story as quite straightforward and makes no allusion to the wonderful circumstances described in the letter of Aristeas. In the Manchester Papyrus we now have before us a sample of an old translation of the Torah which may have been written at the same time as Aristobulus dedicated his book to Ptolemy Philometor. It seems that Aristeas antedated the work of the Alexandrian Commission by about 150 years placing it in the time of Ptolemy II Philadelphus, and in this way identified an older translation of the Jewish Law, in which Ptolemy II Philadelphus may have interested himself, with the work of the Alexandrian Committee on the Bible done by order of the Jewish Community of Alexandria, so as to increase the authority of the work. The 150 years by which Pseudo-Aristeas antedates the revision have to be regarded as part of his propaganda.

Unfortunately the Manchester Papyrus does not contain an example of the Divine name. We now know that the Greek Bible text as far as it was written by Jews for Jews did not translate the Divine name by *kyrios*, but the Tetragrammaton written with Hebrew or Greek letters was retained in such MSS. It was the Christians who replaced the Tetragrammaton by *kyrios*, when the divine name written in Hebrew letters was not understood any more. We must suppose that in this fragment also the divine name was reproduced by the Tetragrammaton, and this is, indeed, most likely. In Deut. xxvi, 17, line 27 of C. H. Roberts' edition, the text breaks off just before the mention of the divine name. Roberts supposed that the scribe must have written the word *kyrios* in full, not in the shortened form used for the *nomen sacrum*. In reality the unabridged Tetragrammaton was written here, and Roberts agreed with me when I pointed this out. The only thing we do not know is whether the Tetragrammaton was written in square letters as in the previously discussed Papyrus Fouad 266 in Cairo and in the Milan Palimpsest of Origen's Hexapla found by Mercati or whether it was written in old Hebrew letters as for instance in the Aquila fragments from the Cairo Geniza published by Burkitt,[1] or in the leather scroll with the Greek text of the Minor Prophets, of which I will speak later on.

[1] *Fragments of the Books of Kings according to the translation of Aquila*, ed. by F. Crawford Burkitt, Cambridge 1898.

6. Fragments from Qumran 4

To these texts, of the Greek Bible written by Jews for Jews, we can now add fragments of three texts of similar kind found in Qumran Cave 4. These fragments were discussed by Monsignor Patrick W. Skehan, of the Catholic Institute in Washington, at the International Old Testament Congress held in Strasbourg in August 1956, and his paper was subsequently published in *Vetus Testamentum*, Supplement iv, Leiden, 1957, pp. 148–160, under the title 'The Qumran Manuscripts and Textual Criticism.' In actual fact, however, only the second part of the article (pp. 155–160) deals with these texts. When we met in Strasbourg, Mgr. Skehan was kind enough to let me have photos of the three fragments, thus enabling me to study them before he had published his paper.

Let us consider the approximate date of the three fragments. 1. the papyrus, 2. the long leather fragment with the text of Leviticus, 3. the fragments of the leather scroll with the text of Numbers. I discussed the matter with C. H. Roberts who, after consulting Professor E. C. Turner of London University, gave me his considered opinion in a letter dated the 8th of August, 1957, from which I quote the following words:

> 1. I too was reminded of the papyrus that Waddell published in *JTS* thirteen years ago. If there is anything in the suggestion that there was a particular style favoured by scribes copying the Greek version of the Jewish Scriptures, it might be worth pointing out that there is a remoter resemblance between your photos (1) and (3) and Papyrus Rylands Greek 458—the papyrus scraps of Deuteronomy dating from about the middle of the second century B.C.
>
> 2. I should assign (1) (the papyrus) and (3) (the fragments of the leather scroll with the text of Numbers) to the end of the first century B.C. or to the opening years of the first century A.D. There are marked points of resemblance between the papyrus and some fragments of the Odyssey (plate in my *Greek Book Hand*, (No. 9b).
>
> 3. I too regard the long leather fragment—No. (2)—as the oldest of the three and would regard a date towards the end of the second century B.C. for this as not out of the question.

I am very grateful to Mr. Roberts for this information.

There can hardly be any doubt that the fragments of the Greek Bible found in Qumran Cave 4 are of Jewish origin, and that it is very likely that they should also be regarded as pre-Christian, so that we now have at our disposal fragments of six manuscripts of the Greek Bible written by Jews for Jews, if we include the leather scroll with the Greek text of the Minor Prophets, of which I will speak later on, specimens of the Greek Bible as it was read when the Christian era began. May I characterize briefly the three texts from Qumran Cave 4.[1]

1. The papyrus containing fragments of Leviticus ii–v is written in a hand closely akin to that of Papyrus Fouad 266, characterized as already mentioned by the fact that the name of God is rendered by the Tetragrammaton in Hebrew square letters (יהוה) not by κυριος as later in Christian MSS of the Bible. The fragment of Qumran Cave 4 renders the name of God by ιαω (written in majuscule letters) and this alone already shows that this papyrus was written by a Jew. The text of the papyrus is not as carefully written as that of the Cairo Papyrus and contains some mistakes which the Cairo Papyrus does not have. Although written somewhat later than the Cairo Papyrus, it belongs to the same category.

2. The second specimen consists of fragments of a leather scroll with the text of Numbers iii, 40–42, iv 6–9, 11–12. The first two parts have been published by Skehan, and he is in the main right when he says that the text is generally speaking that already familiar to us. But he has himself pointed out that the fragments have several readings which do not occur in any of the MSS collated for the greater Cambridge Septuagint. In Num. iii 40 the Hebrew פְּקֹד is translated by αριθμησον, a unique translation, all the otherwise known texts of the Greek Bible reading επισκεψαι. In five places in these short fragments (iv 6, 8, 11, 12) Hebrew בַּדִּים is translated by αρτηρας (not διωστηρας as Skehan supposes) while all the other known sources unanimously read αναφορεις. In Num. iv 9 we find the Hebrew את מנרת המאור rendered by την λυχνιαν της φαυσεως which is again a unique translation. The LXX reads την λυχνιαν την φωτιζουσαν. And in iv 7 we read ιματιον υακινθινον where all other manuscripts of the Greek Bible known to us, read ιματιον ολοπορφυρον. How can one explain this comparatively great number of unique readings in these few pre-Christian fragments?

3. The third specimen is a fragment of a leather scroll of

[1] I am greatly indebted to the Rev. Dr. John Barns for his help in reading these often difficult texts.

Leviticus, containing Lev. xxvi 2–16 in lines each of about 47 letters. These fragmentary lines occupy the full length of one column of 28 lines, with stitching broken away on the left hand side, the margin being intact for the last 12 lines. The upper left hand part of the column and the ends of all the lines are missing, and Skehan describes the fragment quite correctly. But in adding: 'the hand is apparently of the first century A.D.', he is certainly wrong. When I showed the fragment to C. H. Roberts, he immediately said 'This is the oldest of the three', and we have seen that he is inclined to date the fragment in the second half of the second century B.C. The text of the fragment is reproduced and published by Mgr. Skehan on p. 159 of his article with some critical notes on the following page. The text is not very carefully written and contains obvious mistakes; thus on line 4 is written τον ξυλον instead of the neuter, where the Septuagint text has correctly the plural τα ξυλα, and the whole text of the fragment differs greatly from the normal text of the Septuagint. It is hardly possible to complete the 47 letters of each line with the help of the material preserved in the greater Cambridge Septuagint. How can we explain these differences in such an ancient manuscript?

Mgr. Skehan says that the text is in the main the rendering of Leviticus with which we are familiar; nevertheless, he has shown that in the limited fragment of the text at our disposal there are ten separate readings which are unique. Of these, nine are farther from a literal rendering of the Masoretic text than the corresponding readings in the codices of the Septuagint; one is closer, but (i. 15) depends on an inference regarding the amount of text required to fill a gap. None of these unique readings has anything to offer for the criticism of the Hebrew consonantal text. Two of the unique readings, in the opinion of Mgr. Skehan, must be extremely early. In Leviticus xxvi 11, for και ου βδελυξεται η ψυχη μου υμας, the Qumran reading is και ου βδελυξομαι υμας; and in Leviticus xxvi 12, for και υμεις εσεσθε μου λαος the Qumran text has εθν[ος]. Of these two Qumran readings, the former introduces an anthropomorphic term which is not in the original text; and the latter, in rendering עם by εθνος, violates the pattern by which the LXX regularly applies εθνος to the Gentiles, and λαος to the people of Israel. The general impression I form—so Mgr. Skehan writes—is that we have here one more book of the Old Testament in which a single early Greek rendering seems to have undergone even before the time of Origen a considerable amount of what we would to-day call critical revision.

7. The Leather Scroll of the Greek Minor Prophets

The leather scroll of the Greek Minor Prophets was discovered by Bedouin in 1952, but nobody can say exactly where it came from. Milik, in his book of 1957, mentions it on p. 115 under *site non localisé* (Époque de la Seconde Revolte). The scroll is now in the Palestinian Museum at Jerusalem, and I learn from Dr. G. Vermès that more fragments of the scroll were found after D. Barthélemy had written his article on it: 'Redécouverte d'un chainon manquant de l'histoire de la Septante'. (*RB* lx, 1953, pp. 18–29.)

It is certainly of the greatest importance to know when this scroll was written. So I asked C. H. Roberts in Oxford to give me an estimate on the basis of the facsimile published by Barthélemy. He replied:

> The hand belongs to a type known in the Egyptian papyri from the middle of the 2nd century B.C. to the 2nd century A.D. (there is of course considerable development within the type). A characteristic of these hands is the use of decorative script at the top and the foot of the letters. In the Egyptian papyri these normally face to the left; here they face to the right. . . . Some similarities to this particular hand may be noted in Schubart, *Palaeographie*, Abb. 72 (late Ptolemaic) and Abb. 76 (Augustan). I should feel inclined to assign this hand to the century 50 B.C. to 50 A.D.

I have published and discussed this estimate at length elsewhere.[1] As J. T. Milik in his book of 1957 refers to this scroll only via Barthélemy's article (p. 27, n. 1) and dates it in the time of the Second Revolt (p. 115), I asked Wilhelm Schubart for his estimate of the date of the scroll, and on the 2nd July 1957 he wrote to me:

> Gern würde ich Ihre Frage rund und nett beantworten, aber über Ihr eignes Urteil kommt's nicht hinaus. Der Stil der Handschrift gehört zu der Gruppe, die ich in der Paläographie

[1] 'Die im August 1952 entdeckte Lederrolle mit dem griechischen Text der Kleinen Propheten und das Problem der Septuaginta', *ThLZ* 1954, pp. 81–94; A Leather Scroll of the Greek Minor Prophets and the Problem of the Septuagint' in *Opera Minora*, Leiden 1956, pp. 112–37. 'Problems of the Septuagint' *Studia Patristica*, ed. K. Aland and F. L. Cross, Berlin 1957, vol. i, pp. 331–333.

dem Zierstil eingerechnet habe und mit Vorsicht der Zeit des Augustus zuweise. Ob aber a c (=B.C.) oder p c (=A.D.) wage ich nicht zu sagen. Sollte ich in dieser Lage doch Stellung nehmen, so würde ich lieber a c als p c wählen. Aber je älter ich werde, um so mehr sehe ich, dass wir nichts Sicheres wissen und nur allzusehr an Vorurteilen haften, vielleicht haften müssen.

I am very grateful to the great authority on Greek Palaeography for this estimate which agrees in the main with that of Roberts, and we can be nearly certain that this scroll with the Greek text of the Minor Prophets was written in the closing decades of the pre-Christian era or at the beginning of our era. To date this scroll with Barthélemy or Milik at the end of the first or the beginning of the 2nd century A.D. seems to me impossible as long as other evidence is not forthcoming. In other words the scroll has to be regarded as a manuscript of the Greek Bible which was written by a Jew for Jews. We must try to understand it on this presupposition.

The Hebrew text on which the Greek translation is based is in the main our Masoretic text, but with deviations in various details. In Habakkuk it generally agrees with the Hebrew text as explained in the Habakkuk Commentary found in the first Qumran cave. If the whole text of the scroll is published, we may be in a position to reconstruct the Hebrew text which was the basis of the Greek translation in the scroll.

Barthélemy pointed out that this newly found Bible text is in almost exact accordance with the Greek text of the Minor Prophets which Justin Martyr took for his Septuagint and from which he made his Old Testament quotations. The quotation from Micah iv, 1–7 in Chapter 109 of Justin's *Dialogue* shows a very odd text, deviating widely from the Septuagint as we have it in our main manuscripts. The last five verses of this quotation—only these are preserved in the scroll—agree word for word with the text in the newly found scroll. The same applies to the quotation from Zechariah ii, 10–iii, 2 in Chapter 115 of Justin's *Dialogue*; the only preserved verse in the scroll (ii, 12) agrees with Justin in having ἐκλέξεται compared with αἱρετιεῖ in the usual text of the Greek Bible.

According to Barthélemy, further quotations from the Minor Prophets are not to be found in the newly found scroll. But the quoted instances show clearly that the whole text of the scroll is of the same kind. The newly found text agrees in the main with the text of the Minor Prophets quoted by Justin.

8. The Text of Lucian

As a result Justin's quotations from the Minor Prophets take on for us an entirely new importance. More than a hundred years ago, the text of the Bible used by Justin was carefully investigated by the Giessen New Testament scholar Karl August Credner. Speaking of the quotation from Micah iv, 1–7, of which five verses have been preserved in the newly found scroll, Credner says:[1]

> We can recognize that Justin's text is based, though in repeatedly changed form, on the Greek text of LXX. In various parts Justin's reading seems to agree with Aquila, yet it cannot really be Aquila. The basic text is definitely LXX. There are considerable deviations from Aquila. In Micah iv, 4, readings of Symmachus and Theodotion can be detected. That Justin used the Hexapla of Origen is out of the question, as his text was not emended in later times. Besides the obvious and anxious exactness in the affiliation with the Hebrew, peculiar to Aquila, a certain lack of care is apparent, such as one would never expect from Aquila.

Furthermore, Credner shows that the Bible text used by Justin does not agree with Cod B (Vaticanus) of the Septuagint, but with a group of manuscripts which—as we know to-day—show the text of Lucian. He further goes on to report about his investigations of all Justin's quotations from the Minor Prophets and adds the following:

> Some of the corrections agree with Aquila, others with Aquila and Theodotion, others again with Symmachus, whilst in other places Justin's text deviates from all three translations. . . . One verse (Zech. xii, 10) to which Justin adheres together with all three translators against the LXX, can be found in the Apocalypse (i, 7).

This means that already towards the end of the pre-Christian era the Jews were anxious to bring their Greek Bible into accordance with the Hebrew original. Credner concludes his examination by saying that all these corrections must have been

[1] Karl August Credner, *Beiträge zur Einführung in die biblischen Schriften*, Halle 1838, vol. ii, p. 282.

made at a time preceding the three so-called later translators. Now that we have in the Manchester Papyrus a Bible text of Lucianic character which is older than any other part of the Greek Bible preserved to us, and which must have been written at a time before the Alexandrian Committee began the work which resulted in our Septuagint, we can characterize the text of the Greek Bible used by Justin in a quite different way, as a text which had been adapted to the Hebrew original by the Jews some hundreds of years before Origen.

Wilhelm Bousset, while making an investigation of the Gospel quotations by Justin, tried to explain also Justin's Old Testament quotations.[1] Following Credner, he investigated Justin's quotations from Isaiah and Amos and came to the conclusion that the manuscripts of Justin's writings seem to go back to an archetype apparently written for the library of Archbishop Arethas of Caesarea—in a province of the Church where the text of Lucian could be regarded as the approved text. In accordance with this text the quotations of Justin must have been corrected thoroughly.

We have seen that Lucianic readings were found in fragments of the Greek Bible written in the second century B.C., and we find them now in our manuscript of the Minor Prophets written by Jews at the beginning of our era.

On the Lucianic text of the Greek Bible, H. St. J. Thackeray has made some valuable observations. Thackeray, when studying the text of Josephus as co-editor of the Cambridge Septuagint for the books of Samuel, Kings and Chronicles, wrote in his *Note on the Evidence of Josephus* as follows:[2]

> With the books of Samuel (more strictly from i Sam viii onwards), Josephus becomes a witness of first-rate importance for the text of the Greek Bible. Throughout the Octateuch he appears to have been mainly dependent for his Biblical matter upon a Semitic source, whether Hebrew or Aramaic (a Targum), and there has so far been little evidence of his use of the Alexandrian version. Throughout the later historical books, on the other hand, his main source is a Greek Bible containing a text closely allied to that of the 'Lucianic' group of MSS, but anterior by more than two centuries to the date

[1] Wilhelm Bousset, *Die Evangeliencitate Justin's des Märtyrers in ihrem Wert für die Evangelienkritik*, Göttingen 1891, pp. 18–32.

[2] *The Old Testament in Greek*, vol ii, part i: i and ii Samuel, Cambridge 1927, p. ix.

of Lucian, and presenting in I Sam. occasional parallels with the text of Symmachus (I S. xiii, 20; xv, 23, 30; xvi, 21; xvii, 39, 53; xxxi, 4). Besides this Greek Bible the historian still apparently employs a Semitic text as a collateral source. His use of a two-fold text renders his evidence somewhat uncertain. Instances where he agrees with the Masoretic text against all known Greek readings have been neglected in the apparatus to this volume, as presumably derived from his Semitic source. A further element of uncertainty is introduced by his habit of paraphrase; this accounts for the frequency with which it has been found necessary to quote his evidence in the form *Jos (uid)*.

Thackeray is anxious to find out from what part of the world Josephus could have received the 'Lucianic' text in the first Christian century. In reality, the circumstances are quite similar to those of the quotations of Justin from the Greek Bible which we have now rediscovered in a MS written by a Jew for Jews in pre-Christian, or in the earliest Christian times.

In one of his last books[1] Thackeray gives a general review of the results at which he had arrived with regard to the text of the Bible used by Josephus. We find there the following summary:

> Not only can we confidently state in general terms that Josephus used a Greek Bible. We can go further and identify the particular type of Greek text which lay before him. This text was not one contained in our oldest uncial MSS, the codex Vaticanus or Alexandrinus, on which our modern printed editions of the Septuagint are based. It was a text allied to one preserved only in a small group of MSS written not in uncial but in cursive script at a much later date, between the 10th and 14th centuries,[2] and known by the figures assigned to them by the eighteenth-century editors, Holmes and Parsons, as 19, 84, 93 and 103. This type of text . . . was in the nineteenth century identified with a particular recension of the Greek Bible current in Syria and adjacent countries and commonly designated 'Lucianic' after the supposed author, the Christian Lucian of Antioch, who suffered martyrdom under the emperor Maximin in the year 311 or 312. And now that we have in our hands fuller and more accurate editions both of the Septuagint

[1] Thackeray: *Josephus, the man and the Historian*, New York, 1929, pp. 81 f.

[2] Thackeray does not refer here to the *Codex Zugninensis rescriptus Veteris Textamenti*, ed. Eugène Tisserant (*Studi e Testi* xxiii Roma 1911). 127 Palimpsest leaves (122 in Rome, 5 in London) of it are known. They belong to six MSS and are written in uncial script of the fifth/sixth century. The text preserved here is of clear Lucianic type.

and of Josephus, we discover that this 'Syriac' text in an older form was in existence more than two centuries earlier, and can be carried back from the age of the Christian Lucian to that of the Jewish historian.

With regard to the books of Samuel, Thackeray comes to nearly the same conclusion as Adam Mez, who devoted a special investigation to Josephus' Bible quotations in some of the books of the Antiquities.[1] Mez tried to prove the agreement of Josephus' quotations with the 'Lucianic' text by a large number of instances, proper names and positive facts reported by Josephus. He referred also to the observation of S. R. Driver that the Vetus Latina affords independent evidence of the existence of MSS containing characteristic readings of Lucian, and that not infrequently the Peshiṭta also shows passages which agree with the Lucianic text.[2] Josephus, Vetus Latina and Peshiṭta can therefore be regarded as sources for a primitive text of Lucian ('Ur-Lucian') in the first and second centuries of the Christian era.

The statements of Thackeray and Adam Mez that for the historical books of the Bible from Samuel onwards Josephus is of first-rate importance for the Bible text of the Old Testament are of great interest in so far as they are in complete contrast with the conclusions of Alfred Rahlfs on the text of these books of the Bible used by Josephus.[3] Rahlfs' book was suggested by a prize offered in 1907 by the Göttingen Academy:

> Das Verhältnis des sogenannten Lucian-Textes der Septuaginta zu der ihm zugrunde liegenden Überlieferung soll untersucht werden.

Although Rahlfs had limited his investigations to the books of Kings and had failed to give adequate attention to the essential problem, he was awarded the prize.[4]

Rahlfs begins with a sharp criticism of Lagarde's edition of the Lucianic text[5] of the books of Samuel and Kings. Lagarde

[1] Adam Mez, *Die Bibel des Josephus, untersucht für Buch v–vii der Archäologie*, Basel 1895.

[2] *Notes on the Hebrew text . . . of the Books of Samuel*, 2nd edition, Oxford 1913, pp. lxxi and lxxxvii.

[3] *Septuaginta-Studien*, 3: *Lucian's Rezension der Königsbücher*, Göttingen 1911.

[4] *Nachrichten von der Kgl. Gesellschaft der Wissenschaften zu Göttingen*, Geschäftliche Mitteilungen, 1910, pp. 36–40.

[5] *Librorum Veteris Testamenti canonicorum pars prior graece Pauli de Lagarde studio et sumptibus edita*, Göttingen 1883.

had based his edition on MSS containing the Lucianic text. According to Rahlfs, these MSS show two different forms of text, and a relative value only can be attributed to them. Of greater importance are various readings in agreement with quotations by Church Fathers who follow the Lucianic text, and readings which follow Codex B and the Ethiopic version. The text represented by these two sources is for Rahlfs the text nearest to the 'original' Septuagint. He is convinced that the Lucianic text is derived from the 'original' Septuagint. Readings in agreement with Codex B and the Ethiopic version must therefore belong to the oldest parts of the Lucianic text.

On the basis of this reconstructed 'Lucianic' text Rahlfs re-examines the instances of Josephus' quotations from Samuel given by Mez and comes to the conclusion that most of them are no sufficient proof for connecting Josephus' Bible with that kind of text. He himself examined Josephus' quotations from the books of Kings with the result that he found three instances only—one translation, one addition, and the division of the two books—in which the Lucianic text reconstructed by him agrees with the text of Josephus. He concludes that a few scattered readings of Lucian may be of greater antiquity, not the text of Lucian in general, and he supposes that some of these older 'Lucianic' readings may have been influenced by Josephus.

Rahlfs must be accorded the merit of having collected a great amount of material for studying the Septuagint, and his *Verzeichnis der griechischen Handschriften des Alten Testaments* (Göttingen, 1914) is a very useful piece of work. But his preconceived ideas on the origin of the Septuagint and many other shortcomings prevented him generally from making the right use of this material. In this case we have a very clear example of the methods adopted by him. He reconstructs an older Lucianic text, closely related to Codex B, but one which never existed, and shows that this text has nothing to do with the quotations of Josephus. He severely criticizes Lagarde's edition of the Lucianic text made by that great scholar on the basis of actual MSS and does not see—as had been seen by Thackeray—that for the text contained in the MSS published by Lagarde the quotations of Josephus are of first-rate importance. Nobody will be surprised that Rahlfs did not realize the doubtful character of his methods. It is, however, somewhat surprising that the appropriate members of the Göttingen Academy of that time were so much under the influence of these methods that they did not see the vicious circle in which the whole of Rahlfs' deductions moved.[1]

There can be no doubt that the quotations of Josephus from these historical books are in agreement with the text of Lucian. It is another question whether this agreement can be explained in the way suggested by Thackeray and—before him—by Mez. Both these men based their investigations on Niese's critical edition of Josephus.[2] We must remember that among the MSS at our disposal there is not a single one which has preserved the unaltered original text of Josephus. Niese writes:

> Ac primum ne unus quidem (codex) est qui Josephi verba incorrupta tradat. statim enim postquam Josephus maxime a Christianis legi coeptus est, quaedem in eo consulto et de industria mutata sunt, quoniam eum cum libris sacris in linguam graecam olim conversis consentire volebant . . .[3]

From a quotation by Eusebius in which the original reading of Josephus is preserved, Niese is able to show that this reading was altered in all codices of Josephus. From this and similar facts he concludes that all the codices preserved must go back to one archetype:[4]

> Omnium vere codicum et versionis latinae unum archetypum fuisse etiam alia vitia omnibus communia docent.

Niese tries to date this archetype from a time after Origen and before Eusebius. I am somewhat doubtful how far this is really possible. Two things, however, are certain: 1. We have no evidence for the text of Josephus before the formation of the archetype. 2. This archetype was not written before the Lucianic text of the Bible was in existence. We must therefore contemplate the possibility that the striking agreement between Josephus' quotations from the historical books and the text of Lucian may be due to alterations made by Christian copyists who were anxious

[1] In the Academy's report on Rahlfs' book we read: 'Namentlich gibt er (Rahlfs) in allen Fällen, wo eine Gruppe der Lucian-handschriften mit dem griechischen Vulgärtext, eine andere mit B und dem Aethiopen stimmt, der letzteren Gruppe den Vorzug. Dieser Grundsatz, dessen Richtigkeit durch die weitere Untersuchung durchaus bestätigt wird, ist wichtig. Denn es leidet keinen Zweifel, dass der vom Cod. B und dem Aethiopen repräsentierte Texttypus im allgemeinen der ursprünglichen LXX am nächsten kommt' (p. 36).

[2] *Flavii Josephi Opera*, edidit et apparatu critico instruxit Benedictus Niese. 7 volumina, Berolini, 1887–95. The text printed by Thackeray himself and continued by Ralph Marcus as a basis for their English translation in 'the Loeb Classical Library' (1926 ff) depends on the material assembled by Niese.

[3] Vol. i, Praefatio p. xxx.

[4] Ibid., p. xxxii.

—or may have been required—to bring Josephus' quotations into agreement with a Greek text of the Bible which at that time was regarded as particularly authoritative. We shall see that similar conditions prevailed with regard to Philo's quotations from the Greek Pentateuch, and the same has also been proved in other cases.

That the quotations from the historical books in Josephus' text were made to agree with the Lucianic text by later copyists is very likely if we consider that Josephus' quotations from other books of the Bible are of a very different character. According to Thackeray, Josephus made little use of the prophetical books, except Daniel, counted by him among the Prophets. For Daniel he appears to have used a Greek text which combines the peculiarities of both the Greek texts of the book preserved. In the Torah he made little use of the Septuagint. Thackeray thinks that Josephus' main authority in this case must have been a Hebrew text translated by Josephus himself. In the books of Joshua, Judges and Ruth, Thackeray finds no evidence for the use of a Greek text. Where the Hebrew and the Aramaic are concerned, Thackeray suspects, at least in Judges, dependence on an Aramaic Targum.[1]

It is not very likely that Josephus, in the Antiquities, used for the Pentateuch a Hebrew text translated by himself, for the historical books from Samuel onwards a Greek text of exactly Lucianic type, for Judges an Aramaic Targum (again translated by himself), and for Daniel alternatively two Greek translations. Nobody can deny that Josephus' knowledge of Hebrew and of Aramaic was quite adequate. He declares himself that he wrote his *Bellum* first in Aramaic, his mother tongue; moreover he had been educated as a priest and therefore knew Hebrew. His mastery of the Greek language is more doubtful. In any case it is difficult to believe that in his later days when living in Rome under vastly different circumstances from those under which he wrote his *Bellum* he should have translated Hebrew and Aramaic texts into Greek for a book which, with the help of his assistants, he wrote in Greek for non-Jewish readers. The varying character of his quotations must be explained in another way. His Greek Torah, like the Greek Torah used by Philo, may have differed greatly from the 'Septuagint' as used by the Christians. I have already discussed the problem of the Lucianic texts in the quo-

[1] loc. cit. p. 81.

tations from the later historical books. That the quotations from Daniel sometimes agree with the so-called 'Septuagint', sometimes with the so-called 'Theodotion', seems to point to the fact that in addition to the two Greek texts which have come down to us, other texts of Daniel existed in the first Christian century and that one of these texts, now lost, was the Greek book of Daniel used by Josephus.

9. Paul de Lagarde

The Greek translation of the book of Judges is preserved in two different forms. In one of his last publications[1] Paul de Lagarde dealt with the problem of these two texts. He printed Judges i–v according to the two texts side by side, on opposite pages, with the apparatus belonging to each of them, in order to enable the reader to recognize clearly that we have here before us two different translations. He writes:[2]

> Das vorstehende genügt, um folgende Thesen zu stellen:
>
> 1. Die im Codex A . . . stehende Übersetzung des Buches der Richter stimmt im Grossen und Ganzen sowohl mit dem Texte des Origenes als mit dem Texte des lateinisch redenden Westens.
>
> 2. Codex B liefert nicht Varianten zu A, sondern enthält, wie die schwierigeren Stellen zeigen, eine andere Übersetzung des Buches der Richter. Aus B in A, oder aus A in B hinüberkorrigieren darf nur der besonders Kundige und Besonnene. . . .
>
> 3. Ohne Eingehen in den inneren Wert der Codices wird niemand . . . die griechischen Übersetzungen benutzen dürfen. Dies Eingehen ist das von mir 1863 . . . gemeinte 'eklektische Verfahren' das für jeden Herausgeber der LXX nötig wird, der den Urtext dieser Übersetzung finden will . . .

Lagarde saw that the text of Judges as contained in Codex A had a wide circulation in the Christian Church. He admits that the codex has frequently preserved an older translation whereas Codex B only has an excerpt made from later versions.[3] With regard to the book of Judges he is convinced that Codex B contains a different translation. His own interest, however, con-

[1] *Septuaginta-Studien*, Abhandlungen der Göttinger Gesellschaft der Wissenschaften, vol. xxxvii, 1891.

[2] *Septuaginta-Studien*, pp. 71 f.

[3] Lagarde refers here to his *Anmerkungen zur Griechischen Übersetzung der Proverbien*, Leipzig 1863, where he discusses these problems on p. 3 (in text and annotation).

centrates on finding the 'Urtext' of this translation. How can we find an 'Urtext' of two different translations!

Whoever is acquainted with conditions prevailing in older Targums at a time before an authoritative text was fixed will recognize in these two Greek texts typical examples of two forms of an old Targum. The first attempt at translating a difficult Hebrew text into another language was usually not of a high standard. Revisions were made, some with more, some with less ability by different men on different principles. These Targums had no authoritative text. Every copyist could try to improve the text he copied. Sometimes, texts of a higher standard were produced owing to a better understanding of the Hebrew original; at other times we find an adaptation to another Hebrew text. Sometimes the Greek of the translation was improved. But sometimes we see, as Origen did, mere deteriorations in the new texts due to 'the carelessness and indifference of the copyists'.

In this way quite a number of different forms were created and used by Greek-speaking Jews, just as the Samaritans used different forms of their Samaritan Targum and the Jews their different forms of the Palestinian Targum of the Pentateuch.

The Jews soon abandoned the standard text of the Greek Bible, fixed towards the end of the second century B.C. in Alexandria. More and more had they become used to Greek texts which had been assimilated to the Hebrew original. The Hebrew text became more and more the authoritative text for them, and apart from that various Greek texts were used. The Christians were in need of a canonical text of the Greek Bible. Usually they adopted one of the Greek texts used by the Jews. We do not know how it came about that in the book of Judges *two* such texts were adopted. Paul de Lagarde had little experience of the conditions prevailing in older Targums. So he declared the two forms of the Greek text to be two 'different translations' and did not recognize that they were the remains of different forms of a Greek Targum which had been used by Greek-speaking Jews. If Thackeray is right in saying that Josephus' quotations agree with neither of these two forms, Josephus must have had yet another form of the Greek Targum to Judges before him which is now lost. It is quite possible that this form contained such Midrashic elements as to induce Thackeray to believe that Josephus' quotations were translated from an Aramaic Targum.

I come now to the second conclusion we can draw from the

discovery in 1952 of the leather scroll with the Greek text of the Minor Prophets. We can see from it that a MS of the Greek Bible text in circulation among the Jews had already been assimilated to the Hebrew basic text. Of such assimilations Paul de Lagarde spoke in his *Erklärung über die von mir beabsichtigte Ausgabe der Septuaginta*, which he called *Rechenschaftsbericht* and which he had printed in May 1889[1] shortly before his death. Lagarde speaks here about the tasks which face a scholar when he examines a text from Antiquity, and he enumerates them thus: (1) The hearing of witnesses. (2) The classifying of the evidence into groups. (3) The extricating of the oldest available text. Then as (4) he speaks of possibly necessary alterations. In this connection he mentions the variants of the Greek Bible text and points out the following:[2]

> Various readings in the Christian manuscripts of the Septuagint have a distinctive character. Nine-tenths of them are not disfigurations of the original words, due to the carelessness and stupidity of copyists. They are intentional corrections according to a recension of the Hebrew text closely connected with our Masoretic text. It is very likely that they originated from the later Greek translations of the Old Testament unfortunately preserved to us in a very fragmentary form only. . . .

Lagarde here speaks of *Christian* manuscripts. Of Jewish manuscripts nothing was known in his time. But Jewish manuscripts must have preceded the Christian ones. According to Lagarde, Christian manuscripts may take us back to the time of the Apostles. Quotations by Jewish Hellenistic authors, like Philo and Josephus, may take us back to a text about fifty years older. He scarcely doubted that there was a uniform text transmitted by the Jews to the Christians. Christians were made responsible for the various readings and it was supposed that they derived them from the later translations made by the Jews. That was his great error.

For the early Christians, the *form* of the Biblical text was no problem. Their aim was to have a Greek text on which they could rely, since the Hebrew text could no longer be used by them as an authority owing to the fact that they did not understand Hebrew. They had taken over their Greek texts from the Jews, and the letter of Aristeas had given to these texts a special authority.

[1] *Mittheilungen*, iii, 1889, pp. 233–34.
[2] See *Opera Minora*, Leiden 1956, pp. 118 f.

The letter of Aristeas was a letter of propaganda composed in about 100 B.C. or somewhat earlier with a twofold intention: to win acceptance in Jewish communities for a Greek Torah prepared with special care, and also to secure the withdrawal of earlier texts used hitherto which were described as unreliable. The miraculous origin of the translation which was regarded as semi-inspired, for instance by Philo, gave to it the necessary authority. That is the significance of the name *Septuagint* given to the Torah because of the seventy-two men said to have composed it.

The Christians, by extending the name to the *whole* Greek Bible and all the Greek Biblical texts used by them, attributed to these texts the same miraculous origin and the same authority as the letter of Aristeas had relied on to gain approval for a certain Greek Torah among the Jews.

Greek texts of the Bible used by Christians in early times were not the oldest and best which existed. But nobody was concerned with that. We have seen how often the text had been worked over which was quoted by Justin as his Septuagint. The book of Judges still exists in two different forms both of which must have been used by Christians. In the New Testament, the Bible is quoted in forms which differ greatly from the forms of the Greek Bible which have come down to us. The texts were used exactly as they stood by Christians. The letter of Aristeas was quite sufficient to give these texts the necessary authority, and the letter was used by Christians from the beginning of the second century or even earlier.

Irenaeus (died A.D. 202) is already convinced of the miraculous origin of the 'Septuagint', meaning thereby the Greek translation of the whole Bible, and what Philo had said of the divine inspiration of the seventy-two translators of the Torah was said by Irenaeus of the seventy-two translators of the whole Greek Bible. It is of great interest to see to what degree the Christian authors made use of the letter of Aristeas in order to enhance the authority of their Greek Bible. I may refer here to the testimonies collected by Paul Wendland in his edition of the letter,[1] and to his very illuminating article in which he discusses these testimonies.[2] The letter helped greatly to prove the 'canonicity' of the Greek Bible which had become the standard text of the Church. I may

[1] Leipzig, Teubner, 1900, pp. 87–166.
[2] P. Wendland, 'Zur ältesten Geschichte der Bibel in der Kirche', *ZNW*, vol. i, 1900, pp. 267–99.

confine myself to referring to the famous correspondence between Augustine and Jerome in which the views of one of the greatest and most enlightened Christian authorities with regard to the Greek Bible are expressed in a very clear and interesting way.[1]

Augustine cannot understand why Jerome intends to use the Hebrew text as a basis for his new Latin translation of the Bible. He is greatly disturbed by this news. He is astonished to hear that a new understanding of any Biblical passage might be gained from the Hebrew text which had escaped all the many translators, to say nothing of the 'Septuagint', of the miraculous origin and the divine inspiration of which Augustine is firmly convinced. He tries to persuade Jerome to use this 'canonical' text as a basis for the new translation, and he is afraid that Jerome's translation, if based on another text, might bring about a rupture between the Greek and Latin Churches. He declares that it is so convenient to be able to appeal in a debate to the Septuagint as the final authority that it would be very hazardous to refer to a Hebrew original, which could be used by nobody but Jerome, and to abandon so many Greek and Latin authorities.

10. Origen

We know that in deciding to use the Hebrew text as a basis for his Latin translation, Jerome relied on Origen who was the great scholar with a real understanding of the uncertainty of the Greek Bible used in the Church. Origen calls this Bible 'Septuagint', as all Christian authors did in his time. But he attributed to it neither the miraculous origin nor the divine inspiration usually connected with that name. He had studied MSS of the Greek Bible and had seen that these texts did not agree at all with each other. The surviving parts of the 'Septuagint' column in the Hexapla show clearly that he had different texts of the version at his disposal.[2]

But—more important—there were differences between the Greek translation and the Hebrew original. Through controversies with the Jews Origen had become aware of these differences. He was convinced that to the original a greater authority must be attributed than to a translation derived from it. He had a certain knowledge of Hebrew, and we hear from Eusebius that

[1] Wendland, loc. cit., pp. 282 ff, based on Augustine's letters, nos. 28, 40, 67, 71.

[2] Cf. Alexander Sperber, 'New Testament and Septuagint', *JBL*, vol. lix, New York 1940, pp. 210 ff.

he had in his own possession Hebrew Biblical MSS. There can be no doubt that he had been able to procure for himself Hebrew texts which were regarded as authoritative by the Jews of his time. By comparing the Greek Bible with these Hebrew texts he recognized the differences between the two forms of text. But he was not aware that the Hebrew text also had had its history, and that the text which had been the basis of the Greek translation was often not identical with the text regarded as authoritative by the Jews of his time. He could, therefore, see in all the instances where the Greek Bible differed from that text nothing else than deteriorations caused by the carelessness of the copyists. His aim was to repair the disagreements of the Greek Bible according to the authoritative Hebrew text. As his knowledge of Hebrew was not sufficient for doing this directly from the Hebrew text, he used all sorts of Greek translations of the Bible to which he had access, as a help in this task. He could not, however, speak frankly about these problems. He had to be cautious. The 'Septuagint' was regarded as the canonical text, inspired by God. So we only occasionally find in his works a remark on these problems. The chief reference is to be found in his Commentary on Matthew where we read:[1]

> Great differences have arisen in the transcripts, from the carelessness of some of the scribes, or from the recklessness of some persons, or from those who neglected the emendation of the text, or else from those who made additions to the text or omissions from it, as they thought fit. With God's help we were able to repair the disagreement in the copies of the Old Testament on the basis of the other versions. We judged what was doubtful in the Septuagint (on account of the disagreement of the codices) according to the rest of the versions, and retained what was in agreement with them. Some passages we have marked with an obelus, as not to be found in the Hebrew text, since we did not dare to suppress them altogether; some we have added using an asterisk, to make clear that we have added from the other versions something not to be found in the Septuagint, in accordance with the Hebrew text. Whoever wishes may accept them; he to whom this gives offence may accept or reject them, as he thinks fit.

Origen refers here to his great work on textual criticism, the Hexapla. The chief report on it is to be found in Eusebius'

[1] Translated from the critical edition, made for the Berlin Academy by E. Klostermann, vol. xv: *Origenes' Matthäus-Erklärung*, Leipzig 1935, p. 387.

Church History (vi, 16). Eusebius depends here on some notes of Origen's which were published long ago, but the importance of which had not been recognized so that they had been completely forgotten until they were rediscovered and republished by Giovanni Mercati.[1] These notes are contained in an excerpt dealing with some of the sources used by Origen for his great work. Mercati has shown that the excerpt contains original notes by Origen, which were before Eusebius when he wrote his *Church History*.[2] The passage of Eusebius has been discussed in a short, but important article by Eduard Schwartz.[3] I quote the passage of Eusebius in the translation of J. E. L. Oulton,[4] correcting it at two essential points in accordance with statements of Mercati and Schwartz which had escaped the attention of Oulton.[5]

> And so accurate was the examination that Origen brought to bear upon divine books, that he even made a thorough study of the Hebrew tongue, and got into his own possession the original writings in the actual Hebrew characters, which were extant among the Jews. Thus, too, he traced the editions of the other translators of the sacred writings besides the Seventy and[6] discovered certain others differing from the beaten track of translation, that of Aquila and Symmachus and Theodotion, which, after lying hidden for a long time, he traced and brought to light, I know not from what recesses. With regard to these, on account of their obscurity (not knowing whose in the world they were) he merely indicated this: that the one he found at Nicopolis near Actium, and the other in such other place. On the other hand,[7] in the Hexapla of the Psalms, after the four well-known editions, he placed beside them not only a fifth but also a sixth and seventh translation; and in the case of one of these he has indicated again that it was found at Jericho in a jar in the time of Antoninus the son of Severus. All these he brought together, dividing

[1] Giovanni Mercati, 'D'alcuni frammenti esaplari sulla V^a e VI^a edizione greca della Bibbia'. *Studi e Testi*, vol. v, Roma 1901, pp. 28–46.

[2] Mercati, loc. cit., pp. 31–6. See also Mercati's article 'Sul testo e sul senso di Eusebio H.E. VI 16', in *Studi e Testi*, v, pp. 47–60.

[3] Eduard Schwartz, 'Zur Geschichte der Hexapla' (*Nachrichten, Göttinger Gesellschaft der Wissenschaften, Phil.-Hist. Klasse*, 1903, Heft 6.]

[4] Eusebius, *The Ecclesiastical History*, vol. ii (The Loeb Classical Library), London, 1932, pp. 51 and 53.

[5] Oulton's translation is given in both cases in the notes.

[6] 'And beside the beaten track of translation, that of Aquila and Symmachus and Theodotion, he discovered certain others, which were used in turn. . . .' The incorrectness of this translation was indicated by Mercati, who translated 'differenti dalle . . .', cf. p. 39, and Schwartz, p. i, n. 3.

[7] 'At any rate'; but here a new sentence begins, Schwartz, p. 3.

them into clauses and placing them one against the other, together with the actual Hebrew text: and so he has left us the copies of the Hexapla, as it is called. He made a further separate arrangement of the editions of Aquila and Symmachus and Theodotion together with that of the Seventy, in the Tetrapla.

I add here an English translation of the excerpt published by Mercati and reprinted by Eduard Schwartz:

Concerning the fifth and sixth edition further:

The fifth edition which I found in Nicopolis near Actium: the marginal notes in it show how far (another similar text) differs from it.

The sixth edition: found together with other Hebrew and Greek books in a jar near Jericho in the time of the reign of Antoninus (MS: Antonius) the son of Severus.

The translator of the fifth edition, having separated the 10th (Psalm) from the 9th, dividing it into two, goes on with the addition of one until the 69th (Psalm), then, joining the 70th to the 69th, he puts the numbers like those in our MSS, until the 113th (Psalm). From there, by joining some and dividing again others, he concludes with the 148th (Psalm).

In commenting on this text, Schwartz remarks that the last paragraph has to be regarded as a subscription under the seventh column of the Hexapla (containing the Quinta). It must have been written there at the end of the Psalms,[1] as is to be inferred from the contents. In the last paragraph but one we have to see, because of Eusebius' testimony, a subscription at the end of the Psalms under the eighth column (containing the Sexta). The subscription under the ninth column (containing the Septima) is lost, like nearly all of that edition. We do not know under which book Origen had placed the first note on the Quinta.

That the Sexta, not the Septima, was found near Jericho could be inferred already from Eusebius' report. It is proved with certainty by the original subscription of Origen. It is interesting to see to what extent Eusebius is dependent in his description on the original subscriptions in the Hexapla. He preserves the active of εὑρεῖν for the Quinta and uses the passive for the Sexta, like Origen. It seems that besides these notes very little other material was at the disposal of Eusebius. Schwartz remarks that it is

[1] See Mercati, 'La numerazione dei Salmi nella V^{a} edizione', *Studi e Testi*, vol. v, pp. 42–6.

impossible to say at what time and under what conditions Origen was in Nicopolis, and whether he himself or somebody else in his place discovered and acquired the treasure of MSS hidden in the jar near Jericho.

Mercati and Schwartz have seen that Origen's notice concerning the Quinta, as preserved in the excerpt, is incomplete at the end. I have added in brackets the supplement proposed by Schwartz. Origen must have had at his disposal at least two copies of the Quinta, which differed from each other in some respect. In the column of the Quinta, Origen had added to the text of one copy the various readings of the other copy (or copies) in the margin. Mercati has pointed out that the Milan palimpsest contains in the last column—that following the column with the Septuagint—the text of the Quinta, not the text of Theodotion, and that the text of this version is provided in the margin with the various readings added by Origen from the other MS (or MSS) of the Quinta.[1]

We know from Eusebius' report that these anonymous versions (Quinta, Sexta, Septima) occupied special columns in the Psalms of the Hexapla. But a number of readings from these versions

[1] Rahlfs, in his edition of the Greek Psalter (*Septuaginta Societatis Scientiarum Gottingensis*, auctoritate edidit A. Rahlfs, x, *Psalmi cum Odis*, Göttingen 1931) refers to the last column of the Milan palimpsest erroneously as belonging to *Theodotion*, whereas it belongs to the *Quinta*. Mercati had put at his disposal his copy of the complete Milan palimpsest. Rahlfs quotes it very seldom. We can easily control him, as the whole material, on the basis of the same copy of Mercati, was carefully—and correctly—registered in the Oxford *Concordance of the Septuagint*, Supplement II (Oxford, 1906). Rahlfs made also very little use of the Hexaplaric material published by Field—it is especially rich for the Psalter. He did not understand the importance of this material. In the Cambridge Septuagint and in Ziegler's edition of the Greek Isaiah (*Septuaginta. . . .* XIV, *Isaias*, Göttingen, 1938) the Hexaplaric material is carefully registered. Paul de Lagarde, after a long discussion of the importance of this material, declared: 'Eine Ausgabe der Septuaginta ohne vollständige Aufnahme des sogenannten hexaplarischen Materials halte ich für unwissenschaftlich.' See Lagarde, *Mittheilungen*, vol. iii, Göttingen, 1889, p. 234.—Rahlfs's chief interest is devoted to the different forms of the Greek Bible used in the different parts of the Christian Church, the so-called 'recensions', indicated already by Jerome. An exact study of them is of great interest for the history of the Greek Bible in the Christian Church, and their importance is emphasized by Paul de Lagarde. With the help of the material at his disposal, Rahlfs could make here some progress. Arthur Allgeier, however, has shown that his work on some of the sources, especially the Vetus Latina, is quite unsatisfactory, cf. his valuable reviews of Rahlfs's edition in *Deutsche Literaturzeitung*, 1931, cols. 1635–40, and *Theologische Revue*, vol. xxx, 1931, no. 6. By disregarding the other available material which did not interest him, Rahlfs reconstructs, on the basis of the recensions used in the Christian Church, a text which never existed in that form, presents it in the orthography of the third century B.C., and believes that he has pushed back the text 300 years and has arrived at a text closely connected with the 'Urtext' of the translation. Paul de Lagarde saw correctly that we may arrive, with the help of the recensions used in the Christian Church, at a text as old as the beginning of the Christian Church, 'of about the time of the emperor Tiberius'. See *Mittheilungen*, iii, 234.

belonging to other books of the Bible are reported. Very little is known of the Septima. Two readings from the Psalms are reported by Field (p. xlvi). All the rest of this column is lost. Jerome knew more of this version (Field, p. xliii). We know more of the Quinta and Sexta. 'In Psalmis editiones Quinta et Sexta passim laudantur,' remarks Field (p. xliv). To the material for the Quinta given by Field nearly 150 verses of the Psalms have to be added from the Milan palimpsest. For these verses the full text of the Quinta with various readings is preserved. Besides the material from the Psalms, Field quotes from the Quinta: four readings from the Pentateuch, many from the fourth book of Kings, one from Job, several from Canticles and from the Minor Prophets, especially Hosea. Of the Sexta, Field quotes—besides the instances from the Psalms—one reading from the Pentateuch, one from the third book of Kings, one from Job, many from Canticles, one from Amos, and three from Habakkuk. This survey shows that the Quinta and Sexta must have covered quite a number of Biblical books, although very little of these versions is preserved.

No authors of these versions are known. Origen quotes them by the number of the column which they occupied in the Hexapla. They were of Jewish origin. That the MS of the Sexta was discovered—according to Origen—together with *Hebrew* MSS makes this quite certain. But they did not belong to the category of versions made on the basis of the authoritative Hebrew text (Aquila, Symmachus) or brought into accordance with that text (Theodotion). We hear from Eusebius that they had been *hidden for a long time* when they were discovered. This shows that they had been discarded as useless by the Jews.

There can hardly be any doubt that these MSS were discovered by Origen in Jewish Genizas. As a real scholar he was anxious to have the material for his great work on textual criticism as complete as possible. It may be that the Jews themselves indicated to him places where he could find MSS of the Greek Bible. We may regret that he did not give more details of the MSS discovered by him or for him. He had to be cautious in all matters concerning textual criticism, as we have seen. That he himself valued highly these old versions of the Bible we may see from the way in which he made use of them. He would not have provided a special column in the Hexapla for each of these versions had they not differed greatly from each other. He would not have marked various readings in the margins of any of these translations of which he had more than one MS if they had not been of importance for him. According to Eusebius these different columns existed for the Psalms in the Hexapla. We have seen, however, they were not confined to that book of the Bible.

In these versions, carefully collected by Origen, we have to see different forms of the Greek Bible used by Greek-speaking Jews in pre-Christian times and in the first Christian century.[1] They were later replaced by new Greek translations made in agreement with the authoritative Hebrew text. The more this text became predominant among the Jews, the more older forms of the Greek Bible became obsolete; they were put in Genizas that they might do no harm, and might disintegrate there in course of time.

The Christians, during their discussions with the Jews, soon realized the importance of old texts of the Greek standard Bible. They began to look out for them and to find them. The oldest Bible codex, if we do not include the above-mentioned Cairo Papyrus Fuad 266, is the papyrus codex with extensive parts of Numbers and Deuteronomy belonging to Sir Alfred Chester Beatty. It is probable that the codex was written in the first half of the second century A.D. long before Origen lived. The text of Numbers was taken from a scroll which in the main was closely related to the later Codex Vaticanus (B). The text of Deuteronomy was taken from a scroll of which the text was more closely connected with the later Codex Alexandrinus (A). Yet the relation of this codex to the other most important uncial MSS of the Septuagint is also of great interest. Sir Frederic Kenyon has discussed this problem in detail in his introduction to the edition of this codex.

The position is similar with regard to the other papyrus codices in Sir Alfred Chester Beatty's Collection. But even such old and valuable papyrus codices show occasionally alterations to bring them into accord with the Hebrew. This is the case with the Papyrus Codex 967 from the third century, with the text of Ezekiel, of which eight folios are in the possession of Sir Alfred Chester Beatty and twenty-six folios went to John A. Scheide. This codex shows on the one hand assimilations to the Hebrew original; on the other hand various readings can be found in it

[1] It is very likely that various readings in the Hexaplaric material introduced by ὁ Ἰουδαῖος are taken from old Greek translations of Jewish origin. They occur in the Cambridge Septuagint, for instance, in Gen. xl, 9; xliii, 2; xlvii, 31; Exod. xvi, 31. The Rev. Professor G. D. Kilpatrick kindly collected these references for me.

which agree with Aquila, Symmachus and other Jewish translations. Josef Ziegler has made a careful investigation of these alterations and published them in an illuminating article proving that the variations are pre-Hexaplaric! He thinks that the alterations in the text of the codex were made in the first century A.D. He dared not go further back and suspect that the variations were made by Jews and so originate from pre-Christian times. Yet this is probably what happened. The Christians of the first century had more important and different tasks than to adjust a Greek Bible text to its Hebrew original or to revise it according to the usual equivalent texts among the Jews. If the alterations are so old, they must be pre-Christian.

Proof of this assumption is the newly-found Greek text of the Minor Prophets, written before or at the beginning of our era by a Jew for Jews. It is full of assimilations to the Hebrew original and shows readings of Aquila, Symmachus and Theodotion in abundance. It is therefore very likely that a text of Ezekiel, revised by Jews, was the basis for the alterations of the valuable Ezekiel papyrus with a view to assimilating it to the Hebrew original and to the Jewish parallel translations, as Ziegler observed. It is true that these assimilations are extremely important, and Ziegler is quite right when he sees in them the greatest value of these papyrus MSS.

Barthélemy makes the mistake of seeing everywhere this newly found text of the Greek Minor Prophets. He does not realise that there have been many texts deviating in different yet analogous ways. The proper examination of the actual conditions is made so difficult because one usually does not take into account that, after Christianity had become the religion of the State under Constantine, the Jews endeavoured with success systematically to destroy all their literature in Greek, including the Greek texts of the Bible. Greek Bible texts written by Jews have only been preserved in so far as they were taken over and revised by Christians. The newly found scroll of the Greek Minor Prophets, undoubtedly originating from Jews, is the great exception and has only been preserved because about 1900 years ago it was hidden in a cave and remained unnoticed until now.

There are also remains of other texts, differing widely in details from the texts to hand, but which must yet be accepted as analogous. The Washington Papyrus Codex of the Minor Prophets and the just mentioned Ezekiel text are among them.

I wish to refer here to the two Oxyrrhynchus Papyri 656 and 1007, which I have reproduced on plate 12 of my book *Die hebräischen Handschriften aus der Höhle*. The latter is definitely a Jewish text. The Antinoopolis Papyri 10 (1950)—fragments from Ezekiel xxxiii–xxxiv (fourth century), published by C. H. Roberts, show similar conditions in the text to the Chester Beatty-Scheide Papyrus. It is a mistake to try and see standardized, fixed Bible translations in these texts. They can only be seen in their proper perspective if one recognizes in them forms of a Greek Targum which, similar to the Aramaic Targums of older times, were in circulation in different versions, were more and more assimilated to the Hebrew original and influenced each other in many ways. If only we had more Greek Bible texts written by Jews it would become far more apparent that such was the case.

11. Philo's Quotations from the Bible

A very interesting example of the assimilation of the Greek Bible texts circulating among the Jews to the basic Hebrew original can be seen in Philo's Bible quotations. There are some Philo MSS in which the Bible quotations mainly agree with the Greek Bible texts accepted as authoritative by the Church. There is another group of Philo MSS in which the Bible quotations, at least in several books, often differ widely from the text to which we have become accustomed. These generally show a tendency to far more assimilation to the Hebrew original than is usually the case with the Bible text which became authoritative in the Church. The editors of the Philo text, Leopold Cohn and Paul Wendland, did not recognize these facts or, at any rate, greatly underestimated them. Certainly they did not see that the MSS with the divergent Bible quotations also offer in many instances a better Philo text than the MSS in which the Bible quotations agree with the Bible text familiar to us. In consequence we can only gather the most important and interesting readings from the apparatus of this edition of Philo with some difficulty.

During a patristic conference held in May 1940 in Oxford, I drew Mr. Peter Katz's attention to this problem and explained that it would be a worth-while and important task to trace the Bible quotations of Philo, and to examine to what extent aberrant Philo quotations can still be found in the apparatus of the Philo edition by Cohn and Wendland, in order to see what conclusions could be drawn from them for the history of the Septuagint text.

Katz took up my suggestion and after ten years published his book on Philo, in which he collected the relevant material.[1] He has shown that the aberrant text in quotations from the Bible in Philo's writings was more common than we had thought, that it was not restricted to the Philo manuscripts F and U, where it had first been observed by August Schröder (a pupil of Alfred Gehrke, in Greifswald) or to Philo's book *Quod Deus sit immutabilis*. The material collected by Katz is very valuable. The adaptation of the Greek text of the Bible to the Hebrew original in these quotations offers an interesting problem which must be solved. For Katz the matter is very simple. He sees in these adaptations corrections made according to the texts of the so-called *later translators*, Aquila, Symmachus and Theodotion who are said to have lived in the second century and cannot therefore have influenced Philo, a first century author. Consequently the adaptations must have been made later.

Now Rahlfs tried to find a Greek text of the book of Ruth from the 6th century. Although he was not able to find any trace of such a text for Genesis, i.e., a part of the Torah, nor was Katz able to find anything of the kind, he thought that the adaptations to the Hebrew original in the quotations of Philo originated from these later translators.

The development was certainly in the opposite direction. The Greek Bible which Philo had before him was one which was current among the Jews at that time. What a Jewish text of the Bible at the time of Philo looked like we see in the newly-found leather scroll with the text of the Minor Prophets. This text, written by Jews for Jews, is perhaps so old that it could have been used by Philo. It shows very many adaptations to the Hebrew original and to parallel translations in circulation amongst the Jews. The Greek text of the Torah which Philo used may have been similar. A specimen of such a Torah text I have published in my book *Die hebräischen Handschriften aus der Höhle*, plate xii, 3. There can hardly be any doubt that aberrant Bible quotations in manuscripts of Philo's works reveal the Greek Bible text as Philo had it before him. Schroeder conjectured this quite rightly,

[1] *Philo's Bible. The aberrant Text of Bible Quotations in some Philonic Writings and its Place in the Textual History of the Greek Bible*, by Peter Katz, Ph.D. (Cantab.), Cambridge 1950.

and the newly found scroll with the Greek text of the Minor Prophets has fully confirmed his supposition. These aberrant Bible quotations should be carefully collected from the book of Katz. With their help we can form an idea of a text of the Greek Torah in circulation amongst the Jews at the time of Philo.

We know that Philo was one of the Greek-writing Jewish authors from whom the Jews, soon after the destruction of the Temple, turned away. Until the latter part of the Middle Ages Philo's works were unknown among the Jews. It is only due to Jews converted to Christianity that a number of Philo's works have been preserved and only thanks to the Christians that these works were frequently copied. It is conceivable that the Christian copyists corrected the sometimes seemingly odd and aberrant Bible quotations according to the Bible text to which they were accustomed. Happily they could not cope with these corrections and in a number of MSS such original quotations from Philo have been preserved. In view of the newly-found fragments of the Greek Bible we shall have to devote special attention to these aberrant quotations.

The different forms of the Greek Bible were taken over by the Christians in the apostolic period. They are reflected in the New Testament in quotations from and in allusions to the Greek Old Testament. These quotations in the New Testament were not altered according to a later standard text of the Old Testament, the Septuagint, as frequently happened in the case of such quotations from Philo, Josephus and the Church Fathers. The authors of the writings of the New Testament had their own authority.

12. Bible Quotations in the New Testament

These quotations can therefore make a contribution of great importance to our knowledge of the forms of the Greek Bible used by the early Christians. We are not interested in proving that these quotations are more or less in accordance with the 'Septuagint' used by the Christians, the only text of the Greek Bible so far considered. That a large number of these quotations agree with the Christian 'Septuagint' can be explained by the fact that one of the different forms of the Greek Bible used by the early Christians was that which later became the Church's standard text. In other cases there are great differences. These cannot generally be called 'free quotations' from the Christian

'Septuagint' although nobody will deny that sometimes a difference can be explained in this way. Usually we must see in these quotations traces of other forms of the Greek Bible used by the early Christians.

Alexander Sperber has attempted to make a systematic investigation of these differences.[1] He has based his investigations on the readings of Codex B of the Old and the New Testaments but indicated where Codex A and parallels in the Old Testament agree with New Testament quotations. He has dealt with about 300 instances in which New Testament quotations differ from the text of the 'Septuagint' used by the Christians, and has tried to group and classify these various readings according to fifteen criteria: 1. The use of different Greek synonyms. 2. Differences in the exegesis of the same basic Hebrew word. 3. Differences in the use of the possessive pronoun. 4. *Waw consecutivum* in Greek translation. 5. Differences in the use of the personal pronoun. 6. Differences in the use of the article. 7. Collective nouns treated as singulars or plurals. 8. Verb and compound verb. 9. The use of Greek tenses and moods. 10. Differences in Greek syntax. 11. Addition or omission of Greek particles. 12. Hebrew particles in Greek translation. 13. Different interpretation of full sentences. 14. Internal Greek corruptions. 15. Differences resulting from Hebrew *variae lectiones*.

As an example I should like to give here the text of Isa. xlii, 1–4 as quoted in Matt. xii, 18–20. The first line gives the New Testament quotation, the second line the text from the 'Septuagint'. For the first verse I add in a third line the text ascribed to Theodotion. The small numbers added refer to the 'criteria' proposed by Sperber.

Mt. ’Ιδου$_{15}$ ὁ παῖς μου ὃν ᾑρέτισα$_{2}$ ὁ$_{15}$ ἀγαπητός μου ὃν εὐδόκησεν$_{1.2}$
Is. ’Ιακὼβ$_{15}$ ὁ παῖς μου ἀντιλήψομαι$_{2}$ αὐτοῦ ’Ισραὴλ$_{15}$ ὁ ἐκλεκτός$_{2}$ μου προσεδέξατο
Theod. ’Ιδοὺ ὁ παῖς μου ἀντιλήψομαι$_{2}$ αὐτοῦ ὁ ἐκλεκτός μου ὃν ηὐδοκησεν
Mt. ἡ ψυχή μου θήσω$_{1.9}$ το πνεῦμά μου ἐπ’ αὐτόν, καὶ κρίσιν$_{15}$ τοῖς ἔθνεσιν
Is. αὐτὸν ἡ ψυχή μου ἔδωκα$_{1.9}$ τὸ πνεῦμά μου ἐπ’ αὐτὸν κρίσιν$_{15}$ τοῖς ἔθνεσιν

[1] See A. Sperber's article 'The New Testament and the Septuagint', in the Hebrew quarterly *Tarbiṣ*, vi, Jerusalem 1934, pp. 1–29. The material collected here is very impressive. Sperber's later article 'New Testament and Septuagint' in the *JBL*, lix, New York 1940, pp. 193–293, is not always convincing.

Theod. ἡ ψυχή μου
Mt. ἀπαγγελεῖ$_2$ οὐκ ἐρίσει$_2$ οὐδὲ κραυγάσει$_{15}$ οὐδὲ ἀκούσει τις$_{15}$ ἐν ταῖς
Is. ἐξοίσει$_2$ οὐ κεκράξεται$_2$ οὐδὲ ἀνήσει$_{15}$ οὐδὲ ἀκουσθήσεται$_{15}$ ἔξω
Mt. πλατείαις$_1$ τὴν φωνὴν αὐτοῦ. κάλαμον συντετριμμένον$_1$ οὐ κατεάξει$_1$
Is. ἡ φωνὴ αὐτοῦ κάλαμον τεθλασμένον$_1$ οὐ συντρίψει$_1$
Mt. καὶ λίνον τυφόμενον$_1$ οὐ σβέσει, ἕως ἂν ἐκβάλῃ$_1$ εἰς νῖκος$_2$
Is. καὶ λίνον καπνιζόμενον$_1$ οὐ σβέσει ἀλλὰ εἰς ἀλήθειαν$_2$ ἐξοίσει$_1$
Mt. τὴν κρίσιν$_6$. καὶ τῷ ὀνόματι αὐτοῦ ἔθνη ἐλπιοῦσιν
Is. κρίσιν$_6$ . . . καὶ ἐπὶ τῷ ὀνόματι (νόμῳ)$_{14}$ αὐτοῦ ἔθνη ἐλπιοῦσιν

The differences between these two versions of the Greek Isaiah are so great that no one can seriously attempt to explain the one text as a free quotation from the other. Apart from an example of each of Sperber's 'criteria' 6, 9 and 14, we find in these verses seven instances of different Greek synonyms for the same Hebrew word; in five instances the same Hebrew word is understood in a different way; in five instances also the Hebrew text which was the basis of one translation differed in some details from the text from which the other translation was made.

There can be no doubt that here Matthew quoted a translation of Isaiah which differed from the translation found in the Christian 'Septuagint'. Special interest attaches to the third text, added to verse 1 and ascribed to Theodotion. Sometimes it agrees with the translation quoted by Matthew, at other times with the later standard text of the Christian Church. The three forms of text are an excellent example of the character of a Greek Targum in the time before a standard text was created. We can assume that still other forms of text existed in the MSS of the Greek Bible which were in the hands of the early Christians.

In the new edition of the Septuagint text of Isaiah, Josef Ziegler has carefully noted in the apparatus the various readings of the text quoted by Matthew. No MS of the Septuagint used by the Christians supports these readings—except for a few cases where we have to see an influence of the New Testament quotation. It is very noteworthy that a Greek translation of Isaiah which must have been well known in the first Christian century and was quoted by Matthew should have completely disappeared. The Church was in need of a *canonical* text. Differing texts were not copied any longer and disappeared. The standard text of

Isaiah seems to have been established in the Church at a comparatively early stage. In an investigation of the Septuagint text used by Clement of Alexandria,[1] Otto Stählin comes to the conclusion that Clement's quotations often differ from the readings of Codex B, but that they are usually in agreement with A and particularly with Q. On the other hand, if we compare the quotations from Isaiah in the first six books of the *Constitutiones Apostolorum*, based on the quotations from the *Didascalia*,[2] we find that these quotations were taken from a text which was in agreement with the Christian 'Septuagint'. As to the quotations from Ezekiel in this book, Stählin published Ezekiel xviii, 4–9 according to two different quotations taken from Clement, placing them side by side. It is quite evident that these quotations go back to two different translations of Ezekiel, one of which is similar to the Septuagint, while the other one is entirely different.[3] In *Masoreten des Westens* ii, p. 6, I have published a few verses from Ezekiel, which, in the second book of *Constitutiones Apostolorum*, are quoted in a form which bears no relation to the text of the Septuagint. Since then I have collected a large number of further quotations. They all differ from the text of the Septuagint, though not always to the same extent. These matters must be examined carefully. But it is clear that the standard text of the Greek Isaiah must have been generally accepted in the Church long before the standard text of Ezekiel.

13. Theodotion

One of the texts of the Greek Bible used by the early Christians was that of Theodotion. We know very little of the man who bore this name. A text of the Greek Bible is ascribed to him, which he is said to have adapted to the authoritative Hebrew text. As this Hebrew text did not become a standard text before the second century A.D., Theodotion cannot have made his revision before that time. Nor can he have made it much later, as Irenaeus who died in 202 knew it. The best known part of Theodotion is the book of Daniel, since his text of this book was adopted by

[1] *Clemens Alexandrinus und die Septuaginta*, Nürnberg 1901, p. 66. Cf. the further review by Otto Stählin: 'Die hellenistisch-jüdische Literatur', in Wilhelm von Christ's *Geschichte der Griechischen Literatur*, 6th edition by Wilhelm Schmid, ii, 542 ff.

[2] *Didascalia et Constitutiones Apostolorum*, ed. Fr. X. Funk, vol. 1, Paderbonae, 1906; *Constitutiones Apostolorum*, P. A. de Lagarde edidit. Lipsiae, Londini 1862.

[3] Cf. Stählin, loc. cit. p. 69.

the Church and is to be found in nearly all MSS of the Greek Bible. Only one MS from the Chigi-Library in Rome and the Papyrus belonging to Sir Alfred Chester Beatty contain the 'Septuagint' text of this book, for which we have a further witness in a Syro-hexaplaric MS in Milan. In his edition of the Chester Beatty Papyrus,[1] Sir Frederic Kenyon writes:

> Since 'Theodotionic' readings are found in works earlier than the date of Theodotion (in the New Testament, Barnabas, Clement, Hermas, to say nothing of Irenaeus and Tertullian, who were his younger contemporaries), it would appear that Theodotion took over, with or without revision, an earlier translation which has otherwise disappeared except in these few quotations.

In his Commentary on Daniel,[2] James A. Montgomery is anxious to avoid this conclusion. He devotes a special chapter to the problem of Theodotion and presents there the material at our disposal with great care and exactitude. After having discussed the early quotations from Theodotion he sets out a very complicated theory. He tries to explain these quotations by the hypothesis of a Hellenistic oral Targum; but in the end he is obliged to admit:

> Of course such a theory does not exclude the possibility of literary predecessors of the historical Theodotion.

As a matter of fact there can be no doubt that we must see in the text revised by Theodotion an 'earlier translation,' which clearly differed from the text later to become as 'Septuagint' the standard text of the Christian Church, and which was well known and widely used in earlier times. The quotations from Daniel in writings of the first Christian century show that Theodotion could not have altered substantially the text of the older translation when he adapted it to the authoritative Hebrew text. We can only verify with certainty the quotations from Daniel; for the other books of the Greek Bible we must rely, for 'Theodotionic' readings, on scattered notes from Origen's Hexapla. This old form of the Greek Bible must have been held in high esteem. It was widely quoted in its unrevised form during the first Christian century; after its revision by Theodotion, the text of Daniel was taken over by the Church.

[1] *The Chester Beatty Biblical Papyri* . . . fasc. vii, *Ezekiel, Daniel Esther*, London 1937, p. x.

[2] *Critical and Exegetical Commentary on the Book of Daniel*, Edinburgh 1927, see especially pp. 46–50.

One of the characteristics of Theodotion's text is the transliteration of Hebrew words in Greek letters. Field is able to quote more than one hundred of them—names of animals, plants, garments and all sorts of technical terms.[1] Here we depend on occasional quotations from Origen's Hexapla. The translation probably contained many more of these transliterated words. Under the heading 'Hebraisms in Vocabulary' Thackeray writes:[2]

> The influence of Hebrew on the vocabulary of the LXX, though considerable, is not as great as might at first sight be supposed. Apart from a small group of words expressing peculiarly Hebrew ideas of institutions (weights, measures, feasts, etc.), the instances where the Hebrew word is merely transliterated in Greek letters are mainly confined to a single group, namely the later historical books (Jud.–2 Chron., 2 Esdras). Now this is a group in which we have frequent reason to suspect, in the text of our uncials, the influence of Theodotion, and at least one book in the group (2 Esdras) has with much probability been considered to be entirely his work. We know that Theodotion was, whether from ignorance of the Hebrew or in some cases from scrupulousness, specially addicted to transliteration, and many of the instances in the later historical books are probably derived from him. . . .

This view turns the facts upside down. How can we expect that Theodotion, in the second Christian century, should have replaced good Greek translations by transliterated Hebrew words or that such newly-made transliterations should have been substituted for Greek words in some parts of the 'Septuagint'? Obviously the transliterated Hebrew words were used in translations made for Jews. Greek-speaking Jews were familiar with such Hebrew words even if they were not generally able to speak Hebrew. How many Hebrew words are to be found in the Yiddish language which is used by Jews who do not understand Hebrew! They nevertheless understand such Hebrew terms. Theodotion made his revisions for Jewish circles. He did not replace transliterated Hebrew words by Greek translations for he had no cause to fear that the Jews would not understand them.

On the other hand, it is obvious that in MSS of the Greek Bible written for the use of Christians such transliterated Hebrew words had to be eliminated and replaced by Greek equivalents.

[1] Field, *Prolegomena*, pp. xl, f.

[2] H. St. John Thackeray, *A Grammar of the Old Testament in Greek according to the Septuagint*, vol. i, Cambridge 1909, p. 31.

Thackeray's account shows that this was not always done with the same thoroughness in the different books of the Greek Bible. Such transliterated words can, by the way, be found in MSS of the Septuagint used by the Christians, in far greater numbers than could be expected from Thackeray's statements. They are mainly preserved where Greek copyists mis-wrote them because they understood no Hebrew. They corrected them and occasionally Greek words resulted which in the context made nonsense. A famous example is the word עֶרֶשׂ a *couch* or *bed* which, in the old Greek translation was transliterated ιερες according to an old method of transliterating Hebrew words. The Christian copyists changed this into ιερεῖς, so that we now read in Amos iii, 12, *priests* instead of *couch*, which is completely without meaning in the context. Jerome remarks:[1]

> Quod in principio capituli juxta LXX positum est, *sacerdotes* in Hebraico non habetur, sed pro hoc verbo *ares*, quod Aq. interpretatus est *grabatum*; et puto LXX ipsum verbum posuisse Hebraicum, quod quidam non intelligentes pro *ares* legerunt ιερεις.

Jerome transliterates the Hebrew word according to the way in which it was pronounced in his time, in agreement with the methods known to us from the text preserved in the Second Column of Origen's Hexapla. He was no expert in the methods of transliterating Hebrew words used at different times. The transliteration ιερες may have been used in the third or second century B.C. But he saw quite correctly that the transliterated Hebrew word was originally to be found in the 'Septuagint'. Thackeray himself has quoted quite a number of similar cases.[2] Franz Xaver Wutz[3] has made a special study of such slightly deformed transliterated Hebrew words in the Christian 'Septuagint'. He found them especially in the Codex Vaticanus (B). The material collected by him must be regarded as very valuable. These transliterated Hebrew words are among the oldest elements of the Greek Bible. They are certainly no innovation made by Theodotion in the second century A.D.

[1] Quoted from Field, vol. ii, p. 971.

[2] *A Grammar of the Old Testament in Greek*, pp. 37 f.

[3] In his book *Die Transkriptionen von der Septuaginta bis zu Hieronymus* he first deals (pp. 10–36) with transliterated proper names, then (pp. 36–176) with other traces of transliterations in the Greek Bible. The first part of the book was published in Stuttgart in 1925. The conclusions which he tries to draw in the second part (pp. 177–569), Stuttgart 1933, and the theories which he connects with the material can hardly be taken seriously.

Thackeray points out that another Theodotionic text may be preserved in 2 Esdras of the 'Septuagint'. This theory has been developed with much enthusiasm by Charles C. Torrey.[1] Whether or not the theory can be proved, what Torrey has to say with regard to the different Greek texts at our disposal for Chronicles and Ezra is of great interest. He writes:

> When we come to the testimony of the Greek versions, we are here confronted with two somewhat widely differing forms of the history. One agrees quite closely with MT (masoretic text), and has the same extent and arrangement, the other—obviously a mere fragment—begins near the end of Chronicles and extends not quite through the story of Ezra. During the part of the history covered by the two in common, the difference between them lies in (1) the words and phrases of the narrative, the difference here (i.e. in the Greek) being very great; (2) the position of extended passages; (3) material of very considerable amount found in one recension, but not in the other.... And finally, each one of the two forms of the narrative, the 'canonical' and the 'apocryphical' has come down to us in a double Greek tradition, the one embodied in Lagarde's edition, and the other contained in most of the existing MSS.... That is, for a portion of the Chronicler's history amounting to about thirteen chapters, we have at every point to compare four Greek texts.

This is an interesting testimony to the condition of a part of the Greek Bible of which several texts, differing in the whole arrangement of the material and in the translation, are still preserved. These various preserved texts are assuredly of Jewish and not of Christian origin. If Theodotion had really something to do with the text which we find in 2 Esdras in the 'Septuagint' we must presume that he *revised* an older text, not that he *created* the preserved version. 'Lagarde's edition' quoted by Torrey refers to the Lucianic text edited by him. In this case it is especially evident that we have here an old text of the Greek Bible which was revised by Lucian in the third century, not a text created by him.

In the Lucianic text a form of the Greek Esther is to be found which differs widely from the text usually found in MSS of the 'Septuagint'. The editors of the great Cambridge Septuagint write with regard to this text:

[1] See Torrey's article 'The Apparatus of the Textual Criticism of Chronicles-Ezra-Nehemiah' in *Old Testament and Semitic Studies in Memory of William Rainer Harper*, Chicago 1908, vol. ii, pp. 55–111, chiefly pp. 56 f.

> This recension differs so much from the B-text that we found it necessary to print it in full as an appendix. . . . We have printed Lagarde's text . . . without alteration. Fresh collations have been made of the MSS cited by Lagarde.

The Christian martyr Lucian could hardly have been interested in creating a new Greek text of Esther which differed so widely from the form of text usually found in MSS of the 'Septuagint'. He certainly took an old Jewish text for his Greek Bible and may have revised it according to his own principles.

With regard to the text of the book of Tobit the editors of the great Cambridge Septuagint write:

> The presentation of the evidence for the text of Tobit offers special difficulties and we have been obliged to modify our system in several ways. Dr. Swete printed the Sinaitic text 'in extenso beneath the Vatican text, but in smaller type, to denote its secondary character'. He divided the text into verses 'corresponding as nearly as possible with those of the standard text'. We are not prepared to express a definite opinion on the relation of the two Greek texts, certainly not to describe the Sinaitic text as secondary (see p. viii).

These few examples may suffice to show that not only for the Greek Book of Judges, but for several of the later books of the Bible also, different forms of text were preserved in MSS written for Christian readers. These different forms were of Jewish origin and were taken over by the Christians. The Church was more interested in having a canonical text for the Pentateuch and Isaiah than for these later books of the Bible.

I think we must agree with the late Professor T. W. Manson[1] that from ancient times Greek translations of the Bible were in existence which were composed in other places than Alexandria and remained in being as an entirety or in parts. One of these earlier Greek translations seems to have been the Bible text composed in Antioch which circulated widely. Such a text seems to have been the basis on which the revision of the Bible text was made by the martyr Lucian in Antioch. In the Manchester Papyrus we have an example of this text probably written before the text came into existence which we usually call the 'Septuagint'. Manson may also be right in assuming that yet another

[1] Cf. his review of my book *The Cairo Geniza*, in *Dominican Studies*, vol. ii, 1949, pp. 183–94.

form of such an early translation originated from Ephesus and was used as a basis for the text which we name after Theodotion.

No example of this text from pre-Christian times has yet been found; but St. Paul, writing in Ephesus, quotes in 1 Cor. xv, 54 the verse from Isaiah xxv, 8 in a form which is word for word identical with the text of Theodotion and which agrees with the Peshiṭta but differs from the Masoretic text and the Septuagint. In St. John's Gospel xix, 37, probably also written in Ephesus, Zech. xii, 10 is quoted according to Theodotion. It is very likely that we must in fact recognize here Theodotion's Bible text, which was used in Ephesus and in the synagogues of Asia Minor.

But it is of the utmost importance that the leather scroll with the text of the Minor Prophets shows, among others, readings which we know from so-called later Greek translations, used by Origen in his Hexapla. We can observe from this fact that the Jews must have wished even then to adapt their Greek text to the Hebrew original. For them the Hebrew text had become, in ever increasing measure, the really authoritative text in addition to which the translations were only accepted in so far as they agreed with it. It is not merely the existence in pre-Christian times of forms of text related to the Lucianic text which has thus been proved; we also learn from this leather scroll that the Greek Bible texts circulating then were, in wide measure, adapted to the Hebrew original.

14. The Coptic Versions

Father Barthélemy is anxious to discover, in the newly found leather scroll with the text of the Minor Prophets, the source for all the adaptations to be found in the Coptic versions. He points to the important material assembled and worked upon by Willem Grossouw.[1] Against this assumption it must be pointed out that the influence of the Hebrew text can be found in the Sahidic-Achmimic version, in the doublets of this version and also in the Bohairic version. Moreover, the Coptic text of the various versions generally differs from the text of the newly-found scroll and points to a source which agrees far more with the usual Greek Bible translation. For this reason alone it is very unlikely that it should have been only the newly-found text which was responsible

[1] *The Coptic Versions of the Minor Prophets.* A contribution to the study of the Septuagint (Monumenta biblica et ecclesiastica, 3) Roma 1938.

for the Hebraisms in the Coptic versions. Furthermore, both the Sahidic and the Bohairic translations, which exhibit Hebraisms, are independent translations.

One could hold—as Ziegler has suggested—that the Hebraisms in the Coptic versions originate from a number of Greek MSS which, in greater or lesser degree, show such Hebraisms. In his 'Beiträgen zur Koptischen Dodekapropheton—Übersetzung' in which he gave various appendices and rectifications of Grossouw's work, Ziegler concludes,[1]

> . . . when one adds the numerous other agreements of the Coptic translations (mainly the Achmimic-Sahidic one) with the Masoretic text, which are only present in Coptic . . . one sees clearly the Greek origin of the Coptic translations. They still had MSS which, but for a small remainder, have been lost, but have luckily been preserved in the Washington Papyrus Codex and the Bible MS used by Justin. The texts of these MSS had not been revised by way of the Hexapla, but much earlier than that, from the Hebrew text, on the basis of translations which maybe were those of the Aquila- and Symmachus-versions or at least very nearly related to them.

It is conceivable that the newly found text could be one of these Hebraizing texts which influenced the Coptic versions. On the other hand certain facts suggest that we cannot exclude an influence of Origen and his Hexapla. I would like to point out the following in this connection.

My son Paul Eric Kahle, in the introduction to his book on the Bala'izah-texts,[2] has suggested that Sahidic was probably the official dialect of the native population in Egypt and became authoritative long before Christianity established itself there, and that it probably has to be regarded also as the official language of Alexandria. At all events we must suppose that the Sahidic version of the Old and New Testaments was not only the first translation into Coptic, but also constituted the translation officially made by Church authorities.

As proved by Till and others, the Achmimic version of the Minor Prophets has been transcribed from the Sahidic version and only as evidence for this is it of interest to us. The same is true of the rest of the Achmimic MSS of the Bible. If we consider

[1] *Biblica* xxv, 1944, pp. 105–42. I translate his remarks on p. 142.

[2] *Bala'izah, Coptic Texts from Deir el-Bala'izah in Upper Egypt.* Published on behalf of the Griffith Institute, Oxford 1954. I discussed the problems of the Coptic translations at great length with my son and the following account is the result.

what an excellent text was used as original for the Sahidic translation of the New Testament we cannot help wondering how it was possible that such a peculiar text was accepted as basis for the Sahidic translation of the Minor Prophets.

Grossouw showed in his book that there are almost 200 passages in the Sahidic translation of the Minor Prophets in which the Sahidic translation agrees with the Hebrew text, in contrast to all known Greek MSS. Furthermore, numerous doublets can be found in the Sahidic text where either the Hebrew reading has been added to the usual text or they have been mixed. In every case the doublet follows the first text without reference.

Origen reports that he marked with an obelus such passages of the Septuagint in the Hexapla as are not to be found in the Hebrew text, and that on the other hand he added other passages, after the parallel translations, which are in agreement with the Hebrew text and which cannot be found in the Septuagint; these additions he marked with an asterisk.

If we suppose that—as was frequently the case—obelus and asterisk were omitted in Septuagint texts of the Hexapla, we should find there the doublets as they occur in the Sahidic translation.

Grossouw proves that in 175 passages the assimilation of the Minor Prophets to the Hebrew can be seen. In 104 of these passages the readings of the four parallel translations (Aquila, Symmachus, Theodotion, Quinta) are known in full or in parts; in 56 passages it can be proved beyond doubt, and in a further 34 passages it is more than likely. In the remaining 14 cases the translation presupposes a different text, but in no one of these 14 cases do we know the variants of all four parallel translations. It is probable, therefore, in spite of Ziegler, that the adaptations to the Hebrew original in the Sahidic translation have been taken from the Hexapla.

If we now recall the fact that the Sahidic translation emerged from official Christian circles and that it was made about the middle of the third century A.D., the conclusion seems obvious that the official Septuagint text which Origen established for the fifth column of the Hexapla formed the basis of the Sahidic translation. It suggests itself particularly from the unusual doublets. We know from Origen himself how it came about that he included them in his Septuagint text and we find them again in the Sahidic text.

We also know that it was precisely during the third century

that the text of the Septuagint in the Hexapla played an important role and was highly esteemed. We remember how the presbyter Pamphilus and his pupil Eusebius were eager to keep on copying this Septuagint text and to win recognition for it; we also remember the interesting note from the Codex Sinaiticus to which Sir Harold Idris Bell[1] called our attention, that Pamphilus, whilst in his prison cell awaiting a martyr's death, corrected Old Testament Bible texts according to the Septuagint text from the Hexapla. The Church, as is well known, did not take over the Septuagint text from Origen. The Septuagint text which became authoritative in the Church during the fourth century had nothing to do with the text of the Hexapla. It goes back to far older sources.

It is very probable that in the Sahidic version of the Minor Prophets we have evidence for the Septuagint text of Origen which was translated either within Origen's lifetime or at any rate very soon after his death, and which as early as the fourth century is supported by MS evidence (Jonah in Budge, *Biblical Texts*), evidence almost 400 years older than the Syro-Hexaplaric version translated by Paul of Tella in the years 616 to 617, which up to now has been accepted as the main source for the Septuagint of Origen.

15. Earlier Texts of the Greek Bible

The different forms of earlier texts of the Greek Bible are of great interest to us. Traces of them can be found mainly in four kinds of sources:

1. In the so-called 'recensions' of the Christian 'Septuagint', indicated by Jerome and recognized as of importance by Paul de Lagarde. The chief value of these 'recensions' is that they give us some material for the history of the Greek Bible in the various provinces of the Church and are of great help in classifying the MSS of the Greek Bible. Perhaps the most careful work of this kind, carried out according to the principles laid down by Lagarde, is the Greek Joshua edited by Max L. Margolis.[2] The material

[1] *Cults and Creeds in Graeco-Roman Egypt* (Forwood Lectures for 1952), Liverpool 1953, p. 101.

[2] *The Book of Joshua in Greek.* Parts 1–4 were published 1931–38 in Paris (Geuthner). Cf. Margolis' further articles: 'Specimen of a New Edition of the Greek Joshua' (*Jewish Studies in Memory of Israel Abrahams*, New York, 1927 (pp. 307–323)), 'Textual Criticism of the Greek Old Testament'. (*Proceedings, American Philosophical Society*, lxvii, 1928, pp. 187–197). 'Corrections in the Apparatus of the book of Joshua in the Larger Cambridge Septuagint' (*JBL* xlix, 1930, pp. 234–264). See H. H. Rowley, 'The Proto-Septuagint Question', *JQR* xxxiii, 1943, pp. 497–9.

carefully collected and lucidly arranged by him enables us to follow in great detail the different forms of the Greek Joshua in the Christian Church, in Egypt, Palestine, Syria, Asia Minor and Constantinople. Although most of the MSS contain 'mixed' texts—some of them are especially characterized as such by Margolis—they enable us to see in general the development of the standard text of the Church. In a text closely connected with Codex Vaticanus (B), he sees one of the best representatives of the Christian standard text. But this text was only *one* of those used by Jews and early Christians.

2. In quotations from the Greek Old Testament which are found in the New Testament and in other writings from the first two centuries B.C., in so far as they do not conform with the Christian standard text.

3. In older translations made from the Greek Bible. I refer here, as an example, to two Latin Bible quotations to which the Rev. Dr. A. C. Lawson of Shrewsbury drew my attention and which we discussed. They are to be found in the treatise *De Fide catholica contra Judaeos*,[1] written by Isidore, Bishop of Seville (died A.D. 636).

Isidore was a remarkable man. His father belonged to the Visigothic royal family; his mother was a daughter of the Emperor Theodoric (died A.D. 526). It is said that Isidore had been asked by his sister Florentina to supply her with arguments with which she could meet Jewish objections to the faith. He wrote for her the treatise mentioned above, in two books, the first giving the history of Christ according to the Old Testament, the second containing the prophecies in the Old Testament about the rejection of the Jews and the welfare of true believers under the New Covenant.[2] It is here that we find among many others the quotations in question. The first, Hos. vii, 16, is quoted twice (19, 2 and 47, 2 of the first book) in the form: *facti sunt mihi in sagittam reciprocam*. The second, in which A. Lukyn Williams correctly sees an expansion of Jer. iv, 3, is quoted (31, 1 of the first book) in the form: *spinis peccatorum suorum circumdedit populus hic*. The same quotation *spinis peccatorum suorum* is to be found in Isidore's *Quaestiones in Vetus Testamentum*, in *Genesis*[3] (xviii, 11) and also in Pope Silvester's *Discussion with the Jews at Rome*, and

[1] Migne. *Patrologia Latina*, vol. lxxxiii, cols. 449–538.

[2] A. Lukyn Williams, *Adversus Judaeos*, Cambridge 1935, pp. 216 f, and the summary on pp. 282–92.

[3] *Patrologia Latina*, vol. lxxxiii, col. 251.

is presupposed in the Syriac *Letter to the Blessed Sergius.*[1] Neither quotation agrees with the Hebrew text or with the Christian 'Septuagint'. They reflect a midrashic interpretation of the Hebrew text, and I think that we can find at least hints of them in Jewish sources.

In Hos. vii, 16 the 'treacherous bow' (קשת רמיה) is explained by Rashi with the words: 'If you shoot an arrow to the north it will go south'. *Sagitta reciproca* is not very far removed from this explanation.

In Jer. iv, 3 the Hebrew 'You must not sow amongst the thorns' is rendered in the Targum by 'You must not ask for forgiveness whilst you are in sins'. Rashi combines the two ideas by saying: 'You must not cry unto me whilst you are in sins, but when you are repenting, that you may not resemble those who sow a field without having weeded it, as otherwise your seed will turn into thorns.' This is certainly not the quotation of Isidore, yet here also sinners and thorns occur as in *spinis peccatorum.*

It is therefore very likely that these quotations are ultimately derived from a Jewish source. But the direct source for the Christian authors cannot have been a text written in Hebrew or Aramaic. Isidore, for instance, exhibits a certain naïve curiosity in Hebrew, but betrays no knowledge of Hebrew save what he derived from Jerome.[2] The same may be said of other Christian authors who quote such passages. The source must have been a Greek translation of Jewish origin, differing entirely from the Christian 'Septuagint', the readings of which were still used by Christian authors in the seventh century and perhaps later. Dr. Lawson writes with regard to such quotations:

> It seems clear that Old Testament quotations were used by Christians in a variety of ways from very early times. The number tends to increase. The same texts were used in East and West, in Greek and Latin. Isidore's texts occur partly in S. Cyprian's *Testimonia*, partly in Pseudo-Gregory of Nyssa, and in '*De promissionibus et predictionibus Dei*'. So far, in all instances where I have traced them, I have found that he has taken the texts from an author, from a commentary or treatise.... These texts are not always used in the same way....

It is necessary to collect and investigate all the traces of such

[1] MS Add 17 199 of the British Museum. See the references given by Lukyn Williams, loc. cit., p. 342, n. 2.

[2] See *The Legacy of Israel*, Oxford 1927, p. 287.

Greek translations of the Bible carefully. They were once used by Jews and Christians, and we may have to see in them remains of one of the anonymous versions included by Origen in the Hexapla, or of a version similar to them.[1]

4. In the remains of the Hexapla. This great work of Origen is mostly valued only in so far as it gives an indication of alterations in the text of the Greek Bible in accordance with the authoritative Hebrew text. The different versions collected here have, however, their own importance. We have seen that the version adapted to the authoritative text by Theodotion differed from the version which became, as 'Septuagint', the standard text of the Church. Some earlier material may be preserved also in new translations, such as Aquila and Symmachus. Translations of the Bible were hardly made without reference to already existing texts.

Of greater importance are, however, the anonymous versions which were discovered and registered by Origen. Here we have real Jewish texts, not influenced by the Christian standard text.

It was difficult to value this material rightly on the basis of the scattered remains of the Hexapla. The Milan palimpsest discovered by Giovanni Mercati has preserved nearly 150 complete verses of the Psalms in five columns: the Hebrew text written in Greek characters, Aquila, Symmachus, Septuagint, and Quinta. The edition of these valuable fragments, prepared by Cardinal Mercati, will make possible their careful examination. It is certain that a new era in the study of the Hexapla will begin with the publication of these texts.[2] But the whole problem of the Septuagint will be greatly affected. The task which the Septuagint presents to scholars is not the 'reconstruction' of an imaginary 'Urtext' nor the discovery of it, but a careful collection and investigation of all the remains and traces of earlier versions of the Greek Bible which differed from the Christian standard text.

[1] Lukyn Williams has seen the problem rightly. He writes with regard to the 'Selected Testimonia from the Old Testament against the Jews', attributed to Gregory of Nyssa (*Adversus Judaeos*, p. 124): 'To most readers perhaps its chief interest lies in the character of the Greek version of the Psalms and Prophets which he uses. For this often differs much from the Vaticanus text'; and he adds the annotation: 'I cannot find that it has been the subject of any special study in this respect. And until the Cambridge Larger Edition of the LXX has reached the Psalms and the Prophets (in several years' time), it is almost impossible for a non-specialist to make any profitable study of the various readings that the Selections exhibit.' It is clear that Rahlfs's edition of the Psalms is completely insufficient and of no value for an investigation of that kind. Ziegler's editions of *Isaias* (1939), *xii prophetae* (1943), *Ezekiel* (1952), *Daniel* (1954), *Jeremias* (1957) are quite different.

[2] Eduard Schwartz, *Zur Geschichte der Hexapla* (Göttinger Nachrichten 1903), p. 7.

THE PESHIṬTA

1. Its Relation to the Hebrew and Greek Bible

We have no information whatsoever about the origin of the Peshiṭta, the Syriac translation of the Old Testament, and even Theodore of Mopsuestia (died 428) did not know by whom or where it was made.[1] For the Pentateuch we have, besides the text represented by most of the MSS, some of which were written as early as the sixth century, another text of which Genesis and Exodus are to be found in the British Museum MS Add 14425, dated A.D. 464, the oldest dated Biblical MS so far known = D.[2] This text differs in many places from that of the other MSS and is here generally in agreement with the Hebrew text. In his *Pentateuchus Syriace* edited for the British and Foreign Bible Society London 1914, Professor W. E. Barnes published the text found in the majority of MSS and he thinks that this recension must be as ancient as that found in MS D, and that it may be a more reliable copy of the original Peshiṭta.[3]

John Pinkerton, one of Professor Barnes's collaborators, in a special study devoted to these two texts comes to somewhat different conclusions.[4] According to him the more literal type is to be found not only in MS D which is the best example of this text, and of which he gives various readings as specimens, but also in other MSS of other books of the Pentateuch; for example in the Florentine MS Laurent Or 58 (ninth century = F) and the British Museum MS Add 14427 (sixth century, containing Numbers, Deuteronomy and parts of Leviticus). Compared with this literal type of text, the other is marked by freedom in translation and by greater fullness and smoothness. These features Pinkerton attributes to the Christian Church's amplifying and improving the style of the original translation, in accordance with exegetical principles of the time and the genius of the language. From the

[1] The words are quoted for instance by Swete, *Introduction*, p. 112.

[2] Numbers and Deuteronomy in this MS are written by another hand and have a different type of text. Leviticus is not contained in the MS.

[3] Cf. his article: 'A New Edition of the Pentateuch in Syriac' in *JTS*, xv 1914, pp. 41–4.

[4] 'The Origin and Early History of the Syriac Pentateuch in Syriac' *JTS*, xv, 1914, pp. 14–41.

fact that Aphrahat, writing in 337 and 345, used a text which followed the Hebrew text more closely than did the text in common use in the sixth century, and that Ephraem (died 373) is more familiar with the text in D than with that of the later MSS, and that the agreements not only outnumber the disagreements but also outweigh them in value and importance, Pinkerton concludes that we have to see in D the *older* text of the Syriac Pentateuch, and that this text cannot be the result of a later revision according to the Hebrew text. A text like the archetype of D has to be regarded as the work of a Jewish translator, made for the use of a Jewish community. This Jewish translation was taken over by the Christian Church. Here it was gradually amplified and improved in style, and a certain form of this enlarged text, not the result of a systematic revision, was accepted as a standard text; henceforth all codices were made to conform more or less with this type. This must have happened about the fifth century; in the end the older text was ousted by the standard text.

At present it is not possible to control in detail the results of Pinkerton's researches. The principles of the British and Foreign Bible Society did not allow Professor Barnes to add a critical apparatus to his edition of the text. The new edition was for the use of the Syrians of Mardin and its surroundings and it has obviously served its purpose well.[1] An investigation of the text of Codex D has been undertaken by Professor Ignatius Ortiz de Urbina S.J., the Director of the Pontifical Oriental Institute, and he is now preparing a new edition of the Peshiṭta for the Spanish Polyglot. Until we know what his findings are we must restrict ourselves to the material which Pinkerton has published from Codex D and related codices of the Pentateuch. At present the conclusions drawn from this material seem to me convincing.

We must inquire whether these features exist only in the Pentateuch of the Peshiṭta or whether they are also to be found in other parts of the Syriac Bible. In the case of Ezekiel, C. H. Cornill[2] carefully compared the text with the Codex Ambrosianus, published in facsimile by Ceriani (=A); the Codex originates from the sixth century. He found that this MS agrees in very

[1] The latest attempt to publish the Peshiṭta Pentateuch (*Peshiṭta in Hebräischer Schrift, Mit erläuternden Anmerkungen* Von Ch(aijim) Heller, Teil i, Genesis, Berlin 1928; Teil ii, Exodus, Berlin 1929), cannot be taken seriously. The author is not aware of the real problems; like the other books published by Heller this one also tends to assume an apologetic character.

[2] *Das Buch des Propheten Ezekiel*, Leipzig 1886.

many places with the Hebrew text against all the other recensions of the Peshiṭta—of which, however, he only knew printed texts all depending on the same source. He also found that the Milan MS had been altered to a large extent in accordance with the Hebrew text and he concludes from this that the MS offers the worst of all accessible texts.

Rahlfs already saw[1] that these statements of Cornill cannot be correct. He believed the Milan MS to have in many places a text which, somewhat naïvely, he terms the *right* text. Professor W. E. Barnes, who consulted MSS in addition to the printed texts used by Cornill, sums up as follows:[2]

> After a careful examination of test passages in eight or ten MSS (some of the highest importance) I am led to the conclusion that Professor Cornill's judgment on Cod. A cannot be maintained. Cod. A in its agreement with the Masoretic text does *not* stand alone to the extent suggested by Cornill words. The reverse is often the case. . . . The agreement of the Codex Ambrosianus with the Masoretic is no doubt a fact, but the whole truth seems to be that a text formed from the best and oldest MSS would agree as frequently as Codex A with the Masoretic and would disagree as frequently with the printed text.

The most important MS for Barnes is here the Florentine Codex Laurent. Or 58, already mentioned by Pinkerton (=F). With regard to the text it offers, Barnes declares:[3]

> The text of Codex F is peculiar. While resembling that of Cod. A in many striking instances, it frequently departs from A (and from all other MSS which I have examined) in other instances equally striking to agree with the Masoretic text. . . . It seems quite probable that in Chronicles at least its text has been so freely conformed to the Masoretic, that its value to the text of the Peshiṭta is seriously lessened. Yet where A is silent through loss of text, F should surely be heard, for it seems sometimes to preserve the reading of the last mutual ancestor of A and F. . . .

And in his book on the Psalter[4] we find the following statements on the same Florentine MS

> In text this MS differs not seldom from all other known authorities. The exact coincidences with the Hebrew in places in

[1] 'Beiträge zur Textkritik der Peschiṭta', in *ZAW* ix, 1889, pp. 180–91.
[2] *An Apparatus Criticus to Chronicles in the Peshiṭta Version*, Cambridge, 1897, p. xxii.
[3] Ibid., p. xxxii.
[4] *The Peshiṭta Psalter according to the West Syrian Text*, Cambridge 1904, pp. xvii f.

which the rest of the MSS of the Peshiṭta diverge from the original are especially striking. . . . The relation of F to Nestorian authorities raises some important points. . . . In some cases however F has a double coincidence, i.e. with the Masoretic Hebrew on the one side and with the Nestorian authorities on the other; and it is possible that in such cases the reading of F is due to an assimilation which was intentional as regards the Hebrew, but accidental as regards the Nestorian text. . . . It is also possible on the other hand that the agreement of both F and the Nestorian text with the Hebrew points to a reading belonging to the earliest form of the Peshitta; I should be sorry to reject the suggestion on our present evidence, but I should be still more sorry to accept it at the present stage of Peshitta investigation.

Gustav Diettrich in his book *Ein Apparatus criticus zur Pešitto zum Propheten Jesaia*[1] has devoted a special study to a group of MSS to which belong the MSS A and F already mentioned, and the British MSS Add 14432 (sixth century). According to him these codices often have readings in agreement with the text of the Peshiṭta used by Ephraem in his Commentary on Isaiah. Many of these special readings in all three codices agree with the Hebrew text and it is just these that are often confirmed by the text used by Ephraem.

Here I may perhaps be allowed to quote the conclusions of S. R. Driver with regard to the Peshiṭta of the Books of Samuel:[2]

The Hebrew text presupposed by the Peshiṭta deviates less from the Masoretic text than that which underlies the LXX, though it does not approach it so closely as that on which the Targums are based. It is worth observing that passages not infrequently occur, in which Peshiṭta agrees with the text of *Lucian*, where both deviate from the Masoretic text. In the translation of the Book of Samuel the Jewish element alluded to above is not so strongly marked as in that of the Pentateuch; but it is nevertheless present, and may be traced in certain characteristic expressions, which would hardly be met with beyond the reach of Jewish influence. . . .

I think we can deduce from these quotations that the character of the Syriac text in other books of the Old Testament is not entirely different from that of the Syriac Pentateuch, and it

[1] Beihefte zur *ZAW*, viii, Giessen 1905, pp. xxvi–xxxii.
[2] *Notes on the Hebrew Text . . . of the Books of Samuel*, 2nd edition, Oxford 1913, p. lxxi.

is clear that we shall have to regard agreements with the Hebrew text in MSS in general as belonging to the oldest parts of the Peshiṭta. On the other hand, we shall have to regard instances of the influence of the Septuagint as due to Christian amendments of the Peshitta text. This influence differs in the various books of the Old Testament. Professor Barnes, in his article 'On the influence of the Septuagint on the Peshiṭta'[1] summarized his conclusions as follows:

> The influence of the Septuagint is for the most part sporadic, affecting the translation of a word here and of a word there. The Syriac translators must indeed have known that their own knowledge of Hebrew was far in advance of the knowledge possessed by the Septuagint, and yet the stress of Greek fashion had its way now and again. The Syriac transcribers on the contrary were ignorant of Hebrew and ready to introduce readings found in a Greek version or recommended by a Greek father. So the Peshiṭta in its later text has more of the Septuagint than in its earlier form. It is only in the Psalter (so it seems to me at the present stage of my work) that any general Greek influence bringing in a new characteristic is to be found. That characteristic is a dread of anthorpomorphisms from which the Syriac translators of the Pentateuch were free.

In spite of all the valuable work done by Ceriani, by Professor Barnes and his collaborators, by Diettrich and others, we must admit that a really critical edition of the Old Testament Peshiṭta does not yet exist. But I think we are now beginning to see the direction which further critical work on this version will have to take.[2]

That the Syriac translation of the Old Testament is of Jewish origin agrees with the conclusions to which other scholars have come. It may suffice to quote here what Professor Burkitt says about the version:[3]

> It is clear that the translators had a good knowledge of the general meaning of the text and an excellent acquaintance

[1] *JTS*, ii, 1901, pp. 186–97.

[2] At the Congress in Strasbourg of the International Organization of Old Testament Scholars (August 27–September 1, 1956) it was agreed that a critical *editio minor* of the Old Testament Peshitta should be prepared and published. Dr. W. D. McHardy, Professor of Old Testament Studies in the University of London was invited to act as Editor-in-Chief. Scholars in various countries are assisting in the collation of manuscripts. At present they are working mainly on the Minor Prophets. The basis of the edition will be Codex Ambrosianus.

[3] *Evangelion da Mepharreshe*, Cambridge 1904, vol. ii, p. 201.

with Jewish tradition. To such an extent is this the case that it seems impossible to avoid considering the Peshiṭta as the work of Jewish scholars.

It is generally assumed—even by Burkitt—that the translation was made by Jews for Christians, namely the Christian community in Edessa, since there is no evidence that Jews ever used this version. But Pinkerton thinks that this translation, above all of the Pentateuch—which is Pinkerton's main concern—was made for the *Jewish* community. The problem is, therefore, whether a Jewish community can be identified which required a Pentateuch translated into Syriac. It must have been a community in a Syriac-speaking country which had close connections with Jerusalem. Joseph Marquart pointed out, as long ago as 1903, that the country could only have been Adiabene (חדיב), a kingdom situated between the two rivers Zab, to the east of the river Tigris, which formed a part of the great Parthian Empire.[1]

2. The Jews in Adiabene

In the twentieth book of Josephus' *Antiquities* we read that Izates II,[2] king of Adiabene, son of Monobazos I and his sister Helena, had been won over to the Jewish religion while he was still in Spasinu Charax,[3] which was ruled by King Abennerig[4] to whom Izates had been sent for safety. The king had given him in marriage his daughter Symmacho.[5] A Jewish merchant named Ananias (=Ḥananya) had been admitted to the king's harem and had interested not only some of the ladies in the Jewish religion but Izates as well. When the latter was recalled by his father,[6] Ananias accompanied him. On his return home, Izates found that Queen Helena, his mother, had also been converted to the Jewish

[1] J. Marquart, *Osteuropäische und ostasiatische Streifzüge*, Leipzig 1903, pp. 288.

[2] In the name Izates (*ized*, 'the venerable', a technical term in the religion of Zoroaster) Marquart sees a special omen, but this is hardly justified, as the father of Monobazos and Helena was also called Izates.

[3] At the mouth of the river Tigris, near the present Baṣra; it may be identical with the kingdom of Mesene; cf. Rostovtzeff, in *Cambridge Ancient History*, vol. xi, 1936, p. 113.

[4] Abd Nerig, 'servant of Nergal' (Mars), cf. Marquart, *Streifzüge* p. 289, n. 2. On coins he is called Adinerglus or Abinerglus; cf. N. C. Debevoise, *A Political History of Parthia*, Chicago 1938, p. 165, n. 72. Here the original *l* in the name is still preserved.

[5] Summacho—Syriac ܣܘܡܟܐ 'recreation'. In Niese's edition xx, 23, it is wrongly printed.

[6] His father made him Governor of Corduene, bordering on Adiabene's northern frontiers. For καρρων in Josephus one has to read καρδου, cf. Marquart, loc. cit. n. 4.

religion by another Jew and that she observed the Jewish rites. After the death of his father Monobazos, Helena arranged[1] that Izates succeeded to the throne. He postponed his official conversion to Judaism on the special advice of Ananias and his mother who feared the opposition of the aristocracy of the land, the majority of whom adhered to the Zoroastrian religion. But under the influence of a Jewish zealot named Eleazar who had come from Galilee to Arbela, the capital of Adiabene, the official conversion took place about the year 40. When Queen Helena saw that it had no serious consequences she made a pilgrimage to Jerusalem where she remained for many (14?) years. We are told that Izates sent five of his sons to Jerusalem for their education. Queen Helena and several other members of the royal family owned palaces in Jerusalem and we hear of valuable presents given by Helena and her son Monobazos II to the temple there.[2] After Izates' death, his elder brother Monobazos, who succeeded him as King of Adiabene about A.D. 58, sent his remains and those of his mother, who had died shortly after Izates, to Jerusalem to be buried in the 'tomb of the Kings', called 'Pyramids' by Josephus, a mausoleum erected by Helena herself for that purpose; it can still be seen.[3] Monobazos II was also converted to the Jewish faith and many of his relations and of his entourage followed his example.[4]

Josephus intended to give further particulars of Monobazos II and the benefits Jerusalem had received from these Jewish kings of Adiabene,[5] but he failed to carry out his plan. We only hear by chance[6] that two members of the royal family of Adiabene, Monobazos and Kennedaios, fought on the side of the Jews in the war against the Romans. No more is heard of the Jewish kings of

[1] Josephus' report about Helena's arrangements is interesting, cf. Rostovtzeff, loc. cit. p. 114. This happened in A.D. 36, see Debevoise, loc. cit.

[2] The palaces are mentioned in, for instance, *Bellum*, v, 6, 1 (252, 253) and vi, 6, 3 (355). The gifts to the Temple are mentioned in the Mishna, Yoma 3, 10.

[3] Ed. Pococke senior (died 1691) correctly identified these tombs with the burial-place of the royal family of Adiabene.

[4] According to Josephus opposition flared up amongst the leading people of the kingdom against the Judaism of the king, and the conflict between Izates and the king of the Parthians, Vologases, was partly due to similar reasons. Marquart (loc. cit. p. 292) thinks this may be correct especially as Vologases is known to have been a zealous Zoroastrian, interested in the maintenance of the Avestic literature, the 'Avesta and Zend'. But the passage in the Denkart, referred to by Marquart, does not necessarily mean that there was a written Zend (a commentary). Besides, Professor Henning informs me that it is not clear whether Vologases I or Vologases II (148–191) is meant. Rostovtzeff doubts whether these suggested reasons for the conflict can be accepted as historical facts (loc. cit. p. 112).

[5] *Antiquities*, ed. Niese xx, 53, p. 96.

[6] *Bellum* ii, p. 520.

Adiabene. The sources at our disposal are of Roman origin and they show no interest in such matters. The last king of whom we hear, Mebarsapes, was one of the chief opponents of Trajan in his Eastern campaign of 116. He was defeated and Adiabene became part of the Roman province of Assyria. We do not know whether the dynasty was later restored by Hadrian. Members of the dynasty seem to have played a certain role in Edessa at the end of the first and the beginning of the second century. But the Jewish interests of the dynasty had disappeared after A.D. 70.

What we know of the Jews and their influence in Adiabene in the middle of the first century B.C. is sufficient to suggest that the Jewish community there, particularly the members of the royal family and the other new converts many of whom belonged to the most prominent families in the land, needed a Bible written in a language they were able to understand. The language spoken in Adiabene was an Aramaic dialect, called 'Syriac'. We can take it for granted that at least parts of a Syriac Old Testament, and in the first instance the Torah were introduced into Adiabene during the time of its Jewish kings, i.e. in the middle of the first century B.C.

3. Peshiṭta and the Palestinian Targum

That the Syriac translation of certain books of the Old Testament, especially that of the Pentateuch, is not much else than a Jewish Targum has been recognized since 1859, when J. Perles wrote his *Meletemata Peschittoniana*. But it was difficult to show the exact connections. The only Targum of the Pentateuch then known was the Targum Onḳelos and this Targum is of much later origin; and besides, it has a special halachic character of which we find nothing in the Syriac Pentateuch. But to-day there can be no doubt that the closest relationship existed between the Syriac Pentateuch and the old Palestinian Targum, of which we found the first specimens in the Old Cairo Geniza. We have seen that this Targum existed already in pre-Christian times. So the Jews of Jerusalem had already an Aramaic translation of the Pentateuch when the newly converted Jews of Adiabene were in need of an Aramaic Bible. This Targum was composed in the Aramaic dialect spoken in Palestine. The Jews of Adiabene must have been able to understand it. Josephus sent his first edition of the *Jewish Wars*, composed in the language of his own country, i.e. Aramaic, to the 'Upper Barbarians' (τοῖς ἄνῳ βαρβάροις) and describes them as the 'Parthians, Babylonians, the remotest Arabians and those of our nation beyond the Euphrates, with the Adiabenes.'[1] This history of the Jewish Wars was primarily intended for the real Jews in those countries where Aramaic, as spoken in Palestine, was understood. But we must assume that Biblical texts intended for the newly converted Jews had to be translated into the Aramaic dialect as spoken in Adiabene and to be transcribed into the Syriac alphabet used there. Some of the Jews who had come from Palestine and had been in Adiabene for years would have no difficulty in fulfilling this task.

But we are faced with other problems. We know that most fragments of the Palestinian Targum of the Pentateuch contain special haggadic explanations for some of the verses which are not to be found in the Syriac Bible. At the same time we must remember that this Targum had no fixed text and that no one can tell whether or not MSS of this Targum without these haggadic elements existed in ancient times. In any case the oldest specimen of this Targum preserved in the Cambridge MS T-S, 20,155,=MS A, containing parts of Exodus xxi and xxii, offers no haggadic explanations. Yet the Syriac Pentateuch known to us follows, in the translation of Exod. xxii, 4 and 5, the usual Jewish interpretation and not the one in the Cambridge fragments mentioned above. We must therefore suppose that this fragment represents an older type of the Targum than the one which may have been sent to Adiabene. In any case we have to compare carefully the fragments of the Palestinian Targum with the Syriac Pentateuch, particularly with its older text referred to by Pinkerton which is closely connected with the Hebrew text. We have always to remember that the Palestinian Targum existed in many different forms and we cannot expect that the fragments of the Targum found in the Geniza, written probably in the period between the sixth and the ninth centuries, contain the exact text which may have been sent to Adiabene during the first century A.D. On the other hand it is evident that the Syrian Pentateuch, especially the older type of it, has to be regarded as a valuable source for our knowledge of the old Palestinian Targum of which we have otherwise only small fragments.

[1] *Bellum*, Prooemium, 1, 2; cf. H. St. John Thackeray, *Josephus. The Man and the Historian*, New York 1929, p. 24.

4. The Chronicle of Arbela

The conversion of the royal family in Adiabene no doubt greatly strengthened the missionary power of the Jewish religion in the Parthian Empire, and the Jewish mission amongst the pagan population must have helped to pave the way for the Christian mission. Joseph Marquart has suggested that the Christian mission did not start among the pagan population of Edessa, the later centre of Christianity in the East, but amongst the Jewish population in Adiabene.[1] This suggestion has been proved to be correct by the Chronicle of Arbela composed in the sixth century in Syriac by Meshīḥā Zkhā. This chronicle was discovered by A. Mingana and published by him in 1907 in Syriac with a French translation.[2] Eduard Sachau carefully investigated the text and in 1915 published a German translation with a valuable introduction.[3] The value of the chronicle can hardly be over-estimated. Based on local traditions and reliable sources it describes the history of Christianity in Adiabene and other countries in the East from the beginning up to the sixth century, and in spite of some gaps in the chronology it can generally be regarded as trustworthy even when dealing with the oldest times. Adolf Harnack seems to be right when he maintains that we have here a very valuable document for the history of the Christian mission during the second and third centuries which can be rivalled by no other document from the provinces of the Roman Empire.[4]

[1] *Osteuropäische und Ostasiatische Streifzüge*, pp. 298 f.

[2] *Sources Syriaques*, vol. i, Mshiha Zkha (Texte et Traduction) . . . par A. Mingana, Mossoul, Leipzig 1907.

[3] *Die Chronik von Arbela. Ein Beitrag zur Kenntnis des ältesten Christentums im Orient* (Abhandlungen der Berliner Akademie, 1915). For further Literature see Baumstark, *Geschichte der Syrischen Literatur,* p. 134, f. A Latin translation published by Fr. Zorell, *Chronica Ecclesiae Arbelensis* . . . (*Orientalia Christiana*, viii, Rome 1927). Cf. further G. Messina, *La Cronaca di Arbela* (*Civiltà Cattolica*, lxxxiii, 1932). P. Peeters, the Bollandist, first and foremost has raised doubts as to the chronicle, by pointing to inconsistencies between the chronicle and the true martyrologies of Adiabene and to the fact that the Nestorian literature does not refer to the chronicle ('Le Passionaire d'Adiabene', in *Analecta Bollandiana*, vol. xliii, Bruxelles 1925, pp. 261–304). It seems to me that the Rev. P. Peeters goes too far here with his criticism. The inconsistencies alluded to by him are not so conclusive and the fact that the Nestorian literature does not mention the chronicle does not prove much. Furthermore the legends about Addai are to be explained otherwise than Fr. Peeters thinks. But it is clear nevertheless that a renewed investigation is necessary regarding the codex found by Mingana, incomplete as it is at its beginning and end. What Mingana says in his introduction to the edition is very inadequate. Father Ignatius Ortiz de Urbina S.J. in his Bonn thesis *Die Gottheit Christi bei Afrahat* (Pont. Institutum Orientalium Studiorum, Roma 128. 1933, pp. 28 f,) was quite right in mentioning this.

[4] A. v. Harnack, *Die Mission und Ausbreitung des Christentums*. . . . 4th edition, 1924, p. 684.

We find here the apostle Addai as a very active missionary in the mountain villages of Adiabene. A certain Pḳīdhā is baptized by him and, after having been his disciple for five years, is sent by Addai to Arbela, the capital where, for the next ten years, he worked as the first Bishop of the Christians. We hear all sorts of details about him and his successors who at first had names from the Old Testament (Samson, Isaac, Abraham, Noah, Abel) whereas in later times Christian names prevail. The first leaders of the Christian Church in Arbela seem to have been either converted Jews or Christians of the Jewish population of Arbela. In one passage the chronicle informs us that the parents of the later Bishop Noah, coming from Jerusalem, settled in Arbela 'because many Jews were there'.[1] We must remember that in the sixth century when the chronicle was composed there were no dealings between Jews and Christians. A synchronism which enables us to date the beginnings of Addai's mission in Adiabene some years before A.D. 100 is of special importance. We know that Addai was also active in other places. He is mentioned, together with Mari, as the first missionary in Karka, the present Kirkuk,[2] and several other places claim to have institutions dating back to the time of this apostle.[3] Of special interest is the report in the chronicle that in A.D. 224, when in Persia the rule of the Sassanid kings began, more than twenty bishoprics were established in the lands adjacent to the Tigris, of which seventeen are described in detail in the chronicle.[4]

But Christianity must at that time have spread far beyond the frontiers of Mesopotamia. From the newly-discovered Manichaean texts we learn that Mani went to India about A.D. 240 before he began his mission in A.D. 241 in his home country.[5] There can hardly be any doubt that he followed the tracks of St. Thomas, the apostle of the Indians, and that he knew beforehand something of the legendary history of that saint, as reported in the Acts of Thomas. That the whole framework of these tales belongs to the countries washed by the Euphrates and the Tigris, and that the famous 'Hymn of the Soul' must have been written

[1] Sachau loc. cit., p. 50.

[2] Georg Hoffmann, *Auszüge aus Syrischen Akten persischer Märtyrer* (*AKM*, vii, 3, Leipzig 1880, p. 45).

[3] Hoffmann, loc. cit., pp. 180, 371.

[4] Harnack, *Mission*. . . . pp. 689 f. Sachau, loc. cit. pp. 17 ff; Sachau, 'Zur Ausbreitung des Christentums in Asien' (*Abhandlungen der Berliner Akademie*, 1919) gives important details for the later period.

[5] H. H. Schaeder, 'Ein Mani-Fund aus Ägypten', in *Gnomon* ix, 1933, pp. 348, 350f.

before the year A.D. 224,[1] when the Parthian Empire was destroyed, is as well known as the fact that these Acts were originally written in Syriac. This was the language of Mani and it later became very popular amongst the Manichaeans.[2] Mani must have expected to find Christians in India and he was not disappointed. We are told that he 'made a good selection', which is as much as saying that he founded a community there.[3]

5. The Beginnings of Christianity in Edessa

Under these circumstances it is very improbable that Burkitt is right when he maintains that Christianity east of the Roman Empire started in Edessa about A.D. 160–170.[4] What do we know about these beginnings? Adolf von Harnack makes the following statement in this connection:[5]

> Das Christentum in Edessa, sofern es noch von dem katholischen verschieden war, knüpft (für uns) an drei Personen an, an den 'apostolischen' Missionar Addai, um das Jahr 100, der aber einstweilen noch im Dunkeln steht; an Tatian, den 'Assyrer', und an Bardesanes (geb. 154).

Harnack here dates Addai in accordance with the Chronicle of Arbela, but he admits that in reality nothing is known of his activity in Edessa. Burkitt rejects the evidence of the Chronicle of Arbela. According to him Addai was a contemporary of Tatian. But he has little to say about the activity of either. Since in the legend Addai is connected with the introduction of the Diatessaron into Edessa, of which on the other hand we know that Tatian is the author, Burkitt, in his last attempt to write the history of Eastern Christianity[6], tried to prove that both men were the same, and that the man who in the West was called Tatian may have been called Addai in the East. This shows how uncertain the whole matter is and we must ask: Are we really entitled to connect the beginnings of Christianity in Edessa with the names of these two men? It is certainly remarkable that

[1] F. C. Burkitt, *Early Eastern Christianity*, 1908, pp. 205, 216.
[2] W. Bousset, 'Manichäisches in den Thomasakten' *ZNW*, xviii, 1918, pp. 1–39.
[3] H. H. Schaeder, loc. cit. p. 348.
[4] Burkitt, *Cambridge Ancient History*, xii, 1939, p. 492.
[5] *Mission und Ausbreitung*. . . . p. 680. Cf. Rubens Duval, *Histoire politique, religieuse et littéraire d'Édesse jusqu'à la première croisade*, Paris 1892, chapters 5 and 7.
[6] 'Syriac speaking Christianity', in *Cambridge Ancient History* xii, p. 493. This identification had already been suggested by Burkitt in his article 'Tatian's Diatessaron and the Dutch Harmonies' in *JTS* xxv, 1924, pp. 113–30, particularly pp. 129 f.

in the most reliable source for the history of Christianity there, the Edessene Chronicle,[1] only the last of the three men referred to by Harnack—Bardesanes—is mentioned. How can we account for the names of the other two being omitted if they had been of any interest for the town?

There can be no doubt that Bardaisan was of importance for Edessa. I would recall here the fine characterization of him by Burkitt in the fifth of his St. Margaret's Lectures on the Syriac-speaking Church.[2] After giving a very attractive survey of Bardaisan's dialogue *On Fate*, the only book of his which is preserved, Burkitt outlines his impression of the man and his work as follows:

> It is difficult to realize how an ancient work of this kind appeals to other people; but to myself, coming from the study of ordinary Syriac ecclesiastical literature, the first impression made is of the independence of the writer's mind. It gives me the impression of being the thoughts of one who had learned to think for himself, one who had read much and thought much, and who was not content at the end merely to repeat the formulas of a school. Bardaisan brings out of the storehouse of his learning things new and old, and his imagination has woven them into a new and independent pattern. Such work is of a different order from that of men whose whole achievement is to reproduce as much of the philosophy of someone else—of Aristotle or of Proclus—as they have been able to understand.

Burkitt shows how great a tragedy it was that the Syriac-speaking Church was not able to attract or even tolerate the best scientific intellect of the time. In his 'Introductory Essay' to the important material deciphered by C. W. Mitchell from a palimpsest in the British Museum, published after the author's death by his teachers, Professor Burkitt and Professor A. A. Bevan, in 1921,[3] Burkitt

[1] This chronicle is preserved on excellent ancient parchment in the Vatican Library, in Stephan Euod. Assemani Bibliothecae apost.—vatic. Codic. manuscript. Catal. pars I tom. III p. 329, No. CLXIII: Codex in fol membraneus pervetustus folios 6 constans. Joseph Simon Assemani has published it in his Bibliotheca Orientalis Clementino-Vaticana with a Latin translation (vol. i, pp. 387–417). A new edition with a German translation and a careful investigation has been made by Ludwig Hallier, 'Untersuchungen über die Edessenische Chronik' (*Texte und Untersuchungen* ix, I) Leipzig 1892. Hallier thinks that the chronicle was composed in Antioch, and that it cannot be the work of an Edessenian historian or chronicler,—'that is confirmed also by the fact that the Chronicle has not the specific Edessenian reports' (p. 41). But Hallier is here entirely wrong. We shall see that the chronicle is reliable for historical facts, but that it does not contain Edessene legends.

[2] 'Bardaisan and his Disciples' in *Early Eastern Christianity*, London 1904, pp. 155–92. Cf. especially pp. 186 f.

[3] *St. Ephraim's Prose Refutations of Mani, Marcion, and Bardaisan* transcribed from the Palimpsest Brit. Mus. Add. 14623, by the late C. W. Mitchell and completed by A. A. Bevan and F. C. Burkitt, vol. ii, London 1921, pp. cxxii–cxxxi.

devoted a special paragraph to the 'System of Bardaisan'. Under the influence of Ephraem's polemic Burkitt is much more reserved in his opinion. He doubts whether Bardaisan had a first-hand knowledge of Greek philosophy and whether he really composed the Hymns attributed to him.

In an instructive article published in 1932[1] H. H. Schaeder made new contributions to a real understanding of the man; he was able to use, besides the material made known by Mitchell, a new translation of Ephraem's 'Hymns' (Madrashe) against the heretics, made by Professor A. Rücker on the basis of Syriac texts largely improved from MSS. Schaeder characterized Ephraem's method of dealing with Bardaisan in the following way:

> The valuation of these passages is made difficult by Ephraem's peculiarities of intellect and authorship. He is neither inclined to deal with the ideas of the opponent he attacks, nor is he able to do so. It is sufficient for him to pick out single disconnected expressions of his opponents and to handle them with an extravagant array of words and of moral pathos. We can clearly see from Ephraem what a condition the Church had reached in his time, when it could not bear a spirit like Bardaisan. What in Bardaisan is intellectual clarity and power of comprehending truth, is to him confinement in a gross and primitive theology which does not illumine truth for him, but conceals it. As Bardaisan and his followers had influenced Christian people by their poetry, Ephraem felt compelled to oppose them in poetry. The poetic form in which he clothes his polemics makes them quite unbearable. . . .

In a quotation from Bardaisan preserved by Theodor bar Konai (end of the eighth century), Schaeder recognized a fragment from an original cosmological hymn of Bardaisan.[2] There can hardly be any doubt that Bardaisan was a poet and that he was the author of the hymn-book ascribed to him. This poetry made him popular amongst the Syriac-speaking Christians. But the specific prosody used by him—and later adopted by Mani—was different from that used by Ephraem. Ephraem's verse with a fixed number of syllables is clearly influenced by the metre of the Greeks, and this kind of metre may have been introduced into Syriac poetry by Bardaisan's son Harmonios who had studied in

[1] 'Bardesanes von Edessa in der Überlieferung der griechischen und syrischen Kirche', in *Zeitschrift für Kirchengeschichte*, ii, 1932, pp. 21–74.

[2] loc. cit. pp. 46 ff.

Athens. It was accepted by Ephraem and followed by all the later Syriac poets. Schaeder made every effort to examine impartially all the sources, Greek and Syriac, which mention Bardaisan. He ends his article with the following remarks:[1]

> By examining and comparing information preserved more or less at random, in a more or less fragmentary condition, we have had to try to find outlines of the intellectual constitution of the man. As we have seen, already in the fourth century the positive conception of it had disappeared in the Syrian Church as well as in the Greek. In both East and West everything had been done to obscure his memory and to consign him to oblivion; and Mani, who came after him, was not so much his heir as the destroyer of his thoughts. In Bardaisan's mind Greek civilization and philosophy are still in vigorous and productive tension with the Christian interpretation of life and moral energy. This tension was lost in the dualism and asceticism of the Manicheans. Bardaisan, in his spiritual freedom and his originality, was in a hopeless position in Edessa during the early years of the Eastern Church. In the Greek-speaking Church, more fortunate men took up the work he had begun and continued it. The problem of life, of Christian humanity, to which he devoted himself, is as actual and as urgent to-day as it was in his time.

I think there can be no doubt that it was chiefly due to Bardaisan that Edessa became the centre of Eastern Christianity. He was the famous Syriac classic. He was the gifted poet. It cannot have been easy to break the influence of this man whose real importance we only now begin to understand. We know very little of the details of the struggle. We only see what pains a man like Ephraem had to take in order to refute him—and other heretics like Marcion and Mani, who must both have been of a certain importance for Edessa, since both are mentioned in the Edessene Chronicle.[2] We also see Ephraem eager to compose hymns in order to supplant Bardaisan's very popular hymns. But eventually it was not Ephraem who made an end of Bardaisan's 'heresy' but Bishop Rabbula of Edessa (died A.D. 435). In the *Vita Rabbulae*,[3] composed

[1] loc. cit. p. 56 f. Schaeder quotes Sozomen's *Church History*, iii, 16, where the fate of Syriac poetry and the differences between the poetry of Bardaisan and that of Ephraem are clearly described.

[2] Cf. paragraphs 6 and 10 of the *Chronicle*.

[3] *S. Ephraemi Syri, Rabbulae Episcopi Edesseni, Balaei aliorumque Opera Selecta*, ed. J. Josephus Overbeck, Oxonii 1865, p. 192.

shortly after the bishop's death, we find the following striking report about the end of the struggle:

> The evil teachings of Bardaisan flourished in Edessa until they were condemned and conquered by him (Rabbula). Before that time this accursed Bardaisan had drawn all the leading men of the town to himself by his cunning and the sweetness of his hymns, in order to protect himself by them as with strong walls. The fool had hoped that by erring and leading those who were with him to err, he could firmly establish his errors with the weak assistance of his helpers. This saddened him, (Rabbula), the man wise in the fields of the heart. Not only did he exert himself to root up from that field the choking weeds and to leave behind the many blades of corn—that would have been easy—but in his wisdom he also exerted himself to turn the weeds into corn—this too was necessary. So instead of the frightful blast from the trumpets of Joshua and his followers who trumpeted at the walls of Jericho till they fell, and instead of the annihilation of men and the seizing of their property for the Lord, this victorious general of Jesus the Messiah, in the power of his God and with conciliatory and gentle voice, was able quietly to destroy their church, to carry away all its treasure and to bring it to his own, so that he made use of its very stones.

6. The Doctrine of Addai

We may doubt whether all these endeavours would have succeeded, had not another attempt been made to destroy these heresies and to restore the fame of the Edessene Church which had been somewhat impaired by Bardaisan and the other heretics. The weapon used was a reconstruction of the history of this Church based on the legendary story of its foundation by a direct disciple of Christ Himself, said to have been sent there in fulfilment of the promise given by Christ in a correspondence with the Edessene King Abgar the fifth, Ukkāmā (died about A.D. 50).

The legend was already known to Eusebius in the beginning of the fourth century. He accepted it in his *Church History* as taken from the Syriac original deposited in the archives of Edessa.[1] The apostle sent to Edessa is here Thaddaios, one of the Twelve. In the *Syriac Doctrine of Addai*[2] he is replaced by Addai, supposed to have been a member of the larger group of Christ's disciples.

[1] Eusebius' *Ecclesiastical History*, i, 13.
[2] *The Doctrine of Addai, the Apostle.* . . . ed. by George Philipps, London 1876.

He is said to have been sent there by Thomas, the apostle of the East, whose relics were ceremonially transferred to Edessa and deposited there in a silver shrine in A.D. 232.[1] In the Syriac text the story is given with many more details and connected with other legends. It is astonishing how many persons are mentioned by name. The author is anxious to show how well he was acquainted with conditions at the royal court of Edessa at the time. Most of the men mentioned in the legend are known from other sources to have lived at that time; although they did not belong to the court of King Abgar of Edessa, but to the court of the Parthian kings of the time, Artabanes III (about 12–38), Gotarses II (about 38–50) and Vardanes (about 39–47). This was proved by Joseph Marquart[2] and he drew the conclusion that the legend must have been composed in a land ruled by these Parthian kings and that this land was Adiabene.

It seems that when the land had become to a large extent a Christian country, the historical fact of King Izates' conversion to Judaism of which we have heard was transformed into a Christian legend. We still have traces of this Christian legend of Adiabene. King Izates appears in it under the name of Narsai. In the Edessene *Doctrine of Addai* he is called *Narsai, malkā d'Athōrāyē*, Narsai the king of the Assyrians.[3] More about this legend can be found in the Armenian story as reported by Mose of Khorene.[4]

In Edessa, King Izates-Narsai was replaced by his contemporary King Abgar. Ḥanan, the keeper of the archives (*ṭabōlārā*)[5] said to have been sent to Palestine by the king and to have played a prominent role in the conversion of King Abgar, has his prototype in Ananias (=Ḥananya, Ḥanan), the Jewish merchant who was responsible for King Izates' conversion to Judaism. Queen Helena of Adiabene, Izates' mother, is made the wife of King Abgar of Edessa in the Armenian text of the story.[6] The life of Addai, the missionary of Adiabene and the lands adjacent to the Tigris, for whom we now have a definite date in the Chro-

[1] L. J. Tixeront, *Les Origines de l'Église d'Édesse et la légende d'Abgar. Étude critique*, Paris 1888, p. 155.

[2] *Ostasiatische und Osteuropäische Streifzüge. . . .* Leipzig 1903, pp. 296, f. The years of the Parthian kings are given according to Debevoise, *A Political History of Parthia*, Chicago 1938, p. 270.

[3] Cf. *Doctrine of Addai*, ed. Phillips, p. 37 of the Syriac text, p. 35 of the translation.

[4] Cf. Tixeront, loc. cit. p. 71; R. A. Lipsius, *Die Edessenische Abgarsage*, 1880, p. 39.

[5] This word was read by Eusebius as *tabellārā* and connected with Latin *tabellarius*, and this he translates: ταχύδρομος

[6] Lipsius, loc. cit. pp. 86 f.

nicle of Arbela, had to be antedated by more than sixty years in order to become a disciple of Christ and missionary of Edessa in King Abgar Ukkāmā's time, and he had to be post-dated for more than sixty years in other parts of the legend in order to become the teacher of Bishop Palut in the second half of the second century. In this way he was connected twice with Edessa, which he probably never visited!

It is generally assumed that the reason for importing the legend into Edessa and developing it there was the conversion to the Christian faith of King Abgar IX (ruled A.D. 179–214), with whom Bardaisan is said to have had special connections. But the only *Christian* king of whom we really know is the king of the legend, the contemporary of Christ. In the Edessene Chronicle King Abgar IX is mentioned several times in the well-known report of the great inundation of Edessa in A.D. 201, and other details about him are reported in §9, concerning the year 205–6. But not the slightest allusion is made to the conversion of this king and it is very likely that this 'conversion' should be regarded as a modern legend without historical foundation.[1]

Under such circumstances we must hold that the legend connected with the name of Addai is of no historical value for the beginnings of Christianity in Edessa. As it was adapted in Edessa to the needs of that town, it certainly reflects some of the conditions there at a later time. It was imported into Edessa in order to be used for an idealistic reconstruction of the past. It gives the official history of a correct development of Christianity in Edessa as it should have been according to a later point of view.

Burkitt tries to reconstruct the history of Christianity in Edessa with the help of the legend. Addai, in one part of the legend said to have been a contemporary of Christ, was according to other parts of the legend the teacher of Palut, who is said to have been consecrated as a bishop about A.D. 180 by Serapion. Serapion was Bishop of Antioch from A.D. 182 or 192 to 209 and he is supposed to have been in touch with Zephyrinus who was Bishop of Rome from A.D. 202–218.[2] Through these connections Palut becomes the 'catholic' bishop *par excellence* of the Edessene Church and is the central figure of Burkitt's hypothetical reconstruction.

[1] On this question cf. Marquart, loc. cit. p. 300, n. 3, and H. Gomperz's article 'Hat es jemals in Edessa christliche Könige gegeben?' *Archäol. Epigraph. Mitteilungen aus Österreich-Ungarn*, xix, Wien 1896, pp. 154–57.

[2] These dates do not at all agree with each other. They are given as taken from Burkitt.

On the other hand, Michael the Syrian reports in his chronicle that Bardaisan was converted to the Christian faith by an Edessene Bishop Hystasp who was preceded by Bishop Izani and followed by Bishop Aqai, and Michael puts Palut, of whom he knew from the *Doctrine of Addai*, in the times of the apostles. Michael's list can hardly be brought to agree with Burkitt's reconstruction. 'I think we shall do best to reject Michael's order altogether.' Burkitt writes.[1] He may be right, but it may also be that we have here some remnants of the *real* history which were removed in the idealistic reconstruction. We can only state two facts with certainty:

1. If Bardaisan (born A.D. 154) was converted in Edessa to the Christian faith, a Christian community must have existed there in the second half of the second century.

2. According to the Edessene Chronicle, the sanctuary of the Christian Church was destroyed in the great inundation of 201. This is the earliest reference to a church *building* in Edessa as distinct from worship in private houses. As the 'catholic' bishop, Palut, who must have been bishop of the town at that time, is not mentioned, he cannot have played the important role attributed to him by Burkitt. On the other hand we fully understand why Addai is not mentioned in the Edessene Chronicle.

7. Tatian and the Diatessaron

Tatian, the second man connected by scholars such as Harnack and Burkitt with the beginnings of Christianity in Edessa, calls himself an 'Assyrian', which means that he came from Assyria, the country which, according to the well-known geographer Claudius Ptolemaeus, Tatian's contemporary, lay between the Tigris and Media, from the Armenian mountains as far as Ctesiphon.[2] It has already been noted above that Adiabene, situated to the east of the Tigris, became a part of the Roman province of Assyria[3] after the war of Trajan (A.D. 116). Theodor Zahn may be correct in supposing that Adiabene was Tatian's home country,[4] but we know nothing definite about it. Tatian calls himself a 'barbarian', that is to say he was not Greek. His mother tongue

[1] Burkitt, *Early Eastern Christianity*, p. 32; in the German edition *Urchristentum im Orient*, p. 20. Chronique de Michel le Syrien . . . par Chabot, i, Paris 1899, pp. 184 f.

[2] Theodor Zahn, 'Tatian's Diatessaron', *Forschungen*. . . . Erlangen 1881, vol. i, p. 269.

[3] See above p. 272.

[4] Zahn loc. cit. pp. 270, 273.

was Syriac, the language spoken in Assyria. He was very gifted and a man of importance. He renounced his chance of being given a high position at home and, eager to learn, went abroad to the West. His *Oratio ad Graecos*, the only work preserved for us, shows that he wrote excellent Greek and that he was very well acquainted with Greek philosophy and learning. But he was no admirer of the Greeks. The whole *Oratio* shows that he was proud of being a 'barbarian'.[1]

While in Rome he came in contact with Justin Martyr through whose influence he became a Christian. He must have remained in Rome a few years after his master's death (about 165). We hear of several of his pupils during these years—Rhodon from Asia Minor, Narcissus from Jerusalem and perhaps Clement of Alexandria. His differences with the Church are mentioned by Irenaeus. Epiphanius tells us that he returned to the East. It may be that he left Rome about the year 172. We have no information about the rest of his life. That he went to Edessa is nowhere reported and is only conjectured by modern scholars because they believe that Edessa is the place where Christianity in the East began. He is not mentioned in the Edessene Chronicle[2] nor do we hear that he ever came into contact with Bardaisan, who was born at Edessa in 154. It is much more likely that he returned to his home in Assyria and settled there.

We have seen that a Christian Mission had been launched in Assyria before the end of the first century. It is possible that Tatian knew something about Christianity before he started out for the West. In Rome he learned to regard this religion in a different spirit and became a Christian. If he then returned to Assyria, he must have found there a number of Christian communities. The bishoprics, numbering twenty and more, which existed about 224 in the countries along the Tigris,[3] needed a certain period to develop. Tatian may have tried to contact them. It seems that it was for these Christian communities in Assyria that he composed a Syriac text arranged in the order of the Diatessaron.[4]

[1] Zahn loc. cit. pp. 270–2.

[2] See above p. 276–7.

[3] See above p. 275.

[4] This formulation was suggested by Professor G. D. Kilpatrick, who remarks: 'If the Diatessaron was primarily an arrangement of the Gospel material, then the whole question whether the Diatessaron was first produced in Greek or Syriac becomes of less importance.'

8. The Old Syriac Gospels

The Diatessaron is closely connected with the Old Syriac Gospels, of which we know two MSS. One of them is the Codex Curetonianus, probably written in the fifth century and published by William Cureton[1]. The other one is the famous palimpsest from the Convent of Mount Sinai, discovered in 1892 by Agnes Smith Lewis and published in 1894 as a joint edition by Bensly, Rendel Harris and Burkitt, who had studied the original in the convent.[2] The upper script of the palimpsest contains stories of saints; it was written by a monk Johannes in a convent in Ma'arrat Meṣrān (between Antioch and Aleppo), and was finished in AGr 1090, i.e. A.D. 778. The under script may have been written as early as the fourth century.[3]

These two MSS sometimes differ from each other to such an extent that they have been regarded as two different translations. But this theory, formulated by Julius Bewer[4] under the influence of the material collected by Albert Bonus,[5] is not correct. We have here a translation of the Bible which was never officially recognized. It was subjected to alterations and corrected by copyists who aimed at writing down as perfect a text as possible. They may have adapted the translation to other Greek texts at their disposal. We have an analogue in the Targum and the Septuagint which have occasionally been altered according to other Hebrew texts, and in the forms of the Old Latin Gospels of which we can now form a good idea thanks to the new edition published by the Berlin Academy from material collected by Adolf Jülicher.[6] As soon as we come to an *authorized* version, the conditions are changed. MSS of the Latin Vulgate, of the Syriac Peshiṭta, of the Targum Onḳelos have generally the same text, with few variant readings.

Of the Old Syriac Gospels we only have two MSS and hardly

[1] *Remains of a very ancient Recension of the Four Gospels in Syriac, hitherto unknown in Europe;* discovered, edited and translated by William Cureton, London, 1858.

[2] *The Four Gospels in Syriac,* transcribed from the Sinaitic Palimpsest by the late Robert C. Bensly, and by J. Rendel Harris, and by F. Crawford Burkitt. With an Introduction by Agnes Smith Lewis, Cambridge, 1894.

[3] According to A. Hjelt, *Syrus Sinaiticus,* 1930, p. 24, not later than the beginning of the fifth century.

[4] *The History of the New Testament Canon in the Syriac Church,* Chicago 1900, pp. 3–16.

[5] *Collatio Codicis Lewisiani rescripti . . . cum Codice Curetoniano, . . .* Oxonii 1896.

[6] *Itala. Das Neue Testament in altlateinischer Überlieferung . . .* ed. A. Jülicher. Berlin, i. Matthäus, 1938; ii. Marcus 1940. Subsequently iii. Lucas, has been published.

any quotations by Syriac Fathers, as these usually quote Tatian's Diatessaron.[1] Burkitt, in his great edition of 1904, was able to print the text of one of these MSS and to add the various readings of the other in the notes. The edition was made with great care and is reliable in its details. But we must keep in mind that in earlier times other texts of this version may have existed and that hardly any two MSS will give exactly the same text. Had more of these texts been preserved, we should have to adopt a method of editing the version similar to the edition of the Old Latin Gospels by Jülicher.

It is unfortunate that Burkitt had been asked to publish a new edition of the Curetonian text which was out of print.[2] Although he himself was convinced that the Sinai MS represented a much older form of text, he had to publish the later text according to his commission, and he had to give the various readings of the older text in the notes.[3] Only where the text of the Curetonianus was not preserved was he able to print the older text. The text published by him is therefore not consistent. In most cases it is the later revised text, but in other cases, where the later text is not preserved, he adopts the older unrevised text. He published these texts as if they represented one and the same recension. Both texts are, he thought, of the same type and written in the same idiomatic Syriac. He states that the text is full of peculiarities in grammar and spelling, hardly to be met elsewhere in Syriac literature. But he maintains that there is no question of dialectical variety or rustic idiom. On the contrary, all indications point to the fact that the translator used the vernacular Syriac of Edessa with the simplicity and ease which comes from literary training.[4] There is no doubt that Burkitt underestimated the differences of the two texts and was more impressed by similarities which they have in common against later translations.

[1] There are, however, some passages where the separate Gospels are quoted. Cf. Joseph Schäfers, *Eine altsyrische antimarkionitische Erklärung von Parabeln des Herrn und zwei andere altsyrische Abhandlungen zu Texten der Evangelien. Mit Beiträgen zu Tatian's Diatessaron und Markion's Neuem Testament.* (Neutestamentliche Abhandlungen, ed. M. Meinertz vi, 1, 2, Münster 1917, pp. 226–9.)

[2] *Evangelion da-Mepharreshe. The Curetonian Version of the Four Gospels, with the readings of the Sinai Palimpsest and the early Syriac Patristic evidence*, ed. F. Crawford Burkitt (i, ii, Cambridge 1904).

[3] The commission to re-edit the Codex Curetonianus was first given to Professor Bensly, before the Sinai MS was known. After Bensly's death in 1894, it was given to Burkitt.

[4] See Burkitt's edition, vol. ii, pp. 39 ff.

9. C. C. Torrey's "Documents of the Primitive Church"

The relation between the two texts was examined anew by Charles C. Torrey.[1] He refers to the fact that the Sinai palimpsest shows traces of Syro-Palestinian pronunciation and spelling. Some of these traces had previously been indicated by Wellhausen in 1905.[2] Torrey publishes a large number of such instances which he had collected over a long time from his own reading of these Gospels. He writes with regard to the material which he publishes:

> 'The list makes no claim of completeness, nor on the other hand does it include only such forms and idioms as are not found at all in Edessean Syriac. Any usage which is much more frequent in the 'Western Aramaic' than in classical Syriac may have the right to a place in this investigation.'

The material collected by him is on the whole convincing. He is also quite right in assuming that originally such traces were more numerous in the text, but that they were altered in the course of time by copyists accustomed to correct Syriac. After all, several centuries elapsed between the original date of translation and the copying of the text in the Sinai palimpsest. Torrey arrives at the following conclusions:

> The translators of these Old Syriac Gospels were natives of Palestine, Jews by birth and training but converts to the Nazarene faith, who for a considerable time had been resident in the region of Antioch; men of learning and masters of the Syriac language who nevertheless spoke and wrote with an admixture of Palestinian Aramaic sufficient to give it something of the character of a *patois*. In the Curetonian text we have to see a revision of the Sinai text improving its language in the direction of pure Syriac, removing the conspicuously Palestinian elements and conforming the text to a later form of the Greek.

I fully agree with Torrey's conclusions except for the words 'in the region of Antioch'. From the fact that the upper script of the palimpsest was written in A.D. 778 in a monastery near Antioch we cannot draw the conclusion that the under script—the text of the Gospels—must have been written, three or four centuries earlier, at the same place, to say nothing of the place

[1] Charles C. Torrey, *Documents of the Primitive Church*, New York, 1942, pp. 249 ff.

[2] Wellhausen in his review of Littmann's *Semitic Inscriptions*. *Gött. Gel. Anzeiger*, 1905, p. 683.

where the translation itself may have been made more than six centuries earlier. On the other hand it is clear that, if Torrey is right, the translation cannot have been made, as Burkitt suggests, in Edessa. It may be that a revision of the text was made there. The Curetonian offers such a revised text; here all traces of archaic words and forms have been removed. But this, and other revisions, could have been made in Edessa or elsewhere.[1]

Torrey's conclusions agree entirely with the conditions prevailing in Adiabene where there was a large Jewish population among which a Christian mission had been active since the days of Addai (before A.D. 100). We have seen that this Jewish population had been in the possesion of at least parts of a Syriac Old Testament—made by Jews for Jews—since the middle of the first century. Burkitt remarked quite rightly that the translation of the Gospels into Syriac must have been preceded by a translation of the Old Testament into that language. The correct rendering of Hebrew proper names in the Gospels cannot be explained from the Greek text alone.[2] For 'Jews by birth and education, but converted to the Christian faith who for a long time had been settled'—in Adiabene—the correct rendering of Hebrew proper names would not be difficult. It is very likely that the translation of the Gospels was made in Adiabene where the conditions were precisely such as described by Torrey.

The close connection which obviously exists between the Diatessaron of Tatian and the Old Syriac Gospels can be explained —and has been explained—in two different ways. We can suppose *either* that the Diatessaron was made from the text of the Old Syriac Gospels, which in this case must have existed before the Diatessaron was composed; *or* that the Diatessaron was originally composed in Greek and later translated into Syriac. In this case the Old Syriac Gospels are of a later date than the Diatessaron and must have been translated in close connection with it.

Theodor Zahn, who wrote his fundamental book about the

[1] Important material has been collected by M. Black in his book *An Aramaic Approach to the Gospels and Acts*, Oxford, 1946, cf. Appendix A.: *The West Aramaic element in the Old Syriac Gospels*, pp. 216–221. Most of the instances quoted by Black are from the Sinai text, but there are also examples from the Curetonian. This problem will need a thorough investigation. A second edition of the book was published in Oxford, 1954.

[2] It requires some acquaintance with the Old Testament to know that Ναχωρ in the genealogy given by St. Luke should be written ܢܚܘܪ, but Σαρουχ should be ܣܪܘܓ, and Λαμεχ should be ܠܡܟ. *Evangelion da-Mepharreshe*, II, 202 i. Burkitt gives several more examples in support of his conclusions.

Diatessaron in 1881,[1] came to the conclusion that Tatian composed the Diatessaron on the basis of the Old Syriac Gospels, of which Zahn only knew at that time the Curetonian. Friedrich Baethgen, who in 1885 carefully collated the Curetonian with the Diatessaron, stated that this text shows a great number of harmonistic readings which are difficult to explain unless we admit that they were made under the influence of the Diatessaron. This and other reasons led him to the conclusion that the text of the Curetonian must be later than the Diatessaron and that it cannot be older than the middle of the third century.[2] Zahn was convinced that Baethgen was right.[3]

10. Burkitt on the Sinai Palimpsest

In the Sinai palimpsest traces of great antiquity were discovered. Burkitt, in a long article published in 1894 in the *Guardian*,[4] deals with these various marks of antiquity and concludes:

> The arguments for the priority of the Diatessaron which were satisfactory enough against the Curetonianus break down when applied to Syrus vetus represented by the Sinai palimpsest.

But when, ten years later, he published his text he had completely changed his mind. After a long investigation of the different problems connected with these questions he came to the conclusion that the Diatessaron must have been originally composed from Greek texts in Greek and later translated into Syriac. What were the reasons for this change of view?

Burkitt names several reasons, but one was decisive for him: The Diatessaron shows a large number of 'Western' readings which otherwise are unattested except by the Cambridge Codex Bezae (D) and by some Latin texts. Such 'Western' readings cannot be expected in the East; they must have been imported from the West. This importation must have been made via the Diatessaron, which was composed in Rome from Greek MSS with Western readings, brought to the East by Tatian and there translated into Syriac. A translation of the *separate* Gospels may have been ordered by Palut, the Catholic Bishop of Edessa, mentioned

[1] Theodor Zahn, *Tatian's Diatessaron. Forschungen zur Geschichte des neutestamentlichen Kanons* . . . i Erlangen 1881.

[2] Friedrich Baethgen, *Evangelienfragmente*. Der griechische Text des Curetonischen Syrers wiederhergestellt, Leipzig 1885, pp. 72 f.

[3] Theodor Zahn, *Geschichte des neutestamentlichen Kanons*, i, 1, 1888, p. 405.

[4] 'The Sinai Palimpsest of the Old Syriac Gospels,' *The Guardian*, 31st October 1894.

earlier. He may have been encouraged to give this order by the fact that the Harmony, as composed by a heretic, was not much valued in the Church of Rome. The translation was made on the basis of a Greek text as read in Antioch about 200, and of the Diatessaron to which the Edessenes were accustomed. In this way the 'Western' readings crept into the new translation. But in spite of these supposed endeavours of the Bishop the new translation gained no influence and the Diatessaron remained the Gospel of the Syrian Church during the following centuries.

In the Introduction to his *Evangelion da-Mepharreshe* Burkitt presented this sketch of the development with great caution, as a 'working hypothesis', fully aware of the great difficulties inherent in it.[1] In his second *St. Margaret Lecture* on 'The Bible in Syria', he speaks with much more confidence,[2] and in his last article 'Syriac speaking Christianity'[3] he has somewhat modified his hypothesis under the influence of the Dutch Harmony discussed by Plooij, but in general he does not doubt the correctness of the hypothesis, and here as we have seen, he goes so far as to suggest that Tatian and Addai may be one and the same man.

11. The 'Western' Readings in the Diatessaron

The 'Western' readings in the Diatessaron certainly provide a challenging problem. But I doubt whether it can be solved in the way proposed by Burkitt. I only want to refer here to two facts which have come to our knowledge in recent years.

1. The fragments of the Gospels and Acts among the Chester Beatty Papyri, dated by Sir Frederic Kenyon from the first half of the third century,[4] show these 'Western' readings in great number. After a careful investigation of this MS in connection with other ancient texts, Sir Frederic draws the following conclusions:

> With D and other authorities of the so-called 'Western' type its (i.e. the papyrus') relations are interesting and significant. In all the Gospels there are a considerable number of passages in which it supports readings of this type, including a good

[1] *Evangelion da-Mepharreshe*, ii, pp. 206 ff.

[2] *Early Eastern Christianity*, 1904, p. 76 f.

[3] *Cambridge Ancient History*, xii, 1939, pp. 492–6. See Burkitt's review of Plooij's book '*A primitive text of the Diatessaron*' Leiden 1923 in *JTS*, xxv, 1924, pp. 113–30.

[4] *The Chester Beatty Biblical Papyri. . . .* Fasc. ii, *The Gospels and Acts*, London 1933, p. x.

> many which have exclusively 'Western' support. But it has none of the more notable variants characteristic of this type, and where D and the Old Latin have peculiar readings, the papyrus is usually against them (p. xiv). . . . The general result to which this evidence points would appear to be that this MS is a witness to the existence in Egypt in the first half of the third century of a type of text distinct from that found predominantly in B, and with a strong infusion of readings found in the early authorities which are grouped together as 'Western'. Its 'Western' features do not imply any connection with either Rome or the Syriac Church. It only confirms the conclusion as to the misleading character of the term 'Western'. . . . The readings which do occur in it are not geographically Western or Syrian, but are early readings which did not find a place in B, but which in varying degrees are preserved in Western Syrian, or Caesarean authorities (pp. xviii f).

As we now have a text of the Gospels with 'Western' readings which existed in Egypt in the first half of the third century,[1] we may suppose that much earlier similar texts existed not only in Egypt where a favourable climate preserved them, but also in the East in general.[2] Texts of such a kind must have been the basis of the Old Syrian Gospels.

2. That texts with these so-called 'Western' readings must really be very old is shown in a quite objective way by Professor Wensinck in his investigation of 'The Semitisms of Codex Bezae and their relation to the non-Western text of the Gospel of St. Luke'.[3] By comparing the text of Codex D with that of non-Western MSS of the Gospels he came upon a group of variants originating from a more or less faithful rendering of Semitic expressions and Semitic syntax. Disregarding the variants which owe their origin to editorial tendencies, the variants common to D and non-Western MSS and those common to D and the parallel texts in the other Gospels, about 270 variants remained. Of these more than 200 belong to Codex D and about 50 instances

[1] In connection with these facts it is important to remember that the text used by Clement of Alexandria showed these 'Western' readings in great numbers. See P. M. Barnard '*The Biblical Text of Clement of Alexandria in the four Gospels and the Acts of the Apostles*' (*Texts and Studies* v, 5, London 1899).

[2] Cf. the latest discussion of these problems by G. D. Kilpatrick, 'Western Text and Original text in the Gospels and Acts', *JTS*, xliv, 1943, pp. 24–36. In his article 'Western Text and Original in the Epistles' (ibid., xlv, pp. 60–5) he showed that similar conditions prevail in other parts of the New Testament.

[3] *Bulletin of the Bezan Club*, No. xii, Leiden December 1937, pp. 11–48.

to non-Western MSS, all of them due to differences of reading or translation of an underlying Aramaic text. In a number of cases the reading of the non-Western MSS, as well as of Codex D, gives an unsatisfactory sense which, in the same way, proved to have a simple explanation. From these observations Wensinck concludes: D represents the Aramaic background of the Gospel tradition more faithfully than the non-Western MSS, and seems, from this point of view, to merit precedence.[1]

The so-called 'Western' readings in the Old Syriac Gospels are in reality *early* readings for which the Diatessaron cannot be made responsible. They were already to be found in the Greek text which formed the basis of the Syriac translation. This Greek text must have been a very early one. Torrey writes:

> The Sinai text occasionally renders a Greek text to which it is the only witness, preserving primitive readings which the developing Christian doctrine could not tolerate and accordingly revised.

He refers to the reading Ἰωσὴφ ἐγέννησεν τὸν Ἰησοῦν rendered in Matt. i, 16 together with the support given to this in vv. 20, 24, 25; further, to the reading δαιμόνιόν ἐστιν rendered in Matt. xiv, 26 and Mark vi, 49, and concludes that the oldest of all Syriac translations of the Gospel must date from the early part of the second century. Torrey is assuredly right. It is very unlikely that a Greek text with such readings was used in the church of Antioch about the year A.D. 200, as Burkitt maintained.

By comparing parallel passages in the Gospels of the Sinai text Arthur Hjelt ascertained that the same Greek word has often been translated in the different Gospels by different Syriac words.[2] From this fact he concluded that the Syriac translation of the different Gospels was not made by the same man at the same time. Hjelt thinks he can prove that the Gospel of Matthew was first translated and that of Luke last. I am somewhat doubtful whether we can really go so far. But even Burkitt agrees that a number of the instances collected by Hjelt are sufficiently striking and he admits that they present a formidable appearance

[1] Cf. with Wensinck's conclusion Wellhausen's remark in *Einleitung in die drei ersten Evangelien*; Berlin 1905, p. 15: Im Cantabrigiensis Bezae sind häufig Semitismen stehen geblieben, die im Vaticanus und Sinaiticus beseitigt sind: und dies ist ein Vorzug. Denn es darf als sicher gelten, dass die Semitismen nicht nachträglich eingetragen, sondern ausgemerzt sind. Cf. 2nd edn., Berlin 1911, p. 9.

[2] Arthur Hjelt, *Die Altsyrische Evangelienübersetzung und Tatian's Diatessaron. . . .* Leipzig 1901, pp. 96–107.

to those scholars who are inclined to regard a text practically identical with that of the Sinai palimpsest as the earliest version of the Gospels in Syriac.[1]

12. The Syriac Diatessaron

The Syriac text which was before Tatian when he composed the Diatessaron was certainly *not* practically identical with the text of the Sinai palimpsest. It would be a remarkable coincidence if one of the two forms of text preserved had been the basis for Tatian's work. We must remember that the Syriac translation had no authoritatively fixed text. The differences between the text of the Diatessaron and that of the Old Syriac Gospels cannot be explained by suggesting that Tatian may have used Greek MSS as well as the Syriac Gospels at his disposal. They only show that the Syriac text used by Tatian differed in some respects from the text in the Sinai MS.

On the other hand, the Diatessaron was a great success. In the Syriac-speaking Church the separate Gospels were forced into the background. It is quite natural that the Syriac translation of the Gospels should have been influenced at a later stage by the Diatessaron. Baethgen pointed out such influences in the Curetonian.[2] The error in Baethgen's deduction consisted in his conclusion that the translation could not have been made before A.D. 250. He did not reckon with the alterations to which such old translations were exposed. That an authority like Theodor Zahn was led astray by Baethgen shows that even he was not sufficiently acquainted with the conditions under which such old Biblical translations existed. As the Gospel text in the Sinai palimpsest was probably copied in the fourth century, at a time when the Diatessaron was highly valued in the Eastern Churches, it may well be that it also was influenced by the Diatessaron.[3] But in the main we must see in these Gospel texts descendants of the Syriac text which was before Tatian when he composed the Diatessaron.

The view that the Diatessaron was composed in the East on the basis of an old Syriac translation of the Gospels best explains the fact that we have no real trace of its existence and influence

[1] *Evangelion da-Mepharreshe* ii, pp. 210–12.

[2] See above, p. 289.

[3] See H. J. Vogels, *Die Altsyrischen Evangelien in ihrem Verhältnis zu Tatian's Diatessaron* (*Biblische Studien*, ed. Bardenhewer, xvi, Freiburg 1911).

in the West. It is certainly remarkable that Origen, who was so interested in textual criticism, does not once mention it although he is very well informed about the writings of Tatian.[1] Clement of Alexandria (died about 225) knows of several books written by Tatian and often criticizes his views.[2] But he knows nothing of the Diatessaron, a fact of special importance as he was probably a personal pupil of Tatian.[3] Nor does Irenaeus (died about 202), the first author to mention Tatian as a heretic,[4] know anything of the Diatessaron.

Eusebius (died about 340) mentions the Diatessaron in his Ecclesiastical History (iv, 29). The Greek text has here:

> Tatian, their (the Encratists') first head, brought together a combination and conjunction—I do not know how—of the Gospels, and he called it Diatessaron and this is said still to be found among some people.

The Old Syriac translation of Eusebius shows a few interesting variants:

> Tatian, their (the Encratists') first head, collected and mixed and made an Evangelion and called it Diatessaron, i.e. that of the mixed ones, which still exists among many people up to the present day.

The natural inference from this much discussed passage is that Eusebius never saw a copy of the text.

Epiphanius (died 403) knows that the Evangelion Diatessaron called by some people κατὰ Ἑβραίους is said to have been composed by Tatian.[5] Jerome, in his book *De Viris illustribus*, speaks of the endless series of books which Tatian composed, but he does not mention the Diatessaron.[6]

13. The Greek and the Latin Diatessaron

Until recently not a single line of a Greek Diatessaron text was known to exist. This is no longer so, since on the 5th March

[1] Harnack, *Geschichte der altchristlichen Literatur*, i, 489. It is unlikely that he even knew the title of the book, as Zahn suggests (*Geschichte des neutestamentlichen Kanons*), i, 412.

[2] Cf. besides the references given in note 1: Einar Molland, *The Conception of the Gospels in the Alexandrian Theology*, Oslo 1938, pp. 21 f.

[3] Cf. the references given in n. 1.

[4] Zahn *Forschungen*, i, pp. 14–20; Arthur Hjelt, *Die altsyrische Evangelienübersetzung und Tatian's Diatessaron*, pp. 23 f.

[5] Zahn, *Forschungen*, i, pp. 21 f.

[6] Ibid. pp. 6 f. 'Beachtenswert ist, dass er über das Diatessaron schweigt'. Harnack loc. cit., p. 491.

1933 during a joint excavation by Yale University and the French Academy at Dura, a small piece of parchment was found with fourteen lines of a Greek Harmony which has undoubtedly a close connection with Tatian's Diatessaron. The fragment was published by Carl H. Kraeling.[1] It seems to belong to the third century[2] and is of great value since it clearly shows that a Gospel Harmony in Greek must have existed at an early period. It is of particular importance as it shows some readings which cannot be found in any MS of the Gospels hitherto known. But there can hardly be any doubt that this Greek text is a translation from a Syriac original.[3] Clear evidence of this fact is the name Arimathaea, the place from which, according to Matt. xxvii, 57, Joseph is said to have come. It has the form Ερινμαθαια and we must ask how the ν in the name is to be explained. In Syriac letters the name would have the form ܐܪܝܡܬܝܐ, and this was obviously misread by the translator as ܐܪܢܡܬܝܐ. The Syriac *i* and *n* are often very similar when written. They could easily have been confused by someone who was not familiar with the name. Also the initial *e* of the word can easily be explained if we think of a Syriac original. Dura-Europos was a place where Greek and Syrian influences met. The Diatessaron was read by the Syrian Christians in their churches and the text was translated into Greek for the benefit of the Greek-speaking Christians there.

Kraeling is probably right when he says that the Greek fragment is the earliest Diatessaron document of which we know. But he admits that the Coptic Manichaean texts recently discovered in Egypt provide evidence for the Syriac text which is only slightly later than that which the Dura fragment provides for the Greek text.[4] That the Evangelion quoted by Mani and his disciples was the Diatessaron has already been suggested by the first editors.[5] The texts published since then leave no doubt whatsoever that this is the case.[6] The language used by

[1] *A Greek Fragment of Tatian's Diatessaron from Dura*, ed. Carl H. Kraeling. Studies and Documents. . . . iii, London 1935.

[2] Kraeling, in accordance with the date of the Christian chapel, in the neighbourhood of which it was found, dates the fragment about A.D. 222.

[3] Cf. *Oriens Christianus* 3, iii, 1935, pp. 244 ff.

[4] Kraeling, loc. cit., p. 16, n. 1.

[5] C. Schmidt and H. J. Polotsky, *Ein Mani-Fund in Ägypten*, Sitzungsberichte der Berliner Akademie 1933, pp. 57–59.

[6] *Manichäische Handschriften des Staatlichen Museen*, Berlin. A. Kephalaia, ed. Schmidt, Polotsky, Böhlig, Stuttgart 1935 ff.

Mani was Syriac,[1] and he began his mission in Mesopotamia in 241.[2] The Syriac Diatessaron was well known and generally used at that time. The fragments published by Kraeling show that a Greek text existed. But as far as we know it was not considered to be of great importance.

The same must be said of the Latin text of the Diatessaron which was the source for the Dutch Harmony, the Liège Diatessaron, to which D. Plooij has drawn attention. This Dutch text and similar texts which we know are derived from an old Latin Harmony with a text older than Jerome's Vulgate, and different from the anonymous Latin Harmony found in the sixth century by Victor of Capua which was later brought into accordance with the Vulgate. Plooij thinks that it was an old Latin Harmony which had been forgotten for 1,000 years and which, with the help of the Dutch Harmony, we may be able to reconstruct.[3] He supposes that it was translated directly from the Old Syriac text.[4]

14. The Revised Text of the Syriac Gospels

At the beginning of the fifth century a new text of the New Testament in Syriac was introduced into Edessa. The author was, as Professor Burkitt has made nearly certain, Rabbula, Bishop in Edessa from 411 to 435,[5] whose activity against the followers of Bardaisan we have referred to earlier.[6] In this new translation, the so-called Peshiṭta, the separate Gospels were to be found. Rabbula ordered that priests and deacons should arrange for copies of the separate Gospels to be available in all churches and read there.[7] It seems that he was successful, at

[1] Mani knew besides Syriac some Persian also, but not much. W. B. Henning has published a report about the last audience granted to Mani by King Bahram I, the Sassanid. The report is given by Nuhzadag, who had served as Mani's interpreter on that occasion. Henning remarks: 'Although Mani knew some Persian and had even composed one of his books in—it is true—somewhat halting Persian, he must have felt his knowledge of that language to be insufficient for an audience that was to decide on his life and the future of his community'. Cf. Henning's article 'Mani's last journey', *BSOAS*, vol. x, London 1942, p. 953.

[2] Schaeder, *Gnomon*, ix, 1933, p. 349.

[3] D. Plooij, *A Primitive Text of the Diatessaron*, Leiden 1933.

[4] D. Plooij, *Traces of the Syriac Origin of the Old Latin Diatessaron*, Mededeelingen, Amsterdamer Akademie 1927.

[5] 'Now he translated in the wisdom of God that was in him the New Testament from Greek into Syriac, because of the variation exactly as it was,' *Vita Rabbulae*, ed. Overbeck, p. 172; Burkitt, *Evangelion da-Mepharreshe*, ii, p. 161.

[6] See above, pp. 279–80.

[7] *Praecepta et Monita ad Sacerdotes et Regulares*, ed. Overbeck, loc. cit. p. 220, lines 3–5.

least in Edessa. Other bishops of the Syriac-speaking communities followed his example. Bishop Theodoret of Cyrus (died 457) boasts of having collected and destroyed more than two-hundred copies of the Diatessaron in his diocese alone, and of having forced the churches under his jurisdiction to use the separate Gospels, i.e. the Peshiṭta.

But the introduction of a revised translation of a Biblical text has never been an immediate success. We have seen this in the case of the Targum, the Septuagint and the Vulgate and need not be surprised to find the same story repeating itself in the case of the Syriac Biblical text. The older text of the Syriac Old Testament is to be found in MSS as late as the sixth, even the ninth century.[1] The Diatessaron, in spite of all efforts in the fifth century to replace it by the revised text of the separate Gospels, the Peshiṭta, was for centuries highly valued in the Eastern Churches. It may be that the commentary written on it by so great an authority as Ephraem helped to preserve it. The commentary exists to-day only in an Armenian translation,[2] but is quoted in the Syriac original by Syriac authors of the ninth and later centuries,[3] and a copy of the Syriac Diatessaron made in the ninth century is said to have been the basis of the Arabic translation of which a number of MSS are preserved.

15. The Arabic Diatessaron

The Arabic text of the Diatessaron is known to us in two forms clearly different in details of translation. They are distinguishable even in outward appearance, for one of them has been handed down as anonymous; the other is associated with very full-sounding names of Arab Christians. One form has the genealogies of Christ in the text of the Gospels where one would expect to find them: the genealogy in Matthew i occurs in chapter 2 of the Diatessaron, that of Luke iii in chapter 4 of the Diatessaron. The other form has the genealogies at the end, as a sort of appendix. In the one form the Evangelists are described by the

[1] See above p. 266.

[2] It is to be found in the second volume of the Armenian edition of Ephraem's works, Venice 1836. A Latin translation made in 1841 by J. Baptista Aucher, was published in 1876 by Georg Moesinger (*Evangelii Concordantis Expositio facta a Sancta Ephraemo Doctore Syro*) and became the basis for Zahn's reconstruction of the text in *Forschungen*, vol. i, 1881.

[3] Rendell Harris, *Fragments of the Commentary of Ephraem Syrus upon the Diatessaron*, London 1895.

first two letters of their names, Matthew مت, Mark مر, Luke لو, John يو. In the other form they are each named by one characteristic letter Mt م, Mk ر, Lk ق, Jn ح.

The first form is to be found:

1. In the Vatican MS Arab xiv, called A in the published editions of the text,[1] a MS brought to Rome from the East in 1719 by Joseph Simon Assemani. Originally it consisted of 125 folios, but fos. 17 and 118 are missing and fos. 1–7 are not well preserved. The MS was probably written in the thirteenth or fourteenth century.[2] It begins with the words:

> In the name of the Father, and the Son and the Holy Ghost, who bestows life, the One God in essence (*jauhar*), the Threefold as persons in attributes (*ṣifāt*).

It ends with the remark:

> With God's help the holy Gospel is finished which Tatian has assembled from the four Gospels and which is known as the Diatessaron.

A facsimile of fol. 110 of the MS is published by Marmardji on plate I.

2. In a Beirut fragment, consisting of only three folios which contain the report about the Lord's Supper and the last sentence of the Diatessaron, followed by an interesting colophon.[3] The text is in agreement with Codex A. As the genealogies of Our Lord in this manuscript are not to be found at the end of the Diatessaron, they must have been given in chapters two and four, as in MS A. The manuscript to which the fragment belonged was finished in July 1332. It was connected with a *very old* MS[4]

[1] *Diatessaron . . . seu Tatiani Evangeliorum Harmoniae arabice, nunc primum ex duplici codice edidit et translatione Latina donavit P. Augustinus Ciasca Ord. Eremit.* S. Augustini Bibliothecae Ap. Vaticanae Scriptor, Romae 1888.

[2] According to Ciasca, who follows Assemani, the MS was written in the twelfth century, see Ciasca's article: 'De Tatiani Diatessaron Arabice versione', in Cardinal Pitra's *Analecta Sacra . . .* tomus iv, Parisiis, 1883, pp. 465–87. That in fact the MS must date from a later period has been ascertained by the Swedish scholar J. D. Åkerblad (died 1819). Cf. Zahn, *Forschungen*, i, p. 295.

[3] The fragment was first discovered and published by Louis Cheikho, who deals with it in the *Journal Asiatique* (ix, 10, 1897, pp. 301–5 and in his *Chrestomathia Arabica*, Beirut 1897, pp. 203–5. A further article about the fragment appears in *al-Mashriḳ* vol. iv, 1901, pp. 100–4 and a facsimile of two pages of the fragment is attached. In the Appendix to Sebastian Euringer's book '*Die Überlieferung der Arabischen Übersetzung des Diatessaron*' (*Biblische Studien*, xvii, 2, Freiburg i. Br. 1912), G. Graf has published, on pp. 62–71 a new edition of the fragment.

[4] Unfortunately the date of the *very old* MS is not preserved in the underscript of the fragment.

written in the City of God[1] (Antioch), by three MSS copied from one another in Egypt. The oldest of these three MSS, the one which had been copied directly from the *very old* MS, was written by Anbā Yūsif ben Muḥabrik, Bishop of Fūwah (on the Rosetta Nile) in the first half of the thirteenth century. Codex A was also written in Egypt and no doubt also goes back to the *very old* MS.[2]

The second form is to be found:

1. In MS Borg. Arab. 250 of the Bibliotheca Vaticana (MS B in the editions). It was presented in 1886 to the Museum Borgianum de Propaganda Fide in Rome by its owner, Ḥalīm Dōs Ghālī, a prominent Catholic Copt in Cairo. On fos. 1–85 it contains an introduction which is described by Ciasca, on p. vi of his edition, in the following words:

> Foliis 1–85 habetur praefatio super Evangelia, in qua anonimus auctor, postquam ostendit quibus dotibus liber quilibet ornari debeat. ut revera utilis sit, easque in Evangeliis reperiri, de divinis attributis disserit, in primis vero de unitate ac simplicitate, quae ab Evangeliis potissimum manifestari demonstrat; loquitur insuper de sapientia Dei in novae Legis promulgatione, qua gentes omnes, idolatria excussa, ad Christum venerunt. Quo in tractatu, eruditionis pleno, cuius ob temporis angustias unum dedi argumentum, auctores plures citantur in antiquitate celebriores, uti Zoroaster, Aristoteles, Hermes, Ammonius, Eusebius Caesareensis, Gregorius Armenus. Ibn Attîb non semel, aliique non pauci . . .

On fol. 96–353 the Diatessaron follows. A facsimile of the beginning of the Diatessaron is published by Ciasca (fol. 96v–97r) before the printed text. It reveals the remarkable fact that the first two pages of the Arabic Diatessaron are written in exactly the same way as Sura 1 and the beginning of Sura 2 in a MS of the Koran. The five lines of the text on each of the two pages are short and surrounded by decorations such as we are used to seeing at the beginning of a Koran MS. But a further facsimile of two later pages of the MS (fol. 324v/325r)—on Plate II in

[1] *City of God* (*medīnat Allāh*) is a translation of Theupolis. This name was given to Antioch by Justinian when he restored the town after it had been destroyed by Khusrau Anūshīrwān, the Sassanide ruler, in A.D. 538. The town belonged from 637 to 969, and again after 1084, to the Arabs. It was held by crusading princes from 1098 to 1268.

[2] Euringer loc. cit., pp. 32–56, tries to deduce more from these colophons than is really possible and he makes very curious mistakes. But the final result seems to be correct.

Marmardji's edition—shows that the whole MS is written in a way similar to Koran MSS.

Ciasca suggests that this MS was written in the fourteenth century, but the artist who decorated the first two pages of the MS seems to have been familiar with decorations of the Renaissance period, so that it can hardly date back further than the sixteenth century.[1]

In the preamble of the MS which Ciasca prints at the beginning of his edition, we read:

> We begin with the help of God the Sublime, with the writing down of the pure Gospel and the flowering garden which is called Diatessaron; the explanation of this expression is the fourfold (*ar-rubāʿī*) and it is this which Titiyanus the Greek has assembled from the four Evangelists Mattay, the chosen one (*muṣṭafā*)—his sign is *m*—and Marcus, the chosen one (*mujtabā*)—his sign is *r*—and Luka, who is acclaimed (*murtaḍā*)—his sign is *q*—and Yuḥanna the one giving answer (*mujīb*)—his sign is *ḥ*. It was translated from the Syriac into the Arabic by the noble, learned priest Abulfaraj ʿAbdallāh b. aṭ-Ṭaiyib—God have mercy on him—and he begins with the words: The beginning of the Gospel of Jesus, the Son of the living God. . . .

The postscript of the MS reads as follows:

> Finished is the Evangelion which Tatian assembled and which he called Diatessaron, which means the fourfold (*rubāʿī*), assembled from the four gospels of the holy apostles, the four excellent evangelists, blessed may they be! It was translated by the excellent learned priest Abulfaraj ʿAbdallāh b. aṭ-Ṭaiyib—God have mercy on him—from the Syriac into the Arabic from a MS in the handwriting of ʿĪsā b. ʿAlī, the physician, pupil of Ḥunain b. Isḥāḳ—may God give grace to both of them—Amen.

2. In MS 202 of the Library of the Coptic Patriarchate in Cairo, finished on 27th Bashnes A. Mart. 1511 (22nd May 1795) and consisting of 114 folios. A facsimile of fol. 25 is published as Plate III in Marmardji's edition which he has based on this MS called by him MS E. The MS was written much later than A and B and not very carefully, even if one does not overrate

[1] This was also the view of Dr. Hugo Buchtal of the Warburg Institute, whose advice I asked. However, according to him, it is impossible to make a suggestion, after merely having seen a photograph, as to what date after 1500 these decorations may have been made, since they still occur in the nineteenth century.

the importance of the seventy odd mistakes in the vocalization which Marmardji claims to have discovered on every page; the Maronite Marmardji was a fanatical champion of the form of his mother tongue which he had learned at school. That he based his edition entirely on this MS can be explained by the simple fact that the École Biblique in Jerusalem, where he taught, had a photograph of the MS in its library. The preamble of the MS is the same as the one in MS B. The postscript reads as follows:

> Completed is the Evangelion which Tatian assembled and which he called Diatessaron, which means the fourfold. It is assembled from the four gospels of the holy apostles, the four excellent evangelists, blessed may they be. The completion of this revered Evangelion took place on the 27th of the blessed month Bashnes of A. Mart. 1511. And power and dominion and magnitude and glory to our Lord Jesus Christ in truth to all eternity. Amen, Amen, Amen.[1]

3. In MS 1020 of the Library of Père Sbath.[2] This MS was copied by the deacon (*shammās*) Ibrāhīm Abū Tibl b. Sam'ān al-Khawānikī, one of the servants of the martyr Merkurios Abū Saifain in Old Cairo,[3] in A. Mart. 1512 (A.D. 1798). The MS has the same preamble as MSS B and E. A postscript is so far not known.

4. In MS Arab e 163 of the Bodleian Library in Oxford.[4] It contains three Christian-Arabic texts: (a) an introduction to the four life-giving Gospels and the ten Canons (fols. 5–31); (b) a compendium on Christian truth; and (c) the Arabic Diatessaron (fols. 140–288).

16. The Oxford MS and al-Ghazālī

This MS with the three texts is called at the beginning and end *al-muṣḥaf ash-sherīf*, a name which as a rule is used for a MS of the Koran. The copyist, a certain Antūnī Sa'd, who finished the second text in July 1805 and the third text in January 1806, declares at the end of the MS that, following the orders

[1] In the 'Catalogue de Manuscrits Arabes Chrétiens conservés au Caire', *Studi e Testi*, vol. lxiii, 1934, p. 87, Georg Graf gives wrongly the date of the MS as A. Mart. 1512 instead of 1511.

[2] *Bibliothèque de Manuscripts Paul Sbath.* Catalogue, vol. ii, Cairo, 1938, p. 135.

[3] The church has been described by A. J. Butler, *The Ancient Coptic Churches of Egypt*. Oxford, 1884, vol. i, pp. 75–154.

[4] Cf. the notice about the MS by A. F. L. Beeston. 'The Arabic Version of Tatian's Diatessaron,' *JRAS*, 1939, pp. 608–10.

he had received, he had made an exact copy of a MS which had been completed on the 13th Rejeb AH 500 (15th March A.D. 1107). In the Bodleian MS the beginnings of the first and third texts are written exactly in the same way as the first and the beginning of the second Sura in manuscripts of the Koran.

The author of the first text whose name is not mentioned declares that whoever wishes to study a Gospel with profit must do so under the following aspects. He must pay attention to its purpose (*gharad*): eternal life; its profit (*manfa'a*): salvation from the captivity of Satan; its rank (*martaba*): continuous reading and keeping of its rules is necessary; its characteristics *wasm*: its divine message; its relation to God (*nisba*): the Evangelists are apostles or disciples of apostles; its authority (*isnād*): the report of what Christ did on earth; its divisions (*fuṣūl*): which have to be regarded carefully, as reports on the same things are to be found in the different Gospels. The author enumerates: 219 chapters (Matt 68, Mark 48, Luke 83, John 20), 1165 canons (Matt 355, Mark 236, Luke 342, John 232), 287 Coptic sections (Matt 101, Mark 54, Luke 86, John 46), the ten canons of Ammonius and Eusebius, the Testimonia (Messianic prophecies from the Old Testament) (Matt 95, Mark 53, Luke 73, John 39). Short prefaces to the Gospels follow containing chiefly biographical notes about the evangelists. (Between fols. 22 and 29 there are eight instead of six folios.)

The second text is of particular interest. It is entitled:

tiryāḳ al-'uḳūl fī 'ilm al-uṣūl (*ad-dīnīye*)

'Antidote of the minds in the matter of the (divine) principles.'

In the preamble of the text we are told that the book was written at the request of a Muslim ruler who had expressed the wish to have a compendium of the Christian faith with reference to the various Christian parties, in which questions which had been raised by a prominent Muslim concerning the Trinity and the Divinity of Christ were answered. The text contains a compendium of Christian dogmatics (24 chapters) and ethics (5 chapters). In the concluding part (*khātime*) the questions of the prominent Muslim are answered. It emerges that this Muslim is no other than the great theologian and mystic al-Ghazālī, of whose work *ar-radd al-jamīl* long quotations are given on fols. 129 and 133 of the Oxford MS, and to which many allusions are made.

The full title of al-Ghazālī's book is *ar-radd al-jamīl li-ilāhīyat*

'Īsā 'alā ṣarīḥ al-injīl 'The fine answer to the divinity of Jesus according to the genuine Gospels'. Louis Massignon drew our attention to this interesting text[1] and showed that what al-Ghazālī knew in the earlier period of his life about Jesus was exclusively based on material to be found in Islamic tradition, chiefly '*logia*' of an ascetic character. This material had also been the only source for his main work the *Iḥyā 'ulūm ad-dīn*, *The Revival of the Sciences of Religion*, written after his famous conversion in 1095. He was living at that time in Jerusalem in total seclusion from the world. The approaching Crusaders who in 1099 captured Jerusalem forced him to go to Alexandria for a time. It is very likely that he wrote *ar-radd al-jamīl* in about 1101 in Alexandria. It gives the conclusions at which al-Ghazālī arrived from a study of the Gospels themselves.

Al-Ghazālī's book was published on the basis of two Aya Sofia MSS (2246 and 2247), which Massignon had already used, and a Leiden MS (Catalogue 2084) in which the name of the author is not preserved and which had not been recognized previously; the editor was Robert Chidiac, S.J., one of Massignon's pupils, and a preface was written by Massignon himself.[2] The quotations from al-Ghazālī's book which form part of MS Arab. e 163, the Arabic Diatessaron in the Bodleian Library, have been published by Père Sbath from his own MSS.[3]

Chidiac added a valuable French translation to al-Ghazālī's book and, in a detailed introduction, he dealt in a careful way with the various problems. He showed beyond doubt that the text contained in the three MSS is rightly ascribed to al-Ghazālī although al-Ghazālī himself makes no reference to it in his later works.

In the compendium on dogmatics and ethics of which the Oxford MS of the Arabic Diatessaron contains a copy we see the reply of the Copts, which the Muslim ruler had requested from them, to the arguments set out by al-Ghazālī. It is very probable that we have a copy of the original of the Coptic answer dated A.D. 1107 in the text of the Bodleian MS. The Muslim governor

[1] *Revue des Études Islamiques*, 1932, pp. 523–36.

[2] Al-Ghazālī, *Réfutation excellente de la Divinité de Jésus-Christ d'après les Evangiles.* Texte établi, traduit et commenté par Robert Chidiac, S.J., Préface de M. Louis Massignon (*Bibliothèque de l'École des Hautes Études . . . Sciences Religieuses*, live volume, Paris 1939).

[3] Paul Sbath, *Vingt traités philosophiques et apologétiques d'auteurs Arabes Chrétiens du ixe an xive siècles . . .* Cairo 1929, pp. 176–78. Sbath published these texts according to his MS 1580, dated AH 715 A.D. 1315, and refers to his MS 47, dated A.D. 1863.

of Egypt to whom the preface of the Coptic text refers was therefore al-Malik al-Afḍal, who succeeded his father, al-Bedr al-Jamālī, the famous al-Emir al-Juyūshi.[1] A certain interest in Christian matters can be expected on the part of an influential and broadminded Muslim like al-Afḍal at a time when Jerusalem was in the hands of the Crusaders. We may suppose that al-Afḍal sent a copy of al-Ghazālī's work to the Copts soon after its publication, requesting their comments. The MS dated 1107 represents their answer.

17. The Copts and the Arabic Diatessaron

We can now understand why the Copts gave their MS the title *al-muṣḥaf ash-sherīf*, a title normally reserved for a copy of the Koran, and why the Arabic text of the Diatessaron—and other texts of the MS, were written in the form of a Koran. The Copts may have hoped to make in this way a greater impression on their Muslim rulers. The MS was written by pious members of the Aulād al-'Assāl, a prominent Coptic family which flourished in Egypt for several centuries. One member of the family, who is simply called Ibn al-'Assāl, is said to have been the author of the text. The Copts may have entrusted him with the task of writing the answer to al-Ghazālī's book. He was the grandson (*sibt*) of the old and venerable Shaikh Buṭrus as-Sadamantī, a well-known Coptic author of the eleventh century.[2] In the introductory remarks to the text, Ibn al-'Assāl is described as an eminent scholar, but the epithets given to him must not be taken too seriously. They were chosen to make an impression on the Muslims for whom the treatise had been written.

Three brothers belonging to the Aulād al-'Assāl were well-known thirteenth century authors. One of them was commissioned to make a new Arabic translation of the Gospels (650/1252). In the British Museum MS Or 3382 (Rieu Supplement 7) his name is given as Abulfaraj Hibatullāh, son of Abulfaḍl As'ad, son of Abū Isḥāḳ Ibrāhīm, son of Abū Sahl Jirjis, son of Abulbishr Yuḥannā, son of Ibn al-'Assāl. The six generations

[1] Cf. C. H. Becker's article 'al-Afḍal' in *Encyclopaedia of Islam*, vol. i, p. 153.

[2] See, Louis Cheikho, *Catalogue de manuscrits des auteurs arabes chrétiens*, Beirut 1924, p. 62. Georg Graf mentions Buṭrus in his *Geschichte der Christlichen Arabischen Literatur*, vol. ii, pp. 351–6. He places him in the thirteenth century, because of an alleged date 1260 in his writings.

mentioned in the colophon take us back from the thirteenth to the eleventh century.[1]

The compendium of Christian dogmatics and ethics is, however, ascribed in other MSS to other authors. A note of the copyist in the Paris MS 178 (thirteenth century) reports that the text was composed by a certain Abulkhair, called Ibn al-Ghaib in Ḥoms (Emesa) in A.D. 1052. In MS Sbath 47 (dated 1863) Abulkhair b. aṭ-Ṭaiyib is named as author, and Sbath, who makes of him a Jacobite priest of the eleventh century, seems to identify him with the author mentioned in the Paris MS. Professor Massignon remarks very aptly that a book referring to a work composed by al-Ghazālī cannot have been written before Ghazālī had composed the work. For the same reason Severos b. al-Muḳaffa (tenth century), mentioned as author in the Cairo MS 338 (dated 1746), cannot have composed the text.

In two MSS of the Bodleian Library, Hunt 240 (Uri 38, dated 1549) and Hunt 362 (Uri 50, dated 1476) a certain Abulkhair is named as author. But the name is only to be found on the title-pages and these, in both cases, are late additions. In MS Hunt 240 the title-page was added by a very incompetent person who indicated the contents of the book quite wrongly. He calls the author Rashīd Abulkhair. In MS Hunt 362 the first eleven folios are missing. A later hand has supplemented the beginning of the text by eight folios and here Abulkhair b. aṭ-Ṭaiyib is named as author on the first page, just as in MS Sbath 47.[2] In three MSS of the Bibliotheca Vaticana described by Angelo Mai under Nos. 105, 118, and 119, all written in the fourteenth century, Abulbarakāt b. Kibr is mentioned as the author of a text with the slightly different title of *jalā al-'uḳūl fi 'ilm al-uṣūl*. According to Graf these MSS contain practically the same text as those mentioned above. Abulbarakāt is a well-known Coptic author, a great compiler who died at the age of ninety in 1363.

[1] Concerning the family see Duncan B. Macdonald's article 'Ibn al-'Assāl' in *Encyclopaedia of Islam*, which is chiefly based on articles published by Alexis Mallon. Some new material is assembled by Georg Graf, 'Die koptische Gelehrtenfamilie der Aulād al-'Assāl und ihr Schrifttum', *Orientalia*, Nova Series, Roma 1943, pp. 34 f, 129, f, 193 f. In his *Geschichte der Christl. Arabischen Literatur*, vol. ii, 1947, pp. 387–414, he only speaks of members of the family who were living in the thirteenth century. Already Macdonald pointed out that the family must have enjoyed a certain fame in earlier times. For this we have now definite proofs.

[2] Moritz Steinschneider refers to the two Bodleian MSS in his book: *Polemische und apologetische Literatur in Arabischer Sprache* (Abh. für die Kunde des Morgenlandes vi, 3, Leipzig 1877), p. 37, but does not mention that the title-pages in both MSS were added later. He is inexact in other ways also, for instance he quotes MS Marsh 649 instead of Hunt 240.

In the Cairo MS 391 (eighteenth century) Ibn al-'Assāl, the grandson of Buṭrus as-Sadamantī, is mentioned as author, just as in the Bodleian MS Arab e 163 and in the original of 1107, from which the MS was copied. The Cairo MS 711 (seventeenth century) is incomplete at the beginning and no author's name has been preserved.

In these circumstances it is somewhat surprising to find Georg Graf declaring[1] that the MSS of the compendium—with a few exceptions—name Abulkhair b. aṭ-Ṭaiyib as author of the text, whom Graf makes the *son of a physician* by confounding the words *ṭaiyib* and *ṭabīb*, and to whom he gives the name Rashīd, found on a very doubtful title-page of one MS only.

According to Graf, all MSS of the text have an appendix (*corollarium*) at the end. Yet the appendix is missing in two MSS from Cairo, described by Graf himself (338 and 391), and in the Bodleian MS Arab e. 163—as well as in the original of A.D. 1107 from which it was copied.

Graf states that the appendix added to the text consists of seven parts:

1. On prayer, with quotations from the Didascalia.
2. Quotations from Maimonides.
3. Another quotation from the Didascalia.
4. A quotation from Fakhreddīn ar-Rāzī.
5. The Climates of the Stars.
6. A quotation from ii Timothy.
7. On the right faith, as preached to the world by the apostles.

Graf depends here on the three MSS of the Bibliotheca Vaticana and did not notice that they had been enlarged and worked over by Abulbarakāt. In the two MSS of the Bodleian Library Hunt. 240 and 362 the appendix has only four parts:

1. Quotations from Jer vii, 16–18 and Amos v, 25, 26.
2. Quotations from the Didascalia, chap. 23 and Acts xiv, 11f.[2]
3. Quotations from Maimonides.
4. Quotations from Fakhreddīn ar-Rāzī.

Graf maintains that the appendix was added by the author himself and that the quotations from Maimonides (d. 1204)

[1] See his article: 'Zum Schrifttum des Abulbarakat und des Abulkhair,' *Oriens Christianus* iii, 8, 1933, pp. 133–43.

[2] The quotation from the Arabic Didascalia can be found in the Oxford MS Hunt 31 (Uri 61) in chap. 30 on fol. 109.

and from Fakhreddīn ar-Rāzī (d. 1209) prove that the book could not have been written before the thirteenth century. In both Bodleian MSS—Hunt 240 and 362—the appendix is introduced with the words:

> What is to be found at the end of the book from which this MS was copied—and it is clear that it is not by the author—and what I have copied, is the clear proof that the people of the Seven Climates adored the Seven Planets.

It is very likely that the appendix to the Paris MS 178 was introduced by the same notice. Slane's description in the catalogue is not very clear and Graf has completely misunderstood it.

We can now see quite clearly that the compendium *ṭiryāḳ al-'uḳūl* . . . is preserved in at least three different forms, attributed to different authors:

1. The text attributed to Ibn al-'Assāl, the reply to al-Ghazālī's book *ar-radd al-jamīl* . . . composed between 1101 and 1107.

2. The text attributed to Abulkhair b. aṭ-Ṭaiyib, containing various additions to the former text, especially an appendix consisting of four parts as described above. Quotations from Maimonides and Fakhraddīn ar-Rāzī in the appendix show that this form cannot be older than the thirteenth century.

3. The text touched up by Abulbarakāt and published under a slightly altered title in the fourteenth century.

We have seen that the appendix was enlarged and altered by him. How far he changed the text in other directions can only be ascertained by a careful investigation of the whole text.

It may be that even more forms of this text existed. It is, for instance, very likely that Ibn al-'Assāl, when before 1107 he wrote the answer to the book of al-Ghazālī, used an earlier composition for his work, and that a kernel of truth may lie in the statement that at least parts of the book were written in 1052 or must even be connected with Severus b. al-Mukaffa. It is interesting to see how the various Christian Arabic authors quite unscrupulously put forward older texts with slight alterations as their own work. A true history of such a text can only be written after a careful investigation of the entire material at our disposal. In any case it is evident that problems in connection with such texts cannot be solved by the methods adopted by Graf.

The third text in the Bodleian MS Arab e 163 is the Arabic Diatessaron. It has the same preamble as MSS B and E and the

MS Sbath. Its text conforms with that of MSS B and E and probably also with that of the MS Sbath. The postscript reads as follows:

> Finished is the accomplishment of this fourfold honoured Evangelion which was assembled from the four Gospels of the holy Apostles, the four excellent Evangelists—may they be blessed. The excellent learned priest Abulfaraj ʻAbdallāh ben aṭ-Ṭaiyib—may God be pleased with him—has translated it from the Syriac into Arabic, from a copy in the handwriting of ʻĪsā b. ʻAlī, the physician, the pupil of Ḥunain b. Isḥāḳ—may God the Almighty have mercy on both of them.
>
> And he (the copyist) copied this as it was, not rearranging (anything) in the copy, but observing the orders, on the 8th Tobah A. Mart. 1522—25th Shawwāl AH 1220 (January A.D. 1806).

A comparison of this postscript with that of MS B shows that a few slight differences can be found at the beginning of the Bodleian MS and that the note of the copyist at the end has been added. But in the main part of the postscript the MSS agree. They must have been copied from the same original. MS B may have been copied from the MS dated in 1107, two or three centuries before the Bodleian MS was copied from it. The fact that MS B and the Bodleian MS are written in a form imitating a copy of the Koran can best be explained if one supposes that the original was written in the same way.

There is, however, a clear difference between the two MSS which needs to be explained. In the Bodleian MS the Diatessaron is preceded by *two* texts, as no doubt was the case in the original of 1107. In MS B the Diatessaron is preceded by only *one* text. This text, the introduction, has more or less the same title as the first text in the Bodleian MS but it cannot have the same contents. In MS B the text takes up 85 folios, in the Bodleian MS only 31 folios. Since admittedly the Bodleian MS is more closely written—B has 8 lines to the page whereas the Bodleian MS has 13 lines—the introduction to the Bodleian MS could possibly take up 45–50 folios in MS B, but not 85 folios. Ciasca's description of the introduction to MS B has been quoted above. An introduction like that in the Bodleian MS could not be described in this way. But the authorities said by Ciasca to be quoted in the introduction of MS B throw light on the relationship between the two introductions. Ammonius and Eusebius are names which occur in the first text of the Bodleian MS; the other authorities are to be found in the second text, and they all occur together in the third chapter of the first part of the compendium, which is devoted to the Trinity and the Divinity of Christ. In the introduction to MS B we are faced therefore with a compilation made from the two texts which precede the Diatessaron in the Bodleian MS and in the original of 1107 from which the Bodleian MS was copied.

MS E contains only the Diatessaron, does not exhibit the external form of a Koran MS and does not mention the three Christian Arabic scholars, connected in MS B and in the Bodleian MS with the text. But all other circumstances make it clear that it goes back directly or indirectly to the same original, as must also be supposed in the case of the MS Sbath.

Abulfaraj ʻAbdallāh b. aṭ-Ṭaiyib (died 1043) is mentioned in the preamble of all four MSS and in the postscript of two of them as the translator of the Arabic Diatessaron. But who was this man? What Georg Graf,[1] Sebastian Euringer[2] and Marmardji[3] have to say about him is taken exclusively from Christian sources. But it is essential to remember that Abulfaraj b. aṭ-Ṭaiyib had a great reputation among Muslims and that valuable accounts of him are to be found in Muslim sources, from which the information supplied by Christian authors largely derived. Barhebraeus, for instance (d. 1286) whose report is quoted by Euringer and by Marmardji, simply repeats what he found in Ibn al-Ḳifṭī's (d. 1248) *Ta'rīkh al-Ḥukamā* (*History of the Scientists*)[4] and Barhebraeus himself refers to this source. It is somewhat unfortunate that Marmardji should choose this passage, in which there is not a single word which is not copied from the book of the Muslim author al-Ḳifṭī, in order to illustrate the kind of Arabic written by Barhebraeus. On the other hand, Euringer misunderstands the word *al-Ḳifṭī*, meaning the man from al-Ḳift, the ancient Koptos, a town in Upper Egypt, and takes it to mean *al-Ḳibṭī*, 'the Copt', in this way turning the famous Muhammedan scholar and Ḳāḍī into a Coptic Christian.

[1] *Die christlich-arabische Literatur bis zur fränkischen Zeit*, 1905, pp. 63 ff. Graf deals at great length with him in his *Geschichte* . . . vol. ii, 1947, pp. 160–7, where he has assembled all the material known to him.

[2] 'Die Überlieferung der arabischen Übersetzung des Diatessaron' (*Biblische Studien*, xvii, 2, Freiburg i. Br. 1912), pp. 9 ff.

[3] *Diatessaron de Tatien*, Beyrouth 1935, pp. lxxxv ff.

[4] Ibn al-Qifti's *Ta'rīkh al-ḥukamā*. Auf Grund von Vorarbeiten August Müller herausgegeben von Julius Lippert, Leipzig 1903, p. 223.

The most important notice on Ibn aṭ-Ṭaiyib is provided by Ibn Abī Uṣaibi'a (d. 1270) who devotes a long article to him in his great work on the Classes of Arab Physicians.[1] He mentions more than forty learned books composed by him, commentaries on Aristotle, Hippocrates, Galen, and other works, including a commentary on the Gospels. As Ibn aṭ-Ṭaiyib was a very busy man, he used to dictate his books to his secretaries. But Ibn Abī Uṣaibi'a is very proud of having found a note-book of this eminent scholar in his own handwriting, dated 406/1016, which had served him as a basis for some of his famous lectures on medicine, delivered at the 'Aḍūdīye Hospital in Baghdād. He remarks that his contemporary, the famous Ibn Sīnā (Avicenna) valued highly Ibn aṭ-Ṭaiyib's works on medicine, but did not think that his works on philosophy reached the same standard.

Ibn Abī Uṣaibi'a reports an interesting story which he had heard from his pupil Muwaffaḳ addīn Ya'ḳūb b. Isḥāḳ b. al-Ḳuff an-Naṣrānī (d. 1286) which well illustrates the high esteem in which Ibn aṭ-Ṭaiyib was held among Muslims:

> Two young Muslims came from Persia to Baghdād intending to study medicine under Ibn aṭ-Ṭaiyib. At his house they were told that he was in church. There he was shown to them, an old man vested as a priest, censer in hand, offering incense. When they saw him later in his house and told him why they had come to Baghdad, he asked them whether they had made the pilgrimage to Mecca. 'No,' was the reply. So he recommended them to go to Mecca first and when they returned he would accept them as pupils. When they came back, tired and weary, he asked them whether they had done all they were ordered to do, including throwing stones in the valley of Mīna. They had done all. 'That is good,' he told them. What is ordered by divine law must be fulfilled to the letter, without reflecting about it. They had seen him doing so in church; now they had done what was ordered by their own law. They became his pupils and were later famous physicians in their home country.

Ibn Abī Uṣaibi'a gives a long list of famous physicians in all the lands of Islam who had been his pupils, and he admits that Ibn aṭ-Ṭaiyib was a devout Christian priest who, as secretary to the Nestorian Patriarch in Baghdād, had a great influence among the Christians there.

[1] *'Uyūn al-anbā fī ṭabaḳāt al-aṭibbā*, ed. August Müller, Cairo and Königsberg 1882 and 1884, vol. i, pp. 239–41.

Ḥunain b. Isḥāḳ (d. 873) who is mentioned in the postscript of MS B and of the Bodleian MS was the foremost Christian scholar of the ninth century. Through his excellent translations of Greek and Syriac texts into Arabic he more than anyone else acquainted the Muslims with the achievements of classical science. He was himself an authority in the medical field and physician in ordinary to the ʿAbbāsid Caliph al-Mutawakkil (d. 861).

Ḥunain had founded a school of translators who worked according to his methods and whose translations he corrected.[1] One of the most prominent of his pupils was ʿĪsā b. ʿAlī who is mentioned as the third in the postscript.[2] He was physician in ordinary to the ʿAbbāsid Caliph al-Muʿtamid (d. 892), and a scholar of renown. He is well known as the author of the first Syriac-Arabic dictionary (Bar ʿAlī) for which he was able to use material which had been collected by his teacher Ḥunain himself.

Three outstanding Christian Arabic scholars, all very well known among Muslims, are connected through a group of MSS with the Arabic Diatessaron. First and foremost Abulfaraj b. aṭ-Ṭaiyib, of whom we know that he had made a translation of the Gospels from the Syriac into Arabic.[3] Marmardji published specimens of this translation and of other writings of his dealing with Christian matters[4] which show that he was an able stylist who could write very well classical Arabic. Marmardji rightly concluded that he cannot be the translator of the Arabic Diatessaron, the language of which is not very correct and certainly not classical. How can we explain his name being connected with this translation?

We have seen that the four MSS of this group of the Arabic Diatessaron go back to an original written in 1107. The preamble in the four MSS and the postscript in two of them were copied from the original, which was written at the request of a Muslim Governor to whom it had to be handed over. The Aulād al-ʿAssāl who prepared the copy were anxious to put it into a form which would make an impression on the Muslims. They tried to do this by giving the manuscript the external appearance of a copy of the Koran, and bestowed upon it a name customary

[1] See G. Bergsträsser, *Ḥunain Ibn Isḥāḳ und seine Schule*, Leiden 1913.

[2] *wahua min ajall talāmidhihi* 'and he belonged to the most prominent of his pupils', says Ibn Abī Uṣaibiʿa, vol. i, 203.

[3] Graf, *Geschichte* . . . vol. i, pp. 150 f.

[4] In the Introduction to his edition, pp. xciii–c. See D. S. Margoliouth's review of Marmardji's book in *JTS*, xxxviii, 1937, pp. 76 f.

for such a copy. Ibn al-ʿAssāl, the author of the second text, was given a number of epithets so that he might be regarded as a great scholar. They further enhanced the value of the Arabic Diatessaron by connecting it with the names of three outstanding Christian Arabic scholars who were held in high esteem among the Muslims. Thus Ibn aṭ-Ṭaiyib, the famous professor of medicine and devoted Christian priest, who was known as author of the commentary on the Gospels, and who had translated some of the Gospel from Syriac into Arabic, was mentioned as translator of the Syriac Diatessaron into Arabic, ʿĪsā b. ʿAlī, the well-known physician, the great authority on the Syriac language and outstanding pupil of the famous Ḥunain b. Isḥāḳ, was named as the copyist of the Syriac text from which the Arabic translation of the Syriac Diatessaron is supposed to have been made. The text handed over to the Muslims was to be supported by the greatest possibile authority. In reality none of these Christian Arabic scholars had anything to do with the Arabic Diatessaron.

This discussion of the MSS of the Arabic Diatessaron leads us to the following conclusions:

1. Ghazālī had based his polemic against certain doctrines of the Christians on an Arabic translation of the Gospels which at that time was used in the Coptic churches. This translation had been made from the Coptic text, and R. Chidiac proved that it is in the main identical with the text published later by Erpenius.[1] If the Copts in A.D. 1107 handed over to the Muslims, together with an answer to Ghazālī's polemic, a copy of the Arabic Diatessaron, they must have been convinced at the time that this text was more reliable than their own Arabic Gospels.

2. Although the Christian Arabic scholars mentioned in the preamble and postscript of the text had actually nothing to do with the Arabic Diatessaron, it is nevertheless beyond doubt that it was introduced into Egypt from Mesopotamia and that it was translated from Syriac into Arabic. The text presented to the Muslims must still have been in existence in Egypt at the beginning of the nineteenth century, when the MS now in the Bodleian Library was copied from it. It may yet come to light again.

[1] *Novum D. N. Jesu Christi Testamentum Arabice.* Ex Bibliotheca Leidensi. Edente Thoma Erpenius, Leidae 1616. See for Erpenius the excellent characterization given by Joh. Fück, *Die arabischen Studien in Europa vom 12. bis in den Anfang des 19. Jahrhunderts*, Leipzig 1944, pp. 143–57—Chidiac speaks of the text of the Gospels used by Ghazālī in chapter vii of his book *Les sources Evangeliques*, pp. 71–7. The investigation needs to be made on a broader basis. The Biblical quotations in *tiryāḳ al-ʿuḳūl* must also be investigated with care.

Until then the four MSS of the second form of text which we know must be used to help reconstruct the common original.

3. The two MSS of the first form go back to a 'very old' MS which was brought to Egypt from Antioch before 1200. We know that this text was copied several times in Egypt during the thirteenth and fourteenth centuries.

4. For about 900 years these two forms of text have not influenced each other. They must be accepted as two of the various forms of text which existed in the eleventh century. Both of them were brought to Egypt. There they were copied and in this way saved. All traces of other forms which may have existed have now been lost.

5. We cannot derive one of these forms from the other and cannot reconstruct an 'Urtext' of the Arabic Diatessaron from them. They must be dealt with separately. Ciasca's attempt to publish a mixed text from both these forms was a mistake.[1] Marmardji's attempt to create a 'new' text on the basis of these two forms by improving the Arabic and adapting it to the text of the Peshiṭta, which he supposed to be the Syriac original, shows that he had not any real understanding of the actual problems.

6. The value of the Arabic Diatessaron consists in the amount of help it gives for finding out readings of the Syriac Diatessaron as Tatian composed it. This is limited. The Syriac Diatessaron from which the Arabic translation was made already included alterations made in Tatian's work in order to make it conform with the Peshiṭta. In so far as the Arabic translation agrees with the Peshiṭta, it is of little value. But it is of great importance when it implies a Syriac text different from the Peshiṭta. Here we may find traces of the genuine text of Tatian. Such passages must be carefully picked out and investigated with the help of the Old Syriac Gospels on the one hand and the Peshiṭta on the other. They must be discussed in connection with all the other material of the Diatessaron at our disposal. The task is not easy. It cannot be done on the basis of a translation; the original texts must be investigated. This demands a sound linguistic equipment and a good grasp of the existing problems. Yet it is beyond doubt that in such a way a great service could be rendered to New Testament textual criticism.

[1] This was noticed by Hope W. Hogg in his translation of the Arabic Diatessaron (Ante-Nicene Christian Library, Additional Volume, Edinburgh 1897, p. 36 f.) and by Hjelt, *Die altsyrische Evangelienübersetung und Tatian's Diatessaron*, Leipzig 1901, p. 61.

APPENDIX I

Compare p. 39 supra.

NOVELLA 146 *FROM THE YEAR* 553

The Emperor Justinian to Aerobindus, the most honourable Praefectus Praetorio.

Preamble

The Jews, when they heard the Holy Scriptures, ought not to have clung to the mere letter, but should have turned their attention to the hidden prophecies which foretell the great God and Saviour of the human race, Jesus Christ. But although they have given themselves over to irrational explanations and have, to this day, gone astray from the true interpretation, when we heard they were divided among themselves we could not leave their differences unresolved. For from reports made to us we have learned that some hold to the Hebrew language and wish to use it alone for the reading of the Holy Scriptures, whereas others wish to use the Greek language as well, and in this matter they have long disagreed. Informed of this, we have found those more praiseworthy who wish to have the assistance of the Greek language for the reading of the Holy Scriptures [or, indeed, any language which, in relation to the place, is more suited to and better understood by the audience].

Chapter I

We therefore decree that, wherever there are Jews who so desire, the Holy Scriptures may be read in the synagogues in Greek [or in our mother tongue (that is in Latin) or in any other language which suits the place where the reading is given] so that the text may be understood by those present and they may live and act according to it. The Jewish interpreters (ἐξηγηταί) shall not be allowed to corrupt the Hebrew text on account of their being the only ones who understand it, relying, as they do, on the ignorance of the people who do not notice the corruption. Those, however, who read in Greek are to use the Septuagint, the most accurate translation of all, which is to be preferred especially because of the miracle which occurred when it was made, the translators, working only in pairs and in different places, producing one and the same text.

1. Who, moreover can fail to marvel when he considers that these translators, who lived a long time before the saving appearance of our great God and Saviour Jesus Christ, foresaw it and, full of the spirit of prophecy, translated the Holy Scriptures? All shall therefore prefer this translation to others. But, in order that we may not seem to deny the Jews the other versions, we give them permission to use, if they so wish, the translation of Aquila, although the author is of an alien race and his translation shows not inconsiderable differences from that of the Septuagint.

2. But we strictly forbid what they call Deuterosis, as it is neither included in the Holy Scriptures nor transmitted of old through the Prophets, but is an invention of men who spoke merely with earthly wisdom and were not divinely inspired. They shall read the holy words themselves, opening the Holy Scriptures with their own hands, and hiding nothing of what is written by adding worthless and vain phrases of their own which are not contained in the text but only invented in order to corrupt the pure text. Since this permission has been granted by us, those who use the Greek [and other languages] shall neither be punished nor hindered by anyone. Nor shall those called Archipherekitae or elders or teachers be entitled to prevent this by cunning or by curse, unless they wish to be made wise by corporal punishment and to forfeit their property to us who will and order the better course and the one more pleasing to God.

Chapter II

But if any of them dare introduce godless and vain teachings denying the Resurrection, the Last Judgment, or that the angels are the work and creation of God, it is our will that he shall be expelled from every place and shall not be allowed to utter such blasphemous language devoid of the knowledge of God. For those who dare say such things shall be subjected to the most severe penalties so that we may thereby purge the Jewish people of the error thus introduced.

Chapter III

We wish to admonish those who hear the Holy Scriptures read in one language or the other to beware of the wickedness of their interpreters; they should not cling to the letter, but penetrate into the matter itself and grasp the truly divine sense so that they may come to know what is better, and finally cease to err and sin in regard to the most essential thing: we mean hope in God. For this is the reason why we have given them the optional use of (the Greek) [every] language for the reading of the Holy Scriptures, so that in future all, one after another, may by acquiring knowledge become more receptive of what is better. For everyone will agree that a man who has been brought up in the Holy Scriptures and has little left in him needing correction will be much more able to distinguish and choose what is better than one who knows nothing of Scripture but only clings to the name of divine service, cleaving to it as to a holy anchor and believing to be divine doctrine what in reality must be termed sheer heresy.

Epilogue

This our will and what is decreed by the present sacred law is not only to be observed by your Highness and those under you but by everyone who holds the same office. Under no circumstances shall he permit the Jews to undertake anything against it; he shall rather subject those who dare to resist it or hinder it in any way to corporal punishment first, then force them to live in exile and confiscate their property, so that they may not act disrespectfully against God and the Emperor. He shall also send orders to the provincial prefects, commanding them to obey our law and to publish it in every town when they have studied it and have realized that everybody must necessarily observe it for fear of arousing our displeasure.

Given at Constantinople, 13th February, in the 26th year of the reign of the Emperor Justinian, in the 12th of the consulate of Basilius, V.CL. (=AD 553).

Note: The above translation of Justinian's Novella was made jointly by Professor Fritz Schulz (of the Law-Faculty of Bonn and Berlin) and myself. Schulz realized that originally the Law dealt, apart from the Hebrew language, only with the Greek. The laws of Justinian were first introduced in Italy one year after the decree, in AD 554, and the sentences relating to other languages, particularly Latin, were inserted later. These parts are included in square brackets. One word was left out after the interpolations, and this is included in round brackets.

APPENDIX II

Compare p. 155 *supra*

THE PRONUNCIATION OF HEBREW BY THE SAMARITANS

as recorded at Nāblus in 1917 by HELLMUT RITTER *and* ARTHUR SCHAADE

Edited by A. MURTONEN

Gn i 1–23. This section is recorded by H. Ritter. Its most important special characteristics compared with the texts recorded by Schaade are the very scanty use of ʾ especially at the beginning of words, its use of ʿ even at the end of many words, and its use of the acute accent even for long vowels, where Schaade practically everywhere has the circumflex accent. The latter is in accordance with the observations of the present writer and also of all other students of this dialect with whom I have been in contact. It may be that Ritter intended to indicate only the main stress in general, not differentiated into species. Regarding the ʿ at the end of words, Ritter writes to me that he may have been influenced by the written text. I have, nevertheless, always retained it in the text, since the matter is not quite certain, and the use of this sound varies strongly between different persons. There are people who hardly pronounce it at all, while others utter it fairly regularly at the beginning of words (even in place of a written ʾ occasionally), some people even in the middle of words, curiously merged with the vowel. The same variation of frequency in the use of ʾ may also be observed, even in recitation by one and the same person at different times. These phenomena will be dealt with in greater detail in a grammar of the dialect which will follow in due course. I have placed accents upon monosyllabic words where they seem to be required by the rhythm; Ritter has not marked the accentuation of these words, except where they have another similar one as an enclitic (e.g. *kī́-ṭŏb*). In the division of sentences into words I have followed the normal Hebrew pattern, except in the case of the preposition אל, which I have attached to the word next following, since it is pronounced just like ל, with which it seems to be completely interchangeable in this dialect. Monosyllabic words which can with certainty be recognized as proclitics or enclitics are connected with their main words by means of a hyphen. Other punctuation marks come from Ritter's pen, whose original manuscript I have seen and copied, but not used when redacting the final text.

Gn i 1 Bā̀rā́šit bā́rā̆ ǣ̀lū́wĕm it eššā́mem wit ā́reṣ. 2 wā́reṣ ǣ̀jjā́tā̆
tḗʼū ubḗʼū. wā́šek al fā́ni tū́m urū ǣ̀lū́wem emrā̀ǣ́fat ʿal fā́ni émmim.
3 ujā̀ṓmer ǣ̀lū́wem jā́ʼī ŏr wejā́ʼī ŏr. 4 ujǣ́ræ ǣ̀lū́wem it ā́or kí-ṭŏb

ujébdel ǽlūwem bin ấor ubin ấšek. 5 wjíḳra ǽlūwem lấor jốm
wlấšek ḳấra líle ujấ'i ǽræb ujấ'i bǽḳær jōm ấd.
6 ujàốmer ǽlūwem jấ'i árḳiʿ éftok émmim ujấ'i mébdil bin mem
ʿǽl-mim. 7 wījāš ǽlūwem it árḳiʿ ujébdel bin émmim, ǽšar mittất
lárḳiʿ, ubin émmim ǽšar míjel lấrḳiʿ (?) wjấ'i kĕn. 8 wjíḳra ǽlūwem
lấrḳiʿ šấmem wjấ'ī ǽræb wjấ'i bǽḳær jōm šǽni.
9 wjà'ốmer ǽlūwem jiḳḳấbu émmim mittất eššấmim ʿal mấḳom
ấd turrū́'i ejjabbấša wjấ'i kĕn. 10 ujíḳra ǽlūwem eljabbấša ấriṣ (-eṣ)
welmáḳwa émmim ḳấrā jámmim. ujǽræ ǽlūwem kí-ṭŏb. 11 ujàốmer ǽlūwem tǽdǽšī áreṣ dǽšæ ǽšæb mæzríʿ zǽræʿ bus-fíri ʿấšī fíri
elmínu ǽšar zèrấ'u bū ʿal ấriṣ wjấ'ī kĕn. 12 tū́ṣī áreṣ dǽša ǽšæb
mezrí zǽræ alminǽ'ū̆. wis ʿấši (?) fíri ǽšar zǽrấu bū́ elminǽ'ū̆.
wjǽræ ǽlūwem kí-ṭob. 13 wejấ'ī ǽræb wjấ'ī bǽḳær jōm šǽlíši.
14 wjà'ốmer ǽlūwem jấ'i màū́rot bǽrḳiʿ eššấmim. lấ'ær al ấreṣ
ulấbdil bin éjjom ubin ellíle. 15 wấjū lū́tot welmuwấdim weljấmem
šấnem. wấjū elmàốrot bérḳiʿ eššấmem lấ'ær al ấreṣ. wjấ'i ken.
16 wjāš ǽlūwem it šǽni ammà'ū́rot eggàdélem, it ammấ'or eggấdol
elmemšấlat éjjom. wit ammấ'or eḳḳấtan elmemšấlet ellíle wit kùkấ-
bim. 17 jítten ŏtímma ǽlūwem bérḳiʿ eššấmem lấ'er al ấreṣ.
18 lǽmšal béjjom ubellíle lấbdil bin ấ'or ubin ấšek wjǽræ ǽlūwem
kí-ṭŏb. 19 wjấ'i ǽræb wejấ'i bǽḳær jōm rǽbiʿ.
20 wejàốmer ǽlūwem išrǽšu émmim šǽræṣ nấfiš ʿájja uf-iấfæf
al ấreṣ ʿal fấni érḳiʿ eššấmem. 21 wjíbra ǽlūwem it attànímem
eggādélim wít-ḳal nấfiš ʿájja arrấmšæt ǽšar šàrấsu émmem elmíni-
jímmæ wít-ḳal ōf ḳấnif elminḗ'u wjǽræ ǽlūwem kí-ṭob. 22 wejǽ-
bǽrræk ŏtímma ǽlūwem límur fǽrū umælấ'ū it émmem bejjámmem
wa'ốf jírbi bấreṣ. 23 wejấ'i ǽræb wejấ'i bǽḳær jōm æmíši.

Gn i 24 sqq. The texts recorded by A. Schaade begin here and continue to the end. My principles of redaction are the same as in the preceding section. The punctuation marks come from Schaade, except that the accentuation is added where the rhythm requires it and no doubt can arise regarding the stressed syllables and the quality of the stress. When I was preparing the text, Schaade's manuscript was available to me. The text is based upon Schaade's *original* notes. The mark for the circumflex accent is ^ (used also by S. along with ^̄).

24 wjā'ômer ẹlûwėm tûṣi ârėṣ nâfėš ʿájja ẹlmîna bîmmæ wrǣmæš
wǽjjæt ârėṣ elmîna wjā'ī-kĕ́n. 25 wjāš ẹlûwėm it ʿájjat ârėṣ elmîna
wėt ebbêma elmîna wít-kal rǣmæš adâma elmīnê'u wjệrẹ ælûwėm
kî-ṭob. 26 wjā'ômer ælûwem nǣši âdam afṣālamânu kādệmutânū
wjírdū efdêkėt ǽjjam wbūf eššâmim ubebbîmmæ wéfkæl ârėṣ wéfkæl
errǣmėš errûmėš ʿal âreṣ. 27 wjíbrā ælûwėm it âdam afṣālâmu

afṣâlam ǣlûwem bâra ûtu zākārunaḳâba bârā ōtímmæ. 28 wjǣbǽrrėk ōtímma ǣlûwem wjā'ômær læ̂mma ǣlûwem fæ̂rū wræ̂bū wmǣlâ'u
ėt ârėṣ wkæ̂bašûæh wræ̂dū æfdêkėt ájjām ubūf eššâmim wéfkel
'âjja errâmšėt 'al ârėṣ. 29 wjā'ômẹr ǣlûwėm ínnā nātáttī lākímma
it-kal-æ̂šėb zarî zæ̂ra æ̂šar 'al fânī kal âreṣ wėt-kal-îṣ æ̂šar bū fîri iṣ
zārî zæ̂ra lākímma jæ̂jji lākâlẹh. 30 wálkæl 'ájjat ârėṣ wálkæl ōf
eššâmim wálkæl ærræ̂mėš 'al ârėṣ æ̂šar bū nâfeš 'ájja ét-kæl jæ̂rėḳ
æ̂šėb lākâlæh wjā'i-kén. 31 wjæ̂ræ ǣlûwėm ét-kæl æ̂šar 'âšæh
wæ̂nnah ṭob mæ̂'od. wjâ'ī æ̂rėb wjâ'ī bæ̂ḳar jom ėššíšši.

ii 1 wjikẹ́llu eššâmėm wârėṣ wkæl ṣâbæ'ímmę. 2 wjǣkǽllæ
ǣlûwėm bǽjjom eššíšši mālâktu æ̂šar 'âšah wjíšbat bǽjjom æššǣbî
míkkæl mālâktu æ̂šar 'âšah. 3 wjǣbǽrrėk ǣlûwėm ét-jom æššǣbî
wjiḳẹ́ddiš ôtu kî-bu šâbat míkkæl mālâktu æ̂šar bârā ǣlûwėm lâššut.

4 ílla tôldat eššâmim wârėṣ bǣbbâra'ímmę ébbjom 'ášjot šæ̂mah
ǣlûwėm šâmėm wâreṣ. 5 wkæl-šī eššâdī ṭæ̂rėm jæ̂ji bârėṣ kæl
æ̂šėb ėššâdī ṭæ̂rėm jaṣmæh kī lā ámṭær šæ̂mah ǣlûwėm 'al ârėṣ wâdam
īn læ̂bbad ėt ādâma. 6 wėd jæ̂lli mæn ârėṣ wâšḳa ét-kæl fânī
ādâma. 7 wjâṣar šæ̂mah ǣlûwėm . . . 'âfar mæn ādâma wjébbah
bébbuh nāšæ̂mat 'ájjim wjâ'ī âdam elnâfiš 'ájja.

8 wjíṭṭa šệmah ǣlûwėm gan bæ̂dėn miḳḳệdem wjâšem šẹ́mma it
âdam æ̂šar jâṣar. 9 wjaṣmîh šệmah ǣlûwėm mæn ādâmah ít-kæl
iṣ næ̂mmad elmārî wṭob elmâkal wiṣ 'âjjim éftok éggan wiṣ eddât
ṭob wrâ^{h}. 10 wnâr jâṣa mījệden lâšḳot it éggan wmiššẹ́mmah
jibárrad wẹ́jjah lẹrbâ^{h} râšim. 11 šam ā'æ̂d fîšun ū-ėssûbab ít-kæl
ârėṣ ābbîla æ̂šar šẹ́mmah ẹzzâb. 12 wzâb ârėṣ ā'î ṭob mệ'od
wšẹ́mma abbádla wâben eššâm. 13 wšem ennâr eššênī gîjon
ū-ėssûbab ít-kæl ârėṣ kuš. 14 wšemm ennâr eššǣlîšī ẹddæ̂ḳḳėl ū
âlek ḳídmat âšur. wannâr erræ̂bī ū fârat.

15 wjíḳḳa^{h} šệmah ǣlûwem it âdam wjinnījệ'u éfgan ệden. 16 wjẹ̄-
ṣâbę šệmah ǣlûwėm 'al âdam lîmor: míkkæl iṣ éggan âkal tā'ôkėl.
17 wmîṣ ėddât ṭob wrâ lā tā'ôkėl mimmínnu kī ébjom ẹ́klak mimmínnu mot tæ̂mot.

18 wjā'ômẹr šæ̂mā^{h} ǣlûwėm lâ-ṭůb ájjůt âdam ẹlbǽddu æ̂šji lū
'âzar kānígdu. 19 wjâṣar šệma^{h} ǣlûwėm ūd mẹn ādâma ít-kæl
'ájjat ėššâdī wít-kæl ū̆f ėššâmim wjîbi ẹlâdam ẹlrâ'ot mā-jíḳrā lû^{h}
wkæl æ̂šar jíḳrā lûh âdam nâfėš 'ájja ū šệmu. 20 wjíḳrā 'âdam
šệmot 'ẹ́lkæl ebbîmma ulûf ėššâmim wẹ́lkæl 'ájjat ėššâdī lâdam lā-
mâṣa 'āzar kānígdu.

21 wjẹ́bbæl šæ̂ma^{h} ǣlûwem tẹrdîmmæ^{h} 'al âdam wjîšan wjíḳḳa^{h}
'âd miṣṣīlā'ûto wjésgir bâšar tāttîjję. 22 wjíbni šæ̂ma^{h} ǣlûwėm it
aṣṣîlę æ̂šar læ̂ḳa^{h} mẹn âdam líššẹ̄ wjībîjjâh ælâdam. 23 wjā'ômẹr

âdam zǽ'ot ebbâm ʿâṣam mījjāṣâmī wbâšar mibbāšârī ęlzǽ'ot jiḳḳârī
íššæ kī mîša lǣḳîjjâh zǽ'ot. 24 ʿál-kęn jázzab īš it ābîjju wit ímmu
dâbiḳ bíštu wę̂jja miššęnījjímma ęlbâšar ʿâd. 25 wjâjju šęnijjímma
ʿārę̂mėm âdam wíštu wlā jìtbeššâšu.

iii 1 wennâš ájja ʿârum míkkæl ʿájjat eššâdī ǣšar ʿâša šǣma^{h}
ǣlûwėm wjā'ûmęr ęlā'íšša éf-ki âmar ǣlûwėm lā tā'ūkęlū míkkæl iṣ
éggan. 2 wtā'ômęr ā'íšša ęlennǣš miffîri iṣ éggan nā'ôkel. 3 wmif-
fîri ā'íṣ ézzę ǣšar éftok éggan âmar ǣlûwėm lā tā'ōkęlu mimmínnu wlā tiggâ'u bū fęn tǣmûtun. 4 wjā'ômęr ennâš ælā'íšša:
lâ-mot tǣmûtun. 5 kī jâda ǣlûwėm kī ébjom æklākímma mimmínnu wnę̂fāḳâ'ū īnīkímma wā'ītímma kā'ælûwėm jādâ'ī ṭob wrâ.
6 wtę̂rę ā'íšša kî-ṭob ā'îṣ ęlmâkal wkī tâwa ū lînim wnǣmmad ā'îṣ
lâškęl wtíḳḳa^{h} miffîro wtā'ôkęl wtítten gam lîša ímma wjā'ōkǣlu.
7 wtǣfāḳâna înī šęnījjímma wjādâ'ū kī ʿārę̂mim ímma wjitfâru ʿâlī
tîna wjâššu lǣmma āgę̂rot. 8 wjišmâʿu ít-ḳol šę̂ma^{h} ǣlûwėm mǣtâllak
bę̂ggan ęlrǣbę ǣjjom wjētâba âdam wíštu miffânī šǣma^{h} ǣlûwėm
éftok iṣ éggan. 9 wjíḳra šǣma^{h} ǣlûwėm ælâdam wjā'ômęr lū:
'îka? 10 wjā'ômęr: it ḳôlak šāmâtī béggan wā'îra kī ʿârom ānâkī
wā'íbba. 11 wjā'ômer: mīn ę̂ggėd lak kī ʿârom átta? âmęn
ā'îṣ ǣšar ṣābîtęk ęlbíltī âkal mimmínnu ākálta? 12 wjā'ômęr
âdam: ā'íšša ǣšar nātátta 'immâdī 'ī nētînæ lī męn ā'îṣ wę̄'ûkęl.
13 wjā'ûmær šę̂ma^{h} ǣlûwem lā'íšša: mā-zǽ'ot ʿašîti? wtā'ômęr ā'íšša:
ęnnâš eššījjâni wę̄'ûkęl.

14 wjā'ômęr šę̂ma^{h} ǣlûwėm ęlennâš: kī ʿăšîta zę̂'ot, ʿârur átta
míkkæl ebbîma umíkkæl ʿájjat ęššâdī. ʿal gā'ônak tę̂lak wâfar tā'ôkęl
kæl jâmī ʿájjik. 15 wījjâbę ʿâšėt bînak wbin ā'íšša wbin zęrâk wbin
zęrâ^{h}. ū jęšûfak rę̂'oš wátta tęšūfínnu ǣḳib. 16 węlā'íšša âmar:
ǽrbī ęróbbī 'āṣābûnėk węrrījjûnėk bāṣâbun tęlâdī bânim welîšėk
tǣšūḳâtėk ū jímšal bęk.

17 wlâdam âmar: kī šāmâtta ę̂lḳol íštak tā'ôkęl męn ā'îṣ ǣšar
ṣābîtek lîmor lā tā'ôkęl mimmínnu ʿārûra ādâma bębûrak bāṣâbon
tā'ōkęlínna kęl jâmī ʿájjęk. 18 wḳoṣ wdárdar taṣmî lak wākálta it
ǣšęb eššâdī. 19 efzât ębbęk tā'ôkel lę̂m ʿad šûbak 'ęlādâma kī
mimmínna lęḳîta kī ʿâfar átta węl ʿāfârak tęšub. 20 wjíḳra âdam
šęm íšto 'ábba kī 'î 'ajjâta ęm-kal-ʿáj. 21 wjāš šę̂ma^{h} ǣlûwėm
lâdam wlíšto kittânot ûr wjęlbīšímma. 22 wjā'ômęr šǣma^{h}
ǣlûwėm: ęn 'âdam 'ájja kād mimmínnu aldât ṭob wrâ wâtta fęn
jęšǽlla jędu lęḳa gæm mīṣ ʿâjjim wâkal wī lûlam. 23 wjęšǽllā'ę̄'u
šęma ǣlûwėm miggan-ę̂den lębbad it ādâma ǣšar lęḳī miššęmma.
24 wjēgęrrėš it âdam wjéšken miḳḳędėm ęlgan ę̂den it ekkęrûbim
wít-lāt 'ârib emmētāfę̂kėt líšmar it dęrek iṣ ʿâjjim.

iv 1 wâdam jâda it 'ábba 'íštu wtâr wtâlad ít-ḳin wtā'ômęr ḳānîti
'îš ęt šęma^{h}. 2 wtâṣif lęllêdėt it 'â'o it ębel wjâ'ī ębėl râ'ī ṣę'on wḳen
ǽjja ʿâbed 'ādâma. 3 wjâ'i míḳḳeṣ jâmim wjîbi ḳėn miffîri ādâma
mānâh elšęma^{h}. 4 wębel îbi gæm 'ū mibbākûrot ṣę'ûnu wmìjjēlâ-
bijjínna wjâša šęma^{h} ęl'ębel węlmānâttu. 5 węlḳėn węlmānâttu lâ
šâ wjâr ęlḳėn mę'od wjāfâlu fânu. 6 wjā'ômęr šęma ęlḳėn lęma
'ârā lak wlęma nāfâlu fânėk. 7 ālû 'ęm tîṭib šât wámlā tîṭib ęlfęta
'ętât rêbaṣ wîlėk tęšūḳâttu wátta tímšal bū. 8 wjā'ômęr ḳėn ęl'ębel
'â'o: nęlâka eššâdī wjâ'ī bājūtímma beššâdī wjâḳam ḳėn ęl'ębel 'â'o
wjârāgę'u.
9 wjā'ômęr šęma^{h} ęlḳėn: 'ájje 'ębel ʿâjak? wjā'ômęr: lā jādâtti
āšômęr ʿâ'ī 'ānâkī? 10 wjā'ômęr: mā ʿašîtta? ḳol dam ʿâjak ṣâ'iḳ
îli męn ādâma. 11 wâtta ʿârur átta męn ādâma ǽšar fāṣâtta it
fîjjah ęlḳêt ít-dam ʿâjak mījjędak. 12 kī tębad it ādâma lā tûsif tet
kûwwah lak nâ wnęd tęjji bârėṣ. 13 wjā'ômęr ḳėn ęlšǽma^{h}: gâdol
ônī minnâšę. 14 ęn gęrrísta ûtī ęjjom mîjjal fânī ādâma umiffânėk
issâtir wā'ìtī nâ wnęd bârėṣ wêjja kal māṣâ'ī jārāgânī. 15 wjā'ômer
lū šǽma^{h}: ęlkėn kæl 'âreg ḳėn šibbūwātâ'ėm jíḳḳam wjâšem šęma^{h}
ęlḳėn 'ût ęlbílti ękkot 'ûtu kæl māṣâ'u. 16 wjíṣṣā ḳėn męn fânī
šęma^{h} wjâšab bârėṣ nęd ḳídmat 'ęden.
vi 9 'ílla tôldat nâ^{h}: nā 'îš ṣâdiḳ tâmim 'ájja 'efdūrûto 'ét-'ā'ælûwėm ęttâllak nā^{h}. 10 wjûlėd nā šęlâša bânim ít-šėm wit ʿâm wit
jęfėt. 11 wtíššat 'ârėṣ ęlfânī 'ā'ælûwėm. timmâlī 'âreṣ 'âmės.
12 wjęrę ælûwėm it 'âreṣ węnna niššâta kī ʿāšît kæl bâšar it dírku ʿal
ârėṣ.
13 wjā'ômęr æl. ǽl-nā: ḳęṣ kæl bâšar bā alfânī kī mālâ ârėṣ âmės
miffânījjímmæ winnânī māšītímma ėt ârėṣ. 14 ęšī lak tîbat îṣī gâ-
far ḳínnėm tęš^{j}ī it ėttîbę wkāfárta ûta míbbit mîjoṣ efkâfar. 15 wzę
ǽšar tǽš^{j}ī 'ûta šęlaš-mâ'ot ámma ârek ėttîbę wǽmíššėm ámma
rǽbbah šǽlâšėm ámma ḳūmâta^{h}. 16 ṣâr tǽšji lėttîbah walámma
tęḳęllínnah milmâlah fętah ėttîba afṣíddah tâšim ṭęṭṭim šǽnim
wšǽlīšâ'ėm tǽšji.
17 wânī 'innâni mîbī it emmębbol męm ʿal ârėṣ lāšît kæl bâšar
'ǽšar bū-rû ʿájjim mittęt ėššâmim kæl ǽšar bârėṣ jígbæ. 18 wīḳímtī
it bērîtī 'íttak wbâtta ælęttîba átta wbânęk wíštak wínši bânęk íttak.
19 wmíkkæl ʿâjja míkkęl abbâšar šênim míkkæl tîbī ælættîba lîjjot
ittak zâkār unāḳâba. 20 węjja mæn ā'ôf ęlmīnê'u wmæn ębbîma
elmînæh wmíkkæl ǽšar ręmėš ʿal ādâma elmīnījjímma šênim míkkæl
jābâ'ū îlėk lîjjût. 21 wátta ḳâ-lak míkkal mâkal ǽšar 'ījjâkėl
wāsífta 'îlėk wêjja lak wlęmma lākâlęh. 22 wjâš nā^{h} kâkal ǽšar
ṣâbæ ûtu æl. kėn ʿâša^{h}.

vii 1 wjā’ômęr ’æl. ǽlnā^{h}: bā-’átta wkel bîtak ęlettîba^{h} kī ûtak
rā’îtī ṣâdiḳ ælfânī béddur ę́zzė. 2 míkkal ebbîma^{h} aṭṭāę̂rę^{h} tíḳḳā lák
šābâ^{h} šābâ^{h} zâkār unāḳâba^{h} wmæn ebbîma^{h} ’ǽšar lā ṭā’ę̂ra^{h} ’ī šênim
šênim zâkar unāḳâba^{h}. 3 wgæm mījjûf eššâmim aṭṭâ’or šābǽ^{h}
šābǽ^{h} zâkār unāḳâba^{h} lījjůt zę̂ra^{h} ‘al fânī kæl ârėṣ. 4 kī lējjâmim ūd
šābâ^{h} ānâkī mánṭir ‘al ârėṣ ęrbîm jom węrbîm lîle wmǽ’îtī ít-kæl
æjjǽḳum ǽšar ‘ašîtī mîjjal fâni ādâma. 5 wjâš nā^{h} kâkal ǽšar
ṣābê’u šę̂ma^{h}.
6 wnâ^{h} bęn šęš mâ’ot šę̂na^{h} węmmǽbbol ’ájja mėm ‘al ’ârėṣ.
7 wjâba^{h} nā^{h} wíštu wínši bâno íttu ęlęttîbę miffânī mī ęmmǽbbol.
8 męn ębbîmæ aṭṭā’ę̂rę wmęn ębbîmæ ǽšar īnínna ṭā’ę̂rę^{h} wmęn
’ā’ôf wmíkkæl ǽšar rę̂mėš ‘al ādâma. 9 šę̂nim šę̂nim bâ’u ‘ál-nā^{h}
ęlėttîbę^{h} zâkār unāḳâba^{h} kā’ǽšar ṣâbæ šǽma^{h} ít-nā^{h}.
10 wjâ’ī ęlšābǽt ajjâmim wmî æmmǽbbol ájju ‘al ’ârėṣ. 11 ’æf-
šę̂nat ’ę́ššaš mâ’ot šę̂na^{h} léjjī nā^{h} bâdėš eššę̂ni ęfšābǽ^{h} ‘âšar jom
lâdėš bǽjjom ę́zzė nibbāḳâ’u kǽl-mājânot tûm rábba^{h} wę̄rábbot
aššâmim niffattâ’u. 12 wjâ’ī ęggâšam ‘al ârėṣ ęrbîm jom węrbîm
lîlę. 13 bâṣam ǽjjom ę́zzė bâ nâ^{h} šęm ’âm wję̂fėt bâni nā^{h} wíššat
nâ^{h} šǽlâšat ínšī bâno ǽtímma ęlėttîba^{h}. 14 ímma wkal ‘âjja
ęlmîna^{h} wkęl ęrrǽmeš ęrrûmėš ‘al ’ârėṣ ęlmīnę̂’u kæl ā’ôf ęlmīnê’u
kæl ṣíbbor kæl kânęf. 15 jābâ’u ǽlnā^{h} ælęttîba^{h} šênim šênim
míkkæl bâšar ’ǽšar bû-rū ‘ájjim. 16 wabbâ’im zâkār unāḳâba^{h}
zâkār unāḳâba^{h} míkkal bâšar bâ’u kā’ǽšar ṣābā-’ûtu ǽl. wję́sgir
šǽma^{h} bę̂ddu. 17 wjâ’ī ęmmę́bbol ęrbîm jom ‘al ârėṣ wjírbū
émmim wjiššâ’u it ėttîbæ^{h} wtâram mîjjal ârėṣ. 18 wjiggabbâru émmim wjírbū mę̂’od ‘al ârėṣ wtâlak ęttîba^{h} ‘al fânī ę́mmim. 19 wę́m-
mim gēbę̂ru mę̂’od mę̂’od ‘al ârėṣ wjēkéssū kæl ’ârėm eggābǽ’im
ǽšar tę̂t kæl ęššâmim. 20 ‘ámmėš ‘āšâra^{h} ámma^{h} milmǽla^{h} gēbę̂ru
émmim wjīkéssu ’ârim. 21 wjígbā kæl bâšar ęrrǽmėš ‘al ârėṣ
būf ubėbbîma^{h} ubâjja^{h} wę́fkal ęššę̂rėṣ ėššûrėṣ ‘al ârėṣ wkæl âdam.
22 kæl ǽšar nāšę̂mat rū ‘ájjim bę́bbo míkkal ǽšar bārę̂ba^{h} mę̂tu.
23 wjimmî^{h} ít-kal ajję̂ḳum ǽšar ‘al fânī ādâma mījjâdam ‘ad bîmma^{h}
‘ad rǽmėš ‘ad ūf ęššâmim wjimmûh męn ârėṣ wjiššâr ę́k-nah wǽšar
íttu bėttîba^{h}. 24 wjiggabbâru émmim ‘al ârėṣ ǽmíššėm wmât jom.
viii 1 wję̄zâkar ǽl. ít-nā^{h} wít-kæl ‘âjja wít-kæl ebbîmma^{h} ǽšar
íttu bėttîba^{h} wjâbbir ǽl. rū$^{(h)}$ ‘al ârėṣ wjiššâku émmim. 2 wissęk-
kâru mājjânot tûm wērábbot ėššâmim wję̄ḳę́lla ęggâšam męn ęššâmim.
3 wjāšâbu émmim mîjjal ârėṣ ’alâku wšâbu wjāsâru émmim míḳḳėṣ
ǽmíššėm mât jom. 4 wténna^{h} ėttîba bâdėš eššēbî efšābǽ^{h} ‘âšar
jom lâdėš ‘al ’ârī ārârat. 5 wémmim ’ájju ālâku wāsâru ‘ad âdėš
ā’ę̄šîrī bā’ę̄šîrī bǽd lâdėš nirrâ’ū râšī ’ârėm.

6 wjâ'ī míḳḳėṣ 'ęrbîm jom wjíftaʰ nāʰ it 'âlon ėttîba ǽšar ʿâša.
7 wję̄šǽlla it ʿârėb wjíṣṣā jâṣa wšęb ʿad ję̄bę̂šat émmim mîjjal 'ârėṣ.
8 wję̄šǽlla it ajjābânæʰ mījjíttu ęlrâ'ot āḳâlu émmim mîjjal fânī
ādâma. 9 lā māṣâ ajjābânaʰ mānû ę́lkaf ríglaʰ wtâšab îlo ęlėttîbaʰ
kî-mim ʿal fânī kæl ârėṣ wję̄šǽllaʰ it ję̂du wjiḳḳâh wjîbī 'ûtah îlu
'ęlėttîbaʰ. 10 wjâ'ęl 'ūd šābât jâmem ā'ę̂rėm wjâsef šǽllaʰ it ajjābânaʰ męn ettîbaʰ. 11 tābā-'îlo ajjābânaʰ lēt 'êrib wę̂nnaʰ ʿâlī zit
ṭârėf bāfîjjaʰ wjâdā nāʰ kī ḳâlu émmim mîjjal ârėṣ. 12 wjâ'ęl ūd
šābǣt jâmim ā'ę̂rėm wję̄šǽllaʰ it ajjābânaʰ wlā jāṣę̂faʰ šûbaʰ îlo ūd.
13 wjâ'ī bǣt šėš mâ'ot šę̂na barrā'îšůn bǽd lâdėš ārâbu émmim
mîjjal ârėṣ wjîsir nāʰ it mēkéssī ėttîbaʰ wję̂rę wę̂nnaʰ ārâbu fânī
ādâma. 14 wbâdėš eššênī efšābǣʰ wíšrim jom lâdėš ję̄bę̂ša ârėṣ.
15 wję̄débbėr ǣl. ǽlnāʰ lîmor. 16 ṣâ męn ittîbaʰ átta wíštak
wbânėk wínšī bânėk íttak. 17 wkæl ʿâjjaʰ ǽšar íttak míkkal bâšar
bûf wbębbîmmaʰ wę́fkæl ęrrę̂mėš ęrrûmėš ʿal 'ârėṣ ûsī íttak šę̄rêṣu
bârėṣ wfę̂ru wrę̂bu ʿal ârėṣ. 18 wjíṣṣa nāʰ wbâno wíštu wínši bâno
íttu. 19 wkæl ʿâjja wkæl ā'ôf wkæl ęrrǽmėš ęrrûmėš ʿal ârėṣ
ęlmęšfûttījjímmæ jāṣâ'u męn ėttîba. 20 wjíbni nāʰ mę́zbæʰ
ęlšę̂maʰ wjíḳḳaʰ míkkæl ębbîmmaʰ aṭṭā'ę̂rąʰ wmíkkæl ā'ôf aṭṭâ'or
wjâllī ʿâlot bęmmę́zbæʰ. 21 wjārîʰ šę̂maʰ ít-rī ennîjjaʰ. wjā'ômęr
šǽmaʰ ęllíbbu lā ûsif ūd ęlḳǽllėl it ādâma bę̂bor âdam kī ję̂ṣir leb
âdam rā min nǽro wlā ûsif ūd lâkot ìt-kal-ʿáj kā'ǽšar ʿašîti. 22 ʿád-
kæl jâmi ârėṣ zę̂ra wḳâṣir ḳur wâm ḳėṣ wírrėf jûmam wlîla lā jišbâtu.
ix 1 wję̄bę́rrik ǣl. ít-nāʰ wit bâno wjā'ômęr lę̂mmaʰ fę̂ru wrę̂bu
wmę̄lâ'u it ârėṣ. 2 wmārākkímma wātatkímma ję̂jji ʿál-kal ʿájjat
ârėṣ wę́l-kæl ūf ęššâmim wę́fkal ǽšar tę́rmėš ādâma wę́fkal dêgī
ájjam ébbjėdkímma nàtattîjju. 3 kæl rǽmėš ǽšar 'ū ʿaj lākímma
ję̂jji lākâlaʰ kājêrėḳ ʿę̂šėb nātáttī lākímma it ę́kkal. 4 ęk bâšar
ębnę́fšu dę́mmu lā tā'ūkę̂lu. 5 wít damkímma ęlnęfšū̀tīkímma
ídraš mîjjęd kæl ʿaj idrāšínnu mîjjęd âdam mîjjęd 'îš wâ'o ídraš it
nâfėš 'âdam. 6 šǽfėk dam 'âdam bâdam dę́mmu jiššâfik kī afṣâlam
ǣl. ʿâšaʰ it âdam. 7 węttímma fę̂ru wrę̂bu šę̄rę̂ṣu bârėṣ wrę̂bu baʰ.
xi 1 wjâ'ī kal ârėṣ éšfāʰ ʿāt wdę̄bârėm ʿâdėm. 2 wjâ'ī ebnâsā'ímma miḳḳę̂dėm wjimṣâ'u bāḳâʰ bârėṣ šinnîjjar wjāšâbu šę́mmaʰ.
3 wjà'ūmę̂ru 'īš 'ęlrę̂'u âbaʰ nilbânaʰ líbnim wnišrâfaʰ ęlšērîfaʰ wtâ'ī
lǽmma ęllíbnaʰ lâbėn wa'îmar 'ájja lǽmma lîmar. 4 wjà'ūmę̂ru
âbaʰ níbniʰ lânu 'īr wmę́gdal wrę̄'ûšu bęššâmim wnę̂šji lânu šêm
fęn nâfuṣ ʿal fânī kæl ârėṣ. 5 wjârad šǽmaʰ ęlrâ'ot it ā'îr wit
ęmmę́gdal ǽšar bânu bânī âdam. 6 wjā'ômęr š. ę́n ʿam ʿâd wéšfa
ʿât ę̀lkęllímma wzę̄ʰ ā'ę̄límma lâššut wâttaʰ lā ję̄bâṣar mījjímma kæl
ǽšar ję̄zāmę̂nu lâššut. 7 âbaʰ nę̄râda wnę̄bę́lli šǽmma ęšfâtim

ǣšar lā jíšma ’īš et ’ę́šfat rę̂’u. 8 wjîfiṣ š. ōtímma miššę́mma ‘al
fâni kæl ârėṣ wjādâlu líbnot it ā’îr wit emmę́gdal. 9 ‘ál-kėn ḳârā
šę̂ma^{h} bâbėl kī šę́mma bállal š. it ’ę́šfat kæl ’ârėṣ wmiššę́mma īfīṣímma
š. ‘al fânī kæl ârėṣ.

xii 1 wjā’ômęr š. ęlábram lík-lak mījję́rṣak mimmūlę̄dę̂tak
wmíbbėt ’âbęk ęlârėṣ ǣšar arrâk. 2 wę̂ššak ęlgûwwi gâdol wę̄bęr-
rǣkak wegdîla^{h} šêmak wę̂bī bārâka. 3 wę̄bǽrręk ęmbęrrę̂kėk
wėmḳallêlėk ę̂’ar wnibbarâku bak kæl męšfâ’ot ādâma. 4 wjâlak
ábram kā’ǣšar dę́bbėr îlo š. wjâlak íttu loṭ wábr. bęn ‘ámmėš šę̂nim
šābêm šę̂na^{h} ęfṣījjâtu mījjérran. 5 wjíḳḳa^{h} ábr. it šérri^{h} íštu wít-loṭ
bęn ‘â’o wít-kal rākūšímma ǣšar rākâšu wit annâfėš ǣšar ‘âšu bárran
wjiṣṣâ’u lęllę̂kėt árṣā kānân wjābâ’u árṣā kānân. 6 wjâbbar ábr.
bârėṣ ‘ad mâḳom éškėm ‘ad ‘âlon mûra^{h} wakkānânnī ęz bâręṣ.
7 wjírrâ’ī š. ęl’ábr. wjā’ômęr lū ęlzę̄râk íttėn it ârėṣ ęzzę̂’ot wjíbni
šémma mę́zba^{h} ęlš. ęnnirrâ’ī îlo. 8 wjâttaḳ miššę́mma ’âra miḳ-
ḳę̂dėm ęlbít’ęl wjaṭ ā’ôlu bít’el mîjjam wā’î miḳḳę̂dėm wjíbni šę́mma
mę́zba^{h} ęlš. wjíḳra ę́fšęm š. 9 wjéṣṣa^{h} ábr. âlok wnâsa ennígba.

10 wjâ’ī rāb bârėṣ wjârad ábr. miṣrîma^{h} ę́lgor šǽmma kī kâbėd
ęrrâb bârėṣ. 11 wjâ’ī kā’ǣšar ǽḳrib lābû miṣrîma^{h} wjā’ômęr
ęlšę́rri íštu ínna nā jādâtti kī íšša ję̂fėt mārî ę́tti. 12 wę̂jja kī
jęrę̂’u ûtėk ęmmíṣrėm wāmârū íštu zę̂’ot wārâgu ûtī ^{u}ûtėk jâjju.
13 ǣmârī nā ‘ā’ûti ’ę́tti ęlmân jīṭáb-lī bę̄bûrėk wajjâta nę́fšī efgę̄lâlėk.
14 wjâ’ī kābû ábr. miṣrîma^{h} wjęrę̂’u ęmmíṣrėm it ā’íšša kī ję̂fæ^{h} ’ī
mê’od. 15 wjęrę̂’u ’ûta^{h} šârī fâru wjāllę̂lu ûta^{h} ęlfâru wtúḳḳa^{h}
ā’íšša bîta^{h} fâru. 16 wlábr. ā’îṭab bę̄bûra^{h} wjâ’ī lū ṣę̂’on wbâḳar
míḳnī kâbėd mę̂’od. ‘ābâdėm wašfâ’ot węmûrėm wittûnot wgāmâlėm.
17 wjęnégga^{h} š. it fâru nę̄gǣ’im gadę́llėm wit bîtu ‘al dę̂bar šę́rri
íššat ábr.

18 wjíḳra fâru lǽbram wjā’ômęr mā zę̂’ot ‘ašîtá-lī lǽma lā eggìttá-lī
kī íštak ’ī. 19 wlǽma āmárta ‘ā’ûtī ’ī? wíḳḳa^{h} ûta^{h} lī líšša wâtta
ínna íštak ḳā́ wlík. 20 wjęṣâba ‘âlo fâru ǣnâšem wjęšællâ’u ûtu
wit íštu wít-kal ǣšar lū wlot ímmu.

xviii 1 wjirrâ’ī îlo šǽma^{h} bālûnī mémrī ^{u}’ū jêsib fę̂ta^{h} ’â’ol kâm
’ájjom. 2 wjíššā îno wjęrę wênna šǽlâša ’ǣnûšėm nęsîbėm ‘âlo
wjêrę wjâraṣ ęlḳērāttímma miffę̂ta^{h} ’â’ol wjištâbbī ’árṣa. 3 wjā’ômęr
ādénnī ’ém-nā māṣâttī ’an bīnīkímma ǽl-na tābbârū mîjjal ‘abdākímma. 4 jíḳḳa^{h} na mâṭ mėm wrâšu rę̄gālīkímma wiššā’înu tę̂t
’ā’îṣ. 5 wíḳḳa^{h} fat lǽm wsâdu lę̂babkímma wâ’ęr tābbârū kī ‘ál-ken
‘abbartímma ‘al ‘abdākímma wjā’ōmę̂rū ken tę̂šji kā’ǣšar debbírta.
6 wjęmâ’er abr. ’ā’ôla^{h} ęlšę́rra wjā’ômęr mā’ę̂ri šǽlaš sîm ḳâma sâlet
lûšī wę̂šī ’íggot. 7 wæl’abbâḳar raṣ abrâm wjíḳḳa^{h} bęn bâḳar rak

wṭob wjítten ęlennâr wję̄mâ'er lāššûtu. 8 wjíḳḳa^{h} āmâh wâlab
wít-bęn abbâḳar ǣšar 'âša^{h} wjíttėn ęlfānījímma ^{u}'ū 'âmėd 'ālījímma
tę̂t 'ā'îṣ wjā'ōkę̂lu. 9 wjā'ōmę̂ru 'îlo: ǽjjė^{h} šárra^{h} 'íštak? wjā'ômęr
'ínna^{h} bâ'ol. 10 wjā'ômęr šob 'ǣšob 'îlėk kâ'ėt 'ájja wênna^{h} bęn
ęlšę́rra^{h} 'íštak wšę́rra^{h} šāmât fę̂ta^{h} 'â'ol wī 'ā'ôro. 11 wabrâm
wšárra^{h} zāḳînim bâ'im bęjjâmim âdal lâjjot ęlšę́rra^{h} 'âra^{h} kā'ínšim.
12 wtęṣâ'iḳ šárra 'efḳírba^{h} lîmor: 'ā'ôrī bālîtī 'ajjâtâ-lī 'ídna wādę́nnī
zâḳęn.

13 wjā'ômęr šǣma^{h} ęlabrâm lęma zę̄ ṣā'ę̂ḳa šę́rra^{h} lîmor: 'âf
'āmę̄nímma ę̂lad wânī zāḳántī. 14 'ājíflā^{h} miššǣma^{h} dę̂bar lęm-
mûwad 'ǣšob 'îlėk kâ'ėt 'ájja walšárra bęn. 15 wtę̄kâ'ęš šárra
lîmor: lā ṣā'íḳtī kī jārâh wjā'ômęr lā^{h} kī ṣā'íḳtī. 16 wjāḳâmū
miššę́mma 'ā'ǣnûšim wjišḳâfū 'al fânī sâdim wabrâm 'âlek immímma
ęlšęllā'ímma.

xxii 1 wjâ'ī 'â'ėr ęddębârėm 'ā'ílla wā'ǣlûwėm nássa^{h} it abrâm
wjā'ômęr 'îlo: 'abrâm! wjā'ômęr 'innânī! 2 wj. ḳâ-na it bę̂nak it
jā'îdak 'ǣšar 'ā'íbtā it ję̄ṣâḳ wlík-lak ęl'ârėṣ 'æmmūrîjja^{h} wâllǣ'u
šę́mma 'âla 'al 'âd 'ârėm 'ǣšar 'ǣ'ûmėr 'îlėk. 3 wjíškam 'abrâm
bebbę̂ḳar wjâbbęš it ę̄mûru wjíḳḳa^{h} it šênī nâro 'íttu wit ję̄ṣâḳ bę̂nu
wjæbâḳa^{h} 'îṣi 'âla^{h} wjâḳam wjâlak ęlammâḳom ǣšar 'âmar lu 'ā'ælûwėm. 4 bǽjjom ęššǣlîšī wjíšša abrâm it 'îno wję̂rę it ammâḳom
mirrâḳ. 5 wjā'ômęr abr. ęlnâro šę̂bu lākímma fā 'ėm 'ā'ę̂mor wânī
wannâr nę̄lâka 'ád-ka^{h} wništâbbī wnę̂šob 'īlīkímma. 6 wjíḳḳa^{h}
abr. it 'îṣī 'âla^{h} wjâšėm 'al ję̄ṣâḳ bę̂nu wjíḳḳa^{h} ėbję̂du it 'ā'ę́š wit
'ammākę̂lėt wjālâkū šę̄nījímma jâddu.

7 wjā'ômęr ję̄ṣâḳ ęlabr. 'ābîjju wjā'ômęr: âbī. wj.: 'innânī bę̂nī.
wj.: ínna^{h} 'â'eš wā'îṣėm wę́jjæ^{h} 'ę́š^{j}ī lâlla^{h}. 8 wjā'ômęr abr.:
ǣlûwėm jērê'ī lû-šī lâlla^{h} bę̂nī. wjālâku šę̄nījímma jâddu. 9 wjābâ'ū
ęl'ammâḳom 'ǣšar 'âmar lū ā'ę̄lûwėm wjíbnī šę́mma abr. it ęmmę́zba^{h}
wjârręk it 'ā'îṣim wjâḳḳėd it ję̄ṣâḳ bę̂nu wjâšėm 'ûtū 'al ęmmę́zba^{h}
mimmîjjal lā'îṣim. 10 wjæšǽlla^{h} abr. it ję̂du wjíḳḳa^{h} it 'ammāk-
kę̂lėt ęlšâṭ it bę̂nu.

11 wjíḳra 'îlo mālâk šǣma^{h} męn ėššâmim wjā'ômęr abr. abr. wj.
'innânī. 12 wj. æl tę̄šǽlla^{h} ję̂dak 'al 'ėnnâr wal tę̂š^{j}ī lū mæ'ûma^{h} kī
'átta^{h} jādâttī kī jârī ǣlûwėm 'átta^{h} wlā 'āšę́kta it bę̂nak it jā'îdak
mimmínnī. 13 wjíššā abr. it 'îno wję̂rę wênna^{h} 'īl 'ād nâ'ėz efsâbak
efḳārêno wjâlak abr. wjíḳḳa^{h} it 'ā'îl wjāllę̂'u 'âla^{h} tât bę̂nu. 14 wjíḳra abr. it šæm ammâḳom 'ā'ô šǣma^{h} jęrę̂'ī 'ǣšar 'ījjâmer 'ájjom
bār šǣma^{h} jirrâ'ī. 15 wjíḳrā mālâk šǣma^{h} ęl'abrâm šênit męn
aššâmim. 16 wjā'ômęr bī niššābbâttī nām šǣma^{h} kī jān ǣšar
'ašîta it ęddǣbar ę́zzė wlā 'āšǽkta it bę̂nak it jā'îdak mimmínnī.

17 kī bírrok æbęrrækak wę́rbī 'æróbbī it zęrâk kākū[k]âbī ęššâmim
wkâ'ol 'æšar [ʿa]l 'ę́šfat 'ájjam wjîraš [z]ęrâk it šār 'īj̄âbo.
xxxvii 1 wjâšab jâḳob bârẹ̇ṣ mēgérrī 'ābîjju bârẹ̇ṣ kānân. 2 'ílla
tûldat jâḳob jûsėf bęn šâbæ^{h} ʿāšâra^{h} šênė^{h} 'ájja râ'ī 'et ʿâ'o 'æfṣę̂'on
'^{u}'ū nâr et bânī bālâ^{h} wet bânī zílfa 'ínšī 'ābîjju wjîbī jûsėf 'it dabbâ-
tímma rā^{h} 'æl'ābījímma. 3 wjišrâ'el ʿâ'ėb 'it jûsif míkkæl bâno
kī bęn zāḳînim 'ū lū. wjâš lū kittânėt féssėm. 4 wjērê'u ʿâ'o kī
'ūtu 'â'eb 'ābījímma míkkæl bâno wjašnâ'u 'ûtu wlā jākâlū dēbâro
ælšâlom.
5 wjǽllam jûsif 'ǽlom wjéggėd lâ'o wjūsîfu 'ūd šânā-'ûtu. 6 wjā-
'ômęr 'īlījjímma šę̄mâ'ū nā 'ā'ę̂lom ézzė 'ǽšar ʿālámtī. 7 wênna
ānânnu mālémmėm 'ālémmėm éftok eššâdī wênna ḳā'ę̂ma 'ælimmâtī
wgæm nę̄ṣîba^{h} wênna tissābínna 'ælimmâtīkímma tištābījjínna lælim-
mâtī. 8 wjā'ōmę̂rū lū ʿâ'o: 'āmâlok tímlak ʿālînu? 'æmmâšal tímšal
bânū? wjūsîfū 'ūd šâna 'ûtu ʿal 'ęlâmo węl dēbâro.
9 wjǽllam 'ūd 'ǽlum 'â'er wjęsâfėr 'ûtu lâ'o wjā'ômęr 'ínna
ʿālámtī 'ǽlum 'ūd wę̂nna eššîmėš wajjâra wâd ʿâšar kūkâbim mištâb-
bim lī. 10 wję̄sâfir lābîjju wlâ'o wjāggâr bū 'ābîjju wjā'ômer lū
mā 'ā'êlum ézzėh 'ǽšar ʿālámta 'âba nābû 'ânī wímmak wâ'ėk
lę̄štâbbot lak 'árṣā. 11 wjæ̂ḳėnnâ'u bū ʿâ'o wābîjju šâmar it
ęddę̂bar. 12 wjālâkū ʿâ'o ęlrâ'ot it ṣę̂'on 'ābījjímma béškim.
13 wjā'ômęr jišrâ'el æljûsif: 'ālû ʿâ'ėk râ'im béškim: lík wę̂šællâk
'īlījímma wjā'ômęr lū 'innâni. 14 wjā'ômęr lū lík-nâ wrê'ī 'it šâlom
ʿâ'ėk wit šâlom aṣṣę̂'on wīšībânī dę̂bar wję̄šællā'ǽ'u mījję̂miḳ 'íbron
wjâbā ęškêmę^{h}. 15 wjimṣā'ę̂'u 'ā'îš wênna^{h} tâ'ī bėššâdī wję̄šā'ęlê'u
ā'îš lîmor: mā tę̄bæ̂ḳḳėš. 16 wjā'ômęr 'it ʿâ'ī 'ânī mābæ̂ḳḳėš ęggîda^{h}
nâ-lī 'îfa^{h} 'ímma râ'im. 17 wjā'ômęr 'ā'îš nāssâ'u mízzė^{h} kī šāmāt-
tímma 'āmǽrėm nęlâka^{h} dūtîna wjâlak jûsėf 'ā'ôrī ʿâ'o wjimṣā'ímma
efdûtėn. 18 wjērê'u 'ûtu mirrâḳ weftę̄rėm jíḳrab 'īlījímma wjitnęk-
kâlū 'ûtu līmîtu. 19 wjā'ōmę̂ru 'īš ęl ʿâ'o: 'ínna bâl 'ā'ælâmot
'állaz bâ. 20 wâtta^{h} lîkū nārāgę̂'u wnæšlīkę̂'u bād æbbûrot wāmā-
rínnu ʿájjā râ^{h} 'âkālíttu wnērê'ī mā jêjjī 'ælāmûto. 21 wjíšmā
rę̄'ûben wjaṣṣîlu mījjēdímma wjā'ômęr lā nekkínnu nâfėš. 22 wjā-
'ômęr 'īlījímma rę̄'ûben 'æl tišfâkū dám, ešlîkū 'ûtu ęlę́bbor ézzė^{h}
'ǽšar bęmmę́dbar wjed 'ęl tę̄šællâ'u bū ęlmân 'áṣṣel 'ûtu mījjēdímma
līšîbu 'ęl'ābîjju.
23 wjâ'ī kā'ǽšar bā jûsėf æl'â'o wjafšîṭu 'it jûsėf 'it kittántu 'it
kittânėt efféssėm 'ǽšar ʿâlo. 24 wjiḳḳâ'u wješlîku 'ûtu 'ę́bbor
wę́bbor rīḳ în bū mém. 25 wjāšâbū lâkal lę̂m wjiššâ'u 'īnījjímma
wjērê'u wę̂nna^{h} 'ārât jišmā'îlėm bâ^{h} miggālâd wgāmālījjímma našâ'ėm
nę̄kât ^{w}sárrī wloṭ 'ālǽkęm lûrid miṣrîma^{h}. 26 wjā'ômęr ję̄'ûda^{h}

'æl 'â'o: mā bǽṣa kī nârag 'it 'ajânu wkessînu 'it démmu. 27 lîkū
nēmekkērínnu læjjišmā'īlėm wję̄dânu 'ęl tę̂jjī bū kī 'ājânu wbāšárnu
'û. wjišmâ'u 'â'o. 28 wjābbâru 'ę̄nâšem meddjânėm sérrim
wjimšâkū wjâllū 'it jûsif męn ę̄bbor wję̀mekkêru 'it jûsėf læjjìšmā'īlėm
bíšrėm kâsif wjībîjju 'it jûsif miṣrîma^{h}.
29 wjâšab rę̄'ûben 'ęl'ę̄bbor wênna^{h} 'īn jûsėf bę̄bbor wję̄ḳárra 'it
bę̄gâdo. 30 wjâšab 'ęl 'â'o wjā'ômęr 'æjjâlėd 'īnínnu wânī 'âna
'ânī bâ. 31 wjiḳḳâ'ū 'it kittânėt jûsėf wję̄šâṭṭu šīr 'ízzėm wjiṭbâlu
'it kittânėt . . . . 32 . . . efféssėm wjībījjūwwâ^{h} 'æl'ābījjímma
wjā'ômęru zę̂'ot māṣṣânnu ékkir-nâ 'ākittânet bę̂nak 'ī? 'ám-lā?
33 wjækkę̂rę^{h} wjā'ômęr kittânėt bênī 'ī; 'ájjā râ^{h} 'ākālíttu; ṭârėf ṭârėf
jûsėf. 34 wjēḳérra jâḳob šāmālûtu wjâšem šeḳ bemtâno wję̄tâbal
'al bę̂nu jâmim rábbim. 35 wjāḳâmu kæl bâno kæl bānûto
ęlnā'ę̂mu wjimmâ'en lę̄tnâm wjā'ômęr kī 'ę̂rad 'al bênī 'ę̂bęl šījjûla^{h}
wjēbékkī 'ûtu 'ābîjju. 36 wemmeddjânėm mekkêrū 'it jûsėf
miṣrîma^{h} ęlfūṭîfar sârės fâru^{h} šar aṭṭābîm.
xxxix 1 wjûsėf 'ūwwârėd miṣrîma^{h} wjiḳnā'ę̂'u fūṭîfar sârės fâru^{h}
šar aṭṭābîm 'īš míṣrī mîjjed ajjišmā'īlėm 'ǽšar 'ūrīdę̂'ū šę̄mma^{h}.
2 wjâ'ī šǽma^{h} 'ęt jûsėf wjâ'ī 'īš máṣlī wjâ'ī bit 'ādénno emmíṣrī.
3 wjêre 'ādénno kī šǽma^{h} 'íttu wkæl 'ǽšar 'ū 'âšī šǽma^{h} máṣlī
ebjêdu. 4 wjímṣā jûsėf 'an bînī 'ādénno wjēšérret 'ûtu wjefḳīdę̂'u
'al bîtu wkæl 'ǽšar ję́š-lu nâtan ebjêdu. 5 wjâ'ī mîjjaz éfḳed 'ûtu
bābîtu wél-kæl 'ǽšar ję́š-lu wjēbérrek šǽma^{h} 'ít-bėt emmíṣrī evgǽlal
jûsėf wjâ'ī bārâkat šǽma^{h} éfkal ǽšar ję́š-lu bébbėt wbèššâdī.
6 wjâzzab kæl 'ǽšar lū ébjed jûsėf wlā jâdā 'íttu mę̄'ûmæ^{h} kî-'ėm
'ællǽm 'ǽšar 'û 'âkėl wjâ'ī jûsėf ję̂fa^{h} târ wję̂fa^{h} mārî.
7 wjâ'ī 'â'er ęddę̄bârėm 'ā'ílla wtíšša 'íššat 'ādénno it 'īnîjja^{h}
'ęljûsėf ^{w}tā'ômęr šę̄kâbah 'ímmī. 8 wjimmâ'ėn. wjā'ômęr 'ęl'íššat
'ādénno 'en 'ādénnī lā jâdā 'íttī mę̄'ûma^{h} bābîtu wkæl 'ǽšar ję́š-lū
nâtan ebjêdī. 9 'īnínnu gâdol bébbet 'ézze^{h} mimmínnī wlā 'âšak
mimmínnī mę̄'ûma^{h} kî-'em 'ûtek bǽšar 'éttī 'íštu wik 'ę̂šš^{j}ī 'ærrâ^{h}
'aggādélla^{h} ęzzę̂'ot wātîtī lælûwwėm.
10 wjâ'ī kāddę̄bbę̂ra^{h} ęljûsėf jom wjom wlā šâma 'īlējja^{h} líškab
'íṣla^{h} lâjjot 'ímma^{h}. 11 wjâ'ī kǽjjom ézzė^{h} wjâbā jûsėf ebbîta^{h}
lâššut mālâktu bébbėt wīn 'īš mījjēnâšī ébbet šémma bébbet. 12 tit-
fašę̂'u bābę̄gâdo lîmor: šēkâba^{h} 'ímmī wjâzzab bę̄gâdo ebję̂da^{h}
wjânas wjíṣṣā 'ā'ûṣa. 13 wjâ'ī kārā'ûta^{h} kī 'âzab bę̄gâdo ebję̂da^{h}
wjânas wjíṣṣa 'ā'ûṣa^{h}. 14 wtíḳra lę̄nâšī bîta^{h} wtā'ômęr lǽmma
lîmor rę̂'ū 'ībī lânū 'īš 'íbrī ęlṣâ'ėḳ bânū bā 'īlī líškab 'ímmī. wíḳra
éfḳol gâdol. 15 wjâ'ī kāšāmâ'u kī 'ārę̂mī ḳûlī wíḳra wjâzzab bę̄gâdo
ebjêdī wjânas wjíṣṣā 'ā'ûṣa^{h}. 16 wténna bę̄gâdo 'íṣla^{h} 'ád-ba

'ādénno 'ælbîtu. 17 wtēdébbir 'îlo keddēbârėm 'ā'ílla lîmor: bâ
'îlī 'âbed 'ā'íbrī ǽšar 'ībâtta lânū ælṣâ'ėḳ bī. 18 wjâ'ī kārę̂mī ḳûlī
wíḳra wjâzzab bę̄gâdo 'íṣlī wjânas 'ā'ûṣa^{h}.
19 wjâ'ī kāšâma 'ādénno 'it dę̄bârī 'íštu 'ǽšar dębbę̂ra^{h} 'îlo lîmor:
keddę̄bârėm 'ā'ílla 'âša^{h} lī 'ábdak wjâr ébbu. 20 wjíḳḳa 'ādénnī
jûsėf 'ûtu wjittēnê'u 'élbet assâr mâḳom 'ǽšar 'āsûrī ammâlėk āsûrėm
wjâ'ī šǽmma bâbet assâr. 21 wjâ'ī šǽma^{h} 'et jûsėf wjaṭ 'îlo 'êsėd
wjíttėn 'ínnu bînī šár-bet assâr. 22 wjítten šár-bet assâr ébjed
jûsėf 'ít-kæl 'asûrėm 'ǽšar bâbet assâr wít-kal 'ǽšar 'âšim šę́mma 'ū
'ájja 'âšī. 23 'īn šár-bėt assâr rê'ī 'ít-kal mę̄'ûma^{h} ebję̂du bǽšar
šǽma^{h} 'íttu wkæl 'ǽšar 'ū 'âšī šǽma^{h} máṣlī.
xl 1 wjâ'ī 'â'er eddę̄bârėm 'ā'ílla 'ātâ'u méšḳī mâlek míṣrim wâfa^{h}
lādénnījjímma ęlmâlėk míṣrim. 2 wjíḳṣaf fâru^{h} 'al šênī sārîso
'ál-šar emméšḳim wę́l-šar 'âfim. 3 wjítten 'ūtímma bemméšmar
bít-šar aṭṭābîm élbet assâr wmâḳom 'ǽšar jûsėf 'âsor šémma. 4 wjéf-
ḳed šar aṭṭābîm 'it jûsėf 'ę̄tímma wję̄šérret 'ūtímma wjâjju jâmėm
bemméšmar. 5 wjęllâmu 'ǽlom šēnījjímma 'īš 'ílmu eblîla^{h} 'âd
'īš kāfítrun 'ílmu emméšḳī wâfa 'ǽšar ęlmâlėk míṣrim 'ǽšar āsûrėm
bâbet assâr. 6 wjâbā 'īlījjímma jûsėf bębbǽḳar wję̂rę 'ūtímma
winnímma zêfim. 7 wję̄šâ'el 'it sārîsī fâru^{h} 'ǽšar 'íttu bemméšmar
bit 'ādénno lîmor: meddû fānīkímma râ'em 'ájjom? 8 wjā'ōmę̂rū
'îlo: 'ǽlom 'ālámnu wfûtęr 'īn 'ûtu wjā'ômęr 'īlījjímma jûsėf 'ālû
lǽlûwwėm fitrânėm sēfârū nâ-lī.
9 wję̄sâfir šar emméšḳėm 'it 'ílmu ęljûsėf wj. lū bę̂lmī wênna^{h} gâfen
ęlfânī. 10 wbeggâfen šǽlâša^{h} širrûgėm wī kāfrât 'ālâta náṣṣa^{h}
ibšîlu iškūlūtîjja^{h} 'ę̄nâbėm. 11 wkûwwas fâru^{h} ebjêdī wíḳḳa 'it
'ā'ę̄nâbėm węšât 'ūtímma 'al kûwwas fâru^{h} wítten 'it ekkûwwas 'ál-
kaf fâru^{h}. 12 wjā'ômęr lū jûsėf: zę̄^{h} fitrânu šǽlâšat ešširrûgėm šǽlâšat
jâmėm 'ímma. 13 būd šǽlâšat jâmėm jíšša fâru^{h} 'it rę̄'ûšak wīšîbak
'al kínnak wnātátta kûwwas fâru^{h} ebjêdu kemméšfat arrā'îšon 'ǽšar
'ā'îta mėšḳê'u. 14 kî-'ėm zākartânī 'íttak kā'ǽšar jīṭáb-lak weššîta
nā 'immâdi 'ǽsėd wāzgirtâni 'ælfâru^{h} '^{u}'ūṣāttânī męn ébbet 'ézze^{h}.
15 kī gânob niggānábtī mījjârėṣ 'ā'íbrėm wgǽm-fa^{h} lā 'aššîti mę̄'ûmæ^{h}
kī šâmū 'ûtī bę́bbor.
16 wję̂rę šar 'âfim kî-ṭob fâtar wjā'ômęr 'æljûsėf 'æf 'ânī bêlmī
wênna^{h} šǽlâša séllī 'ârī 'al rē'ûšī. 17 wbással 'ālîjjon míkkæl mâkal
fâru^{h} mâšš^{j}ī 'âfa^{h} wā'ôf 'âkel 'ūtímma mîjjal 'ással mîjjal rē'ûšī.
18 wjān jûsėf wjā'ômęr zę̄^{h} fitrânu: šǽlâšat ęssėllim šǽlâšat jâmėm
'ímma. 19 būd šǽlâšat jâmėm jíšša fâru^{h} 'it rē'ûšak mījjâlik wtâla
'ûtak 'al 'ā'îṣ, wâkal ā'ôf 'it bāšârak mījjâlik. 20 wjâ'ī bǽjjom
ęššǽlîšī jom 'ūlę̂dėt 'it fâru^{h} wjâš méštī ę́lkal 'ābâdo wjíšša 'it rę̄'oš

šar emméšḳėm wit rę̂'oš šar 'âfim éftok 'ābâdo. 21 wjîšeb 'ít-šar
emméšḳem 'al mešḳę̂'u wjítten 'it ekkûwwas 'ál-kaf fâru^{h}. 22 wít-
šar 'âfim tâla kā'ǣšar fâtar lǣ[m]ma jûsėf wlā zâkar šar emméšḳėm
'it jûsėf wjiššāḳā'ę̂'u.

Ex ii 1 wjâlak 'īš míbbėt lîbī wjíḳḳa^{h} ít-bæt lîbī. 2 wtâr 'ā'íšša^{h}
wtâlad bęn wtę̂rę 'ûtu kî-ṭob 'ū wtaṣfīnę̂'u šǣlâša jērîm. 3 wlā
jākâla^{h} 'ūd 'aṣfīnę̂'u wtìḳḳâ^{h}-lu 'ímmu tîbat gâmī tāmâra bî-
mar węfzę̂fet wtâšėm bā^{h} it 'ajjâlėd wtâšem bássaf 'al 'ę́šfat 'ájjar.
4 wtittîṣab 'ā'ûtu mirrâḳ ęldât mā 'ījjâšī lū. 5 wtârad bæt fâru^{h}
ęlrâṣ 'al 'ájjar wnārūtîjja^{h} 'ālǣkat 'álījėd 'ájjar wtę̂rę it ėttîba^{h} ę́ftok
ássaf wtę̄šǽlla^{h} it 'āmâta^{h} wtiḳḳâ^{h}. 6 wtiftâ^{h} wtę̂rę it 'ajjâlėd wênna^{h}
nâr bâkī. wtâmal 'âlo bæt fâru^{h}.... 7 wtā'ômęr 'ā'ûtu 'ę́lbæt fâru^{h}
'ā'ǣlak wḳārâttī lik 'íšša mīnḳot męn 'ābrîjjot ^{u}'ūtîníḳ-lik 'it 'ajjâlėd.
8 wtā'ômęr lā^{h} bæt fâru^{h} lîkī wtâlak 'ālîma^{h} wtíḳra 'ít-'æm 'ajjâlėd.
9 wtā'ûmęr lā^{h} bæt fâru^{h} 'ālîkī it 'ajjâlėd ézzė wīnīḳê'u lī wânī íttėn
it šékrėk wtíḳḳa^{h} 'ā'íšša^{h} it 'ajjâlėd wtīnīḳę̂'u. 10 wjígdal ęnnâr
wtībījjê'u ę́lbæt fâru^{h} wjâ'ī lā^{h} ę́lbęn wtíḳra it šêmu mûši wtā'ômęr:
kî-męn émmėm māšīttîjju.

11 wjâ'ī bėjjâmėm 'ā'ímma wjígdal mûšī wjíṣṣa ęl'â'o wję̂rę
ęfsābālūtímma wję̂rę 'īš míṣrī mékkī 'īš 'íbrī mījjâ'o. 12 wjâfan
kā^{h} wkā^{h} wję̂rę kī 'īn 'īš wjékkī it ėmmíṣrī wiṭmānę̂'u būl. 13 wjíṣṣa
bǽjjom eššênī wênna^{h} šênī ę̄nâšim 'íbrim nâṣim wjā'ômer lėrrêša
lǣma^{h} tékkī rêk. 14 wjā'ômęr mī šâmak līš šar węlšûfaṭ 'ālînu
'âlārāgânī 'átta 'âmar kā'ǣšar 'ārígta it emmíṣrī? wjîrā mûšī wjā'ômęr
'âkėn nûda ęddǣbar. 15 wjíšma fâru^{h} it ęddǣbar ézzė wję̄bǽḳḳeš
lârag it mûšī wjíbra mûšī miffânī fâru^{h} wjâšab bârėṣ médjan wjâšab
'al ébbir.

16 węlkâ'en médjan šâba bânot wtābā'ínna wtidlā'ínna wtimlā'ínna
it arrâṭim lâšḳot it ṣę̂'on ā̀bījjínna. 17 wjābâ'u ęrrâ'im wję̄gę́rrē-
šúmma wjâḳam mûšī wjūšījjínna wjéšḳī it ṣę̄'ōnímma. 18 wtābā'ínna ęlrâwel ābījínna wjā'ômęr męddû mā'írtėm bā 'ájjom?
19 wtā'ōmērínna 'īš míṣrī 'aṣṣīlânu mîjjed ęrrâ'ėm wgæm dâla dâla
lânu wjéšḳī it aṣṣę̂'on. 20 wjā'ômęr ęlbānûto wę́jjė^{h} lǣma^{h} zę^{h}
'āzábtėn it 'ā'îš ḳērîn lū wjā'ôkel lǣm. 21 wjâ'ęl mûšī ęlšǣbęt ęt
'ā'îš wjítten it ṣibbôra^{h} bíttu ęlmûšī líšša. 22 wtâlad bęn wjíḳra
it šêmu gíršam kī 'âmar ger 'ā'îtī bâręṣ nikrîjja.

23 wjâ'ī bæjjâmim 'arrábbim 'ā'ímma wjâmat mâlek míṣrim
wjānâ'u bânī 'išrâ'el męn 'ā'æbîda wjǣṣā'ǣḳu wtǣl šūwwātímma
'æl'ā'ælûwwėm męn 'ā'æbîda^{h}. 24 wjíšma^{h} 'ælûwwėm 'it nę̄ḳā-
tímma wję̄zâkar 'ǣl. 'it bērîtu ęt abr. węt ję̄ṣâḳ węt jâḳob. 25 wjêre
'ǣl. 'it bânī jišrâ'el wjâda ǣl. **iii** 1 wmûšī 'ájja râ'ī 'it ṣę̂'on jítru

ʿātênu kâʾen médjan wjęnâʾig ʾit aṣṣêʾon ʾâʾer ʾæmmǽdbar wjâbā
ęlʾar ʾāʾæl. ʾūrîba^{h}. 2 wjirrâʾī ʾîlo mālâk šǣma^{h} æblāʾębat ęš
míttok ęssânī^{h} wjêre wênna^{h} assânī^{h} bâr bêš wassânī^{h} ʾēnínnu ʾêkėl.
3 wjāʾômęr mûšī ʾęsor nā wērêʾī it ammārî eggâdol ʾézzė^{h} męddû lā
jibbâr ʾassânī^{h}. 4 wjêre ʾǣl. kî-sar ęlrâʾot wjíḳrā ʾîlo ʾǣl. míttok
assânī^{h} wjāʾômęr: mûšī, mûšī! wjāʾômęr ʾinnânī! 5 wj.: æl tíḳrab
ʾǣlam šęl nâlek mîjjal rēgâlek kī ammâḳom ʾǣšar ʾáttā ʿâmed ʿâlo
ʾādâmat ḳâdeš ʾī. 6 wjāʾômęr ʾānâkī ʾælûwi ʾābûtėk ʾælûwwi ʾabr.
wælûwwi jęṣâḳ wælûwwi jâḳob wjéster mûšī fâno kī jârā mījjábbeṭ
ʾælʾāʾælûwwėm.

7 wjāʾômęr šǣma^{h} râʾū rāʾîtī ʾit ʿánnī ʿámmī ʾǣšar bāmíṣrim wit
ṣāʾiḳtímma šāmâttī miffânī nęgîšo kī jādâttī ʾit mākāʾûbu. 8 wērâda^{h}
lāṣṣîlu mîjjed míṣrim wlālûtu męn ʾâreṣ ʾāʾī ælʾâreṣ zâbat ʾâlabudâbaš
ʾæl mâḳom ękkānânnī āʾíttī wāʾęmérrī wæffērízzī weggirgêšī wāʾíbbī
węjjębûsī. 9 wâtta^{h} ʾínna ṣāʾęḳat bânī ʾīšrâʾel bâ ʾîli wgæm rāʾîtī
it ʾallâṣ ǽšar míṣrim lāʾęṣėm ʾūtímma. 10 wâtta^{h} lík wǣšællâk
ʾælfâru^{h} ʾ^{u}ūṣâtta ʾit ʿámmī bânī jišrâʾęl mimmíṣrim. 11 wjāʾômęr
mûšī ʾælʾāʾæl. mī ʾānâkī kī ʾǣlak ʾælfâru^{h} wkī ʾūṣî it bânī ʾīšrâʾęl
mimmíṣrim. 12 wjāʾômęr kī ʾǣjjī ʾímmak wzę̂-lak ʾāʾôt kī ʾānâkī
šællâttėk būṣîjjak ʾit ʿâm mimmíṣrim tābbâdun ʾit ʾāʾælûwwėm ʿal
ʾâr ézė^{h}. 13 wjāʾômęr mûšī ʾælʾāʾælûwwėm ʾínna ʾānâkī bâ ʾælbânī
jišrâʾęl wāmártī lǣmma ʾælûwwī ʾābūtīkímma šællâni ʾīlīkímma
wāmârū lī mā šêmu? mā ʾæʾûmęr ʾīlījímma?

14 wjāʾômęr ʾǣl. ælmûšī ʾǣjjī ʾǣšar ʾǣjjī wjāʾômęr: kā^{h} tāʾômęr
ælbânī jišrâʾel: ʾǣjjī šællânī ʾīlīkímma. 15 wjāʾômęr ʾūd ʾælûwwėm
ʾælmûšī kā^{h} tāʾômęr ælbânī jišrâʾel šǣma^{h} ʾælûwwi ʾābūtīkímma
ʾælûwwi ʾæbrâm wælûwwi jęṣâḳ wælûwwi jâḳob šællânī ʾīlīkímma
zę̄^{h} šêmī lûlam wzę̄^{h} zékrī ęldar wdór. 16 lík wāsífta ʾit zāḳînī bânī
jišrâʾel wāmártā ʾīlījímma šǣma^{h} ælûwwī ʾābūtīkímma nirrâʾī ʾîlī
ʾælûwwī ʾæbrâm wjęṣâḳ wjâḳob lîmor fâḳad fāḳáttī itkímma wit
ʿāšûwi lākímma bāmíṣrim. 17 wæmęra ʿâlli ʾitkímma mījjénī
míṣrim ʾæl âréṣ ękkānânnī ʾāʾíttī wāʾæmérrī węffērízzī wėggirgêšī
wāʾíbbī węjjēbûsī ʾælʾâréṣ zâbat ʾâlabudâbaš. 18 wšęmâʾu ʾælḳôlak.
wbâtta ʾátta wzāḳînī īšrâʾel ʾælmâlek míṣrim wāmartímma ʾîlo šǣma^{h}
ʾælûwwī ʾāʾíbrėm niḳḳâra ʿālînu nēlâka^{h} nā dêrek šǣlâšat jâmėm
bemmédbar wnizbâ^{h} ʾælšǣma^{h} ʾælūwwînu. 19 wânī jādâttī kî-la
jíttėn ʾitkímma mâlek míṣrim lâlek ʾālû ébjed ʾāzęḳa^{h}. 20 wšęllâttī
ʾit jêdī wākkîtī ʾit míṣrim éfkal niflāʾûtī ʾǣšar ʾǣšš^{j}ī efḳírbu wāʾōrī ken
jęšǣlla ʾitkímma. 21 wnātáttī ʾit ʿan ʿâm ʾézzė bînī míṣrim wę̂jja
kī tęlâkon lā tęlâkon rîḳėm. 22 ^{w}šâʾęl ʾīš mîjjad rêʾu wíšša^{h} mîjjed
rāʾûtah meškínta wemgîrat bîta^{h} kîlī kâsef wkîlī zāb wšāmâlut

wšemtímma ʿal bānīkímma węl bānūtīkímma wnasṣeltímma ʾit mísṛim. **iv** 1 wjān mûšī wjāʾômęr wén-lā jāmę̂nū lī wlâ jišmâʾu ʾælḳûlī kī jāʾômę̂rū lā nirrâʾī ʾîlėk šǽmaʰ.

2 wjāʾômęr ʾîlo šǽmaʰ mâ-zeʰ ebjêdak? wjāʾômęr máṭṭī. 3 wjā-ʾômęr: ešlīkę̂ʾu ʾárṣā wješlīkę̂ʾu ʾárṣā. wjâʾī ʾælnâš wjânas mûšī miffâno. 4 wjāʾômęr šǽmaʰ ʾælmûšī šǽlla jêdak wâʾez efzānâbu wjēšǽlla jêdu wjâzziḳ bū wjâʾī ʾælmáṭṭi efkébbo. 5 ʾælmân jāmę̂nu kī nirrâʾī îlek šǽmaʰ ʾælûwwi ʾābūtímma ʾælûwwī ʾæbrâm wælûwwī jęṣâḳ wæl. jâḳob.

6 wjāʾômęr šǽmaʰ lū ʾūd ʾîbi nā jêdak bîḳak wjîbī jêdu bîḳu wjūṣījjâʰ mîḳu wênnaʰ jêdu emṣarrât keššêlag. 7 wjāʾômęr ʾîšeb jêdak ælʾîḳak wjîšeb jêdu ʾælʾîḳu wjūṣījjâʰ mîḳu wênnaʰ šâbæʰ kābā-šâru. 8 wǽjjaʰ ʾém-la jāmę̂nū lak wlā jišmâʾu ʾǽlḳol ʾāʾôt ʾęrrāʾîšon wāmę̂nū ʾǽlḳol ʾāʾôt ʾāʾę̂ron. 9 wǽjjaʰ ém-lā jāmę̂nu gæm ælšênī ʾāʾûtot ʾāʾílla wlā jišmâʾu ʾælḳûlak wlę̄ḳâtta mimmîmī ʾǽjjar šāfákta ʾajjabbâša wâjjū émmėm ʾǽšar tíḳḳa męn ʾájjar jâjju ʾę́ldam ebjab-bâšat. 10 wjāʾômęr mûšī ʾælšǽmaʰ bī ʾādânī lā ʾīš dę̄bârėm ʾānâkī gæm mittâmol gæm miššę́lšom gæm mîjjaz dębbę̂rak ʾælʿábdak kī kâbed fāʰ wkâbed líššun ʾānâkī.

11 wjāʾômęr šǽmaʰ ʾîlo: mî-šam fāʰ lâdam ʾû mī jâšem ʾíllam ʾū ʾârėš ʾū fêḳīʰ ʾū ʾáwwėr ʾālû ʾānâkī šǽmaʰ. 12 wâttaʰ lik wānâkī ʾǽjjīʰ ʾęm fîjjak ʾᵘūrîttek ʾǽšar tēdébbir. 13 wjāʾômer bī ʾādânī šǽlla nā ébjed tę̄šǽlla. 14 wjâr ef šǽmaʰ bāmûšī wjāʾômęr ʾālû ʾârron ʿâjak ellîbī jādâttī kī débbir jēdébbir ʾū wgæm ʾínna ʾū jíṣṣa ʾælḳērâttak wrâk wšâma eblēbâbo. 15 wdebbírta ʾîlo wšámta ʾit eddēbârėm bāfîjju wānâkī ʾǽjjī ʾęm fîjjak węm fîjju. ʾᵘūrîttī ʾitkímma ʾit ʾǽšar tǽššun. 16 wdébbėr ʾū lak ʾælʿâm wǽjja ʾū jǽjjī lak ʾǽlfāʰ wátta tǽjjī lū lælûwwėm. 17 wit ʾæmmáttī ézzė tíḳḳa ebjêdak ʾǽšar tǽššʲī bū ʾit ʾāʾûtot. 18 wjâlak mûšī wjâšab ʾæljítrū ʿātênu wjāʾômer lū ʾēlâkaʰ nā wēšûbaʰ ʾælʿâʾī ʾǽšar bârėṣ mísṛim wērêʾī . . . .

NOTES

Gn i 6 *éftok*: R. *éftot*, obviously an error. 7 *wījāš*: R. *wījās*, either an error (cf. v. 16) or due to Jewish influence, which does not seem very probable. Even in the Samaritan Hebrew, it is true, the two *šin*'s were perhaps originally differentiated (contrary to the opinion of other scholars), but the original *śin*, where not pronounced like *š*, appears nowadays as *šj* (*šʲ*), cf. *ʿášjot* ii 4, *ʾę́šʲī* xxii 7, &c. 10 *welmáḳwa*: the stressed *a* must be short; if R. has *ā́*, it is unquestionably an error, since the form would be without any parallel; Obadiah Ṣedaqah recited to the present writer with *ắ*. 11 R. *mäzrīʿ* (Betonung unklar); Ob. Ṣed. recited *mæzrî*, which is in accordance with parallel forms (see further in the grammar). 12 *wis*:

nowadays *ṣ* can often be distinguished from *s* only by a very sensitive ear, at times not at all. The same is the case with *ṭ* and *t*, while *ḳ* has never been identified with *k*, but resembles rather ʾ. In accordance therewith, I have corrected every *k* which appears in the place of *ḳ*, but left *s* and *t* in similar cases unchanged, though there naturally must be cases where the omission of the point below is due to an oversight, as it always is in the case of *k* = *ḳ*. 14 *mằṻrot*: R. *mằṻt*, error. 18 R. *lā̊mšal*. The long vowel, however, is inexplicable, since there is no guttural after it. 19 *rǽbiʿ*: the regular form is *ræbî* (so Ob. Ṣed.), but the variant in the text is also used sometimes. It has without doubt arisen through the analogy of *šǽnī*, *šíššī*, &c. 20 *išrǽšu*: *ṣ* > *š*, probably through the influence of the first *š*, except that the two sounds resemble one another rather closely. The initial *j* before an *i* is occasionally neglected in pronunciation. *uf-iā̆fæf*: R. *ufi ā̆fäf*. 21 *attằnīmem*: sic R.; retrograde assimilation supported by partial dissimilation (to avoid the accumulation of dentals). R. *eggādélim*. *wít-ḳal* (bis), *ḳā̆nif*: confusion of the so-called emphatic and non-emphatic sounds also occurs in this way, and in this case *k* can be pronounced as *ḳ* (cf. v. 12). *šằrā̆su*: cf. v. 12. *elmīnijimmæ*: R. *el-mīni jimmäm*, the word being divided probably because of the two main accents. There are, however, analogous cases, e.g. ii 22, 23. The final *m* is obviously an error, either of the reader or of the scribe.

Gn i 24 *wrǽmæš*: S. here and in v. 25 *rǽmæš* with acute, but everywhere else with circumflex, which seems to be the correct one here also. 26 *efdêkėt*: sic S., cf. v. 28. 27 *zākārunaḳâba*: sic S., and Ob. Ṣed. also read these words very closely together, as one word, but only in this verse; everywhere else they can clearly be recognized as two words, unlike *ʾâlabudâbaš* Ex iii 17 which is everywhere pronounced as *one* word. In the present passage, perhaps some myth about the First Man being originally a hermaphrodite was the original cause of this reading.

ii 1 *wjikę̄llu*: S. 'Wohl Hörfehler für *u̯i̯ikkę̄llu*; vgl. Pet. S. 77, zum Pual der Verba', but the quite regular form is Puʿal (or Feʾal, in Sam. Hebrew), which Petermann did not recognize; similarly Ob. Ṣed. 2 S. *eššiši*, mistake. 3 *ôtu*: S. 'fast wie *ûtu*'. 5 *jaṣmæh*: sic S.; the normal accentuation would be *jáṣmæh*, but Ob. Ṣed. pronounced *jaṣmǽh*; the latter perhaps influenced by *wjaṣmîh* v. 9, where the circumflex on the final syllable is regular. 7 before *ʿâfar* S. omitted *it âdam*. 10 *wmiššę́mmah*: S. 'Die Verdopplung des *m* habe ich hier *nicht* notiert', mistake. 11 *šam*: S. 'sic! wohl *šä̆m* gemeint?', but it is not necessary, cf. *ʾan/ʾínnu* xxxix 4, 21, *kal/kæl/kel* (passim); the vowel might be coloured by the following one, in Sam. Hebrew there being a strong tendency towards vowel harmony, though not universally. *āʿǽd*: ʿ in the middle of a word, certainly due to the form without article. 14 *wšemm*: S. 'sic!' *errǽbī*: cf. i 19. 18 *šǽmā*ʰ: S. 'so notiert; das lange *a* ist aber wohl nur Schreibfehler!' (probably so). *ṭůb*: S. *ṭōb*, with note: '$\overset{u}{o}$ = Mittellaut zwischen *o* und *u*'; I have changed the character to facilitate the printing, though the sound has developed from *o*; the interchange of *o* and *u* is so frequent that this cannot add much to the confusion; moreover, the Samaritans themselves regard *o* and *u* as one and the same sound. 19 *ū̊f*: S. *ōf*, with note: 'fast wie *ūf*'. 20 S. (*w*)*lâdam*, and note with reference to (*w*): 'von mir nicht notiert, aber wohl bloß überhört', which is hardly the case. The omission of this *w* in pronunciation is frequent, and might represent a new phase in the development of this 'dead' dialect. So I have omitted it everywhere where it is lacking in S.'s original notes; where it is afterwards added to them, I have placed it above the line. 21 S. *wjẹbbǣl*, which is simply impossible; Ob. Ṣed. *wjébbæl*. 22 *wjī-bîjjâh*: cf. i 21. 23 *lǣḳîjjâh*: cf. i 21. 24 *jázzab*: regular *jâzzab*, but occasionally (quite irregularly) the lengthening of the vowel is dropped.

iii 5 *wnệfāḳâ'ū*: cf. i 21. 6 S. *wtẹ́rẹ*, with note: 'so notiert!', but the form would be anomalous. 7 *wtǣfāḳâna*: cf. i 21. 8 *wjišmâʿu*: sic; influenced by the written text? 10 *šāmâtī*: sic (for regular *šāmâttī*). 11 *mīn*: S. 'so notiert'. 12 *nētînæ*: sic!; the form is Qal passive, but this sense seems impossible; perhaps there is some mythical story behind it. 14 *ʿăšîta*: S. 'für die erste Silbe habe ich ausdrücklich *kurzes a* notiert', a phenomenon which is fairly regularly observed in the perfect of this verb. *ʿârur*: sic. 15 *ʿâšét*: sic. *wbin*: in the plain copy S. has *ụbîn* (3 times), but I have never observed in this word, when unsuffixed, a long vowel or any stress, which agrees with S.'s original notes also. 16 S. *ẹ̄robbī*, with note: 'so, mit *o*, notiert! Darüber ein nicht mehr erkennbares Zeichen, vielleicht.' The sign seems to be ʹ, which grammatically also is the only possible one. 17 *ʿārûra*: sic, cf. v. 14. Ob. Ṣed. pronounced ' in both places. 22 *aldât*: S. 'so notiert: *al-*!'; cf. ii 11. 23 *wjẹ̄šǣllā'ệu*: cf. i 21. 24 *wít-lāt*: sic; cf. i 12.

iv 2 *wtâṣif*: sic; cf. i 12, 21. 5 S. *lâ-šâ*, but the two words, both having a circumflex accent, cannot be very closely attached to each other. 7 *'ẹ̄tât*: cf. i 12. 8 *wjâḳam*: S. in the plain copy *wjêḳam*, with note: 'das *e* unsicher; könnte auch *o*, vielleicht sogar *a* sein'. As far as I can see, the character is not *o*, and of the two other possibilities *a* is more probable, since it appears everywhere else in this form of the verb and of all the others of the same type (the so-called hollow roots). It would be too hazardous to suppose the existence of a variant on the ground of one uncertain example. *wjârāgệ'u*: cf. i 21. 11 *ʿârur*: cf. iii 14, 17. 15 *ẹlkén*: S. *ẹlḳén*, with note: 'Ich habe *elḳen* = לקין notiert; wohl Hörfehler!'

vi 12 *ʿāšît*: sic; cf. iii 14, 15 a.e. 14 *mîjoṣ*: S. in the plain copy *mî(i̯)i̯oṣ*, with note: 'nur ein *i̯* notiert!' Dropping of the gemination occurs occasionally, in *j* and *w* more frequently than in the other consonants, cf. *jǣji* ii 5, *mījệden* ii 10, *tâwa* iii 6, &c. 16 *ṭẹ̄ṭṭim*: sic S., with note: 'so, mit 2 *ṭ* (!) notiert! Hörfehler', but it is no mistake. Ob. Ṣed. pronounced the word exactly so, too, and cf. i 12, 21 a.e. 18 *'íttak*: so in the original notes, though somewhat obscure (and not *'íttek*, which in addition would be highly exceptional).

vii 3 after *zệra*^{h} note: 'Bis hierher reicht die Reinschrift. Scha.', but in fact it appears to be continued to v. 22, where it ends abruptly in the middle of the word *mík/kal*. 4 *mánṭir*: sic; partial assimilation. 13 *'âm*: S. 'sic!' *ǣtímma*: S. 'sic!' 15 *bû-rū*: S. 'so gesprochen, *ru* enklitisch an *bu* angelehnt!' Such a pronunciation, which pays no attention to the sense, is not very infrequent in Sam. Hebrew. It might indicate that the recitation has grown mechanical. 16 S. *ṣābā'ûtu*, with note: '*ṣaba* proklitisch!' 23 *wjimmî*^{h}: sic S. (regular).

viii 7 *jẹ̄bệšat* is apparently intended. 11 *bāfîjja*^{h}: sic S. (regular).

12 *jâmim ā'ęrêm*: sic S. *jāṣęfa^h*: sic; cf. i 12, 21; iv 2. 21 *leb*: originally *lebb*, but the second *b* struck through. *lâkot* (for *lâkkot*): cf. vi 14.

ix 2 *ébbjėdkímma*: cf. i 21. 3 *ʿęšéb* scripsi; in the notes of S. it looks like *ʿą̂šéb*, which is quite anomalous; the first vowel is probably corrected twice.

xi 2 S. *wjâ'ī*, as normally. *wjimṣā'u*: sic S. (regular). 9 *šęma^h* scripsi; S. *š*. (confused with the Divine Name).

xii 4 *šābêm*: or *-îm*? 6 *wjâbbar*: sic S. (regular); the second *b* added above the line. *ʿâlon*: sic; cf. iii 14 a.e. 11 originally *jādāti*. 18 S. *ʿašîtā lī, eggíttà lī*, which does not seem possible. With the text cf. *jīṭáb-lī* v. 13. 19 *wlǣma*: sic S. (regular). *ḳá*: with acute, a sign of unusual (probably stronger) stress.

xviii 1 *'ā'ol*: sic S. (regular). 2 *nęsîbêm*: cf. i 12 a.e. 5 *wsâdu*: sic S.; the point below the *s* unintentional.

xxii 1 *nássa^h*: sic S. 6 *'ā'éš*: sic S., but 7 *'â'eš* (like Ob. Ṣed. in both places). 12 *tęš^jī*: sic S. (and not *-ššī*). 14 *'ā'ô*: sic S. 17 *'ǣróbbī*: sic S. (like iii 16).

xxxvii 1 *mēgérrī*: sic. 3 *ʿā'ėb*: sic S. (cf. iii 14), but v. 4 *'â'eb* (like Ob. Ṣed. in both passages). S. *zâḳīnim*, which is quite anomalous. 4 *wjašnā'u*: sic. 5 S. *šānā'ûtu*. 8 or *šâna'ûtu* (= *šâna-'ûtu*)? 13 *węšællâk*: sic S. (the sign above *æ* struck through). 20 *rá^h*: sic (unusual stress). 21 *nâfėš*: sic (and not *nê-*). 27 *nēmekkērínnu*: sic (the last *n* added above the line). 29 S. *bęgádo* (anomalous). 31–32 omission caused by homoeoteleuton. 32 *wjā'ômęru*: cf. i 21 a.e.

xxxix 5 *evgǣlal*: S. *ewgâlal*, with note: 'sic! mit labiodentalem *w*!' (so Ob. Ṣed., too). 9 *wātîtī*: cf. i 12 a.e. 10 *kāddębbęra^h*: sic. 21 *šárbet* apparently intended by S.

xl 1 *ʿātā'u*: cf. i 12 a.e. 2 *emméšḳim*: sic S. (and not *-á-*). 3 *élbet* apparently intended. 5 *'ílmu*: sic (bis). *eblîla^h*: sic (regular). 10 *kāfrât*: sic. 14 *zākartânī*: sic S. (and not *-ênī*). *wāzgirtâni*: sic (partial assimilation).

Ex ii 3 *wtìḳḳā^h-lu* scripsi; S. seems to have *wtí-*, which is anomalous. 5 *'ālǣkat ʿálījėd*: sic S. 6 the end omitted (homoeoteleuton). 7 *mīnḳot*: sic. S. *^w'ūtî níḳlik*. 25 originally *'īšrā'el*.

iii 1 *'ūrîba^h*: sic S. (regular). 2 S. *bêš, 'ēnínnu*, with note: '*ē* geschlossen'. 7 S. *mākā'ubû*: with note: 'ohne Verdopplung!', which shows that he did not understand the principles of gemination in connexion with the disappearance of the gutturals. The form is quite regular, except that S. has placed the accent on a wrong syllable; Ob. Ṣed. ut scripsi. 8 *'âlabudâbaš*: sic, pronounced as one word (cf. Gn i 27), might represent one conception, something very good or delicate stuff. 10 *jišrā'ęl*: originally *'īš-*. Similarly vv. 13, 14, 15. 15 *ęldar wdór*: sic S., and so Ob. Ṣed., too (with short vowels in both forms). Probably to be connected with the two infinitive forms of the so-called hollow roots. 16 *jišrā'el*: orig. *īš-* (without '). *fâḳad*: sic S. (and Ob. Ṣed.). 17 *mījjénī*: sic. *'âlabudâbaš*: as always, cf. v. 8 and Gn i 27. 20 *'ǣšš^jī*: S. 'sic!' 22 orig. *meškínta wemgîrad*; corrected afterwards. orig. *bêta^h*; corr. immediately.

iv 1 *wén-lā*: sic S. *jā'ômęrū*: cf. Gn i 21 a.e. 4 S. *efzāzānâbu* (mistake). 7 *šābæ^h*: sic (and not *šābâ^h*). 10 *'ādânī*: sic (to God; to men *'ādénnī*). Similarly, v. 13. 17 *'æmmáttī*: sic, cf. Gn i 12 a.e.

APPENDIX III

Compare p. 68 *supra*

A PALESTINIAN/TIBERIAN TEXT OF THE HEBREW BIBLE

The folio published and discussed here was discovered by Professor Alejandro Diez Macho of the University of Barcelona in the Library of the Jewish Theological Seminary of America, New York, where it is listed as MS 594, Box B, Envelope 12, one folio on vellum containing parts of the text of Eccles xi, 1–9, xii, 3–9 and Lam i, 1–4, 7–11. Unfortunately the upper part of the folio is badly damaged. Diez Macho sent a photo of it to me and was kind enough to revise my copy twice against the original (see above, pp. 68 f., 151 f.). Subsequently Dr. Murtonen compared my copy with the original in America.

Diez Macho has discussed this folio in the Volume of the 1956 Strasbourg Congress, *VT*, Supplement iv, Leiden, 1957, pp. 28 f. He believes that the text is important because it forms a transitional stage between the Palestinian and Tiberian systems of punctuation, and he tries to explain several features of the text on this hypothesis.

I do not think that his characterization is quite correct. In my opinion this text shows the ancient Palestinian punctuation, added by the copyist himself in a reddish-brown ink, superseded by the Tiberian one. It is not a case of a transitional stage in which an old form of punctuation is supplemented by another, but of Palestinian punctuation replaced by Tiberian punctuation, the masorete responsible using black ink for the purpose and disregarding the original punctuation. One has the impression that the Tiberian signs were added at a time when this method of punctuation was not yet fully developed, and in my view it is the differences from the mature Tiberian system that are of special interest. Consequently we cannot always explain the punctuation of the fragment exactly in the same way as Diez Macho has done.

I publish this valuable Old Testament text, giving each line of the original twice. In the upper line of each pair the Palestinian signs are added to the text, in the lower line the Tiberian signs, in both cases so far as they are preserved in the original.

It is difficult to present such an ancient punctuation adequately in a printed text if one is dependent on the Hebrew signs normally used in printed Bibles. These signs were formed with a somewhat curious embellishment at about A.D. 1500 and have not been changed since. They are very different from those which we find in ancient manuscripts of the Bible which are now available. When I began working on Kittel's *Biblia Hebraica* in Leipzig in 1926 I myself had to design vowels, accents and diacritical signs in order to ensure that they would correspond to those in the manuscripts used as a basis for the text, and I have tried to do the same in conjunction with the Monotype Corporation in London for the types to be used in the new edition of the *Biblia Hebraica* to be printed in Stuttgart. Such types were not available here. In the present case the reader will be able to see how far the printed signs differ from the signs in the original as both pages of the fragment are given in facsimile.

The parchment is creased in places, making some individual letters in several lines invisible on the photograph.

I am adding as annotations what Murtonen has appended to my copy of the text, as these remarks come from an expert after a careful study of the original. In one case only do I disagree with him. In Lam i, 12 the Tiberian hand has clearly written a Zarḳa on אליכם which precedes the Segolta on דרך. Murtonen wrongly takes ם with a Zarḳa to be a ל (from the following word).

In the fragment two masoretic notes are to be found. To שוממין in Lam i, 4 we find ל̇ בנון דסופה. In Lam i, 16 we find שוממים written with final ם.

In Lam i, 10 we find the note ד̇ דגשין בכל קרייה against בקהל, referring to the four places where in the word קהל a ק with Dagesh follows the prefixed ב. The four places are Jud xxi, 5, Job xxx, 28, Lam i, 10 and 2 Chr xxx, 17. A reference to the masoretic note is given by a small sign, and the same sign introduces the masoretic note in the margin at i, 4.

ANNOTATIONS TO APPENDIX III

Eccles xi, 1–9

1. יא in the margin; תִּמְצָ]נוּ Tib.
2. תֶּן־חֵלֶ]ק Tib.; in the mg. לא קרי
3. אם Tib.; גֶּשֶׁ]ם Tib.; גשׁ]ם Pal.; וְאִם־יִפּוֹל Tib.; בַּצָּפוֹן Tib.; שׁיפּ]ם Pal.
4. רוּחַ Tib.; לֹא Tib.; לֹא Tib.

5. דֶּרֶךְ Tib.; בבֿטן Pal.; בבַטֶן Tib. pm, but destroyed and written בְּבֶטֶן; אֲשֶׁר Tib.; יעשה Pal. (no points)

6. אֶת־זַרְעֶךָ Tib.; אֵינְךָ (א preserved) Tib.; יִכְשַׁר Tib.; וְאִם־ Tib.; טוֹבִים Tib.

7. הָאוֹר Tib.

8. [יחיה] Tib.; בְּכֻלָּם sic! Tib.; ישמח Pal.; הָבֶל־ Tib.

9. בִּילְדוּתֶיךָ Tib.

Eccles xii, 3–9

3. הראות Pal.; הָרֹאוֹת Tib.

4. בשוק Pal.; בַּשּׁוּק Tib.; בִּשְׁ[פַ]ל Tib.; הטחנה Pal.; לְקוֹ[ל] Tib.; הצפור Pal.

5. בַּדֶּרֶךְ Tib.; וְתָפֵר Tib.; האביונה Pal.; הַסֹּפְדִים Tib.

6. ירחק Pal.; חֶבֶל sic! Tib.; הזהב Pal.; כַּד Tib.; ונרץ (ḥolem not preserved in Tib.)

7. הֶעָפָר Tib.; הארץ Pal.; הָאָרֶץ־ Tib.

8. אָמַר Tib.; הבל Pal.

9. למד Pal.; לִמַּד־ Tib.

Lam i, 1–4; 7–12

1. בָדָד Tib.; במדינות Pal.; לָמַס Tib.

2. בלילה Pal.; לָהּ־ Tib.; מִכָּל Tib.

3. גָּלְתָה Tib.; no points Pal.; יהודה Pal.; מעני Pal.; עֲבֹדָה Tib.; הַמְּצָרִים Tib.

4. אבלות Pal.; אֲבֵלוֹת Tib.; מועד Pal.; כָּל Tib.; מר Pal.

7. מימי not preserved, except for vowels; בִּנְפֹל Tib.

8. רָאוּ Tib.; וַתָּשָׁב Tib.; ותשב Pal.; אָחוֹר Tib.

9. בשוליה (= bĕšwale(h), cf. דְּוָדִים, שְׁוָרִים) Pal.; מְנַחֵם Tib.; ראה Pal.; אויב Pal.

10. צַל Tib.; מחמדיה Pal.; לָךְ Tib.

12. אליכם: pm אליכל (from the following word), the accent is not there [so Murtonen, but see my remark above]; כל Pal.; מַכְאֹ[וב] Tib., no accent preserved

Tiberian and Palestinian signs are sometimes difficult to distinguish, since the ink has faded, but the above list should be fairly accurate (A. Murtonen).

Eccles xi, 1–9

תמ[צא]נו : 2 תן חל[ק

תִּמְ[צָאֶ]נּוּ תֶּן חֵלֶ[ק לשבעה וגם לשמונה

כ֯י לא תדע מה [

כִּי לֹא תֵדַע מַה יִהְיֶה רָעָה [על הארץ]

3 אם ימלאו העבים גש[ם

אִם יִמָּלְאוּ הֶעָבִים גֶּשֶׁ[ם על הארץ

יריקו ואם יפול עֵץ [בדרום ואם

יָרִיקוּ וְאִם־יִפּוֹל עֵץ [בדרום ואם

בצפון מֶקום שֶׁיִּפ[ול

בַּצָּפוֹן מְקוֹם שֶׁיִּפּ[וֹל העץ שם יהוא

4 שֹׁמר רוח לא יזרע וראה בעבים

שֹׁמֵר רוּחַ לֹא יִזְרָע וְרֹאֶה בֶעָבִים

5 לא יקצור׃ 5 כאשר אינך יודע מה

לֹא יִקְצוֹר כַּאֲשֶׁר אֵינְךָ יוֹדֵעַ מַה

דרך הרוח כַעצמים בבטן המלאה

דֶּרֶךְ הָרוּחַ כַּעֲצָמִים [1] בְּבֶטֶן הַמְּלֵאָה

ככה לא תדע את מעשה האלהים

כָּכָה לֹא תֵדַע אֶת מַעֲשֵׂה הָאֱלֹהִים

6 א]שר יעשה את הכל׃ 6 בבקר זרע

אֲ]שֶׁר יַעֲשֶׂה אֶת הַכֹּל בַּבֹּקֶר זְרַע

את זרעך ולַערב אל תַנח ידך כי

אֶת־זַרְעֶךָ וְלָעֶרֶב אַל־תַּנַּח יָדֶךָ כִּי

אינך יודע אי זה יכשר הזה או זה

אֵינְךָ יוֹדֵעַ אֵי זֶה יִכְשַׁר הֲזֶה אוֹ זֶה

[1] pm בבַטן ? corr. in בְּבֶטֶן

7 ואם שניהם כאחד טובים: 7 ומתוק
וְאִם־שְׁנֵיהֶם כְּאֶחָד טוֹבִים וּמָתוֹק

האור וטוב לַעינים לראות את
הָאוֹר וטוֹב לַעֵינַיִם לִרְאוֹת אֶת

8 השׁ]מש: 8 כי אם שנים הרבֵה
השׁ]מֶשׁ כִּי אִם־שָׁנִים הַרְבֵּה

יחיה] האדם בכלם ישמח ויזכר
יחיה] הָאָדָם בְּכֻלָּם יִשְׂמָח וְיִזְכֹּר

את ימי החשך כי הרבה יהיו
את] יְמֵי הַחֹשֶׁךְ כִּי־הַרְבֵּה יִהְיוּ

9 כל שבא הבל: 9 שמח בחור
כָּל־שֶׁבָּא הָבֶל שְׂמַח בָּחוּר

בילדותיך ויטיבך לבך בימי
בְּיַלְדוּתֶיךָ וִיטִיבְךָ לִבְּךָ בִּימֵי

Eccles xii, 2–9

2 הֶעָבִ]ם אחר הגשם]

3 ביום שיזעו ש]מרי הבית ו[התעותו
ביום שֶׁיָּזֻעו ש]מְרֵי הַבַּיִת ו[התעותו

אנשי] החיל ובטלו הט]חנות כי מעטו
אנשי] הֶחָיִל וּבָטְלוּ הַטֹּח]נות כי מעטו

4 וחשכו] הראות בארבות: 4 וסגרו דלתים
וחשכו] הָרֹאוֹת בָּאֲרֻבּוֹת וְסֻגְּרוּ דְּלָתַיִם

בשׁוק בשׁ[פ]ל קול הטחנה ויקום לקול

בַּשּׁוּק בִּשְׁ[פ]ל קוֹל הַטַּחֲנָה וְיָקוּם לְקוֹל

5 גם : הצפור וישׁחו כל בנות השׁיר

גַּם   הַצִּפּוֹר וַיִּשַּׁחוּ כָּל בְּנוֹת הַשִּׁיר

מֹגֹּבֹה יראֹו וחתחתים בדרך ויֹנֹאֹץ

מִגָּבֹהַ יִרָאוּ וְחַתְחַתִּים בַּדֶּרֶךְ וְיָגֵאץ

השׁקֹד ויסתבל החגב ותפֹר האבּיוֹנֹה

הַשָּׁקֵד וְיִסְתַּבֵּל הֶחָגָב וְתָפֵר הָאֲבִיוֹנָה

כי הֹלֹך האדם אל בית עֹלֹמֹו וסֹבבו

כִּי הֹלֵךְ הָאָדָם אֶל בֵּית עֹלָמוֹ וּסָבְבוּ

6 בשׁוק הסֹפדים : 6 עד אשׁר לא יֹרֹחֹק

בַּשּׁוּק הַסֹּפְדִים   עַד אֲשֶׁר לֹא־יִרחק

חֹבל הכֹסֹף ותֹרֹץ גֹלת הזהב ותשׁבר

חֶבֶל הַכֶּסֶף וְתָרֻץ גֻּלַת הַזָּהָב וּתְשָׁבֵּר

כֹד על המבֹוע ונֹרֹץ הגלגל אל הבֹור :

כַּד עַל הַמַּבּוּעַ וְנָרֹץ הַגַּלְגַּל אַל הַבּוֹר

7 וֹישֹׁב העפר על הארץ כשׁהיה והרוח

וְיָשֹׁב הֶעָפָר עַל־הָאָרֶץ כְּשֶׁהָיָה וְהָרוּחַ

8 תשׁוב אל האלהים אשׁר נתנֹה : 8 הבל

תָּשׁוּב אֶל־הָאֱלֹהִים אֲשֶׁר נְתָנָה   הֲבֵל

9 הבליֹם אמר הקוֹהֹלת הכל הבל : 9 וֹיֹתֹר

הֲבָלִים אָמַר הַקּוֹהֶלֶת הַכֹּל הָבֶל   וְיָתֵר

שהיה קהלת חכם עוד למד דעת את

שֶׁהָיָה קֹהֶלֶת חָכָם עוד לִמַּד־דַּעַת אֶת

Lam i, 1–4

1 איכה | ישבה בדד העיר רבתי עם היתה

אֵיכָה | יָשְׁבָה בָדָד הָעִיר רַבָּתִי עָם הָיְתָה

כאלמנה רבתי בגוים שרתי במדינות

כְּאַלְמָנָה רַבָּתִי בגוים שָׂרָתִי בַּמְּדִינוֹת

2 היתה למס: 2 בכה תבכה בלילה

הָיְתָה לָמַס בָּכה תִבְכֶּה בַּלַּיְלָה

ודמעתה על לחיה אין לה מנחם מכל

ודִמְעָתָהּ עַל לֶחֱיָהּ אֵין־לָהּ מְנַחֵם מִכָּל־

אהביה כל רעיה בגדו בה היו לה

אֹהֲבֶיהָ כָּל רֵעֶיהָ בָּגְדוּ בָהּ הָיוּ לָהּ

3 לאיבים: 3 גלתה יהודה מעני

לְאֹיְבִים גָּלְתָה יהוּדָה מֵעֹנִי

ומרב עבדה היא ישבה בגוים לא

וּמֵרֹב עֲבֹדָה הִיא יָשְׁבָה בַּגּוֹיִם לֹא

מצאה מנוח כל רדפיה השיגוה בין

מָצְאָה מָנוֹחַ כָּל רדְפֶיהָ הִשִּׂיגוּהָ בֵּין

4 המצרים: 4 דרכי ציון אבלות

הַמְּצָרִים דַּרְכֵי צִיּוֹן אֲבֵלוֹת

מבלי באי מועד כל שעריה שוממין ‏ לֿ בנון דסופה

מִבְּלִי בָּאֵי מוֹעֵד כָּל שְׁעָרֶיהָ שׁוֹמֵמִין

כהניה נאנחים בתולתיה נוגות והיא מר

כֹּהֲנֶיהָ נֶאֱנָחִים בתולֹתֶיהָ נּוּגוֹת־[הִיא מַר

Lam i, 7–12

7 מ

עניה ומרודיה כ]ל מַחֲמֻדֶיהָ[

אשר היו מימין] קדם בנפל עמה

אשר היו מִימֵין] קֶדֶם בִּנְפֹל עַמָּה

ביד צר ואין] עוזר לה ראוה צרים

ביד צר ואין] עוֹזֵר לָהּ רָאוּהָ צָרִים

8 שחקו על מש]בתיה: 8 חטא

שחקו על מש]בַּתֶּיהָ חֵטְא

חטאה ירושלם] על כן לנדה היתה

חטאה ירושלם] עַל־כֵּן לְנִדָּה הָיָתָה

כל מכבדיה הזילוה כי ראו] ערותה

כָּל מְכַבְּדֶיהָ הִזִּילוּהָ כִּי רָאוּ עֶרְוָתָהּ

גם היא] נאנחה ותשב אחור:

גַּם הִיא נֶאֶנְחָה וַתָּשָׁב אָחוֹר

9 טמאתה בשוליה לא זכרה

טֻמְאָתָהּ בְּשׁוּלֶיהָ לֹא זָכְרָה

אחריׄתה ותׄרד פלׄאים אין מנחם לה
אַחֲרִיתָ֔הּ וַתֵּ֣רֶד פְּלָאִ֔ים אֵ֥ין מְנַחֵ֖ם לָ֑הּ

ראׄה יהוׄה את עׄניי כי הגדיל
רְאֵ֤ה יְהוָה֙ אֶת־עָנְיִ֔י כִּ֥י הִגְדִּ֖יל

10 אויׄב : 10 ידׄו פרש צׄר על כל
אוֹיֵֽב׃ יָדוֹ֙ פָּ֣רַשׂ צָ֔ר עַ֖ל כָּל־

מחמדׄיה כי ראתה גויׄם באו מׄקדשׄה
מַחֲמַדֶּ֑יהָ כִּֽי־רָאֲתָ֤ה גוֹיִם֙ בָּ֣אוּ מִקְדָּשָׁ֔הּ

ד דגשין בכל קרייה
אשר צׄויתה לא יבׄאו בקׄהל לׄך :
אֲשֶׁ֣ר צִוִּ֔יתָה לֹא־יָבֹ֥אוּ בַקָּהָ֖ל לָֽךְ׃

11 כל עׄמה נאנחיׄם מבקשים
כָּל־עַמָּ֤הּ נֶאֱנָחִים֙ מְבַקְּשִׁ֣ים

לׄחם נׄתנו מחמדיהם באׄכל להׄשיב
לֶ֔חֶם נָתְנ֧וּ מַחֲמַדֵּיהֶ֛ם בְּאֹ֖כֶל לְהָשִׁ֣יב

נׄפש ראה יהוׄה והבׄיטה כי היׄיתי
נָ֑פֶשׁ רְאֵ֤ה יְהוָה֙ וְֽהַבִּ֔יטָה כִּ֥י הָיִ֖יתִי

12 זוׄלׄלה : 12 לוא אליכם כׄל עׄברי
זוֹלֵלָֽה׃ ל֣וֹא אֲלֵיכֶם֮ כָּל־עֹ֣בְרֵי

דׄרך הביטו וׄראׄו אם יש מכאׄוב
דֶרֶךְ֒ הַבִּ֣יטוּ וּרְא֔וּ אִם־יֵ֤שׁ מַכְאוֹב֙

כמכאוׄבׄי אשר עׄולׄל לי אשר הוגׄה
כְּמַ֣כְאֹבִ֔י אֲשֶׁ֥ר עוֹלַ֖ל לִ֑י אֲשֶׁר֙ הוֹגָ֣ה

APPENDIX IV

Compare p. 143 *supra*

AL-FARRĀ' (*died* A.D. *821*) *on Reading the Korān*

MS. Arab. 705 of the Chester Beatty Collection, foll. 4–7

قال الفرّاء وقد رأينا اهل القراءة الذين يعرفون الكتاب والسنّة من اهل الفصاحة اجتمعوا على انّه نزل بأفصح اللغات فاعترض فى ذلك اقوام ممّن ينظر فى الاشعار وايّام العرب فقالوا انما فضّل القران من فضّله لما اوجب الله من تعظيم القران فإذا صرنا الى الفصاحة وجدناها فى اهل البوادى واختلفوا فى ذلك فقال اهل الكوفة الفصاحة فى أسد لقربهم جوارهم منهم فقال اهل البصرة الفصاحة فى عُليا تميم وسُفلى قيس من عُكْل وعُقيل وقال اهل المدينة الفصاحة فى غطفان لانهم جيرانهم وقال اهل مكّة الفصاحة فى كنانة بن سعد بن بكر وثقيف فاحببنا ان نردهم بالآثار والقياس والاعتبار الى تفضيل لغة قريش على سائر اللغات فقلنا ما بال قريش فضلت الناس فى حسن صورها والنبل فى رايها والبسطة فى اجسامها قالوا نحن اعلم الناس بهذا انما اتاهم النبل والجمال ان العرب كانت تاتى البيت الحرام للحجّ والعمرة نساءهم ورجالهم فيطفن النساء بالبيت حواسر ويشهدن المناسك سوافر فيتخيّرونهنّ على العيان فيبغون الشرف والجمال فمن ذلك اتاهم الفضل معما خُصُّوا به قلنا فكذلك كانوا يسمعون من احياء العرب اللغات فيختارون من كل لغة احسنها فصفى كلامهم ولم يخالطه شىء من اللغات الشنعة الا ترى انك لا تجد فى كلامهم عنعنة تميم ولا عجرفية قيس ولا كسكسة ربيعة ولا الكسر الذى تسمعه من قيس وتميم مثل تِعْلمون تِعلم ومثل بِعير وشِعير بكسر التاء والباء والسين والشين فاتتهم

الفصاحة من تخيرهم الكلام كما اختاروا المناكح فكان فى هذا كسر لقولهم ورجوع الى قول من هو اعلم بالقران منهم

قال وقد بلغنا مع ذلك ان عمر بن الخطاب قال يٰرسول الله انك لتاتينا بكلام من كلام العرب ما نعرفه وانّا لنحن العرب حقّا فقال رسول الله صلى الله عليه وسلم انّ ربى علّمنى فتعلّمت وادّبنى فتادّبت فانّ فضل القران على سائر الكلام كفضل الله على خلقه

قال وسمع عمر بن الخطاب رجلا يقرأ عتى حين يريد حتّى حين فقال من أقرأك هذا قال عبد الله بن مسعود قال فكتب الى عبد الله ان القران نزل بلغة قريش ولم ينزل بلغة هذيل فأَقْرِئْهُ الناس بلغة قريش ولا تقرئنّهم بلغة هذيل

وقال ابو بكر الصديق رحمه الله ان إِعْراب القران لأحب الىّ من حفظ بعض حروفه

وروى ابو هريرة قال قال رسول الله صلى الله عليه وسلم تعلّموا القران والتمسوا غرائبه

وقال ابن مسعود جَوِّدُوا القران وزيّنوه بأحسن الاصوات وأعربوه فانه عربىّ والله يحبّ ان يُعْرَبَ وكان ابن عمر يضرب ولده على اللحن

وقال مجاهد لَأَن أُخْطِئَ بالآية احبّ الىّ من ان أَلْحن فى كتاب الله

وقال ومرّ عمر بقوم يتناضلون فلحن احدهم فقال عمر سوء اللحن اقبح من سوء الرمى

وروى عبد الملك بن عمير قال قال عمر بن الخطاب لا يُمْلِيَن مصاحفنا الّا غلمان قريش وثقيف

قال محمد بن سعدان حدثنا عبد الوهاب بن عطاء الخفّاف عن سعيد عن قتادة عن زرارة بن اوفى عن سعد بن هشام عن عائشة عن النبى . . . قال الماهر بالقران مع السفرة الكرام البررة والذى يقرأه وهو عليه شاقّ يتتعتع فيه فله أجران

INDEX OF SUBJECTS

INDEX OF NAMES

INDEX OF BIBLE QUOTATIONS

LIST OF THE PLATES

P

Cambridge Unive

Psalm Scroll with Palesti

: I

Library, T-S 20, 54.

Punctuation. Ps. xxxv-xl.

PLATE 2

Bodl. MS Heb. d 55, fol. 4a.

Liturgical Poetry with Palestinian vowels.

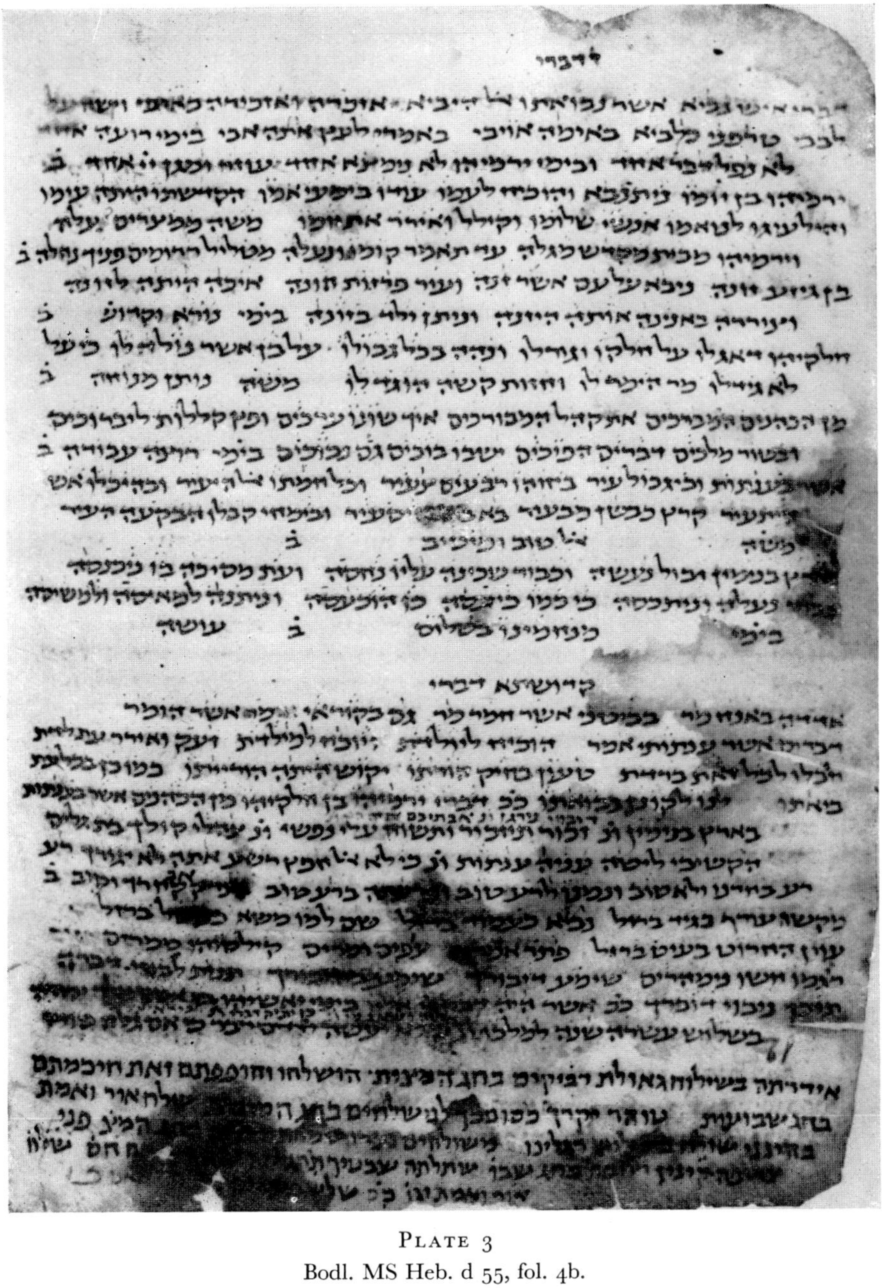

PLATE 3

Bodl. MS Heb. d 55, fol. 4b.

Liturgical Poetry with Palestinian vowels.

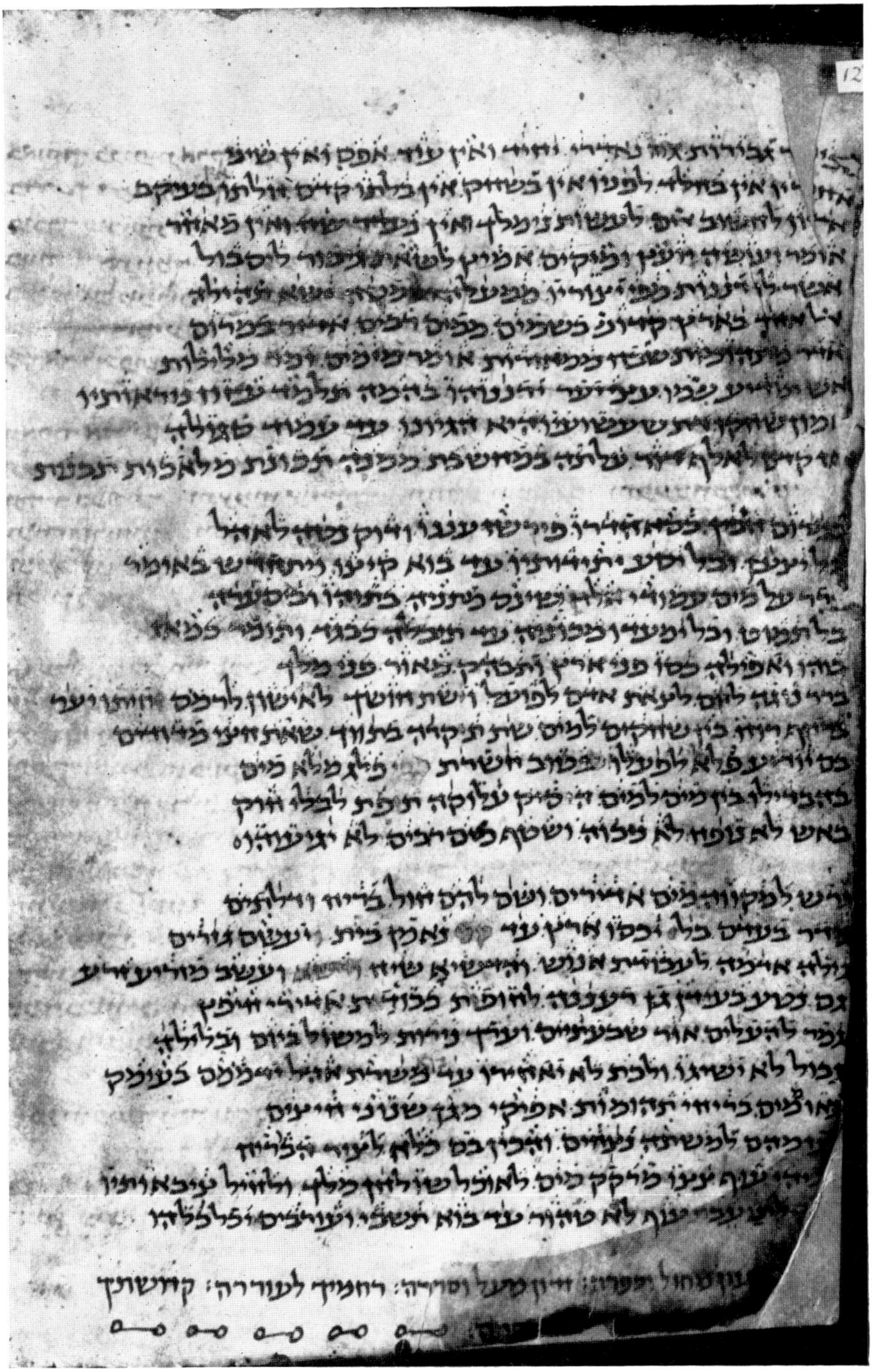

PLATE 4

Bodl. MS Heb. d 55, fol. 12a.

Liturgical Poetry with Palestinian vowels. Jose b. Jose, ʻAboda for Kippur.

PLATE 5

A Palestinian/Tiberian Text (p. 68).

(Jew. Theol. Seminary of America MS 594 Box B Env 12.)

Eccl. xi 1–9, xii 3–9.

Appendix III, pp. 338–341.

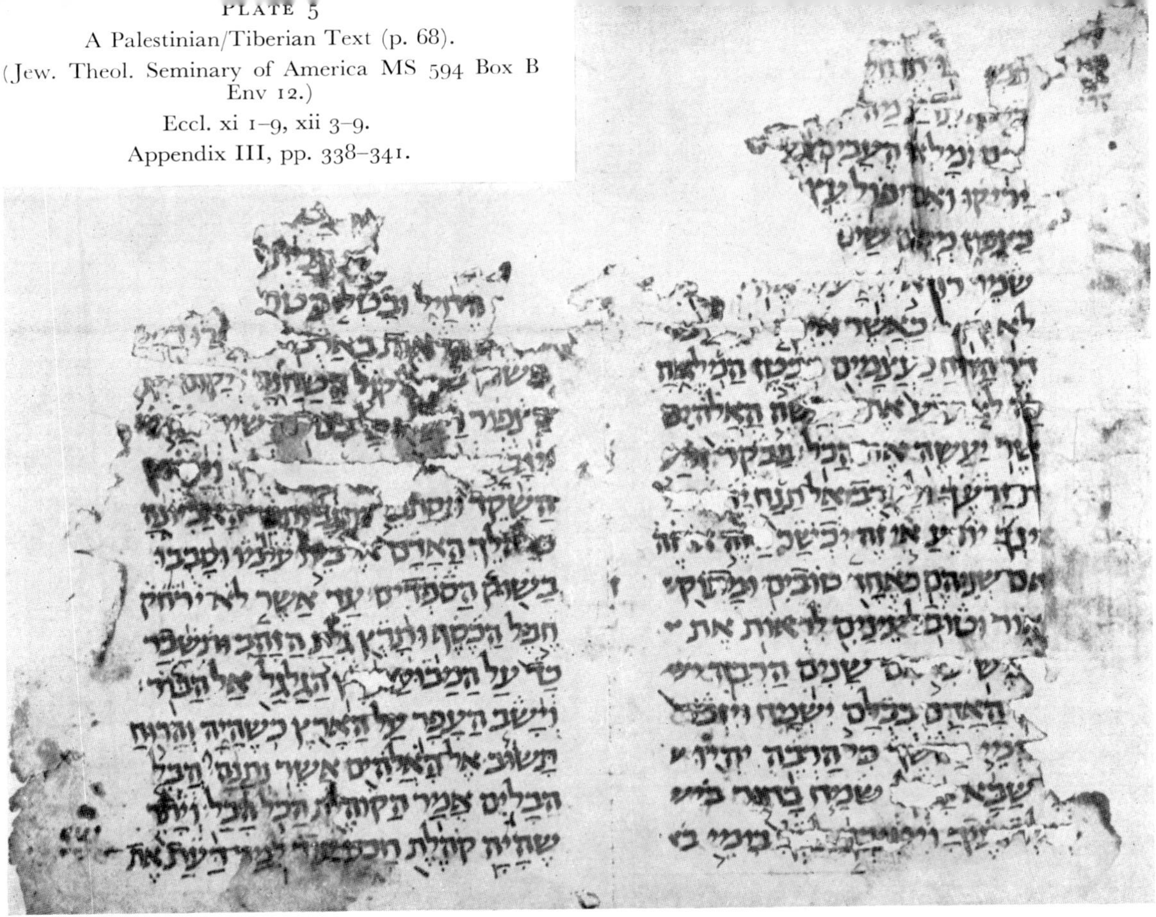

PLATE 6

A Palestinian/Tiberian Text (p. 68). (Jew. Theol. Seminary of America, MS 594, Box B Env. 12.)

Lam. i 1–4, 7–11. Appendix III, pp. 342–344.

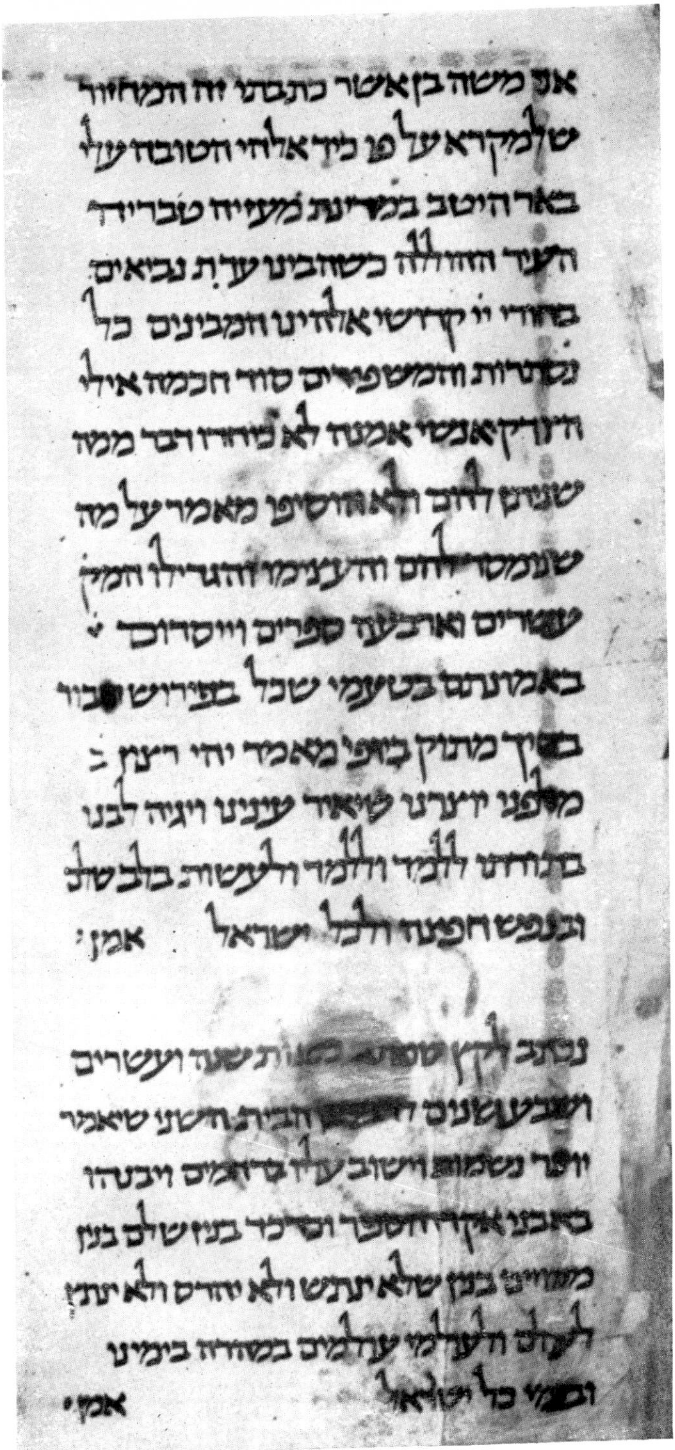

אני משה בן אשר כתבתי זה המחזור
של מקרא על פי כיד אלהי הטובה עלי
באר היטב במדינת מעזיה טבריה
העיר ההוללה כשהבינו עדת נביאים
בחירי יי קדושי אלהינו המבינים כל
נסתרות והמשפירים סוד החכמה אילי
הצדק אנשי אמנה לא כחדו דבר ממה
שנתן להם ולא הוסיפו מאמר על מה
שנמסר להם והעצימו והגדילו המק'
עשרים וארבעה ספרים ויסדוהו
באמונתם בטעמי שכל בפירוש דבור
בחיך מתוק ביופי מאמר יהי רצון
מלפני יוצרנו שיאיר עינינו ויגיה לבנו
בתורתו ללמד וללמד ולעשות בלב שלם
ובנפש חפצה ולכל ישראל אמן :

נכתב לקץ [illegible] מאות ועשרים
ושבע שנים [illegible] הבית השני שיאמר
ויפר [illegible] וישוב [illegible] ויבנהו
באבני אקדח וספיר [illegible] בנין
משוכלל בנין שלא יתנתש ולא יהרס ולא יתנתץ
לעולם ולעולמי עולמים במהרה בימינו
ובימי כל ישראל אמן :

PLATE 7. Karaite Synagogue, Cairo.
Moshe ben Asher's Colophon, Codex of the Prophets, dated 827 after the destruction of the Temple (A.D. 895).

PLATE 8. Karaite Synagogue, Cairo.
Ya'bes b. Shelomo's order for the Codex of the Prophets, written by Moshe b. Asher in A.D. 895.

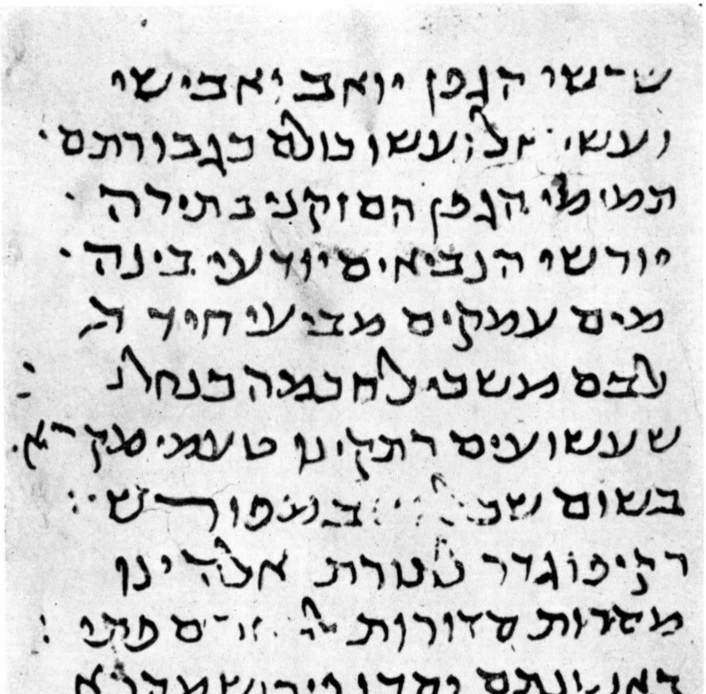

ש
ת
מ
ש
ה
ב
נ
א
ש

PLATE 9

Moshe ben Asher's Song of the Vine.

Last verses with Acrostic משה בן אש[ר]

Cambridge Or 1080, Box V 1 (via Jerusalem)